THE ARMIES
OF THE
FIRST FRENCH REPUBLIC

THE ARMIES

OF THE

FIRST FRENCH REPUBLIC

AND THE RISE OF THE MARSHALS
OF NAPOLEON I

THE ARMÉE DU NORD

By the late
Colonel RAMSAY WESTON PHIPPS
formerly of the Royal Artillery

VOLUME I

The Naval & Military Press Ltd

Published by

The Naval & Military Press Ltd
Unit 5 Riverside, Brambleside
Bellbrook Industrial Estate
Uckfield, East Sussex
TN22 1QQ England

Tel: +44 (0)1825 749494

www.naval-military-press.com
www.nmarchive.com

In reprinting in facsimile from the original, any imperfections are inevitably reproduced and the quality may fall short of modern type and cartographic standards.

PREFACE

My father, the author of this book, served for twenty-seven years in the Royal Artillery. Commissioned at the age of seventeen, he joined in 1855 in the Crimea, and thus at the outset of his career came in friendly contact with the French army, whose history he has studied so deeply.

Indeed, his interest in France may perhaps be called an hereditary one, for his father, Colonel Pownoll Phipps of the Honourable East India Company's service, had been one of a family of English children whom the war had cut off in France from their parents, and who, growing up at Caen between the years 1792 and 1798, probably obtained a better understanding of the French than was common in those days among Englishmen.

From the time when he retired from the army in 1882, my father devoted to the study of the Napoleonic period all the time he could save from many public duties. His first interest was in the Ministers of the Empire, but, in collecting notes on them, he was struck with the difficulty of obtaining facts about the Marshals, and decided to devote himself to these.

He continually increased his library upon this subject, particularly by buying, as they came out, all those personal memoirs of the period of which so many have appeared in France in our generation. In 1885 he edited for Messrs. Bentley a revised edition of Bourrienne's *Memoirs of Napoleon Bonaparte*,[1] in which it will be seen that Chapter XXIV on the 'Cent Jours' and Chapter XXVI are by him.

In 1888 he edited for the same publisher a new edition of

---

[1] *Memoirs of Napoleon Bonaparte*, by L. A. Fauvelet de Bourrienne. Revised edition edited by R. W. Phipps. 3 vols. London, R. Bentley & Son, 1885, 8vo.

O'Meara's *Napoleon at Saint Helena* : [1] the long and important Introduction to this book is by him, and was praised at the time as a convincing exposition of the case against the treatment of Napoleon.

There is also an edition of Madame Campan's *Private Life of Marie-Antoinette*, which contains notes by my father.[2]

His library of books and maps relating to the period, more than two thousand volumes, my father gave in 1920 to the College of All Souls at Oxford, with which the Professorship of Military History at Oxford is specially connected, and that College, after distributing to other libraries any of the books of which they themselves possessed copies, has placed the rest, that is, the great majority of them, in the Codrington library.

More than once the impending issue of my father's *Lives of the Marshals* was announced by Messrs. Bentley, but its publication was delayed by two causes ; first by the constant appearance of new material, which had to be collected, checked, and digested, and secondly by the author's conviction of the great importance, for his subject, of the early years of the Republican armies, so little known to English readers, yet of such far-reaching influence on the future careers of the Marshals.

This latter consideration had the effect of increasing the scope of the work. In dealing with the Marshals the problem, of course, had been to avoid covering the same ground several times over, and the author's solution was to describe fully, in the life of each Marshal, only the campaign or campaigns in which he had been most prominent, and to summarize his share in others. Even this system, however, would have involved some duplication, if the effect of the revolutionary atmosphere on his early services were to have been brought out fully in the case of every Marshal.

Accordingly my father wrote both an Introduction to his work and a summary of the histories of the armies of the

---

[1] *Napoleon at Saint Helena*, by B. E. O'Meara. 2 vols. London, R. Bentley & Son, 1888. 8vo.

[2] *The Private Life of Marie-Antoinette*, with notes by R. W. Phipps. 2 vols. London, R. Bentley & Son, 1883.

Republic and Consulate, from 1791 to 1804; at certain points he pauses to review the positions of the various future Marshals and of other well-known Generals at that moment, and to reflect upon the development of their experience, the acquired characteristics of their leadership, and their relations to one another, and to the Emperor. This summary he afterwards enlarged into a detailed history of each army, with chapters on the various *coups d'état* in the Capital, such as those of Fructidor 1797 and of Brumaire 1799, ending with an account of the establishment of the Marshalate, with the author's criticisms of the appointments to that body.

Altogether, the great mass of typescript left by my father at his death in June 1923 includes:

(1) An Introduction.

(2) A summary of the armies of the Republic and Consulate and of their campaigns, showing the future Marshals at various stages.

(3) A detailed history of these armies and of the *coups d'état* in Paris.

(4) A complete history of the French armies in Spain, 1808 to 1814, dealing of course with a number of Marshals: in the same way there are accounts of Napoleon's 1814 campaign, of the Marshals under the first Restoration, of the campaign of 1815, and of the Marshals under the second Restoration.

(5) The lives of the individual Marshals, some practically ready for printing, others requiring further revision.

(6) Notes on the Ministers of the Empire, in a rough stage.

This material, by far the greater part of which was carefully revised and checked by the author, with detailed reference to authorities, the result of patient and laborious research, undoubtedly forms a valuable addition to Napoleonic literature, and one that ought not to be lost to history. It had been my father's hope that something at least might be done by his children to let his work try its fortune in the world. For this purpose he made some provision for the publication of, perhaps, a portion of the matter that he left, and the questions to be decided were accordingly those of selection and of abridgement. After careful consideration it has seemed best to present this first volume, which contains my father's Introduction and his detailed history of the important Armée du Nord, in the hope of eliciting opinion or advice as to the line that a second volume should follow.

Abridgement of course has been considered, but I judged that neither in knowledge nor in skill should I be qualified to attempt any material alteration of the work, at any rate until I had prepared this first volume for the press: with the experience thus gained and the attainment of some degree of leisure I dare to hope that the case is altered.

For a future volume the alternatives appear to be either to continue the detailed history of the Republican armies, or instead to give my father's summary of these armies up to the establishment of the Empire, together with his characteristic appreciations and criticisms of the men concerned. Such a volume would, I think, be practicable: whether it is possible to look farther ahead and to contemplate the publication of the lives of any of the Marshals must depend on the extent to which the present volume may attract readers.

The title chosen is longer, and perhaps more clumsy, than would normally be desirable, but it does, I think, show what was in my father's mind when, instead of publishing the lives of the Marshals, he committed himself to a second undertaking.

The kindness of Sir Charles Oman has enabled me to refer to the various authorities quoted by my father and now in the 'Phipps bequest' at the Codrington library, and I am most grateful to Mr. Algernon Whitaker, to whom I have constantly written about many doubtful points in the references, and who has taken a great deal of trouble in solving difficulties for me in the Library.

My father designed his work to be a history of men and of the times they lived in, rather than a critical study of military operations. Accordingly the maps have been made as simple as possible. Maps of the period and maps contained in the authorities quoted have been consulted for details, and, where questions of accuracy can be settled, the maps issued by our army Map Department during the war have been used.

Names of places in France and Flanders have been spelt as in the latter maps, because it is under this spelling that they are now known to so many of us. For places in Holland or Germany the spelling used in those countries has normally been followed.

The method of writing French military ranks, titles, and names of regiments and institutions varies greatly in both French and English books : every effort has been made to keep to a uniform system, and, where apparent variations occur, they are in reality due to some logical subtlety of distinction.

In any hands but his own the preparation of my father's work for the press was bound to suffer, but it will be a deep satisfaction to his children that some fruit of the labour and devotion they watched so long should at last be offered to the student of history and to the general reader interested in a great period.

CHARLES F. PHIPPS,
Colonel, late R.A.

COLLINGDON,
  CRANLEIGH,
    15 *May* 1926.

CONTENTS

	PAGE
LIST OF AUTHORITIES QUOTED . . .	xv

INTRODUCTION

I. SCOPE OF THIS WORK 1

II. TRANSFORMATION OF THE ARMY OF THE MONARCHY INTO THAT OF THE REPUBLIC . 11

III. THE 'AMALGAME' 30

IV. THE FUTURE MARSHALS CLASSIFIED . . 42

THE ARMÉE DU NORD

V. DECEMBER 1791 TO MAY 1792.

Famous names associated with this army. The group of armies covered by the term 'Nord'. Rochambeau, Lafayette, Luckner, and Dumouriez. Colonel Berthier and Captain Mortier in the first engagements . . 62

VI. MAY TO AUGUST 1792.

Luckner in command. The great value set on Berthier as a staff officer. Influence of the political situation on the armies. The *Chassé-croisé*. Lafayette's action against the Assembly and his failure 84

VII. AUGUST AND SEPTEMBER 1792.

The Valmy campaign. Daring of Dumouriez. His nervous army saved by the regular troops of the Armée du Centre. Kellermann 109

VIII. SEPTEMBER TO DECEMBER 1792.

Retreat of Brunswick. Dumouriez's invasion of Belgium and victory at Jemappes. Lieut. Murat writes home: prospects and family affection 133

CONTENTS

PAGE

IX. JANUARY TO APRIL 1793.
The French invasion of Holland interrupted by the Allies' advance. The Neerwinden campaign and loss of Belgium. Failure of Dumouriez's attempted *coup d'état*. Lieut.-Colonel Davout's decisive action. Dilemmas of Colonel Macdonald 150

X. APRIL TO JULY 1793.
The Representatives with the armies take control. Loss of Famars and Valenciennes. Difficulties and death of Dampierre. Custine's discipline and popularity with the army. His trial and execution. Captain Murat's run of promotion. Colonel Macdonald denounced. . . . 171

XI. JULY AND AUGUST 1793.
The Allies attack the Camp de César and Kilmaine withdraws. Houchard in command: moves to relieve Dunkirk, besieged by the Allies. Tribulations of Lieut. Ney. Davout and the spies. Evil and mysterious influence of General Brune. Captain Bernadotte 191

XII. AUGUST AND SEPTEMBER 1793.
The Hondschoote campaign and relief of Dunkirk. Important share of General Jourdan in the victory. Loss of Menin and Le Quesnoy. Houchard tried and guillotined 218

XIII. SEPTEMBER 1793 TO JANUARY 1794.
Jourdan's rise to the command of the 'Nord': his advantages and limitations. Campaign and victory of Wattignies. Lieut.-Colonel Mortier wounded. The 'Carnot legend' of Wattignies. Macdonald again denounced, but saved by Souham. Dismissal of Jourdan . 246

XIV. JANUARY TO MAY 1794.
Pichegru in command. Rise of Moreau and Vandamme. Colonel Bernadotte refuses promotion. Generals Souham and Macdonald at the taking of Menin. . . . 275

XV. MAY AND JUNE 1794.
Battle of Tourcoing won by French under Souham. Moreau's risk. Indecisive battle of Pont-à-Chin or Tournai. Siege of Ypres and gallantry of Macdonald's brigade 296

CONTENTS

PAGE

XVI. JUNE 1794 TO APRIL 1795.

The co-operation of the 'Sambre-et-Meuse' enables the 'Nord' to advance. Conquest of Belgium and Holland. Moreau's successful sieges. Retreat of the Allies . . 314

XVII. APRIL 1795 TO OCTOBER 1797.

Moreau in command. Lieut.-Colonel Murat's troubles. End of the 'Nord's' campaigns. Beurnonville succeeds Moreau. General Grouchy and his chances of high command. General Macdonald ill with fever. The 'Nord' as a training-ground for Generals 336

INDEX 353

MAPS

Operations in the Argonne . . *facing p.*	109
Operations in Holland	145
Operations in Northern France and Belgium .	171
Operations in Flanders	213

LIST OF AUTHORITIES QUOTED

Alger, John, *Englishmen in the French Revolution*, London, Sampson Low, Marston & Co., 1889.
Alison, Sir Archibald, *History of Europe from 1789 to 1815*, with Atlas, 9th edition, 12 vols., and Index vol., Edinburgh and London, Blackwood, 1853–5.
Aulard, F. A., *Recueil des Actes du Comité de Salut Public*, 7 vols., Paris, Imprimerie Nationale, 1889–1918, 8vo.

Bajot, *Chronologie ministérielle de Trois Siècles*, 4th edition, Paris, Imprimerie Royale, 1844.
—— *Le Maréchal Canrobert*, 6 vols., Paris, Plon-Nourrit, 1898–1912.
Barras, *Mémoires de*, 4 vols., Paris, Hachette, 1895.
Barthety, *Le Maréchal Bernadotte*, Paris, Champion, 1912.
Belliard, *Mémoires du Comte*, Paris, Berquet et Pétion, 3 vols., 1842, 8vo.
Beugnot, Comte, *Mémoires de (1783–1815)*, 2me édition, 2 vols., Paris, Dentu, 1868.
Biographie universelle des contemporains, ou dictionnaire des hommes vivants et des hommes morts depuis 1788, 2me édition, 5 vols., Paris, 1830–4.
Blocqueville, Marquis de, *Le Maréchal Davout*, 4 vols., Paris, Didier, 1879–80.
—— *Correspondance inédite du*, Paris, Perrin, 1887.
Bonnal, M., *Carnot, d'après les Archives nationales, le Dépôt de la Guerre, et les Séances de la Convention*, Paris, Dentu, 1888.
Bonnal, Le Général H., *La Vie militaire du Maréchal Ney*, 2 vols., Paris, Chapelot, 1910–11.
Bow, E. B., *Jean-Paul Marat*, London, Grant Richards, 1900, 8vo.
Brandt, General Heinrich von, *Aus dem Leben des G.I. H. de Brandt*, Berlin, 1868–9.
Bricard, *Journal du Canonnier*, Paris, Hachette, 1894, 8vo.

Calvert, *Journals and Correspondence of General Sir Harry*, London, Hurst & Blackett, 1853, 8vo.
Campan, Madame, *Mémoires sur la vie privée de Marie-Antoinette*, edited by F. Barrière, 5th edition, 3 vols., Paris, Baudouin, 1823. English edition, 2 vols.
Carnot, *Mémoires sur, par son Fils*, 2 vols., Paris, Hachette et Cie, 1893.
Castellane, *Journal du Maréchal de (1801–62)*, 5 vols., Paris, Plon-Nourrit, 1895–7.

xvi LIST OF AUTHORITIES QUOTED

Charavay, Étienne, *Le Général La Fayette, 1757-1834*, Notice biographique, Paris, Société de l'Histoire de la Révolution Française, 1898, 8vo.

Chassin, *Les Pacifications de l'Ouest, 1794-1801*, 3 vols., Paris, Félix Juven (ancien Dupont), 1896-9.

—— *La Vendée patriote, 1793-1800*, 4 vols., Paris, Félix Juven (ancien Dupont), 1893-5.

Chuquet, Arthur, *Les Guerres de la Révolution* :
 1ère Série :
  I. *La Première Invasion prussienne*, Paris, Cerf, 1888, 8vo.
  II. *Valmy*, Paris, Cerf, 1887, 8vo.
  III. *La Retraite de Brunswick*, Paris, Cerf, 1887, 8vo.
 2me Série :
  IV. *Jemappes et la conquête de la Belgique*, Paris, Cerf, 1890, 8vo.
  V. *La Trahison de Dumouriez*, Paris, Cerf, 1891, 8vo.
 3me Série :
  X. *Valenciennes*, Paris, Léon Chailley (not dated), 8vo.
  XI. *Hondschoote*, Paris, Léon Chailley, 1896, 8vo.

—— *Un Prince jacobin, Charles de Hesse, ou le Général Marat*, Paris, Fontemoing, 1906.

Colin, J., Capitaine d'Artillerie, *Campagne de 1793 en Alsace et dans le Palatinat*, Paris, Chapelot, 1902.

—— Général, *Les Transformations de la Guerre*, Paris, Flammarion, 1916.

—— Capitaine, *La Tactique et la discipline dans les Armées de la Révolution*, Paris, Chapelot, 1902.

Coutanceau, Lieutenant-Colonel H., *La Campagne de 1794 à l'Armée du Nord* :
 Ière Partie : Organisation. Tome i (par H. Coutanceau), Paris, Chapelot, 1905.
  Tome ii, Organisation (par le même), Paris, Chapelot, 1905.
 IIme Partie : Opérations (par H. Coutanceau et le Comte de la Jonquière). Tome i avec Documents et Cartes, Paris, Chapelot, 1907.
  Tome ii (par H. Coutanceau et H. Leplus), Paris, Chapelot, 1908.

Cuneo d'Ornano, Ernest, *Hoche*, 2 vols., Paris, Baudouin, 1892, 8vo.

Daudet, Ernest, *Histoire de l'Émigration pendant la Révolution Française*, 3 vols., Paris : vol. i, Poussielgue, 1904 ; vols. ii and iii, Hachette, 1905, 1907.

—— *La Conjuration de Pichegru et les complots royalistes du Midi et de l'Est (1795-7)*, Paris, Plon-Nourrit, 1901.

—— *Un Amour de Barras*, Paris, Ollendorff, 1895.

David, Le Citoyen, *Histoire chronologique des opérations de l'Armée du Nord et de celle de Sambre-et-Meuse*, Paris, Guerbart, 8vo.

Delhaize, Jules, *La Domination française en Belgique*, 2 vols., Bruxelles, Lebègue, 1908, 8vo.

LIST OF AUTHORITIES QUOTED

Dellard, *Mémoires du Général Baron*, Paris, Librairie Illustrée (not dated), 8vo.
Déprez, *Les Volontaires nationaux (1791–3)*, Paris, Chapelot, 1908, 8vo.
Derrecagaix, Le Général, *Le Maréchal Berthier*, 2 vols., Paris, Chapelot, 1904–5, 8vo.
Desbrière et Sautai, *Organisation et tactique des Trois Armes : Cavalerie*.
    1er Fascicule. La Cavalerie française de 1740 à 1789.
    2me Fascicule. La Cavalerie pendant la Révolution du 14 Juillet 1789 au 26 Juin 1794 : La Crise.
    3me Fascicule. La Cavalerie pendant la Révolution : La Fin de la Convention (du 19 Juin 1794 au 27 Octobre 1795).
Publications of the *Section historique de l'État-Major de l'Armée*, 3 vols., Paris, Berger-Levrault, 1906–7–8.
D'Hauterive, Ernest, *L'Armée sous la Révolution (1789–94)*, Paris, Ollendorff, 1894.
—— *Le Général Alexandre Dumas (1762–1806)*, 2nd edition, Paris, Ollendorff, 1897.
Donntenville, J., *Le Général Moreau*, Paris, Delagrave, 1899.
Dreyfous, Maurice, *Les Trois Carnot, Histoire de Cent Ans (1789–1888)*, Paris, Dreyfous (not dated), 8vo.
Du Casse, A., *Le Général Vandamme*, 2 vols., Paris, Didier, 1870, 8vo.
Dumas, Général Comte Mathieu, *Souvenirs du*, 3 vols., Paris, Josselin, 1839.
Dumouriez, Général, *La Vie et les Mémoires du*, 4 vols., Paris, Baudouin, 1822–3, 8vo. English edition, *Life of General Dumouriez*, 3 vols., London, Johnson, 1796, 8vo.
—— *Lettres sur l'ouvrage intitulé La Vie du, etc.*, Londres, Faulder, 1795, 4to.
Dupuis, Le Capitaine, *La Campagne de 1793 à l'Armée du Nord et des Ardennes*, 2 vols., Paris, Chapelot, 8vo.
    Tome i. De Valenciennes à Hondschoote, 1906.
    Tome ii. D'Hondschoote à Wattignies, 1909.
—— *Les Opérations militaires sur le Sambre en 1794 : Bataille de Fleurus*, Paris, Chapelot, 1907.
Duruy, Albert, *L'Armée royale en 1789*, Paris, Calmann-Lévy, 1888.

Ernouf, Le Baron, *Souvenirs militaires d'un jeune Abbé*, Paris, Didier, 1881.

Fabre de l'Aude, *Mémoires et souvenirs d'un Pair de France*, 4 vols., Paris, Tenon, 1829–30.
Fage, René, *Le Général Souham*, Paris, Picard, 1897, 4to.
Fastes de la Légion d'Honneur, Biographie de tous les Décorés, 5 vols., Paris, Saint-Edmé, 1843–7.
Fersen, Le Comte de, *et la Cour de France*, 2 vols., Paris, Firmin-Didot, 1877, 8vo.

xviii LIST OF AUTHORITIES QUOTED

Fezensac, M. le Duc de, Général de Division, *Souvenirs militaires de 1804 à 1814*, Paris, Dumaine, 1870.
Foucart (Paul) et Finot (Jules), *La Défense nationale dans le Nord*, 2 vols., Lille, Lefebvre-Ducrocq, 1890-3, 8vo.
François, Le Capitaine, *Journal du*, Paris, Carrington, 1903, 8vo.
Frémilly, *Souvenirs du Baron de (1768-1828)*, Paris, Plon-Nourrit, 1909.
Fricasse, Le Sergent, *Journal de marche d'un volontaire de 1792*, Paris, Librairie 13 Quai Voltaire, 8vo.

Gaulot, Paul, *Un Ami de la Reine* (M. de Fersen), 4th edition, Paris, Ollendorff, 1893.
Gavard, Charles, *Galerie des Maréchaux de France*, Paris, Bureau des Galeries historiques de Versailles, 1839.
Gay de Vernon, Le Baron, *Mémoire sur les opérations militaires des Généraux-en-chef Custine et Houchard (1792-3)*, Paris, Firmin-Didot, 1844, 8vo.
—— *Vie du Maréchal Gouvion Saint-Cyr*, Paris, Firmin-Didot, 1856.
Godart, *Mémoires du Général Baron (1792-1815)*, Paris, Flammarion, 1895.
Greville, *Memoirs*, 1st Series, London, Smith, Elder & Co., 1884.
Gribble, *Chateaubriand and his Court of Women*, London, Chapman & Hall, 1909, 8vo.
Griffiths, 'A Pioneer in Military Education, General Gaspard Le Marchant', *Blackwood's Magazine*, May 1904.
Grouchy, Le Marquis de, *Mémoires du Maréchal*, 5 vols., Paris, Dentu, 1873-4, 8vo.
Grouchy, Vicomte de, et Guillois, Antoine, *La Révolution Française, racontée par un Diplomate étranger, Correspondance du Bailli de Virieu, Ministre Plénipotentiaire de Parme (1788-93)*, Paris, Flammarion, 1903, 8vo.

Hamel, E., *Histoire de Robespierre*, 3 vols., Paris, Lacroix, Verboeckhoven et Cie, 1856-67, 8vo.
Hogendorp, *Mémoires du Général Dirk van*, publiés par son petit-fils M. le Comte D. C. A. van Hogendorp, La Haye, Nijhoff, 1887.
Hannet-Cléry, *Mémoires de, Ancien Valet de Madame Royale*, 2 vols., Paris, A. Eymery, 1825.

Jennings, Louis, *The Croker Papers*, 3 vols., London, Murray, 1884.
Jomini, Le Lieutenant général, *Histoire des Guerres de la Révolution*, 15 vols., Paris, Anselin et Pochard, 1820, 8vo.
—— *Vie politique et militaire de Napoléon*, 4 vols., Paris, Anselin, 1827.
Jones, Captain L. T., *Historical Journal of the British Campaign in 1794-5*, London, Egerton, 1797, 8vo.
Jung, Lieutenant colonel Th., *Bonaparte et son temps (1769-99)*, 3 vols., Paris, Charpentier, 1880-1.
——, *Dubois-Crancé (1747-1814)*, 2 vols., Paris, Charpentier, 1884.

LIST OF AUTHORITIES QUOTED

Krebs (Léonce) et Moris (Henri), *Campagnes dans les Alpes pendant la Révolution*, 2 vols., Paris, Plon, 1891–5.

Lahure, L. J., Le Lieutenant général Baron, *Souvenirs*, Paris, Lahure, 1895, 8vo.
La Jonquière, Le Comte de, *La Bataille de Jemappes*, Paris, Chapelot, 1902, 8vo.
—— *L'Expédition d'Égypte (1798–1801)*, 5 vols., Paris, Charles Lavauzelle, 1899–1907.
Landrieux, Jean, L'Adjudant général, *Mémoires*, 3 vols., Paris, Albert Savine, 1893 (one volume only published).
Langeron, Le Comte de, *Mémoires sur les guerres de la Première Coalition* ; included in the volume *L'Invasion austro-prussienne (1792–4), Documents publiés par L. Pingaud*, Paris, Picard, 1895, 8vo.
Lanzac de Laborie, L. de, *La Domination française en Belgique*, 2 vols., Paris, Plon-Nourrit, 1895, 8vo.
Las Casas, *Mémorial de Sainte-Hélène, 10 Novembre 1816*, Paris, L'Auteur, Rue du Bac No. 59, 1823.
Lavalette, Mémoires et souvenirs du Comte, 2 vols., London, Bull, 1831.
Lavaux, Francis, *Mémoires de, Sergent au 103me de Ligne (1793–1814)*, Paris, Dentu, 1894.
Le Grand, Général, Baron de Mercey, *Mémoires et souvenirs du (1755–1828)*, Paris, Berger-Levrault, 1903.
Lejeune, *Mémoires du Général, De Valmy à Wagram*, Paris, Firmin-Didot, 1895.
Lombard, Jean, *Un Volontaire de 1792*, Paris, Savine, 1892, 8vo.
Lumbroso, Albert, *Correspondance de Joachim Murat (1793–1808)*, Turin, Roux Frassati, 1899.

Macdonald, *Souvenirs du Maréchal*, Paris, Plon-Nourrit, 1892, 8vo.
Mahan, Captain A. T., *The Influence of Sea Power upon the French Revolution and Empire, 1793–1812*, 4th edition, 2 vols., London, Sampson Low, Marston & Co., 1892.
Marbot, *Mémoires du Général Baron de*, 3 vols., Paris, Plon-Nourrit, 1891.
Marmont, *Mémoires*, 9 vols., Paris, Perrotin, 1856–7.
Marmottan, Paul, *Le Général Fromentin et l'Armée du Nord (1792–4)*, Paris, Dubois, 1891.
Martin, *Histoire de France depuis 1789 jusqu'à nos jours*, 2me édition, 8 vols., Paris, Furne-Jouvet et Cie, 1878.
Masson, Frédéric, *Josephine de Beauharnais (1763–96)*, Paris, Ollendorff, 1899.
Maurel, *Les Trois Dumas*, Paris, Librairie Illustrée, 1896.
Maye, Le Général Hippolyte, *Marceau*, Paris, Martin, 1889.

xx LIST OF AUTHORITIES QUOTED

Michaud, *Biographie universelle, ancienne et moderne*, 52 vols., Paris, chez Michaud Frères, 1811–28, 8vo ; Supplément, vols. 55–85, Paris, chez L. G. Michaud, 1832–62, 8vo.

Mockler-Ferryman, *Annals of Sandhurst*, London, Heinemann, 1900.

Money, J., Maréchal de Camp, *History of the Campaign of 1792*, London, Harlow, 1794, 8vo.

Moreaux, Léon, *Le Général René Moreaux et l'Armée de la Moselle (1792–5)*, Paris, Firmin-Didot, 1886.

Murat, S.A. le Prince, *Lettres et documents pour servir à l'histoire de Joachim Murat (1767–1815)*, Paris, Plon-Nourrit, 1908.

Musset-Pathay, M. D., *Relations des principaux sièges faits ou soutenus en Europe par les armées françaises depuis 1792*, Paris, Magimel, 1806, 4to.

Napoléon I, *Correspondance de, publiée par l'ordre de l'Empereur Napoléon III*, 32 vols., Paris, H. Plon, J. Dumaine, 1858–70.

Napoléon, Louis, *Mémoires sur la Cour de*, Paris, Ladvocat, 1828.

Ney, *Mémoires du Maréchal, publiés par sa famille*, 2 vols., Paris, Fournes, and also 2 vols., London, E. Bell, 1833.

Nollet, Jules, *Histoire de Nicolas Charles Oudinot, Maréchal d'Empire et Duc de Reggio*, Paris, Dumaine ; Bar-le-Duc, Rolin ; Nancy, Grimblot et Raybois ; et Gouet, 1850.

Pajol, Général le Comte, *Kléber, sa vie et sa correspondance*, Paris, Firmin-Didot, 1877.

Panmure Papers, The : *being a selection from the correspondence of Fox Maule, second Baron Panmure*, 2 vols., London, 1908, 8vo.

Parfait, Noël, *Le Général Marceau*, Paris, Levy, 1892.

Pelleport, Général Vicomte de, *Souvenirs militaires et intimes de 1793 à 1853*, 2 vols., Paris, Didier, 1857, 8vo.

Philebert, Le Général, *Le Général Lecourbe*, Paris, Lavauzelle, 1895, 8vo.

Piérart, Z. J., *Wattignies*, Maubeuge, Cagny-Bayot, 1893.

Pingaud, Léonce, *Bernadotte, Napoléon, et les Bourbons (1797–1814)*, Paris, Plon-Nourrit, 1901.

Pouget, Le Général Baron, *Souvenirs de Guerre*, Paris, Plon-Nourrit, 1895, 8vo.

Pouget de Saint-André, *Le Général Dumouriez*, Paris, Perrin, 1914

Révérend, Le Vicomte, *Armorial du Premier Empire, Titres, Majorats, et Armoiries concédés par Napoléon I*, 4 vols., Paris : vol. i, Bureau de l'Annuaire de la Noblesse de France et chez Alphonse Picard et fils, 1894 ; vols. ii, iii, iv, Paris, Dentu, 1894–7.

Révolution Française en Hollande, La, Paris, Hachette, 1894, 8vo.

Revue de Paris, 15me Année, No. 18, 15th September 1908 (Valmy, Letters of Generals Servan and Dumouriez) ; 15th October 1908.

LIST OF AUTHORITIES QUOTED xxi

Rioust, N., *Carnot*, Gand, G. De Busscher, 1817.
Rose, J. Holland, and Broadley, A. M., *Dumouriez and the Defence of England against Napoleon*, London, Lane, 1909, 8vo.
Rousselin, Alexandre, *Vie de Lazare Hoche*, 2 vols., Paris, Buisson, An VI de la République (1797–8), 8vo.
Rousset, Camille, *Les Volontaires (1791–4)*, 4th edition, Paris, Didier, 1882.

Saint-Cyr, Le Maréchal Gouvion, *Mémoires sur les campagnes des Armées du Rhin et de Rhin-et-Moselle de 1792 jusqu'à la Paix de Campo-Formio*, 4 vols., Paris, Anselin, 1829.
Saint-Sauveur, Grasset, et Labrousse, *Costumes des Représentants du Peuple*, Paris, Deroy.
Savary, Duc de Rovigo, *Mémoires de*, 8 vols., Paris, Bossange, 1828.
Ségur, Le Général Comte de, *Histoire et Mémoires*, Paris, Firmin-Didot, 1873.
—— *Mélanges*, Paris, Firmin-Didot, 1873.
Sérignan, Le Comte de Lorte de, *Un Duc et Pair au service de la Révolution, le Duc de Lauzun* (Général Biron) (1791–2), Paris, Perrin, 1906, 8vo.
Sérignan, Le Commandant de, *Les Préliminaires de Valmy, la Première Invasion de la Belgique*, Paris, Perrin, 1903, 8vo.
Sicotière, L. de la, *Louis de Frotté et les Insurrections normandes (1793–1832)*, 3 vols., Paris, Plon, 1889.
Soult, *Mémoires du Maréchal-Général, Duc de Dalmatie, publiés par son Fils*, 3 vols., Paris, D'Amyot, 1854.
Stanhope, Philip Henry, 5th Earl, *Notes of Conversations with the Duke of Wellington (1831–51)*, London, Murray, 1888.
Susane, Le Général, *Histoire de l'Infanterie française*, 5 vols., Paris, Dumaine, 1876.
—— *Histoire de l'Artillerie française*, 2me édition, Paris, Hetzel, 1874.
—— *Histoire de la Cavalerie française*, 4me édition, 3 vols., Paris, Hetzel, 1874.

Thiébault, Général Baron, *Mémoires*, 5 vols., Paris, Plon-Nourrit, 1893–5, 8vo.
Thiébault, Paul, Adjudant-Général, *Manuel des Adjudants-Généraux*.
Thiers, M. A., *Histoire de la Révolution Française*, 4 vols., Bruxelles, Meline Caus et Cie, 1888.
Thomas, Jules, *Correspondance inédite de La Fayette (1793–1801)*, Lettres de Prison, Lettres d'Exil, Paris, Delagrave (no date).
Thoumas, Le Général, *Le Maréchal Lannes*, Paris, Calmann-Lévy, 1891.
Tiersot, Julien, *Rouget de Lisle*, Paris, Delagrave, 1892.
Tissot, P. F., *Mémoires historiques et militaires sur Carnot*, Paris, Baudouin, 1824.

xxii LIST OF AUTHORITIES QUOTED

Victoires et Conquêtes, Désastres, Revers, et Guerres Civiles des Français de 1791 à 1815, par une Société de Militaires et de Gens de Lettres, 27 vols., Paris, Panckoucke, 1817–22, 8vo.

Vigier, Le Comte, *Davout*, 2 vols., Paris, Ollendorff, 1898, 8vo.

Vogel, *Karte des Deutschen Reichs*, Gotha, J. Perthes, 1891.

Wallon, Henri, *La Révolution du 31 Mai et le Fédéralisme en 1793*, 2 vols., Paris, Hachette, 1886.

—— *Les Représentants du Peuple en Mission et la Justice révolutionnaire dans les Départements en l'An II (1793–4)*, 5 vols., Paris, Hachette, 1889–90.

—— *Histoire du Tribunal révolutionnaire de Paris avec le Journal de ses Actes*, 6 vols., Paris, Hachette, 1880–82.

Wilson, General Sir Robert, *Life*, 2 vols., London, Murray, 1862, 8vo.

—— *Private Diary*, London, Murray, 1861.

Worth, Joseph, *Le Maréchal Lefebvre, Duc de Dantzig*, Paris, Perrin, 1904.

Wouters, Félix, *Histoire chronologique de la République et de l'Empire (1789–1815)*, Bruxelles, Wouters Frères, 1847.

INTRODUCTION

I

SCOPE OF THIS WORK

TWENTY-SIX men were made Marshals by Napoleon. Their successes and defeats, their merits and defects during the wars of the Empire, had much to do with the result of the long contest between France and Europe. As Wellington was matched against several of them their careers should be interesting to English readers. Yet I doubt whether many Englishmen have correct ideas on Napoleon's Marshalate. Nothing is more difficult than to get a true English list of the Marshals.[1] General Junot almost always figures in this rank, in which I have seen Fouché, the Minister of Police, included. Also the relative positions of the Marshals and of Napoleon are misunderstood. All owed their *bâtons* to him: some he made Dukes, a few Princes, and one a King; yet in many cases it was not he that first raised them to eminence. A few rose with him, and only by him. Others had won distinction as commanders of great armies while he was but a junior and unknown officer. Kellermann, leading one of the armies of France, had checked Brunswick at Valmy in 1792, and Jourdan with the main army of France won Wattignies in 1793, stopping the advance of the Allies, when Napoleon was only a Captain. Had Napoleon never existed, or had he found his way young to the scaffold, a reader of the present day would know nothing of such men as Bessières, Lannes, Marmont, Murat, or Victor, but no historian could have helped mentioning Jourdan, Kellermann, Macdonald, Moncey, and Pérignon, as commanders of important armies and leaders in battles, while others, such as Masséna and Saint-Cyr, would probably have won their way to fame.

[1] For list see Chapter IV of this Introduction.

INTRODUCTION

Now, to understand the history and characteristics of the Marshals, as well as their relative positions and their feelings towards one another, we must go back to the schools in which they were trained, the armies of the First Republic.

The first years of an officer's service are his most plastic time. It is then that the style of warfare that he sees, the characteristics of his chiefs and of his comrades, even the nature of the country in which he operates, tell most on him. For almost all the future Marshals the years from 1792 to 1797 were the years of education, and I have considered that it was, as a rule, not until each had reached the rank of General of Division, corresponding to Major-General in our Army, that his character was fully developed.

But, by the time that the first organization of armies was broken up and a new world was beginning under Bonaparte, they had formed friendships, rivalries, and hatreds which were to be permanent. When Marshal Ney, Duc d'Elchingen, broke the combinations of Marshal Soult, Duc de Dalmatie, in the campaign of 1809 in Spain, he was much influenced by the feelings which Colonel Ney had entertained towards General of Brigade Soult when they were serving together in the Armée de Sambre-et-Meuse in 1795 and 1796. The clues to many such actions are to be found in the story of the years when Empire and Marshalate were yet undreamed of.

The Monarchy was still existing when, on 14th December 1791, three armies were formed to defend the North-Eastern frontier—the Armée du Nord, the Armée du Centre (which in October 1792 changed its name to Armée de la Moselle), and the Armée du Rhin. Then in the south an Armée du Midi was formed. These armies were soon subdivided, and fresh forces were raised to meet the insurrection in La Vendée. Gradually they grew until, under decree of the Convention, 30th April 1793, eleven armies encircled France on the coast, as on the land frontiers, facing the ring of fire in which the Allies hoped that the Republic, scorpion-like, would sting itself to death. The accompanying table of the strength of these armies in 1794 will be useful, if only as showing their comparative importance at that time.[1]

[1] Wouters, 77.

SCOPE OF THIS WORK

Armée du Nord		245,822
,, des Ardennes		37,630
,, de la Moselle		103,323
,, du Rhin		98,390
,, des Alpes		43,042
,, d'Italie		60,551
,, des Pyrénées-Orientales		70,508
,, des Pyrénées-Occidentales		50,782
,, d'Ouest		22,519
,, des Côtes de Cherbourg		27,388
,, des Côtes de Brest		34,379

In 1794 the Armée de Sambre-et-Meuse was formed from part of the 'Nord', the 'Ardennes', and the 'Moselle', and the Armée de Rhin-et-Moselle was formed from the 'Moselle' and the 'Rhin'.

My task is to give the histories of these armies, tracing in them the fortunes of the men who afterwards became famous leaders. In this volume I give that of the Armée du Nord.

Had the wars of the Revolution all been fought on one frontier, or had one theatre become pre-eminent, as did that of the Peninsula for the English, a continuous account would suffice for the history of the early services of the Marshals. But, as it was, the contest was waged simultaneously on very different frontiers, and the future Marshals soon fell into separate and well-defined groups in these theatres. There was a certain amount of passage between armies, and in a few cases future Marshals shifted from one theatre to another, becoming members of groups other than those with which they had hitherto served. Still, to the officers engaged on one frontier, the war there had no immediate connexion with that carried on elsewhere, especially in the earlier years. Even when a victory of Bonaparte's in Italy told on affairs in Germany, that mainly concerned the commanders of armies, not the officers leading divisions or brigades. That Jourdan won Fleurus in the north in 1794 was no direct help to Moncey, who soon commanded an army on the Pyrenees. Bonaparte's victories in Italy in 1796 had the greatest personal interest for Augereau, Berthier, Bessières, Lannes, Marmont, Masséna, Murat, Sérurier, Suchet, and Victor, who were with him; but they had only a strategic value for Jourdan, and did not affect in any way the actual fighting of Davout, Lefebvre, Mortier, Ney, Oudinot, Saint-Cyr, and Soult in Germany.

For these reasons I prefer my plan of writing the history of each army in turn, as it enables me to follow the fortunes, say, of Jourdan and of the group round him, as long as I can, instead of sandwiching what Jourdan did (which did not affect Moncey) with what Moncey did (which did not affect Jourdan). The very grouping of the Marshals invites such a course.

At first they fell into two groups, one in the north and on the Rhine frontier, and the other in the south. Then those in the first group split in two, one body fighting on the Northern frontier, and the other operating on the Rhine. By the end of 1794 both these bodies had joined together again on the Rhine and so continued to serve until the peace in 1797, although they preserved separate identities, one in the army of the Sambre-et-Meuse, under Jourdan, and the other in the Rhin-et-Moselle, under Moreau.

In the south we may take one group of future Marshals as fighting on the Pyrenees, and another in the two sister armies of the 'Alpes' and 'Italie'. The summer of 1795, bringing peace with Spain, sent most of the group from the Pyrenees to join those with 'Italie'; so grouped they fought until the peace of 1797. Consequently, during the eventful years 1795-7, when Jourdan and Moreau penetrated far into Germany and when Bonaparte all but saw Vienna, the future Marshals fought in three groups round (*a*) Jourdan, (*b*) Pichegru and Moreau, and (*c*) Bonaparte; all of course in one common interest, but with different fashions of thought and action.[1]

Now it is no technical or artificial division when I group a number of officers together and call a certain army their school. Each of these armies acquired a history, style, prejudices, and reputation of its own. Their efforts in a common cause did not prevent a sharp rivalry between them and much criticism, often bitter enough, sometimes hostile, of one another. The separation of military bodies is apt to cause each part to produce a certain *esprit de corps* of its own, even where the whole was originally homogeneous. It may be that the

[1] See Chapter IV, p. 58.

French troops were especially liable to this feeling, for the army-corps of the Empire displayed much the same spirit towards one another as the armies of the Republic.

The cause was partly the different origin of the armies. Each of the volunteer battalions, which formed so large a proportion of each force, came from a Department and was recruited from the district which supplied it. Then, when the *amalgame* nominally swept away the local connexion, the different Departments still supplied men to the armies nearest to them.

Naturally, as a rule, the Departments of the north and east had sent their battalions to the armies in that region, and those of the south sent their men to the Spanish or Italian frontiers. The inhabitants of the cold north had different characteristics from those of the hot south, and the Norman and the Gascon had their sharp contrasts. Just as we should not expect, say, Mortier from the north, to act like Murat from the south, so the armies of the north and those on the Rhine frontier acted and thought differently from the army of Italy. Also, though I say this with some diffidence, I think the armies in the north and east were more directly influenced by the action of the Government, and perhaps by the spirit of the Capital, than those in the south. Whatever the cause or causes, the great armies were separate entities. Marceau was plaintively indignant when he thought that his commander, Jourdan, at the end of 1796 was about to degrade himself by accepting the charge of the Armée du Nord, after having been at the head of the 'Sambre-et-Meuse'. In the same year Castelverd, who by drawing back his division of the 'Nord' without cause had forced the 'Sambre-et-Meuse' to retreat, chuckled maliciously over the fact that, if they had retired eight leagues, he had done ten.[1] And in 1797, when Bernadotte and his men from the Rhine frontier joined the Armée d'Italie, they found themselves amid new and hostile surroundings.

Further, the theatres on which the different armies operated affected their style of warfare. The plains and fortresses of the north could not be treated in the same way as the slopes

[1] Macdonald, *Souvenirs*, 46.

of the Pyrenees, and Desaix, after years of war on the Rhine and in Germany, was astonished when he saw the marshes and causeways which had broken the fighting front of the Armée d'Italie.

I have said enough to show the importance of these early years of the Republic to my subject, but it was only after working long at them that I realized why the historians of the Marshals generally glide over that part of their lives. The difficulty of reconciling the inconsistencies of most accounts is very great. Since I began my work the French have poured out a mass of personal memoirs of actors in the great wars of the Republic and Empire. To the excellent works of Chuquet, Foucart, Coutanceau, and Dupuis I owe much, and the French military authorities have given the most valuable accounts of several campaigns; Aulard has enabled me to follow many minute details of the occurrences of the Revolution. I have, indeed, found it necessary to form a special library for my work. This mass of material has greatly assisted me, but its growth has necessarily led to much alteration and reconstruction of my work. At last I believe I can issue the result of my long labour with every trust in its general correctness.

If English writers are often wrong in dealing with the Marshals, the French are liable to trip, especially where the early services of these men are concerned. For instance, Bessières is shown as serving in 1793 in the Armée de la Moselle and Murat in the Pyrenees when in reality Bessières was in the Pyrenees and Murat in the north. One class of error is caused by confusion as to the names of the different armies of the Republic, a very important matter with which I shall deal. The common habit of describing the forces on the Rhine as the ' Armée du Rhin ' is responsible for a complete misapprehension of the relation of Moreau to several of the future Marshals and to a great part of the troops who served on that frontier.

Further, in French books one has but a choice between general histories of the period and separate biographies of individual Marshals, in which their share in events is too often exaggerated, or is not treated with reference to the careers of their comrades.

SCOPE OF THIS WORK

Whilst I dwell on the mistakes of others, I am only too painfully aware of my own liability to err. Still, I must ask my readers not to assume that I am wrong because they find some statement at variance with the ordinary authorities, biographical dictionaries, &c. Once an error is started, such works hand it down one to the other with wonderful exactness. Even statements in memoirs by the Marshals themselves are often wrong. Men sitting down to write accounts of events of their early life, which they think they know too well to need reference to documents, are liable to fall into curious errors. Such mistakes are common, and occasioned me much delay, until I learnt to how much checking the account of an eyewitness should be subjected. However, if, in making my way through a cloud of inaccuracies, I have gone wrong, I am ready to accept correction with much humility and some scepticism.

I have had some difficulty in forming a proper vocabulary. In the case of proper names, for instance those of the Marshals, it is best to adhere to the style by which the men were really known. Thus I write ' Davout '[1] instead of d'Avout, ' Marmont ' instead of Viesse de Marmont, ' Moncey ' instead of Jannot or Jeannot de Moncey, ' Saint-Cyr ' instead of Gouvion, and ' Victor ' instead of Perrin. In such matters, for all the French officers, I try to follow the spelling of names in the *Armorial* of Révérend,[2] which English writers should use. For German geographical names I try, as a rule, to follow Vogel's *Karte des Deutschen Reichs*, a most useful work.

The military vocabulary is not so easily settled. The Revolution swept away many of the terms of the Monarchy. The regiments became *demi-brigades*, and the Colonels *chefs de brigade*. Under Napoleon there was a sensible reversion to the old order, and once more we have regiments and Colonels. I have thought it best to follow the first and final style from beginning to end, as if there had been no interruption in its use. I always translate *demi-brigade* by ' regiment '; *chef de brigade* by ' Colonel '; and *chef de bataillon* for the infantry, or *chef d'escadron* for the cavalry, by ' Lt.-Colonel '. The

---
[1] There is no authority for the common English form of ' Davoust '.
[2] See Révérend, *Armorial*, in list of authorities.

term *maréchal de camp* was used under the Monarchy to include the staff officers, and under the Restoration to mean our 'Brigadier-General', or 'Col. Comdt.'. In the latter case I translate it by General of Brigade, for the French system of having Generals of Brigade and Generals of Division is very simple. The difficulty comes with the Adjutant-Generals. The staff terms of the Monarchy were swept away by the Revolution, and the staff officers became Adjutant-Generals, some being Lt.-Colonels, others Colonels. An army had a General, whether of Division or of Brigade, for its Chief of Staff. The divisions had, as Chiefs of the Staff, Adjutant-Generals, who not only did ordinary staff work but also, often enough, especially when two were present, actually commanded parties and columns.[1] Thus, Ney, Adjutant-General with the rank of Colonel, acting as Chief of the Staff to the division of Colaud of the 'Sambre-et-Meuse' in the 1796 campaign, constantly led its advanced guard. To translate his rank as 'Colonel-on-the-staff' might mislead an English reader. I therefore use the awkward term 'Colonel Adjutant-General' or 'Lt.-Colonel Adjutant-General' for what officially was *adjudant-général, chef de brigade*, or *chef de bataillon*.

In stating the strength of a force I follow the best authorities, but nothing is more difficult than to know the real number of men available for any operation. Even Napoleon, with all his returns and his passion for reading them, seldom if ever knew the exact strength of any part of his army and almost always exaggerated their numbers even in his own mind.[2] Judge, then, how much uncertainty must have prevailed in the early armies of the Republic. Even in times of dead peace few can tell the effective strength of a regiment with perfect accuracy, whilst in war the difficulty of course increases.

Besides the future Marshals, there are certain other Generals, Desaix, Hoche, Joubert, Dumouriez, Moreau, and Pichegru, into whose careers I must go to some extent, as they affected

[1] See this subject in Coutanceau, *Nord*, I^e Partie, i. 139, 152–6, quoting Thiébault's *Manuel*. Desbrière, *La Cavalerie pendant la Révolution : La fin de la Convention*, 188, ascribes this practice in cavalry matters to want of confidence in the regimental officers.

[2] Marbot, i. 247–51 : ' Aussi Napoléon, malgré sa puissance, n'a-t-il jamais su exactement le nombre de combattants dont il pouvait disposer un jour de bataille.'

those of the Marshals and as they occupied positions too high to be passed over. All doubtless would have been Marshals, had not the first three died before the Empire rose, had not Dumouriez fled to the enemy, and had not the last two, Moreau and Pichegru, ruined themselves by their opposition to Napoleon, who is alleged to have been so jealous of Pichegru that he had him 'suicided' in preference to giving him an open trial. I think that an account of the career of Pichegru will show that he was a broken and discredited man after 1797 and that he never had any claim to be considered a great commander. It also will be found that Moreau, a General with strange faults, never had that hold over the army or armies with which he is credited and which might have made him figure as a rival to Napoleon: the idea is chiefly based on a mistake as to the extent of his commands. As for Dumouriez, he is so much bound up with the first campaigns of the Revolutionary wars, that it is not possible to pass him over lightly. Other commanders of the armies of the Republic, such men as Custine, Luckner, Schérer, Dugommier, &c., can be dealt with in less detail, but their characteristics must be described, as their conduct may have had an influence on the lives of the future Marshals that served under them. For minor men I give the references necessary to those who wish for more information about them.

If, then, the reader should ask why he should be expected to follow the campaigns of the Armée du Nord, to know how Dumouriez fled, how Custine and Houchard died, the answer is plain. Nothing can explain the individual actions of the future Marshals except the general events through which they had passed. For instance, that a number of officers, who had begun their careers under the influence of a passion for liberty, should end by consenting to serve under, and to support the arbitrary government of the Emperor, can only be explained by their experience. It was the faults, follies, and crimes of the Revolution, falling on the armies, which presented Napoleon with a body of military chiefs ready to obey the man who would give glory to their arms and tranquillity to their country. The Davout who, to support the Revolution, had fired on his commander, Dumouriez, was changed into the Davout, type of implicit obedience to Napoleon, not merely by his personal history, but by what he had seen of the fate of others. When his commanders had seemed to be linked with the enemies of France, no action was too strong for him to take against them. But then he saw Generals whom he believed to be capable commanders, and knew to be true-hearted Frenchmen, sent to the scaffold and dubbed traitors on account of misfortunes for which they were not responsible. His personal ill treatment he might have forgotten, but not the shambles to which so many had been sent. What he had seen, and what had changed him, must be known before he can be judged fairly. The French officers, who had known the disasters, cruelties, and bewilderment of the Republic, accepted the yoke of the Soldier who could lead them to victory and of the Statesman who could give France internal peace. Their reasons were written in blood.

II

TRANSFORMATION OF THE ARMY OF THE MONARCHY INTO THAT OF THE REPUBLIC

Transformation of the army of the Monarchy into that of the Republic. Complete change in the circumstances of the army. Effect on its feelings towards Napoleon. State of the army at the beginning of the Revolution. The King allows himself to be stripped of troops in Paris. Indiscipline spreads amongst the troops. Emigration of officers. Effect of the raising of a volunteer force. The first good levies. The later bad levies. The *Fédérés*. Composition of the first armies of the Republic. Regulars in white, volunteers in blue. Large emigration of officers and flight of commanders. The establishment of the *Représentants en mission*. Their jealousy. Suspicions of their bravery. Drouet makes himself safe. Slaughter committed by them. Real crime of the commanders often their attacks on the civilian officials. Effect of the system on the Generals. What the soldiers of France feared. Republics and their commanders. Rivalries of the Representatives. Saint-Just and the battery. Fate of many commanders. Faults of the Allies save France. The Representatives in the field. Want of good faith in the orders. Survival of the old army. ' Restoring discipline.' Rapid promotion of officers. Generals fear responsibility. Soldiers' opinion of the Representatives.

AND now, in order that my readers may understand the early careers of the Marshals and of some of the more prominent French officers of the Republic and Empire, I must ask them to follow me in an account of the transformation of the army of the Monarchy into that of the Republic.

The great change came in the years 1791–5. English officers, of whatever generation, whether they marched under Marlborough, floated on the St. Lawrence with Wolfe, or toiled after Wellington, ended, as a rule, their military lives amidst the same surroundings as existed at the beginning of their careers. It was very different with French officers of this period. A new earth, one is tempted to say a new hell, had opened before them. After the interval of the Commonwealth, England settled down to her former sturdy life. In France the

Revolution altered permanently the whole state of the land. The old laws, the old geographical boundaries, the old social distinctions were all changed, and for a long time for the worse, whilst the misery and confusion which ensued were made the bitterer by the bright hopes that had greeted the first beginnings of the new movement. The aimless, foolish butchery of the Convention only gave way to the squalid rule of the Directory, hardly less deadly than its predecessor, for the 'guillotine sec', or transportation, killed as effectively, if more slowly, than the blade which hissed between the posts. There was no question of peace between Frenchman and Frenchman, but only of which party should slay the other. Sick of the struggle, the best manhood of France sought shelter with the armies on the frontiers. There stood officers and men, as if on an embankment between two seas of blood, happy if they did not slip into that behind them.

Except the arms they bore in their hands, everything was changed for the soldiers of France.[1] Uniform, organization, the system of command, were all new ; and, if Fortune seemed to open fresh avenues for advancement, at the end of each stood a guillotine. The horror with which honourable officers must have looked on the Revolutionary masters of the armies can be imagined. Happily the Revolutionary leaders, arrogant in their moment of power, were helpless when their friends presented the knife to their throats, and Danton, after his shout of 'De l'audace, encore de l'audace, toujours de l'audace', went as meekly to the scaffold as any Noble. Then came Napoleon with his sheathed sword and picked the crown from the mud into which it had fallen. At once he gave to France an internal peace, by which the Royalists, who libelled and intrigued under it, were the first to profit. Under him the hostile factions were quelled, and so strong was his arm that soon few realized from what seething misery he was keeping France. Nothing is so pleasant as to pass from the time of the Revolution and to study the working of the sharp sword and clear brain of Napoleon. The Consulate and the Empire cannot be judged until the Revolutionary period has been studied in detail. The army knew and remembered the evil years, and

[1] This refers only to the infantry.

TRANSFORMATION OF THE ARMY 13

it took the forces of all the Powers to wrench it from the man who had saved it.

At the beginning of the Revolution the French army was fine enough. It was well disciplined, and the class of what we should call the non-commissioned officers was especially good. It is often believed that the men were offended by the introduction of corporal punishment by the Minister, the Comte de Saint-Germain. In reality, intending to alleviate the system, he only regulated it, ' but in his time they began to speak much, and consequently to lie much '.[1] The position of the regular troops soon became unsatisfactory, the cavalry being much employed in quelling local disturbances.[2] The Court had seemed to threaten to use the army, without daring to strike, a fatal attitude in front of an excited populace. In 1789 the ' Régiment de Flandre ' had been brought to Versailles, notwithstanding the murmurs of the National Guard. The celebrated dinner given by the ' Gardes du Corps ' to the officers of the garrison of Versailles was the occasion of the march of the Parisians on Versailles, which could easily have been stopped, just as later on the storming of the Tuileries was only possible because the King had allowed himself to be almost entirely stripped of troops. Indeed, even so the unfortunate Swiss would have repulsed the volunteers from Marseilles, had Louis but left them a free hand. An officer of regulars, Bonaparte, looking on, longed for one whiff of grape-shot from his guns to crush the *canaille*. He himself in time was to apply that remedy.

Gradually the new principles spread amongst the men and loosened discipline. The Marquis de Bouillé, who commanded from Switzerland to the Sambre, first had to put down an insurrection at Metz and then to use the same troops against the garrison of Nancy, which had mutinied. A man of energy, he stormed the town and crushed the revolt. The young Savary, the future Police Minister of Napoleon, had just joined a regiment of cavalry in time for the march on Nancy. Most of the officers were opposed to the new doctrines. This was especially the case amongst the heavy cavalry, although

---

[1] Susane, *Inf. franç.*, i. 308.
[2] Desbrière, *La Cav. pendant la Rév.: La crise*, 14–21.

the young Davout in 'Royal-Champagne' was an exception and indeed in 1790 was imprisoned and had to leave the service for protesting against measures taken to punish men in his regiment for insubordination.

The flight of the King at midnight on 20th June 1791 was intended to place him under the protection of the army on the frontier commanded by Bouillé. Posts of cavalry were placed to escort the Royal family; the Chasseur regiment in which Private Murat served furnished the post that should have received them at Montmédy. The incapacity and weakness of the King, and the failure to have him met by an energetic officer who would have crushed the resistance at Varennes wrecked this plan. Bouillé himself, the first of the fugitive commanders, left France, a great emigration of officers began,[1] and the regular army was placed, as it were, in opposition to the Nation, or rather to the new doctrines.

Had the *ancien régime* lasted in France, even a great war would not have materially affected the fortunes of most of the men with whom we are concerned. The civilians would have remained in their classes. Some of the privates might have risen in the lower grades, and a few of the officers might have gained fair rank in the army. France would have largely increased her regular forces, and the war would have run its ordinary course under ordinary conditions. As it was, the Government raised a mass of so-called volunteer battalions, which for some time served alongside of the regulars. Little or nothing was done to maintain the usual recruiting for the latter, who were looked on with suspicion by the patriots. Disgusted with the Revolutionary Government and with the confusion introduced into the army, large numbers of officers of the regulars emigrated. The army fell more and more into confusion, but two fresh channels of promotion were opened. The vacancies left by the *émigrés* had to be filled from the officers that remained; failing them, from the ranks. Thus in November 1791 Bernadotte, then *adjudant*, or, as we should say, Regimental Sergeant-Major, in one regiment of regulars,

---

[1] See Desbrière, *La Cav. pendant la Rév.* : *La crise*, 31–49, for the emigration of officers, but I venture to think his figures do not always show the whole loss, as the vacancies were filled.

TRANSFORMATION OF THE ARMY 15

got his lieutenancy in another regular battalion, which had just been abandoned by a great part of its officers. Then the volunteer battalions, who had the right of electing their officers and who required leaders with some knowledge of drill, gave men that were serving, or had served, in the ranks an opportunity for gaining the higher grades. In this way Soult, a Sergeant in the regulars, going as instructor to a volunteer battalion, soon became an officer; and Jourdan, who had left the army seven years before, got the command of a volunteer battalion. By one or other channel the future Marshals rose with a rapidity and to a height for which they could not have hoped in ordinary times.

All this would have affected, as a rule, the regimental officers only. The commands of armies would have fallen, as they did at first, into the hands of Generals of the old army, such as Kellermann and Dumouriez, or into those of officers of the regulars who had gained promotion by their patriotic sentiments or by their services in the war just begun. Dampierre, whom the Revolution found Colonel, and Houchard, a Captain, belonged to this last class. But the Revolutionary mania for dismissing or beheading Generals and commanders, and the law which prohibited the ex-Nobles from serving, cleared away most of these classes, as well as the senior officers who would have filled the higher grades: this gave a great advantage to such men as Jourdan and Hoche, who had sprung from the ranks and who could hardly be suspected of devotion to the *ancien régime*. The long and continuous war gave men of real merit plenty of opportunities of proving their worth, whilst the way to the top was made the clearer by the well-founded belief, which long prevailed, that a step in the higher grades brought an officer so much nearer to the scaffold. It was under these special circumstances that the future Marshals rose in the army. Some detail is required to explain this.

In 1791 it was determined to make a large increase in the military forces of France. At first the Assembly had intended to raise 100,000 additional men for the army, but in the end it resolved to form 169 new battalions, 101,000 men, all volunteers. These battalions were furnished by the Departments, that of the Nord for instance supplying twenty-three. As a rule these battalions were good, for there chanced to be an exceptionally fine material ready : France had possessed a large and good force of Militia, which formed a reserve for the army and which sometimes served in war.[1] This force had been dissolved on the creation of the National Guard, which nominally amounted to two and a half millions. In the enthusiasm of the moment the National Guard furnished a great number of battalions, and the volunteers received not only a mass of men formerly belonging to the Militia, but an even more important asset, a part of the officers, *sous-officiers* and non-commissioned officers of the Militia battalions. The dissolution of the *Maison du Roi* also furnished good material for the new bodies. Again, a number of men who had served in the regulars during the war in America, and who had been discharged, Jourdan for one, now joined the new force. In a fortnight, says Dellard, the Department of Lot sent three fine battalions to the frontier.[2] Soon almost all of this levy was on the frontiers.

Placed alongside the regulars and, in the Armée du Nord, brigaded with them, these men soon became good troops, although still wanting in confidence in themselves and in their officers. They had the right to elect their officers, but a wise rule restricted the choice to those officers and *sous-officiers* that had served in the regulars or in the Militia.[3] Sent at once to the camps on the frontier and, in many cases, being attached to battalions of regulars, these battalions had some six or eight months of preparation before they were brought into the field. They rendered valuable service during the war, but it is easy to exaggerate their share in the first combats.

Chuquet, speaking of the whole mass of so-called volunteers, says that two armies, that of the 'Nord' and that of the 'Centre', had to make head against the invasion. On 10th August 1792 the first only counted thirty-two, and the second eighteen battalions of volunteers, and these belonged to the first levy of 1791 decreed by the *Assemblée constituante*.[4]

Next, in 1792 more levies of men were ordered, and a fresh

---

[1] Susane, *Inf. franç.*, i. 263–82.
[2] Ibid., i. 319–52 ; Chuquet, *Invasion*, 70–8 ; Dellard, 3.
[3] Chuquet, *Invasion*, 71.   [4] Ibid., 39.

TRANSFORMATION OF THE ARMY

mass of so-called volunteer battalions was formed and eventually sent to the armies. These later levies were not in reality voluntarily enlisted. The number of men that each Department and District was to furnish was settled. The local authorities then assembled the men liable to be enrolled and tried to induce enough of them to enlist in order to avoid the necessity for a ballot, which otherwise was taken. It was what we now call the Conscription, tempered by large voluntary enlistments, but carried out in the absence of system, order, and method.[1] Men much too young, or too infirm, were accepted as were those of bad character. Untrained, mutinous, and prone to excess, the battalions of this, which I style the 'new levy', were a source of weakness and danger to the armies which they joined. 'It is the indiscipline, ignorance, presumption, and cowardice of the greater number of these battalions', says General Susane, 'which caused the disasters of 1792 and which used up all the Generals of the Republic and led to the scaffold commanders whose sole crime was to have written to the Convention, "Send us regular troops and disembarrass us of the sans-culottes".'[2]

Some of the worst of these new levies were the *Fédérés*, a special levy of 20,000 men, who were ordered to be sent to Paris and whose representatives were 'federated' at the *fête* of 14th July 1792. The battalion from Marseilles, which took part in the slaughter of the Swiss Guard after the King had ordered that body to cease firing, was a part of this force.[3] The *Fédérés* were, as a rule, far inferior to the Departmental battalions. Still, even they often selected old soldiers as their officers. Thus the 1st battalion of the Pas-de-Calais chose Godart as their Lt.-Colonel, a man who had been seven years as Private and Sergeant in the regulars. It is, however, true

[1] See the enlistments in Lavaux, *Méms.*, and Fricasse. Lavaux, rejected as unfit in April 1792, was taken later that year. General Pelleport, ii. 131, speaks of himself as 'enlevé par la réquisition de 1793'. Out of seven brothers four were requisitioned in 1793, one enlisted voluntarily, apparently in 1792, another was requisitioned later for the navy; one alone remained at home (Pelleport, i. 4-5).

[2] Susane, *Inf. franç.*, i. 353.

[3] See Lombard's *Volontaire de 1792* for a description of the way in which the *Fédérés* of Marseilles and Montpellier were raised. These battalions and the contingents from Gard, Vaucluse, and Var were all called 'Marseillais' in Paris. Marseilles itself only furnished 500 men.

that, annoyed by the drill through which he put them, these sons of Liberty tried to hang him as a ' despot who despised Liberty and Equality '.[1]

As for the *Levée en masse*, decreed by the Convention on 16th August 1793,[2] and the unfortunate *troupes agricoles* who were, at least on the Rhine frontier, dragged from their homes, these for the most part settled their fate by deserting : the rest either furnished part of the garrisons of the fortresses, or else were absorbed in the volunteer battalions.[3]

The first armies of the Republic consequently were formed of a number of corps, differing in organization, dress, manner of recruiting, length of service, and, indeed, in every respect. First came the battalions of the regulars, now designated by numbers instead of by their old territorial designations. As I have said, little attention had been paid to keeping up their strength : indeed some patriots wished them to disappear. They had been scattered along the frontiers, so that the first battalion of one regiment would be with one army, and its second with another, just as in the English army. For example, one regiment had its first battalion with the army of Miranda, or the ' Nord ', its second with the army of Custine, or the ' Vosges ', by the Rhine, and its grenadiers with the army of Dumouriez in Holland, whilst its depot was at Metz.[4] They retained their white coats. We who have always been accustomed to associate blue with the dress of the French army must remember that it was in white that our great-grandfathers saw their infantry, although most, if not all, of their foreign regiments, including the Irish, wore red.

Then came the Legions and the blue-coated volunteers, many of them really forced into the service and all having very loose ideas as to the length of time for which they were to remain with their corps. Their battalions were called after the Departments whence they came and were numbered after a Departmental list, thus—1st, 2nd, or 3rd ' Vosges ', and so on.[5] It was what we should call a County organization, and their

---

[1] Godart, 8–12.   [2] Aulard, *Recueil*, vi. 3–4 ; Thiers, *Rév.*, ii. 231–3.
[3] Colin, *Campagne de 1793*, i. 176–227.
[4] Jung, *Dubois-Crancé*, i. 342–3.
[5] See Susane, *Inf. franç.*, i. 322–51, and Déprez, *Volontaires nationaux*, 395–515, for list.

TRANSFORMATION OF THE ARMY

commanders corresponded with the Departmental authorities, often giving most minute information, at least in the early days, of the proceedings and achievements of the corps. Next came the battalions of *Fédérés* and a mass of nondescript corps, *Compagnies franches*, &c. These separate units became very numerous, and it was so easy for the volunteer battalions to change their names, to amalgamate with one another, or even to disappear, that the War Office lost all count of them. Even the careful General Susane does not profess to have obtained perfect certainty as to the number of corps that existed.[1] As for their strength, that no one knew.[2] It differed greatly. One battalion had twenty-seven officers and three men. A stiffening was given to this heterogeneous mass by the regular army which still existed in its midst. Always suspected by the patriots, it had been scattered as far as possible, as I have said, the separation of the grenadier companies to form fresh battalions making this easier. The reason given was that it was necessary to break up the suspected mass, but in truth the regulars were needed to leaven the volunteers.

Probably the officers and the system of the regular forces would have mastered the confusion, had it not been for the emigration of the Nobles and their party. A mass of officers poured over the frontier and joined the enemy, serving in one or other of the Royalist corps, that of Condé or of the Princes. Where possible, they induced some of their men to go over. With this dangerous element in their front the regiments had not the usual support of discipline. Worked on by Revolutionary agents and by the vilest literature carefully supplied to their camps, often even by the War Office, urged to distrust and to denounce their officers, the men became thoroughly unsettled, and the bonds of discipline were relaxed to an incredible extent. Generally there is an innate feeling amongst all ranks of an army in favour of the preservation of order and discipline, but the volunteers took long to understand the necessity for order and, when the usual punishments were denounced from Paris, the regulars became ready to listen to the men who preached that obedience was for the slaves of despots, not for the sons of Liberty.

[1] Jung, *Dubois-Crancé*, ii. 70. [2] Ibid., ii. 68.

English soldiers, sprung from a race trained in public meetings, beginning with the Parish Councils, know pretty much what to think of Parliamentary spouters. To the French Private, as to most of his class in the nation at this moment, the New Jerusalem had descended on Paris.[1] In the ranks, as in the cottages, there long existed a pathetic belief in the virtuous aims of the foolish and sanguinary party that had seized the reins of government in France. It was hard not to credit the denunciations against the officers which were showered from Paris with such authority; and when defeat came it was so consoling to believe that some treachery had been at work. The men were assured that the reign of Love and Equality had begun. If no effects were visible, surely that must be the fault of some rebel or traitor? Nor was it one shock only which the army had to bear from emigration. One commander, Marshal Bouillé, had gone over to the enemy on the failure of the King's flight to Varennes. Next another, Lafayette, left his army almost in presence of the enemy and crossed the frontier. Then Montesquiou, commanding in the south, followed this example. The first act we know of the future Marshal Davout was when he fired on the Commander-in-Chief of the main army of the Republic, Dumouriez, the successor of Lafayette, then engaged in an attempt to overthrow the Government in conjunction with the enemy. Small wonder if men looked in each other's faces to ask, 'Are you a traitor?' Matters were made worse by the decree which for a time drove from the army those Nobles, such as Davout and Grouchy, who had remained faithful to the Republic. From this cause, and from the emigration, the changes amongst the officers were enormous. Between 1791 and 17th July 1792 five hundred and ninety-three Generals had been replaced.[2]

Fortunately enough good sense remained to prevent the regulars being altogether submerged. Although here and there some Republican spouter of patriotic sentiments found his way to command, the hard test of war found such men so wanting that they had to be replaced, and fortunately the slayers were apt to turn on their own instruments. No doubt the army, if left to itself, would have rectified the confusion,

---

[1] Clough, Poems, *Amours de voyage*, 235.   [2] Jung, *Bonaparte*, ii. 313.

but the natural growth of discipline and organization was delayed by the action of the Convention, which placed it entirely under the civil power.

After certain essays, on 30th April 1793 it decreed the system of the *Représentants en mission*. Establishing eleven armies, it sent Representatives to them, generally four to each. These men were given the fullest powers. In order to fill all vacancies amongst the officers, they were to act in concert with the Generals, but they were to exercise the most active supervision on the agents of the *Conseil exécutif*, or Council of the Ministers, on the contractors, and on the conduct of the Generals, officers, and soldiers. They could suspend the *agents militaires* and they could replace them temporarily. One article of the decree places the armies in their hands :—' Art. 16. They shall take every measure to discover, to have the Generals arrested, and to have arrested and brought before the *Tribunal révolutionnaire*, every military man, civil agent, and other citizen who may have aided, favoured, or counselled a plot against the liberty and safety of the Republic, or who may have engineered the disorganization of the armies and fleets, and robbed the public funds'. Another article, 18, went on, ' The Representatives of the people sent with the armies are invested with unlimited powers for the exercise of the functions delegated to them '.[1] To make these powers perfectly complete the only thing that remained was to consider any alleged error or fault of a General or officer as a plot against the Republic, that is, as treachery. Alongside every commander was placed a sort of Committee with full powers over him.

To wield an army with effect a commander requires full power and the confidence of his troops, but the Representatives and the Ministers were jealous of all authority except their own. When a commander grew popular with his troops, he became an object of suspicion to these watchers and, if he could not be denounced, he was shifted to another force, so that he could be the more easily dealt with. When a sort of half approval is given to the sanguinary means by which such men as Saint-Just ' restored discipline ' in the army, it is forgotten how discipline came to be so relaxed. One of

[1] Aulard, *Recueil*, iii. 533-41 ; Wallon, *Représentants*, i. 15-19.

the crimes which sent Custine to the scaffold was his attempt to restore discipline in his Armée du Nord. When his successor, Houchard, was arrested, he was at once sent to the common prison, evidently to degrade him as much as possible. What power would Wellington have had, if alongside of him had ridden Wilkes [1] with power to put him in handcuffs at a moment's notice ? French armies before and after this period did not require a civilian with powers of life and death to preserve discipline.

These men might have done much good, as indeed some did, by working with the commanders and assisting them in matters within civil cognizance. Unfortunately they too often aspired to command. Ordering impossible or fatal movements, interfering with each detail of command, seeing treason in everything, indiscriminately inflicting death, and what was worse than death, disgrace, these men dazed the Generals and deprived rank of all prestige. Bewildered, half murmuring, the troops saw Generals that had led them to victory hurried to the scaffold. Had any General won continued success and gained sufficient hold over his men, the wild disorder caused by the Representatives would soon have ended. Unfortunately the desertion of so many Generals and the defeats of others, often caused by the Representatives, robbed the commanders of proper power.

Whatever their bravery really may have been, there was a strong though ill-natured suspicion that the Representatives, especially the Regicides, had a great dislike to exposing themselves to be taken prisoners. The capitulation of Mayence on 23rd July 1793 was attributed to this anxiety on the part of the Representatives not to fall unprotected into the hands of the Allies, and all the Representatives within Cambrai left it when it was in danger. Drouet, the former postmaster at Sainte-Menehould, who had done so much to arrest the flight of Louis XVI at Varennes, being now a Representative, was within Maubeuge when that place was surrounded. He attempted to cut his way out with some Dragoons, but was taken prisoner. When denounced for not sharing the fate of

---

[1] It is, however, unfair to Wilkes, who was never a Wilkite, to compare him with the Representatives.

the garrison, he defended himself in a curious manner. Seeing, so he told the Convention, that the troops were terror-stricken, and hearing them say that their only hope now lay with the Representatives, as their General had abandoned them, the idea struck him to raise the spirits of the men by making himself safe. If the men did but know that he had cut his way out, all anxiety on their part would be removed. Consequently, when an officer commanding a regiment proposed to make his way through the blockade and to inform the Convention of the state of the garrison, Drouet replied that it was better for a Representative to do so. It is not always easy to follow the reasoning of a patriot, but this explanation is found satisfactory by the authors of the *Défense nationale dans le Nord*,[1] while it sounds like an anticipation of a character in that most charming work, *A week in a French country house*,— ' Ursule, there is danger, I leave thee '.[2]

Sometimes the action of the Representatives was so openly ruinous that the troops turned on them. When the Armée du Rhin was retiring from Wissembourg in 1793, the men hooted the Representatives as those officials passed the ranks. So dangerous was the temper of the men that one Representative took refuge in the division of General Ferrey, on whose staff was Saint-Cyr. There, under the stress of the moment and to the marvel of the officers, he became human and even gentle.[3] When they were in safety such men displayed an extraordinary hatred of their fellow countrymen. Fréron, before Toulon, tells his dear Robespierre that he and Barras will not be really happy till they have put that city to fire and sword.[4] When they did get in the slaughter was indiscriminate,[5] although by no possibility could the whole of the population be considered guilty. Even Barras, who in later years represented himself as shedding tears at the prospect of punishing the town, says that the popular class in Toulon was always devoted to the Republic.[6] Now ten righteous men would have saved Sodom.

One crime of the commanders often was not really defeat,

[1] Foucart-Finot, ii. 223–5 ; Chuquet, *Hondschoote*, 290.
[2] Sartoris, Smith, Elder & Co., 1867, p. 94, republished in 1903.
[3] Saint-Cyr, *Rhin*, i. 132.
[4] ' à feu et sang ', Aulard, *Recueil*, vii. 536.
[5] Marmont, i. 46. [6] Barras, i. 128–30.

but that they had attacked the work of the army officials. Men of vigour, such as Dumouriez and Custine, could not see with equanimity the ignorance, sloth, and carelessness of the officials on whom the welfare of their men depended. Few things are so comforting as the ardour and knowledge with which Napoleon attacked such officials. He, almost alone amongst Sovereigns, possessed regimental experience, and shooting a few commissaries was ever his suggestion to a commander in difficulties about supply. But the days of Napoleon were yet far off and at this period the officials had a terrible instrument of defence ready to their hand. The officer who complained of them must be a bad patriot, and for him broad and smooth lay the road to the scaffold. Little knowledge of human nature is required to understand that the Republican system of killing unsuccessful commanders, far from spurring on the survivors, did but dispirit and confound the successors of the murdered Generals. Once in command of an army, a General soon found how much his will was limited by the interference of the Representatives with him, as well as by the disorganization and defects of the army itself. Realizing his difficulties, he saw the gulf before him. Death if he halted to reshape his forces, Death if he attacked and were defeated; whilst, as Houchard found, even victory might not save him. ' Victory or Westminster Abbey ', a glorious success or a splendid grave, were in the thoughts of Nelson as he swept on the enemy's line. A felon's fate, a dishonoured grave and execrated name, were in the minds of the commanders of the Republic. Those who believe that it was the guillotine that drove Generals to victory must remember that the commanders were not executed as blunderers, but as traitors.

Standing on the frontier, the soldiers of France faced her enemies. Those they did not fear. What they did dread was the foe in rear. In the stress of defeat, in the anxious hour of waiting, even in the very moment of victory, the hand they loathed might be laid on them. Then followed the dreary journey to the capital, the squalid imprisonment, often amidst jeering aristocrats, finally the mock trial, sure to end in death, if not in insult worse than death. The man who had hoped to leave at least an honoured name to his children too often died in the belief that his sons would be taught to shrink from his memory. Not for the young Marceau nor for the fallen Desaix need History drop a tear. Let her weep for the brave men who died hoping at best for oblivion for their names. How could they dream that from the dire confusion a soldier chief should rise to do them justice?

A soldier need have no quarrel with any form of Government, and Monarchies, from the time of Belisarius, have been ungrateful enough to their officers. Still, Republics are apt to have a dread of a successful commander, and Venice had a curious way of dealing with her Generals. In the United States General Grant in time succeeded to the Presidency; in France such an elevation of a General was the nightmare of the politicians, and the more so as their own incompetence became evident.

The whole subject of the *Représentants en mission*[1] has been treated by M. Wallon in a work which deserves most careful study to learn how the Revolutionary axe did not fall merely on a few Nobles and timid Generals, but smote the low as well as the high, the bold rather than the coward.

As I have said, these men with the armies might have been most useful in assisting the commanders in their relations with the civil authorities: indeed some were useful, and Jourdan had the good fortune or the tact to be able so to employ those with him. Even then, when they approved of, and worked with the commander of an army, they had a natural but unfortunate habit of identifying themselves with whatever force they were accompanying. In consequence they objected to any reinforcement being drawn from the body to which they were attached; and when two armies should have acted in combination, there was often a struggle between the Representatives with each, as to which General should command and what operation was to be attempted. Nor was this all. When an operation was decided on, it was impossible for a commander to know what check might be put on him at any moment. We shall find Houchard in September 1793 first having his reinforcements reduced and then his right wing immobilized just when he counted on it: this too when he was

---

[1] Wallon, *Représentants* (see list of authorities).

staking his life on success. It was the same in small operations. In 1794, when Jourdan was attacking Charleroi, Saint-Just found a battery in process of construction. He said to the Captain, ' If by six to-morrow it is not able to fire, your head shall fall '. As many men as possible were put on, but the task could not be completed and the Captain died.[1] It is a pleasure to think that but a month afterwards Saint-Just no longer ' carried his head like the Saint-Sacrement '.

Far from the fervour of the Representatives being a cause of the success of the armies, the period of these men's greatest power was also the period of the most foolish warfare and of the greatest waste of men. It was the faults of the Allies,[2] divided as they were in their real objects, not the merits of the Convention nor yet of the Representatives, that saved France from invasion. The withdrawal of the Duke of York from joint action with Coburg to besiege Dunkirk in 1793, and that of the Archduke Charles from before Masséna in 1799, were the undoubted causes of the failure of the Allies in those years. Many a gallant General might have lived to shed fresh glory on his country, if sense and good faith had reigned in Paris. I say ' good faith ', for it is impossible to characterize the animosity displayed towards Custine and Biron as anything but a conspiracy for their destruction. At no time were the Representatives more dangerous than when they appeared in person on the field, even leading a column. If they succeeded, that meant the failure of the commander whose place they had taken : if they were defeated, treachery was at once evident. When General Arthur Dillon was accused of treachery, Camille Desmoulins asserted that his great crime was having led Billaud-Varennes under fire, and then having talked of the fear which the Representative had shown. As for good faith, that of the orders given to the commanders can only be believed if the folly of the writers be assumed. Take part of those given to Jourdan when in command of the ' Nord ', after his victory at Wattignies. ' He is to pass the Sambre, either above or below or at Maubeuge, he is to surround the enemy, he is to envelop them, he is to enclose them in the portion of the territory which they have invaded, he is to cut their

[1] Soult, *Méms.*, i. 156–7.   [2] Thiébault, i. 413.

TRANSFORMATION OF THE ARMY

communications with their own country and to separate them from their magazines, which he will burn if he cannot take possession of them.' Now even the lamented Mrs. Glasse suggested the propriety of first catching your hare, and the idea of Jourdan surrounding Coburg would be most excellent fooling if the lives of brave men had not had to pay for the wild follies of the tyrants at Paris. As for not following such orders, one of the signatories, as Soult significantly remarks, was Robespierre. If this paragraph be bad, the next is worse.

'Nevertheless the French Army will only enter foreign territory with prudence: it will move as close along the frontier as it can and will always keep its communications with the fortresses in safety. It will, as far as possible, carry on a war of posts: it will only engage in a general affair when an occasion shall offer of fighting with advantage and of putting the army of the enemy to complete rout.'[1]

It is hard to believe in the good faith of these instructions, for how could an army by a war of posts surround the enemy, and how could a war of posts be compatible with an instruction given in another, the 5th paragraph, that the General was to keep his army *en masse*? The decree seems framed to make the destruction of the General certain, unless he delivered and *won* a great battle. If he simply skirmished along the frontier, he would be met by the order to surround the enemy. If he fought a battle and lost, he would be met by the order to carry on a war of posts, whilst the fact that he was beaten would be proof that he had disobeyed the order to fight only if he had the advantage. If he pleaded that the advantage seemed certain, that at once would prove his having treacherously thrown it away. Robespierre signed this decree, but so did the 'Organizer of Victory', Carnot!

The extraordinary rapidity with which officers were promoted and degraded by the Representatives and the Revolutionary Government told on the spirit of the army. There is a well-known story of the mad Czar Paul, who, driving one day in his sleigh, stopped as he passed a Private of his Guard. 'Get in, Sergeant.' 'But, your Majesty, I am only . . .' 'Get in, Lieutenant,' replied the Czar. By the time the astonished

[1] Aulard, *Recueil*, vii. 564; Jomini, *Rév.*, iv. 417-19.

Guardsman was inside the sleigh he was Captain, and as they drove along the Czar pointed out objects of interest to the man, now well 'on his promotion', who rose a rank with each remark. At the end of the day he stepped from the sleigh a General. There was, however, a good deal of method in Paul's madness, and in a few days the 'General' found himself requested again to enter the sleigh, but now as a Colonel. By the end of the drive he had fallen to Sergeant. This was an amusing though silly whim, but the follies of the Representatives were not so innocent in their result. The blood of brave soldiers had to be shed to wash out the follies of men wrongly selected for command. Savary, an officer with the Armée du Rhin at the time, tells with a little exaggeration how in the Wissembourg or Lauter lines the troops paraded at eight a.m. to receive Carlenc, a Major of Dragoons, just promoted to be General of Brigade. At eleven they were again called out to receive the same officer as General of Division. Next day he was Commander-in-Chief.[1]

How the soldiers in the end regarded the Representatives is shown by an anecdote of the time. During an action a Representative, not in his official and glaring costume, passed a grenadier who was sitting down some distance from the battle and who took no notice of him. The grenadier refused to give any explanation of his conduct, as the Representative was not in uniform. Any disrespect to themselves made the upholders of equality furious, and the Representative called off a General from the action to ask the man why he was not engaged. To the General the grenadier was all respect. 'I have come from the action,' he said, throwing open his coat and showing a wound through his chest.[2] In reality he had only been waiting for the surgeon, while he watched that his comrades did well, but he considered he owed no explanation to the fussy Representative of the Convention. There was, indeed, much dumb endurance of suffering amongst the soldier tribe. In 1814 under the Empire, a surgeon, who was rapidly adding to a pile of amputated limbs during a battle, noticed a trooper of the Old Guard sitting cloaked on his horse close by, watching him. He questioned the man, who for

[1] Savary, i. 4. [2] Ségur, *Hist.*, vi. 333-4.

answer turned his horse and showed his shattered leg, to which his foot hung only by a sinew. He too was only waiting for the rapid knife. It was the same everywhere. Did not Hardinge, lying after Waterloo in the same room as the future Lord Raglan, know that his comrade's arm had been amputated only by hearing him ask that his wife's ring might be removed from the limb before it was thrown away?

III

THE 'AMALGAME'

Generals regain influence. The *amalgame* or *embrigadement* of the regulars and the volunteers. Infantry become homogeneous. Description of an *embrigadement*. Distribution of officers. Promotion by seniority. Officers must read and write. The army returns to its former state. The artillery left alone, but battalion guns introduced and horse artillery formed. The cavalry enlarged, but otherwise little interfered with. Bonaparte's 'Guides'. The reconstruction of the army, really a reversion to the old system. Napoleon trundles the Revolutionary nonsense into the dustbin. Carnot and Dubois-Crancé trained in the regulars. Tactics of the French. Requisitions. Supply and plunder.

SOME of the effects of the 'fool-fury' of the Revolution lasted long, especially the reluctance of many officers to accept command until the whole military system had again hardened into its usual mould. Still, the Generals and the system of the regulars gradually regained influence. One great change soon came. It was obviously impossible to retain such a mass of separate units, differing in every manner from one another both in organization and in mode of recruiting. The regulars naturally kept themselves apart as much as possible and prided themselves on every mark which distinguished them from the volunteers. At first they had their traditional white coats. Then, forced to adopt the blue of the volunteers, they either wore white off parade, or else retained their old regimental buttons in a manner shocking to all lovers of Republican principles. It was at last resolved to amalgamate all units, regular and volunteer, in fresh regiments, or demi-brigades. This ensured uniformity, whilst the jealousy of the patriots at losing the 'patriotic' force was stilled by representing the measure as the swamping of the regulars by the volunteers. In reality the regulars, as I have said, were needed to leaven the volunteers. One of the members of the Assembly, Dubois-Crancé, who had the advantage of previous service in the

THE 'AMALGAME'

Mousquetaires gris,[1] part of the *Maison du Roi*, said, ' Will it be denied that the battalions of the former line have in their bosom Officers, Quartermasters, and Sergeant-Majors long accustomed to accounts, and that the *Conseils d'administration* of those corps are generally better organized than those of the volunteers ? ' The volunteers, on the other hand, were flattered by being told that their officers, passing into the regulars, would annihilate ' les molécules organiques de l'aristocratie '. The real truth was that the regulars had been the stay on which the army had rested.[2]

This important change, the *amalgame* or *embrigadement*, making the infantry homogeneous, was decreed by the Convention on 28th January 1794, but was really begun in 1793. Whenever possible, a battalion of the regulars was taken as a nucleus for each of the new demi-brigades, and a number of volunteer organizations was added to it. It was impossible to find regular battalions for each demi-brigade, but the plan succeeded: indeed, on the first formation of the armies on the frontier in 1792, Lafayette, followed by Dumouriez in the Armée du Nord, had acted on this principle, brigading two volunteer battalions with one regular battalion. With the disappearance of so many units the armies became much more manageable. So little was known at the War Office as to what corps existed that the *amalgame* had to be left to the Generals or to the Representatives with the armies. Still, too many units remained, for very many corps had been left out of the organization, which sometimes had to be scrambled through whilst an army was on the move. A second *amalgame* in 1796, completed in 1799, swept away the last vestiges of the early confusion and produced the regiments of the Consulate and of the Empire. To show the reduction in units, in the second *amalgame* fourteen corps went to form the 28th demi-brigade of Light Infantry.[3]

We have a curious description of the manner in which this

[1] The *Mousquetaires noirs* and the *Mousquetaires gris*, two of the four *Compagnies rouges* of the *Maison*, were so called from the colour of their horses.
[2] Susane, *Inf. franç.*, i. 358 ; Jung, *Dubois-Crancé*, ii. 67–8.
[3] Susane, *Inf. franç.*, i. 356–421 ; Chuquet, *Invasion*, 57–89 ; Albert Duruy, *L'Armée Royale* ; Ernest d'Hauterive, *L'Armée sous la Révolution* ; Camille Rousset, *Les Volontaires* ; Déprez, *Les Volontaires nationaux*.

work was carried out in the formation of the 9th Light Infantry. The Representative harangued the newly joined battalions and swore to the preservation of several things of value at the time: the drums beat, arms were grounded, and the officers and men of the three battalions, arm in arm, grouped round the Representative, swore an eternal union and an equally eternal war against tyrants and their satellites, until tears of joy flowed from the eyes of the worthy Gillet, one of the Representatives that Jourdan found manageable.[1] It would be curious to trace whither the war against tyrants led these enthusiastic regiments.

'You have no word for "sentiment"', said Guizot to Lord Palmerston. 'Oh yes,' was the answer, 'we have, "Humbug"'; and the sentiment of this scene probably hid a good deal of dissatisfaction.

The volunteer battalions had for the most part been two or three years on active service, so that the amalgamation was more that of three regular regiments than, say, that of an English regular regiment with two ordinary battalions of volunteers. Still, the disappearance of the old proud titles and of the well-known battle cries, which we shall find heard on the field of Jemappes, must have been bitter both to old officers and men. Then came the question of officers. The senior Lt.-Colonel of the three battalions was made *chef de brigade*, or Colonel in command of the whole demi-brigade or regiment. The three next senior Lt.-Colonels took the head of the battalions, and the senior Captains those of the companies. The Captains ranked according to seniority. The companies were distributed amongst the battalions by the *tiercement*; the 1st, 4th, 7th, 10th, 13th, 16th, 19th, and 22nd being in the first battalion. As for the men, one difficulty with them was that the regulars had to serve for their whole engagement, whilst the volunteers were only tied for a campaign.[2]

There must have been many difficulties to overcome and many awkward questions to solve. Promotion from the rank of Corporal to all higher ranks was arranged as follows. Two-

---

[1] Coutanceau, *Nord*, I^e Partie, i. 479–82; Susane, *Inf. franç.*, i. 384. Compare Pelleport, i. 35–6.
[2] Coutanceau, *Nord*, I^e Partie, i. 405–527

thirds of the vacancies were to be filled by election, the rest by seniority : but what was seniority ? This at first was taken not by length of service in the present rank of the claimant, but from his total service, so that, it was complained, Corporals from the regulars would in time pass over the young Captains of volunteers.[1] This obviously was unbearable. Then how about officers who could neither read nor write and those who, unable to read and write in French, could do so in German ? The decision seems odd. It was not sufficient for an officer to know how to sign his name, but he must be able really to read and write: still, if he could do so in German, that would suffice, although he was reminded that it was a duty for every Frenchman to know the language of his country. It is at least doubtful if this prevented the advancement of many illiterate officers, but it is rather amusing to imagine the feelings of a Frenchman passed over by a German or Alsatian, a scholar but a foreigner in language, on account of this quaint arrangement.[2] Oudinot, who was only Lt.-Colonel of a volunteer battalion, got the command of the regiment in which his corps was amalgamated, as the Colonel of the regular battalion had emigrated. No doubt the senior officer of regulars thought he should have had the vacancy in the regiment as well as in the battalion, and accordingly we are told that the officers of regulars grumbled, as was most natural. Lannes had been made Colonel of a regiment under the first *amalgame*, late in May 1795. The second *amalgame* merged his regiment with another, whose Colonel was senior to him, and accordingly he was seconded. It must have taken some time to remove all these difficulties. The men also had their grievances, for, whilst the regulars, as I have said, lost their old titles, the volunteers saw the link cut which bound them to their respective Departments. It is true that it was intended that the regiments should eventually take the names of the Departments, but how this was to be done was a puzzle, and the plan was never carried out. At the moment the loss of the Departmental tie was resented and this caused great desertion. Still in time the

---

[1] Coutanceau, *Nord*, I^e Partie, i. 478, 502, 505.
[2] Ibid., 356–7. See on all this subject Desbrière, *La Cav. pendant la Rév. : La Fin de la Convention*, 1-11.

system worked. The bullet solved many awkward questions of rank, and fresh campaigns and victories gave the new bodies fresh bonds of union and tradition. Thus we may say that, beginning in 1796, the Republic got the army back into much the same state as it had been in under the Monarchy, whose regiments might better have been continued without a break in their history.

Wild work as the Revolution made of most things, it is fair to say that it had the good sense to leave the artillery alone and not to swamp it with volunteers, as in the case of the infantry; a self-restraint for which it was amply repaid, as that excellent arm won Valmy, Jemappes, and Wattignies, and all through the first campaigns did much to cover the shaky infantry. For all practical purposes the cavalry was also left untouched. It is a pity that army reformers in England did not study the formation of the armies of the French Republic, otherwise the Territorial Artillery—but I must keep to France. The seven regiments that together formed the Régiment de Royal-Artillerie had taken precedence after the 64th regiment of infantry. In 1797 this was altered and the Directory settled the precedence as follows: Artillery, Engineers, Infantry, and Cavalry.[1] Clothed in blue, the colour of all artillery, including, I presume, that of Jonathan,[2] and most of its officers sympathizing with the Revolution, the Royal-Artillerie was not obnoxious to the patriots, but, though no fundamental changes were made in it, some alterations may be of interest. The seven regiments had taken the titles of the Artillery Schools to which they were linked.[3] This explains how Napoleon, an artillery officer, in his days as Emperor, having first horrified the Austrian courtiers by speaking of Marie-Antoinette as 'my late Aunt',[4] then scandalized them by talking of the time 'when I was in the regiment of La Fère'. The artillery regiments were now numbered and La Fère, though retaining that title till 1820, became the 1er Régiment d'Artillerie à pied. In 1795 the strength was fixed at eight regiments of foot and eight of horse artillery.[5] The seven

---

[1] Susane, *Art. franç.*, 221.
[2] 1 Samuel xx. 40.
[3] Susane, *Art. franç.*, 188.
[4] His wife, Marie-Louise, was niece to Marie-Antoinette.
[5] Susane, *Art. franç.*, 221.

artillery *régiments provinciaux*, each attached as a reserve to one of the regular regiments, and five others intended to work under the engineers had been dissolved together with the whole body of Militia.

Although, as I have just said, no great volunteer body of artillery was formed, one change was made of very dubious value. In the Seven Years' War the battalions of infantry had had light guns of their own, but these had been suppressed at the peace. Now each volunteer battalion was to include a company of artillery with two guns, 4 pdrs. In February 1793 it was proposed to do the same with the regular battalions, in order to make them uniform with the volunteers for the *amalgame*, but this was found impossible. Indeed, if all the volunteer battalions really had guns, it is curious how little mention is made of them. Pelleport's battalion is described as flying at full speed from a fight for two or three hours: its arms were replaced, but nothing is said about the guns.[1] An interesting account of one such company of volunteer artillery is given by Bricard.[2] This system is generally a sign of some consciousness on the part of the infantry of weakness for their proper work: it is often proposed, sometimes introduced, and always fails. In France this battalion artillery was abolished in 1798. In 1809 Napoleon, finding himself at Vienna with not quite a satisfactory army and a number of captured Austrian guns, reverted to this plan and gave two pieces to each regiment.[3] These guns were all lost in Russia, and the system, which had not been tried in Spain, was again abolished.[4]

I presume that the volunteer companies of the Republic and the artillery of the Legions had received most of the men released from the Militia artillery. One great improvement in this arm must be attributed to the Assembly—the introduction of horse artillery. Lafayette had seen the Prussian flying batteries and had returned loud in praise of them. The three first-formed companies were sent to the armies of the 'Nord', 'Centre', and 'Rhin': these alone had all their

[1] Pelleport, i. 11-12. [2] Bricard, *Journal*.
[3] *Nap. Corr.*, xix. 15272. Napoleon regretted the withdrawal of the *pièces de régiment*.
[4] Susane, *Art. franç.*, 208-9, 216-17, 232.

gunners mounted, an improvement on those of Prussia, where some of the gun detachments were borne on carriages. The other French horse artillery batteries at first carried their detachments on light wagons until enough horses could be procured. Here once for all let me say that the French artillery of the Republic, Consulate, and Empire was a fine body of men, always serving their guns well and faithfully, as we know their successors of to-day to do. Always formidable, it was especially in the first battles, at Valmy and elsewhere, that they did much to cover the somewhat shaky infantry and weak cavalry of France. The story of the formation of the first horse artillery can be read in the Souvenirs of Mathieu Dumas, who carried it out.[1]

The cavalry, like the artillery, was but little interfered with. The personnel already wore blue, except the Dragoons, who had green, and in matters of dress the Revolutionary Government only displayed a passion for the lofty plumes so well known in pictures, and which must have been an agreeable alteration for Murat. The *ancien régime* bequeathed to the new government sixty-two cavalry regiments, some 30,040 men: that is, 26 regiments of cavalry of the line [2] (including 2 of Carabiniers), 18 of Dragoons, 6 of Hussars, and 12 of Chasseurs à cheval. One regiment (of Hussars) emigrated with Dumouriez: the rest retained their existence, but lost their old titles, receiving instead numbers according to the army to which they belonged. Still, as with the infantry, the old style was not forgotten, and so late as 1809 we find a private of the 2nd regiment of Hussars boasting to his Spanish assailants, ' You don't yet know the Hussars of Chamborant '.[3] A large increase was at the same time made to this arm. The numerous Legions that had been formed contained cavalry as well as infantry and artillery, and there were also several corps of volunteer cavalry. When the *amalgame* of the volunteer infantry with the regulars was planned these mounted bodies were not amalgamated with the old regiments of cavalry, but were used to form entirely new regiments, the increase being

---

[1] Dumas, *Souvenirs*, i. 514–16; Susane, *Art. franç.*, 214–16, 350–74; Coutanceau, *Nord*, I^e Partie, ii. 129 77.
[2] Desbrière, *La Cav. pendant la Rév.: La crise*, 8–9.   [3] Marbot, i. 69.

mainly in the Chasseurs, a comparatively recent formation of the Monarchy. A large part of this addition to the horsemen of the Republic was really of officers and men trained under the Monarchy, for the disbandment of the *Gendarmerie* and the *Maison du Roi* left some 10,000 good *sous-officiers* and men available, besides the 30,040 in the ranks of the old regiments.[1] Probably the volunteer bodies and the new regiments contained a good many deserters. For instance, two new regiments of cavalry of the line were formed to get rid of a body of deserters assembled at Paris. The formation of the new regiments facilitated the rise both of Augereau and of Murat, whose professional knowledge was useful for training the men. Still, I think that the future Marshals that began service under the Revolution in the cavalry did not get such a good opening as those with the infantry. This, however, does not apply to Grouchy, who was a Lt.-Colonel in December 1791 and served in that rank, and as Colonel, in three old regiments, oddly enough in three arms, Chasseurs, Dragoons, and Hussars, before he was promoted General of Brigade in September 1792. Eventually the cavalry of the Revolution consisted of two regiments of Carabiniers, twenty-five of cavalry of the line, twenty-one of Dragoons, twenty-five of Chasseurs, and thirteen of Hussars, giving a total of eighty-six regiments. Only one regiment carried the cuirass,[2] the mass of that arm being formed later, under the Consulate. On all these points the excellent works of General Susane give full details of the cavalry, infantry, and artillery, and Commandant Desbrière gives those of the cavalry. It is a pity we have no such useful authorities for the English army.

Before leaving the cavalry let me say a word of the company of Guides organized by Bonaparte in Italy on the 25th September 1796 which, with the Guard of the Directory, in time burgeoned out into the Imperial Guard. It does not seem clear that no such body existed in the Armée d'Italie before 1796. Marmont says that Bonaparte, after being nearly captured by a surprise in Valeggio in June 1796, determined always to have with him

---

[1] Susane, *Cav. franç.*, i. 246; but I take the strength from Desbrière as above, pp. 8–9.
[2] The *Cuirassiers du Roi*, the 7th Regiment. Susane, *Cav. franç.*, i. 154, 178; ii. 65–75.

' a strong escort '.[1] Now in April 1792 the Assembly had decreed that a company of Guides should be attached to each staff ' to accompany the General officers who direct the columns, and who open the march, to watch over the correspondence of the army for the transmission of orders '.[2] Such companies certainly existed in the armies of the ' Nord ' and of the ' Ardennes ' and the ' Rhin '.[3] Pichegru, when in command of the ' Rhin-et-Moselle ', had what Hannet calls a regiment of Guides ; but this body could not get men as its whole uniform was yellow, and the soldiers in a country where ridicule killed could not stand being nicknamed ' Pichegru's canaries '.[4] Hoche had a company of Guides in 1797 with the ' Sambre-et-Meuse '.[5] I think the explanation is that the whole strength of the establishment allowed by the Assembly was twenty-one officers and men, whilst Bonaparte, wanting a strong escort, made his one hundred and sixty. Captain Bessières is stated to have been given the command of the Guides of the Armée d'Italie on the 5th June 1796, that is, immediately after the affair mentioned by Marmont, and he was made *chef d'escadron*, say Lt.-Colonel, in September, when the larger body was organized. These were cavalry, and became the nucleus of the Chasseurs of the Guard. The company of Guides à pied, formed later, was increased to two companies on the 11th August 1797. On the 6th July 1798 at Alexandria the Guides were organized in seven companies, four of cavalry and three of infantry, besides one company of horse and two of field artillery.

To sum up, the formidable army of the Monarchy did not suddenly disappear with the fall of Royalty. It remained as the nucleus of the raw forces formed in 1791 and later years. What the rulers of the French Revolution did do was to destroy the whole framework of the army and the system of obedience on which the existence of an army depends. Then, under the pressure of the needs of war and the advice of the regulars, much of the confusion was gradually swept away, not by introducing novelties, but by reversion to the former

---

[1] Marmont, i. 182–3.   [2] Coutanceau, *Nord*, I^e Partie, i. 156, 174–6.
[3] Desbrière, *La Cav. pendant la Rév.: La crise*, 302–5.
[4] Hannet-Cléry, i. 293.   [5] Cuneo d'Ornano, *Hoche*, ii. 358.

system, although even in 1799 the War Office knew nothing of the real state of the armies. The successful armies of the Republic were produced not by the invention of a new organization, but by reversion to the old system, till finally an officer of the regulars became First Consul and trundled all the Revolutionary nonsense into the dust-bin.

As for the Republican 'organizers of victory' I shall have to discuss the merits of Carnot in this book and to show that, if he organized victory, he also prepared defeat. When, however, his work as an organizer is spoken of, it must be remembered that he had been trained as a Captain of regulars. Dubois-Crancé, another man who had much to do with the reorganization of the armies, had been fourteen years in the *Mousquetaires* of the *Maison du Roi*. Had the advice given by such officers as the experienced Kellermann been taken at first [1] the infantry would have been treated as the cavalry and artillery had to be, and almost all the early confusion and the consequent necessity for the *amalgame* would have been saved.

A word may be said as to the tactics used in the Republican armies.[2] Here again there was no really new departure; the formations to which the regulars and the volunteers of 1791 were trained were the column for movement and the line for fire.

This was more or less of a compromise between the school of Frederick the Great, which ordained stiff lines, depending for their existence on the fire they could deliver, and that of the advocates of the more mobile system of column formations, which had gained in favour since the Seven Years' War. Both theories had been much discussed by military writers before the Revolution.

It was, however, some time before the column system was developed to the stage reached under the Empire. The new troops who soon joined the armies, untrained in manœuvre, tended instinctively to form into line.

The employment of 'skirmishers', so largely adopted by the French, was copied from the Austrian armies. Parties of

---

[1] See Dumouriez on this point, *Vie*, ii. 283-5, and Eng. ed. ii. 374-7.
[2] The reader will find this subject thoroughly discussed in Colin's *Les Transformations de la Guerre* and *La Tactique et la discipline dans les Armées de la Révolution*. See list of authorities.

from thirty to sixty men from a battalion would break into clouds of skirmishers, bleeding the enemy like so many mosquitoes, either in front of the attacking column, or else working on its flanks. Sometimes also whole battalions of Chasseurs, or of ordinary infantry of the line, were employed in this way on broken ground or in woods.[1]

Naturally the other Powers adopted the column system [2] and, equally naturally, their successes in later years were attributed by them, and even by some French officers, to this cause. In 1815 both the Czar and the King of Prussia, talking with the Duke of Wellington, insisted on the superiority of the attack in column. The Duke denied that it ever had been, or could be successful against steady troops on a large scale, and he instanced Waterloo. The two Sovereigns persisted in attributing their own successive defeats to the use of the column by the French, and the Duke at last requested permission to show them his principles at a review of his whole army in the plain of Saint Denis. We are not told that this exhibition converted the Sovereigns.[3] The English superiority in line depended very much on the power of the officers to restrain their men. A French column would approach the British line, which, standing with its officers in front, waited patiently till the word ' Ready ' was given as the enemy drew near. The column, half halting for a moment as the English muskets moved, came on again shouting and firing. Then rang out a volley, followed by the charge, before which the column retired. But always the English obeyed the order to halt and resumed their line.

As regards the other arms, whilst cavalry lost in importance, artillery gained. The former now became less an instrument for gaining victory on the battle-field than for exploiting success and rendering it decisive.

In artillery the Revolutionary armies were weak at first and, although it was able to afford the most important support, as I have already said, to the infantry, still it was usually a good deal dispersed over the front of a battle, and nothing

---

[1] Colin, *Trans. de la Guerre*, Part I, Chap. I, sect. 5.
[2] Jomini, *Vie de Nap.*, iii. 201, note.
[3] Jennings, *Croker Papers*, iii. 274.

approaching the concentrations of guns used by Napoleon was possible.

An important feature of the campaigns of the first Republic was the system by which armies moved without magazines or supplies. This afforded them great mobility, but the men suffered in poor districts and whenever halted for any time. An officer would find himself detached without provisions or money, with kind instructions to ransack the land for food and pay.

There was nothing really wrong in this system if the search were carried out systematically and with proper order. But too often a system of legalized plunder wasted more than the army consumed or wanted, and one corps might be in plenty, while another was starving. The disuse of tents lightened the trains and enabled the troops to halt at the end of the day's march much where they stood, when they rapidly made shelters for themselves, but here again the homes of the inhabitants too often suffered.

As for the effect of the long periods of war on the army as a whole, it can easily be imagined that interminable service in the field, away from homes and country, formed the troops into a class apart or rather, as they were called, a 'nation of camps'. Officers and men served year after year without getting leave, that most precious privilege of the soldier. It was not till after the peace of Amiens that the first discharges of men were made, except for wounds or unfitness; and then, when men of ten years' service were discharged, a good many re-enlisted, getting higher pay and bearing a chevron as badge on their left arms.[1]

If the careers of such men as Soult and Davout be closely followed, the reader will be surprised to see how little time they passed at their homes or indeed in France.

[1] Dellard, 189-90.

IV

THE FUTURE MARSHALS CLASSIFIED

Classification by military experience. Their birthplaces. Their social position. The arms of the service to which they belonged. Their political opinions. Their religions. Musical talents. Importance of experience in the regular army. Groups. Ranks in 1792. Ages.

I HAVE in the last two chapters taken a general view of the setting in which we shall watch the actions of the future Marshals: let us now consider the men themselves as they stood in 1791. In this short review it will probably be of more interest to the reader if I include all the future Marshals, not limiting it to those that we shall meet in the Armée du Nord.

The Marshals may for our purpose be classified as follows:

Officer Class.

    François-Christophe Kellermann.
    Louis-Alexandre Berthier.
    Emmanuel de Grouchy.
    Jean-Mathieu-Philibert Sérurier.
    Bon-Adrien Jeannot (or Jannot) de Moncey.
    Jacques-Étienne-Joseph-Alexandre Macdonald.
    Louis-Nicolas Davout.
    Catherine-Dominique de Pérignon.
    Auguste-Frédéric-Louis Viesse de Marmont.

Soldier Class.

    Michel Ney.
    Joachim Murat.
    Nicolas-Jean-de-Dieu Soult.
    Jean-Baptiste-Jules Bernadotte.
    François-Joseph Lefebvre.
    Nicolas-Charles-Marie Oudinot.
    Jean-Baptiste Jourdan.
    Claude Victor (Perrin).
    André Masséna.
    Pierre-François-Charles Augereau.

THE MARSHALS CLASSIFIED

Civilian Class.
>Jean-Baptiste Bessières.
>Guillaume-Marie-Anne Brune.
>Jean Lannes.
>Louis-Gabriel Suchet.
>Laurent (Gouvion) Saint-Cyr.
>Édouard-Adolphe-Casimir Mortier.

Prince Poniatowski belongs to the Empire period and I do not deal with him.

When the Monarchy really fell in France, that is, when Louis XVI was arrested at Varennes in June 1791, nine of the future Marshals were officers in the army, which then consisted only of regular troops.[1] Ten others were, or had been, serving in the ranks as privates or as non-commissioned officers. The remaining six were civilians. Of the officer class, Kellermann was *mestre de camp*, or General of Brigade. Berthier was a Colonel on the Staff. The Marquis de Grouchy was a Lt.-Colonel, Sérurier was a Major, Moncey was a Captain, Macdonald was a *sous-lieutenant* of five years' service. Davout and Pérignon were both *sous-lieutenants* of six years' service, but the latter had just retired. Marmont was a *sous-lieutenant* with less than a year's service. Bonaparte himself was a Lieutenant of artillery of nearly six years' service, and was living on his pay of one hundred francs a month. All these nine Marshals and the future Emperor consequently began the Revolutionary period with the training and ideas of the old army of France.

Of what I may call the soldier class, Ney had three, Murat four, and Soult six years' service in the ranks. Bernadotte was Adjutant, with ten years' service. Lefebvre, who in 1789 had been sixteen years in the Gardes Françaises, had then become a Lieutenant in the paid National Guard. Others had been in the ranks, but had left the army. Of these Oudinot had served for three, Jourdan six, Victor nine, and Masséna for fourteen years. The last had risen to the rank of *adjudant sous-officier*. Augereau had had some seventeen years' service in France and abroad. All of this soldier class must have

[1] As a rule I use the tables of service in Gavard's *Galerie des Maréchaux de France*.

known, and some of them very well, the ordinary rules and life of the army, what we call its interior economy.

Bessières, employed in the shop of a hairdresser; Brune, a printer; Lannes, in a painter's shop, had thought little of the army and were pursuing their trades. Suchet was probably prepared to follow his father as a silk merchant. Two future Marshals had refused offers for their admission to the army. Saint-Cyr had preferred to be an artist; Mortier, who had actually been given the post of *sous-lieutenant*, had not accepted it.

We thus have amongst the future Marshals nine who were officers of the old army, with the ordinary knowledge, traditions and prejudices of their respective ranks and arms. With this class would come Bonaparte. Another ten had served in the ranks, and possessed considerable experience, training, and discipline. I say ten, for Lefebvre was not an officer of the regulars, and *adjudant* with the French was not the same rank as in England, but lower, so I do not count Bernadotte, Lefebvre, or Masséna as commissioned officers. Only six at most, Bessières, Brune, Lannes, Mortier, Saint-Cyr, and Suchet, were mere civilians without any military knowledge. The case of Lannes, however, is doubtful, for, according to local report, he had enlisted in the regulars, and had become Sergeant-Major. Then, wounded in a duel, he returned home in disgust and meant to take up his trade, but, being assured he would starve on that, he started again to enlist in the volunteers. Although there is no proof of this, still the fact that he was elected *sous-lieutenant* on the same day that his battalion was formed, as if it were known that he had some military experience, seems to corroborate the report.[1] Thus the proper numbers may be nine officers, eleven privates and non-commissioned officers, and only five civilians.

A list of the birthplaces of these men may be of some interest. Taking those in the north of France first, we get at Paris (Seine) Augereau and Grouchy; at Versailles Berthier. Then in the north-east, Mortier at Le Cateau (Nord), Davout at Annoux (Yonne), Macdonald at Sedan (Ardennes), Sérurier at Laon (Aisne), and Marmont at Châtillon-sur-Seine (Côte-d'Or).

[1] Thoumas, *Lannes*, 4–5.

THE MARSHALS CLASSIFIED

On the east were Kellermann at Strasbourg (Bas-Rhin), Lefebvre at Rufach[1] (Haut-Rhin), Moncey at Palisse (Doubs), Ney at Sarre-Louis[2] (Moselle), Oudinot at Bar-sur-Ornain or Bar-le-Duc (Meuse), Saint-Cyr at Toul (Meurthe), and Victor at Lamarche[3] (Vosges).

All the above, except Moncey, Sérurier, and Victor, served first in the north, although Marmont soon went south.

In the central districts of France I presume we may place Suchet, born near Lyons (Rhône), Brune at Brives (Corrèze), and Jourdan at Limoges (Haute-Vienne). Of these Suchet served in the south; Brune, after much time in Paris and the north, did his first real fighting in Italy in 1796, and only Jourdan belongs to the Northern armies.

In the south we have Bernadotte, born at Pau (Basses-Pyrénées), Bessières at Preissac (Lot), Lannes at Lectoure (Gers), Murat at La Bastide-Fortinière (Lot); Masséna, whose family was Jewish, was born at Nice (Alpes-Maritimes) at a time when that place belonged to the King of Sardinia, Pérignon at Grenade (Haute-Garonne), and Soult at Saint-Amans-Labastide[4] (Tarn).

If we go strictly by the limits of the old provinces, Lannes was the only Gascon by birth.

Ney, Oudinot, Saint-Cyr, and Victor came from Lorraine, Kellermann and Lefebvre from Alsace. Neither of the latter spoke French, at least in 1792, at all perfectly. Macdonald, both of whose parents were Scotch,[5] was French by birth and domicile.

It would be interesting to know the exact social position of the future Marshals in June 1791, but it is very difficult for an Englishman to place them properly. We are apt to divide the French nation at this period between the Nobles, the bourgeois class, and the common people. De Castellane, one of Louis-Napoleon's Marshals, says, however, that *un homme de qualité* would have been horrified if he had been called *un noble*, as that would have implied that his family had been ennobled. *L'homme de qualité*, the real blue-blooded aristocrat,

---

[1] Rufach, south of Colmar.
[2] Or Saarlouis.
[3] Lamarche, south of Neufchâteau.
[4] Now called 'Labastide Soult'.
[5] I follow Révérend's *Armorial*, which, I presume, gives the family account.

was a man who had not been ennobled, and whose family belonged to the *ancienne chevalerie*. This explains why such a man as, for example, Marmont, who aped the *grand seigneur*, was never looked on in that light by any one of knowledge in such matters. *Un homme de naissance* was one of the less fortunate beings who had been ennobled, and who came from an illustrious family. Le Comte de Grouchy was one of the happy men who had been invited to enter the carriages of the King. This required him to prove his titles since 1360 without any trace of ennoblement.[1]

Abandoning all hope of assigning the Marshals to their proper places in the French social scale, I will attempt to class them as they would have been looked on in English society, supposing them to have held there rank equivalent to their rank in France. A knowledge of the position of their parents will often assist in this. The father of Berthier, Lt.-Colonel of the Engineers, was a man of considerable position, *Commandant des ingénieurs hydrographes*, having the Cross of Saint Louis. The mother of the Marshal was Marie-Françoise Lhuillier de la Serre. Davout's father was Jean François d'Avout, *Écuyer, Seigneur de Ravières*, a Lieutenant in the Régiment royal de Chartres. His mother was Adelaide Minard du Velard. Grouchy was the son of François-Jacques de Grouchy, *Chevalier, Page de la Grande Écurie*. The family of Kellermann belonged to the *noblesse bourgeoise*, his father being *Premier Échevin* of Strasbourg. He himself had married in 1769 Marie-Anne de Barbé-Marbois. Macdonald was the son of a Scotch lieutenant in the French service. Viesse de Marmont was son of a captain in the regiment of Hainault, who had the Cross of Saint Louis, and who was the owner of an old country estate. Bon-Adrien Jeannot (or Jannot) de Moncey was the son of François-Antoine de Jeannot, nominally *Avocat au Parlement de Besançon*, but really a landed proprietor, living at Moncey. The future Marshal, buying the Moncey estate in 1789, added 'de Moncey' to his name, but dropped the particle when the Revolutionary period began. Pérignon was the son of Jean-Bernard de Pérignon, and himself was a deputy to the *Assemblée législative* from the Haute-Garonne. Sérurier was the son of

[1] Castellane, i. 344–5, note.

THE MARSHALS CLASSIFIED 47

Mathieu-Guillaume Sérurier, Seigneur de Sore et de Saint-Gobert, who served in the Gardes du Corps, a body to enter which, even as a private, one's family had to be either *noble*, or at least *hors du commun*.[1] Bonaparte's father was deputy of the Corsican Nobility to the body called together by Necker in 1779 [2] to settle the distribution of taxation. Bonaparte's own admission to the military school of Brienne was only obtained after proof of the nobility of his family.

As for the soldier class : Augereau was son of a servant or of a fruit dealer, Jourdan of a surgeon, Lefebvre of a miller who had served in the Hussars ; Masséna and Oudinot were sons of merchants or traders, Murat was the son of an innkeeper, a labourer, he said. Ney was the son of an old soldier, who had turned cooper, Soult of a notary. Victor is said to have been son of a well-to-do farmer, who is also described as *huissier royal*. Bernadotte was the son of Henri de Bernadotte, *Procureur au Sénéchal de Pau*, and of Jeanne de Saint-Jean. Their families had intended Bernadotte for the law, Murat for the priesthood, and Victor for the magistrature. Some of these, Bernadotte, Murat, and Oudinot, for example, were well educated. Others, like Masséna and Ney, however little teaching they brought with them, acquired in the army the ordinary good education of a soldier, having to keep accounts and to furnish returns, for if the old saying were true that it took a ton of lead to kill a man, it is also true that in all armies about the same amount of paper is required to keep each man alive.

It is not easy to classify the six civilians. I presume that all except Mortier must be put amongst the *bourgeoisie* at highest. Bessières was son of a well-to-do surgeon. Brune's father was an *avocat*, and his uncle had the Cross of Saint Louis, a military order requiring twenty years' service. Lannes was son of a farmer. Saint-Cyr's father was a tanner who had been a butcher. Suchet's father is said to have been a silk merchant, but he is also styled *Juge Conservateur de la Charité de Lyon*. Mortier must have stood higher than the other civilians. His father, a man of some position, was Deputy from Cambrésis

---

[1] Susane, *Cav. franç.*, i. 210.
[2] Not to the States-General of 1789, as often said.

to the States-General in 1789. The future Marshal himself was given a commission as Lieutenant in the Carabiniers in 1791. This, if it be literally correct, would have included him amongst the class of officers, and the two regiments of Carabiniers were crack corps.[1] The posts in them were given, at least in the time of Louis XIV, to officers too poor to purchase companies in ordinary regiments.[2] Mortier, however, never joined his corps, entering the army through the volunteers. Of this class Lannes was the worst educated, knowing only what we call the three R's. The others had a fair or good education; Brune, for example, was intended for the law and was an author, though he had to enter a printing office to live. Saint-Cyr, whom one would have expected to have come off worst, was well taught.

If I be right in my classification, it follows that all the future Marshals who were, or had served as, officers in the regular army by 1791, that is, Berthier, Davout, Grouchy, Kellermann, Macdonald, Marmont, Moncey, Pérignon, and Sérurier, with Mortier and perhaps Suchet from the civilian class, and possibly Bernadotte from that of the soldiers, a total of twelve, belonged to classes which in England supply the mass of the officers of the regular army. Four, all of the soldier category, Augereau, Lefebvre, Murat, and Ney, belonged to classes which in England have hitherto supplied our rank and file. Five of the soldier category, Jourdan, Masséna, Oudinot, Soult, and Victor, with four civilians, Bessières, Brune, Lannes, and Saint-Cyr, a total of nine, belonged to classes very little represented amongst our officers or rank and file. Still I say this with great diffidence, believing that classification requires a greater knowledge of the exact shading down of the different classes in France than I possess. It is difficult enough to draw a line between different classes in an English village. It may be said that it was open to Brune to follow the example of his uncle and become an officer; and I doubt whether Masséna and Oudinot should not be classed with Ney. Whatever my mistakes, it will be seen that the Marshals cannot be described as a mass of leaders rising from a rough soldiery. Almost all were, or ought to have been, well or fairly educated. Some

[1] Susane, *Cav. franç.*, ii. 187-207.   [2] Ibid., 188.

THE MARSHALS CLASSIFIED

did rise from the ranks, but they took their new position worthily. Murat was the son of an innkeeper, yet Sir Robert Wilson, no lover of Frenchmen, says of a dinner with him in 1814: 'It was impossible for Lord Chesterfield to have done the honours better;' and he hints that even the Prince Regent, 'the first gentleman in Europe', might 'feel a little jealous of his kingly courtesies'.[1] As for those with whom the English came most in contact, whether it were the calm Mortier, rough Soult, violent Ney or hot-tempered Victor, we found the most chivalrous of foes. Safe were our wounded in their hands. If we doubt the impartiality of Napier, it is when he treats of Soult, whose care he, a wounded prisoner, had experienced. Nor was it only to officers that the Marshals' care extended. Ney, following Soult and Moore in the race for Coruña, came on a lot of women which that much married force, the English army, had left behind. He directed them to be taken for safety to a Spanish nunnery. Our Allies objected: the women were heretics. 'I appreciate your scruples,' said Ney, 'and instead will send you a company of grenadiers whose catholicity I will guarantee.' The nuns chose the heretics. This and much of more serious import might have been remembered in 1815.

It is a little difficult to be right technically in assigning the future Marshals to the different arms of the service under the *ancien régime*; for instance, Marmont did not belong to the artillery till 1st March 1792, but the following distribution will serve for all practical purposes. The staff may be said to have given Berthier to the Marshalate, whilst the cavalry gave two already old officers, Kellermann and Grouchy, with Davout, a young one, besides Augereau, who had served in the ranks, and Murat and Ney, who were still serving there in 1791. Although Moncey had served in the *Gendarmerie*, a part of the cavalry, I must place him where most of his service previous to the Revolution lay. Consequently the infantry gave as officers Macdonald, Moncey, Pérignon, and Sérurier, and as privates Bernadotte, Lefebvre, and Soult, all still in the ranks, besides Jourdan, Masséna, and Oudinot, who had left the service. Disregarding Grouchy's first nominal

[1] Wilson, *Diary*, ii. 345.

connexion with the artillery, that arm only gave two Marshals, Marmont and Victor, but it also gave Napoleon. If, however, we look to the arms in which the Marshals had had most experience when they received the *bâton*, and in the term 'infantry' include the command of mixed bodies, then I think we may describe Berthier as a staff officer, Kellermann and Grouchy as officers who had left the cavalry, and Marmont the artillery, to command divisions or armies. Bessières and Murat were cavalry officers, pure and simple. All the rest (and I now include the six who were civilians in 1791), Augereau, Bernadotte, Brune, Davout, Jourdan, Lannes, Lefebvre, Macdonald, Masséna, Moncey, Mortier, Ney, Oudinot, Pérignon, Saint-Cyr, Sérurier, Soult, Suchet, and Victor, rose by infantry service. But this is not quite satisfactory, unless we remember how much Ney and Davout had to do with the cavalry after 1791. By 1792 four of the future Marshals had been in the King's Guard, two in the *Maison du Roi*, the Guard of the *ancien régime*, and two in the *Garde constitutionnelle* of what we may call the short-lived Constitutional Monarchy. Grouchy had been in the cavalry of the *Maison* in the crack corps, the *Compagnie écossaise*, of the Gardes du Corps, and Lefebvre was Sergeant in the infantry of the *Maison*, in the Gardes Françaises. Bessières and Murat served as privates in the cavalry of the *Garde constitutionnelle*, the new body. Another, Moncey, had been very near the *Maison*, having served as private in one of those companies of the *Gendarmerie de France* which only took orders from the King.[1] It is true that he had been turned out of that corps, just as Murat had been practically turned out of the Guard. Indeed, one is inclined to suspect that Grouchy may have had some hint to leave the *Maison*, with whose officers he can have had but little sympathy. The corps to which Lefebvre and Bessières belonged were dissolved, but it was natural enough that Lefebvre should have some (and Bessières a very close) connexion afterwards with the Imperial Guard.

It would obviously be very interesting to know the political opinions of these men in 1791, but the task is so hard that I undertake it with great diffidence. Officers and men passed

[1] Susane, *Cav. franç.*, i. 238-40.

the frontier, remained with their regiments, or joined the army from civilian life, at this period, for many reasons. The causes which made so many officers become *émigrés* are easy to understand. The Nobles were naturally disgusted at the new state of affairs, and in many cases their lives were not safe with their regiments, for the denouncers were already at work, and in some cases the irritated men drove away officers whom they distrusted. Others, who may have sympathized with these, still were retained by circumstances and by a dislike to become wanderers in a foreign land, where many of them were unlikely to get a friendly reception from the extreme Royalists. It was a question of becoming an *émigré*, or staying with the colours, for it was dangerous to retire. Davout, who tried that plan later, after giving full proof of his patriotism, found himself suspected and imprisoned. Further, no one in 1791 could have imagined into what dark misery the armies would fall. Thus, both men who partly sympathized with the new doctrines, and those who found themselves no longer barred from promotion by not being *Noble*, had much inducement to remain.

Meanwhile many civilians and soldiers who had left the service had good prospects if they joined the ranks. The former soldiers saw a new career open to them in the volunteers. As for civilians, in the first place a great wave of enthusiasm had passed over the country, and to many young men it was natural and pleasant to enlist, amidst the applause of their friends, for a short time or for the war. Once the enemy were thrown back and the safety of the country assured, obviously an operation which would not take long, then would come the triumphal return and a glorious memory. Such praiseworthy feelings brought to the ranks men who were to see many fights and many lands and to leave their bones in Egypt, Spain, or Russia, but the enthusiasm with which some of them entered did not always last long. For men who were alarmed at the confusion in the interior, or who had in any way compromised themselves with the patriots, the armies were the best and safest shelter. There those that did not hold high rank had the best chance of escaping from the denouncers, who often enough in civilian life had their own vengeances to satisfy.

All these causes were operating to fill the ranks in 1791. Still, in attempting to get at what was in the minds of the future Marshals at this period, I must take subsequent events into some consideration.

Amongst the *patriots* in this first stage of the Revolution we may safely count Augereau, Brune, Davout, Grouchy, Suchet, Jourdan, Kellermann, and Murat : perhaps also Bernadotte. Of these, putting aside Murat's long personal quarrel with his commander, Landrieux, I know only three, Augereau, Brune, and Suchet, who can be said to have taken any part in the work of denouncing others (when that soon meant the scaffold for the alleged criminal), or who showed any sympathy for the murderous work of the Representatives with the armies. Augereau was always a violent talker, and both his and Suchet's language was probably stronger than their intentions. Brune alone amongst the Marshals bore any of the blood-stains of the Revolution. It is untrue that he was the tall wretch who bore the head of the Princesse de Lamballe through the streets, as the Royalists alleged, and for which they eventually did him to death, as if to show what they too were capable of. The friend of Danton, who called him his ' Patagonian ', a hanger-on of Robespierre's, Brune served in and even commanded one of the vile ' Revolutionary armies ', whose prey was their fellow countrymen. He was engaged in what we may call the conspiracy to destroy such Generals as Custine. Grouchy was a type of the aristocratic Revolutionist, full of ideas of progress, and equally surprised and indignant when he found himself struck at. Kellermann was simply a well-intentioned old officer, admiring the first phrases of the patriots, but too good a soldier not to object to their methods with the army. Davout's attitude I have referred to. It is easily understood and explains how the regimental patriot of 1791 became the stern upholder of order under the Empire. Bernadotte's Republicanism was of a curious sort, not preventing a close eye to his own interests. Murat at this time was a boiling patriot, but he was a weak man and soon cooled. Jourdan, a simple-hearted man, was full of a sincere, partly pathetic, partly ludicrous belief in the efficacy of patriotic phrases, such as ' the country is in danger ', which he retained

THE MARSHALS CLASSIFIED 53

long after his own treatment might well have sickened him of his party. He had nothing to do with the evil measures of the faction to which he nominally belonged. Most probably such men as Lannes, Lefebvre, Masséna, Ney, Oudinot, Saint-Cyr, and Victor were in favour of the Revolution so far as it affected them, and, except Saint-Cyr, none of them was likely to entertain very wide views. Macdonald was at most lukewarm, and indeed might have gone over the frontier, had not his wife been unable to accompany him. It might not be fair to suggest that the canny Scotsman knew that he had good backing in France, but one always suspects him of being a little amused at the capers of the excitable race amongst which his lot was thrown; he certainly knew by family experience the shady side of emigration for a lost cause. Soult no doubt speaks truly in representing himself as taking part with no factions, and I might well class him with the worthy Lefebvre, who had wise ideas as to liberty.

Marmont describes himself as a constitutional Royalist, and that mode of government would probably have suited also Berthier, Bessières, Moncey, Mortier, Pérignon, and Sérurier, but there were differences amongst these. Of Mortier's opinions I know nothing. Moncey's friendships tell a tale: one was with Carnot (but he was considered a moderate) and others with Moreau, always suspected of Royalism, Pichegru, who went over to that party, Willot, a Royalist, and Georges Cadoudal, a most violent Royalist partisan; they all tend to the belief that he might have been contented with the *ancien régime*. Pérignon, elected a member of the *Assemblée législative* of 1791, soon left, alarmed at the excesses of the Jacobins. He seems to have been well content with the First Restoration. Sérurier was exactly one of the men whom one would have expected to have welcomed the Revolution. When he had had every recommendation and every qualification for promotion to Major, for long he had failed to get the step because he had *point de condition*, that is, of birth. Still, he is alleged to have attempted to emigrate and to have failed only from being turned back by a patriot. The story is probably unfounded, but shows what was thought of him. Two of the men who were to be amongst the longest companions of the

Emperor were certainly Royalists. Berthier had good reason for being satisfied with the *ancien régime*, which had treated him well. The patriots had always suspected him, perhaps the more from his having commanded the troops who in the Spring of 1791 put down the mob which was trying to prevent the departure of *Mesdames*, the Aunts of the King, for Rome. Also he was believed to be of Lafayette's party. He was very fortunate in escaping with his life and must have felt at last in the right place when he found himself head of the staff of a firm Ruler. Bessières, having served in the King's Constitutional Guard, remained in Paris when that was disbanded. It may be that he was one of the trusted men whose pay the King, it was alleged, secretly continued. During the assault on the Tuileries on the 10th August he had at least assisted some of the defenders to escape, and had then gone into hiding till he could get back to the south, where he joined the Armée des Pyrénées-Orientales. It was therefore natural enough that he should soon be in command of Bonaparte's Guides, for the rising General knew the value of fidelity. It was also natural that Bessières should be the Marshal who really commanded the Imperial Guard. Cold, reserved, honourable, faithful, his unfortunate death, with that of Duroc in 1813, was not merely a great loss to Napoleon, but also has made the Emperor seem in the eyes of posterity as going into exile a friendless man. Chance no doubt played an important part in the choice of sides, and a camp story makes Moncey decide his fate by throwing into the air his plume, which, fortunately for him, fell towards France.

About their religious opinions we know very little, for we need not take seriously the fervour shown by Soult under the First Restoration, nor the support to Charles X's policy given by Victor under the Second Restoration. Soult got on well with his Protestant wife. Religion was at a discount in the days of the Republic, and, as for the Empire, when Napoleon expressed his wish not to have an army of bigots, de Fezensac remarks that he need have had no anxiety on that point.[1] Still, the honest-hearted Lefebvre was not ashamed to acknowledge that he made an *action de grâces* before going into action,

[1] Fezensac, *Souvenirs*, 36.

THE MARSHALS CLASSIFIED

and doubtless others did not forget early lessons. The only Protestant amongst the future Marshals was Bernadotte ; at least, when he went to Sweden, he said that he had accepted the Confession of Augsburg, later asserting that he had been born a Protestant. It was true that his family name appears amongst those of Protestants,[1] but on birth he was duly baptized as a Catholic.[2]

Of the musical talents of the Marshals we do not know much. Ney, *à l'oreille musicale*, played the clarionet, at least in 1800.[3] Three at least played the violin—Victor (who, however, owed his entry into the service to his skill on the clarionet), Marmont, and Saint-Cyr. Brune is the sort of man one would expect to have been musical. Marmont in his young days had a taste for ' la musique et la bonne comédie ', and in his old age he regretted that he had never been more than a scrabbler on the violin : ' It is an immense resource for a young officer when he plays an instrument, opening the doors of society to him, especially if he have a good education and does not sacrifice his duties to it.'[4] Marmont, however, is speaking of playing amidst his gay society, but Saint-Cyr bent over his violin to console himself when, shaking off for a few hours the golden horde of the Empire, he sat alone at night in the dreary time of 1812, Desaix dead, Moreau no longer to be girded at, and the evil years for France fast coming on. All this music would have been wormwood to Napoleon, who could not endure the high notes of the violin, and who got Méhul to write an opera with no stringed instrument in the orchestra of higher register than the ' alto ' or ' viola '. In such matters Wellington set an excellent example. Once he used to play the violin well and very much, but when he began to take his profession seriously, he realized the danger of the taint he had inherited from his father, ' most musical of Lords ',[5] and burnt his violin, considering that it was not a soldierly accomplishment.[6] Méhul, by the by, complained to Napoleon that he put Italian music first, to which the Emperor replied, ' C'est comme vous, Méhul, vous avez une haute réputation,

---

[1] Pingaud, *Bernadotte*, 106–8.   [2] Barthety, *Le Maréchal Bernadotte*, 7–8.
[3] Bonnal, *Ney*, i. 269.   [4] Marmont, *Souvenirs*, i. 10.
[5] Thackeray, *Ballads*, 232.   [6] Jennings, *Croker Papers*, i. 337, note.

mais votre musique m'ennuie'. 'Eh,' said the thoughtless Méhul, ' qu'est-ce que cela prouve ? ' Then, realizing to whom he was talking, he fled, believing himself disgraced for ever. Napoleon remained struck dumb by this audacity, but eventually overlooked the matter.[1]

The very peculiar conditions under which most of these men rose make it impossible to take their careers as an argument for or against promotion from the ranks. In the case of Masséna and Soult it was their knowledge of drill, not of strategy, which gave them their opportunity. Masséna was General of Division in three, and Soult General of Brigade in little more than two years after they had entered the volunteers, but two years of that time had been steady fighting. Masséna had had six years' experience of war, and Soult much more, before they got independent command of an army. Under ordinary conditions they would at each stage have had to encounter the rivalry of men with greater experience, and, if they had progressed to the same heights, it must have been much more slowly. An army is a machine for immediate work, and the unexpected and extraordinary respites which the Allies gave to France alone saved her whilst she was reconstructing her forces.

It is important not to lose sight of the great influence of the former officers and soldiers of the old Royal army on the forces of the Republic. For example, in 1798, when the Armée d'Orient started for Egypt, it had thirty-two general officers. Of these, fourteen had served in France as officers before 1789, besides two others, Kléber, who had been in the Austrian service, and Zaioncheck in Poland. Eleven others had served as privates or *sous-officiers* before 1789. Thus twenty-seven out of thirty-two came from the old system and only five had entered the army after 1789, that is, under Revolutionary conditions.[2] Considering that the Armée d'Orient was mainly a picked detachment from the famous Armée d'Italie, this

---

[1] *Rev. des Deux Mondes*, 1st May 1911, p. 180.

[2] Sixteen former officers: Bonaparte, Andréossy, Baraguey d'Hilliers, Berthier, Desaix de Veygoux, Dugua, Kléber, de Menou, du Muy de Saint-Maime, Belgrand de Vaubois, Caffarelli du Falga, Davout, de Dommartin, d'Hennezel de Valleroy, Manscourt, Zaioncheck. Eleven former privates: Bon, Chanez, Dumas, Friant, Fugière, Leclerc, Murat, Rampon, Veaux, Verdier, Vial. Five entered after 1789: Belliard, Damas, Lannes, Mireur, Reynier. See La Jonquière, *Égypte*, i. 513, note.

large proportion of the old Royal army amongst it is very striking.

Even the men who had been only privates started with invaluable knowledge, and it was the Marshals who had been in the army of the Monarchy who rendered the most valuable services to France. If we take the six civilians, Bessières, Brune, Lannes, Mortier, Saint-Cyr, and Suchet, it will be seen that it did not fall to any of them to render such services as Kellermann did at Valmy, Jourdan at Wattignies and Fleurus, or Masséna at Zurich, not to mention the achievements of Bonaparte himself. Doubtless Lannes, Saint-Cyr, and Suchet were far superior in ability to many of the Marshals sprung from the regulars; still they did not command in the early campaigns, and had to learn their trade.

Two things should be noted in this connexion. First, the immense difference in the seniority of the Marshals. Secondly, the future Marshals who first held high command, did so under every possible disadvantage compared with those who rose later. The improvement in the troops themselves in self-confidence, discipline, and experience in later days made movements possible which would have been fatal in the first years of the war. Also, the early commanders had not the experience generally possessed before attaining their rank. In two years from the time when he, a former private, had been given the command of a volunteer battalion, Jourdan had to command in a pitched battle, leading the main army of France and without the use of a trained staff. On the other hand, it took Suchet sixteen years from the time he got the command of a regiment till he led the 3rd Corps in Spain. It might be a fairer comparison to take Saint-Cyr, but it is difficult to do so, as, though he took an important position in the army comparatively soon, yet he can hardly be said to have held an entirely independent command in the field till he went to Spain in 1808. Further, by the side of the early commanders stood the irresponsible but all-powerful Representatives, meddling with every movement. Imagine such a man able to check Napoleon at Wagram, when, disregarding the growing defeat of his Left, he pushed on his Right? I am a humble follower of Saint-Cyr and Napoleon in the belief that commanders seldom improve in the higher art of war by experience: yet in many matters experience does tell. It behoves us to be very tender in dealing with the early commanders of the Revolution. Now neither Jourdan, Kellermann, Moncey, nor Pérignon stand in the first class of commanders, but by 1794 all four had commanded important armies of the Republic with success.

And now as to the 'grouping' of the future Marshals, to which I alluded in Chapter I.

If we allot each Marshal of the twenty-five [1] to the army in which he gained his most important experience in these wars, we get the following groups up to the peace or armistice of 1797.[2]

Taking first those who served under the broad heading of 'armies on the Northern and Eastern frontiers', we get:

Armée du Nord	Jourdan and Macdonald.
Armée de Sambre-et-Meuse . .	(formed in 1794 from the Armée des Ardennes, together with part of the Armée du Nord and part of the Armée de la Moselle). Jourdan, Lefebvre, Ney, Soult, Bernadotte, Mortier.
Armée de Rhin-et-Moselle . .	(formed in 1795 from the Armée du Rhin and the Armée de la Moselle). Davout, Saint-Cyr, Oudinot.
Armée du Centre	Kellermann, whom I place here because of Valmy, but his longest experience of these wars was in the south.
Armies in La Vendée	Grouchy.

Then the groups on the Southern frontiers are:

Armée des Alpes	Kellermann.
Armée des Pyrénées-Orientales .	Pérignon.
Armée des Pyrénées-Occidentales	Moncey.
Armée d'Italie	Berthier, Masséna, Augereau, Sérurier, Lannes, Murat, Marmont, Suchet, Victor, Bessières, Brune.

---

[1] Omitting Prince Poniatowski.

[2] After this the armies were broken up and my system of grouping cannot be continued.

THE MARSHALS CLASSIFIED

It will, of course, be understood that the early services of these men were not limited to the groups in which I have put them; for instance, in the ' Nord ' we shall find several besides Jourdan and Macdonald. But I have considered that in each case the experience which had the greatest influence on their character was that which they gained in these particular groups. Both Kellermann and Jourdan I have allotted to two armies.

In such early experience the contrast which is most marked is that between the campaigns of the ' Sambre-et-Meuse ' and ' Rhin-et-Moselle ' groups on the one hand, and the ' Italie ' group on the other.

All that now remains for me to do, before entering on the history of the ' Nord ', is to give the ranks of the future Marshals at the beginning of the Revolutionary wars. By the 20th April 1792, when war was declared with the Emperor, the promotion caused by the emigration of many officers and the formation of the battalions of volunteers had changed the position of most of the future Marshals, and they stood as follows. Kellermann, far the senior, had become Lieut.-General. Berthier was Adjutant-General with the rank of Colonel. Grouchy was Colonel of a Dragoon regiment, Sérurier a Lt.-Colonel, Moncey a Captain, and Macdonald a Lieutenant in the infantry. The young Marmont had passed into the artillery as *élève-sous-lieutenant*, say ' Cadet '. All these were in the regular army. One of those formerly holding commissions in the regulars, Davout, had entered the volunteers, in which he was the Second Lt.-Colonel of a battalion. Pérignon had not yet re-entered the army, but was sitting as member of the Legislative Assembly at Paris. Captain Bonaparte of the artillery was in Corsica, where he had become Second Lt.-Colonel to a volunteer battalion.

Of the five whom the Revolution found in the ranks of the army without commissions, by the 20th April 1792 Bernadotte was a Lieutenant and Lefebvre a Captain in the regular infantry. Murat was still a private in the Chasseurs, to which he had returned from the Gardes à cheval. Ney, on the other hand, had risen to be *maréchal des logis chef* (Sergeant-Major) in the Hussars. Soult, becoming Sergeant in a regular battalion, was now instructor to a volunteer battalion.

INTRODUCTION

Of the five former privates who had left the army, by the 20th April 1792 Augereau was, he said, in the National Guard, but his rank is unknown. The four others were in the volunteers, Jourdan and Masséna as Lt.-Colonels commanding battalions, and Oudinot as a Second Lt.-Colonel. Victor was *adjudant sous-officier*.

Of the six former civilians, Bessières, Brune, Lannes, Mortier, Saint-Cyr, and Suchet, only three had entered the army at the time of the declaration of war. Bessières was a private in the Gardes à cheval du Roi, Brune was *adjudant-major*, and Mortier Captain, in different battalions of volunteers. The three others joined the volunteers later, Lannes as *sous-lieutenant* in June 1792, and the others, apparently, as privates, Saint-Cyr in September 1792, and Suchet between January and July 1793. Thus the first of the future Marshals to enter the army was Kellermann in 1752, and the last Suchet in 1793, a difference of forty-one years.

To give some specimens of rapid promotion, Bernadotte, Adjutant of a regular regiment, in November 1791 entered another as Lieutenant. Hostilities only began in April 1792, but in November of that year he was *adjudant-major*, and Captain in July 1793. Next year, 1794, he became Lt.-Colonel in February, Colonel in April, General of Brigade in June, and General of Division in December. The volunteers gave openings for quick elevation, Davout, a Lieutenant, and the former privates, Jourdan, Masséna, Oudinot, and Victor, becoming Lt.-Colonels, either at a jump, or very shortly after entering. Amongst commanders of volunteer battalions who became Generals of high rank were Championnet, Delmas, Lecourbe, Moreau, Pichegru, and Souham. Bonaparte himself, as we have seen, had had a short experience of one of these battalions.

These sudden changes in rank must have caused much heartburning, and one can fancy how such a man as Lt.-Colonel Sérurier, with his thirty-six years' service, must have looked on some of the now numerous Lt.-Colonels who had not as many days to count. Still, if we give them all their respective ranks and include their future master, we get the following list: Lieut.-General Kellermann; Colonel Berthier; Lt.-Colonels Grouchy, Jourdan, Masséna, Pérignon, and Sérurier;

THE MARSHALS CLASSIFIED

Second Lt.-Colonels [1] Oudinot and Davout ; Captains Moncey, Mortier, Lefebvre, and Bonaparte ; Lieutenants Macdonald and Bernadotte ; *adjudant-majors* Augereau and Brune ; *élève-sous-lieutenant* Marmont ; *adjudant sous-officier* Victor ; *sous-officier* Lannes ; Instructor Soult [2] ; Sergeant-Major Ney ; Privates Murat, Bessières, Saint-Cyr, and Suchet.

In the matter of age, the future Marshals, including this time Poniatowski as well as Bonaparte, stood as follows in April 1791. Far the senior was Kellermann, who was all but 57. Next came Sérurier, 49. These alone were past forty. Berthier and Pérignon were both 38 and Moncey 37, Lefebvre 36, Masséna all but 36, Augereau 34, Jourdan 30, and Poniatowski all but 30. Next came a younger lot. Bernadotte was 29, and Brune all but that age. Saint-Cyr was 28, Victor 27, and Macdonald 26. Murat and Grouchy were 25, and Oudinot all but that age. Mortier was 24 ; Bessières, Lannes, Ney, and Soult were all 23. Bonaparte was 22, and Davout was all but that age. Suchet was 21. Then came the youngest of all, Marmont, who was only 17.

Other French leaders stood as follows : Kléber 39, Pichegru 31, Moreau 29, Hoche 24, Desaix, Joubert, and Marceau, 23. Of their opponents, Wurmser was 67, Alvinzi 66, Souvaroff 62, Brunswick 57, Kutusoff 47, Moore 31, Wellington 23, the Archduke Charles, and also Schwarzenberg 21.

[1] They may have ranked with the other Lt.-Colonels, but did not command a battalion.
[2] I do not know in what rank to put Soult.

V

L'ARMÉE DU NORD, 1791-2

Formation of the first three Armies: Nord, Centre, and Rhin. Position of Berthier, Jourdan, Macdonald, and Mortier at this time, and also of Hoche, Marceau, and Moreau. The *Chassé-croisé* brings in Davout, Grouchy, and Murat. Grouchy leaves before, and Ney joins after Valmy. The Marshals who joined and left this army. Forces furnished by the 'Nord', 'Argonne', 'Ardennes', 'Belgique', 'Hollande'. Combined action with 'Centre'. Commanders of the first three Armies: Rochambeau, Lafayette, and Luckner. Luckner's 'parre'. Bad effect of the quarrels of the Generals. Plans of the Commanders for the Campaign. Intervention of Dumouriez. His character and plans. Advance of the French, and their rout at Baisieux and Quiévrain. Rochambeau resigns. Unfortunate mission of Berthier to Paris. Luckner replaces Rochambeau.

ON the 14th December 1791 the Monarchy then, be it remembered, still existing, three armies were formed to defend the north-eastern frontier: the Armée du Nord, holding the northern fortresses, with its head-quarters at Valenciennes; the Armée du Centre, which in October 1792 became the Armée de la Moselle, head-quarters at Metz; and the Armée du Rhin, head-quarters at Strasbourg. Of these the 'Nord' was the most important force. When first organized it had, including six Swiss battalions, thirty-one battalions of regular infantry and forty-four squadrons of cavalry (all belonging to the old army), 29,446 strong, and eight battalions of volunteers of the 1791 levy, 4,320 strong; or a total of 33,766 men, with 25,502 garrison troops, depots, &c., making a grand total of 59,268, besides four battalions of artillery, which of course were all regulars.[1] This force was commanded by Rochambeau. Except for one thrilling day at Valmy, when the Armée du Centre took the main strain, the history of the 'Nord' is the most important of all the armies of France for the first years of the war, until in 1794 it succeeded in conquering Holland, when the interest turned to other forces on other frontiers.

[1] Sérignan, *Invasion*, 13-15.

Of the two other armies formed at the same time, the Armée du Centre, under Lafayette, and the Armée du Rhin, under Luckner, the first was not quite on a level with the ' Nord ' in importance, whilst the Armée du Rhin was certainly inferior in interest to both.

It may be well to give a list of the future Marshals and other men with whom we are concerned, who served at different times with this army. On its first formation Colonel and Adjutant-General Berthier was on its staff, and Lieutenant Macdonald was in a regular regiment, the 87th ' Dillon ', quartered at Lille.[1] The others were in volunteer battalions. Captain Mortier, of the 1st Nord, was at Dunkirk on the 1st October 1791, going to Lille on the 1st January 1792.[2] Lt.-Colonel Jourdan's battalion, 2nd Haute-Vienne, only formed on the 2nd October 1791 at Villers-Cotterets, came from Étampes to Cambrai on the 20th June 1792, that is to say, after the beginning of hostilities.[3] Lt.-Colonel Moreau's battalion, 1st Ille-et-Vilaine, which had been at Fougères, came up to Arras in May 1792, and then to Lille in June 1792.[4] Two other Lt.-Colonels, Davout of the 3rd Yonne, which had gone to Dormans in December 1791,[5] and Lt.-Colonel Oudinot, of the 3rd Meuse, which had been at Rocroi and Charleville,[6] belonged to the ' Nord '; but both of these battalions passed to the Armée du Centre in May 1792.

In July 1792 the *Chassé-croisé*, explained farther on, sent General Berthier, Chief of the Staff, with Marshal Luckner to the Armée du Centre, whilst Colonel Grouchy with his Dragoon or Hussar regiment, Sergeant Murat in the 12th Chasseurs, and, I think, Adjutant Ney in the then 5th Hussars, joined the ' Nord ', and Lt.-Colonel Davout with his volunteer battalion rejoined from the ' Centre '. On the 1st July 1792 General Dumouriez joined from Paris, rising to command the ' Nord ' in August. Grouchy, promoted General of Brigade on the 7th September 1792, went to the Armée des Alpes a little before Valmy. Then, if we include in the ' Nord ' all its satellites, the Armée des Ardennes, the Armée de la Belgique,

---

[1] Susane, *Inf. franç.*, v. 64.   [2] Déprez, *Volontaires nationaux*, 460.
[3] Ibid., 501.   [4] Ibid., 436.
[5] Ibid., 505 ; Vigier, *Davout*, i. 19–22.   [6] Déprez, *Vol. nat.*, 457.

and the Armée de la Hollande, all of which sprang from it, we may say that after Valmy Lt.-Colonel Marceau and Captain Hoche joined from the ' Centre ', Marceau leaving almost immediately for Paris and La Vendée. Brune, an Adjutant-General, probably a Colonel, is said to have come to this army from Paris in October 1792, but his frequent appearances with it are impossible to follow. In April 1793 Dumouriez emigrated. In July 1793 Davout, then General of Brigade, went to La Vendée and never returned here, passing to the Rhine group in the ' Moselle ', late ' Centre ', in October 1794. Early in September 1793 Captain Bernadotte came with his regiment from the ' Rhin '. On the 22nd September 1793 Jourdan, a General of Division with this force from the 30th July 1793, took command of the ' Nord '. In October 1793 Hoche, made General of Division, went to command the Armée de la Moselle, late ' Centre '. The future Marshals, &c., now with the ' Nord ' were Bernadotte, Jourdan, Macdonald, and Mortier, with Moreau ; Brune, as I have said, sometimes appearing here.

In January 1794 Jourdan was sent into retirement, and Pichegru came from the ' Rhin ' to take command. In April of that year Kléber and Marceau, both now Generals of Division, joined from La Vendée, but only for a time, for in June they both, with Colonel Bernadotte, Lt.-Colonel Mortier, and Captain Ney, passed into the new force, the ' Sambre-et-Meuse '. In April 1795 Pichegru handed over the command of the ' Nord ' to his friend Moreau, and went to the command of another new army, the ' Rhin-et-Moselle '. Lt.-Colonel Murat went to form part of the garrison of Paris in May 1795. Brune, employed on the staff, came into the district of the ' Nord ' on some occasions, especially about April and May 1795, but he cannot be counted as really belonging to this army. In March 1796 Moreau went to succeed Pichegru in command of the ' Rhin-et-Moselle ', and Grouchy, now General of Division, came from the west to be Chief of the Staff to the army under Beurnonville. In August 1796 Grouchy went back to the west. In October 1797 the ' Nord ' ceased to exist as an army, although Macdonald, long a General of Division, remained in Holland, which was its district at that date. Jourdan's association with the ' Nord ' is marked by his first victory, Wattignies, but Macdonald was the only future Marshal who served for a long period in this army. Now for the detail of its history.

The history of the ' Nord ' is complicated by the fact that, like another and later formation, the Armée du Midi, it threw off or detached from itself other armies, but, unlike the ' Midi ', ended by absorbing these in time. But as, during the most complicated period, all these formations were commanded in chief by Dumouriez, we can for some purposes, for instance in describing the shifts amongst future members of the Marshalate, use the term ' Nord ' for the whole northern group of armies. At first its southern portion was described as the ' Camp de Sedan ', or the ' Armée de Sedan ', and when this body marched under Dumouriez into the Argonne to meet Brunswick it was sometimes called, unofficially I think, the ' Armée de l'Argonne '. Dumouriez, however, as soon as he himself arrived at Sedan from the north, styled the force there the ' Armée des Ardennes ',[1] a title which only became official on the 1st October 1792, and which was then intended for the whole body of what was really part of the ' Nord ', serving in the Argonne.[2] This title was transferred, I take it by Dumouriez himself, to that part of the force in the Argonne which followed Brunswick in his retreat, in company with the Armée du Centre, under Kellermann. The rest of the Argonne force went north for the invasion of Belgium, as the Armée de la Belgique. Then part of the ' Nord ', or reinforcements for it from Paris, became the Armée de la Hollande. After the defeat of Neerwinden and the flight of Dumouriez, who had had the chief command of the four armies, ' Nord ', ' Belgique ', ' Hollande ', and ' Ardennes ', the ' Nord ' absorbed the Armée de la Belgique and the Armée de la Hollande. The ' Ardennes ' nominally retained a separate existence, but in reality it was a mere satellite of the ' Nord ', which after Fleurus in June 1794 absorbed its left wing, its right falling to a new force, the ' Sambre-et-Meuse '.

At first, until after Valmy, the ' Nord ' acted in close

[1] *Revue de Paris*, 15th September 1908, 231, note 3, is, I think, obviously wrong in referring this to the Camp de Maulde.
[2] Aulard, *Recueil*, i. 82.

combination with the 'Centre', the 'Rhin' operating apart, but when Brunswick retreated the 'Centre', becoming the Armée de la Moselle, entered into what I may call a partnership with the 'Rhin', which ultimately ended in both being welded together in 1795 as the 'Rhin-et-Moselle'. In describing the first operations in the north when the 'Nord' and 'Centre' acted together, it is best to give much of the detail of both armies in the history of the 'Nord', especially as the two commanders had frequent consultations together. Indeed, as the commanders of 'Nord', 'Centre', and 'Rhin' all met for certain purposes, and as Lafayette commanded in turn two, 'Centre' and 'Nord', whilst Luckner passed from the command of the 'Rhin' to that of the 'Nord' and then to that of the 'Centre', it will be best to give here the description of the three commanders to whom the first armies were entrusted.

Rochambeau,[1] who received the command of the principal army, the 'Nord', was an old soldier in every sense of the word. Born in 1725, he had entered the army as Cornet in 1742 and had served in the Seven Years' War with distinction. Then he had commanded the French corps sent to America in 1780 to support the revolted Colonists, where he had served alongside of Washington, Berthier being his A.D.C. Rough and brusque in manner, cold in conversation, he was absorbed in his profession, and Biron complained that he was always drawing plans of movements on the ground, in your room, on your table, even on your snuff-box if in an unguarded moment you took it from your pocket. He had been liked by the Americans; 'Your General is sober,' one of them had remarked. Active, he took in the lie of the ground in a moment and thoroughly understood war. Also he knew how to appeal to his men, and at the capture of Minorca had made them sober by announcing that those who got drunk in the trenches would not be permitted to have the honour of taking part in the assault. Such a man, with his experience of the colonial troops in America, might now have done much for the armies

---

[1] Jean-Baptiste-Donatien de Vimeur, Comte de Rochambeau (1725-1807), Marshal December 1791. Michaud, *Biog. univ.*, xxxviii. 282-8; Sérignan, *Invasion*, 16-21. For his portrait see Sérignan's *Le Duc de Lauzun*, p. 158.

of France; but he was very independent, and, as we shall see, would not submit to the disastrous interference of the Minister for War, Dumouriez. He must not be confused with his son, the General of the Empire, killed at Leipzig.[1]

Lafayette commanded the army second in importance, the ' Centre ', and to write his history would be to write that of the first years of the Revolution. Born in 1757, he had early in life shown his love of agitation, and in April 1777 he sailed to join the American force, in which he was given the rank of Major-General, although he was only a Captain in France. Joining Washington, he served against the English, and in February 1779 returned to France, when, supporting the efforts of the American envoys, he did much to get France to aid the colonies, himself preceding the expedition which sailed under Rochambeau. After the success of the revolted States, Lafayette came back to France and threw himself into the first movements of the Revolution, becoming the commander of the National Guard of Paris and being styled the ' héros des deux mondes '. He followed, rather than led, the march on Versailles, but on him lay the responsibility of forcing the King to come to Paris, and this was the origin of much evil by exposing Royalty to the mob of the Capital. Then, after a period of wild popularity, he gradually lost the favour of the Parisians. The escape of the Royal Family to Varennes, the Queen almost brushing past him unobserved, when he had engaged that such an enterprise should be impossible, was a blow to him, whilst he began to dread the growing power and vehemence of the Jacobins. Like many such men, he had not realized the danger of the torrent he had let loose. Frederick the Great had been more clear-sighted when the General had appeared at his Court about 1783. ' I have ', he said, ' known a young man who, after visiting countries where Liberty and Equality reigned, wished to establish all that in his own country : do you know what happened to him ? ' ' No, Sire.' ' He was hanged.' Lafayette, who did

[1] Général Baron, Donatien-Marie-Joseph de Vimeur, Vicomte de Rochambeau (1755–1813); surrendered to the English in San Domingo in 1803, prisoner until 1811; employed in 1813. Michaud, *Biog. univ.*, xxxviii. 288–90.

not take the King's meaning, narrowly escaped the guillotine, and that only by flight.¹

On the 8th October 1791, the *Assemblée constituante* having completed its labours and existence, Lafayette laid down his command of the National Guard and retired to the country, the force rapidly being disorganized and losing all power for good. Still it was no doubt a belief in his influence which led to his receiving this command of the ' Centre ', which he mainly owed to the Minister for War, Narbonne, a friend of his. Jomini, who could have but little grounds for his opinion, asserts that Lafayette was the only commander who seized the decisive point and thus proved that he would have made war with distinction had not Fate decided otherwise. His appointment was most unfortunate. He really wished for the preservation of the Constitutional Monarchy, but his past career and the part he had played in the humiliation of the Royal Family at Versailles made the Court distrust him and most unluckily refuse to receive his help, whilst he was bitterly attacked by the Jacobins. From the first he kept his eyes fixed on the Capital and wished to use his army to put down the mob or at least to give the King the means of leaving Paris and joining him. Yet, whilst his support was refused by the Monarch, he had not the moral courage to crush the Jacobins, weak as they then were in armed forces, and he did the most dangerous thing in face of a popular movement: he threatened, but did not strike. Whilst he thus did much to embroil the Generals with the Jacobins, he did nothing to overawe the Clubs. However, much of this was for the future. On the 25th December 1791 he left Paris for his head-quarters, Metz. His departure was a sort of triumphal procession, for he was still loved by the National Guard, and detachments from all its battalions, with a crowd of applauding people, accompanied him to the barriers.²

Luckner, the commander of the ' Rhin ', was a curious contrast alike to that fine style of a General of the *ancien*

---

¹ Marie-Joseph-Paul-Yves-Roch-Gilbert du Motier, Marquis de Lafayette (1757–1834). Charavay, *Le Général Lafayette* ; Michaud, *Biog. univ.*, lxix. 348–405 ; Jules Thomas, *Correspondance inédite de Lafayette*.

² Charavay, *Lafayette*, 280.

régime, Rochambeau, and the political General, Lafayette. Bavarian by birth, he had served against France in the Hanoverian army during the Seven Years' War, passing into the French army as Lieut.-General on the 20th June 1763. Short, with an enormous body, massive head, square shoulders, although now sixty-nine, he could still walk twenty-seven miles or remain twelve hours on horseback, and he was of immense bodily activity. A brave and daring Hussar, he had not the brains of a commander and understood nothing but raids. When Dumouriez, full of far-reaching plans, tried to explain to him the contemplated invasion of Belgium, the old Hussar could only reply, 'Oui, moi tourne par la droite, tourne par la gauche, et marcher vite'. He talked a jargon which might be German, but was certainly not French, and when later on he tried to read a speech to the Assembly the members began laughing, and Narbonne, the Minister, had to save the situation by taking the manuscript himself, whilst declaring that the Marshal, as he then was, had a heart more French than his tongue.[1] It was by the oddest of chances that to such a man was dedicated the Hymn of the Revolution, the *Marseillaise*. He had causes for dissatisfaction with the Monarchy. Louis XVI, with some wisdom, had run a pen through his name when submitted for some promotion, and the old General kept on saying, ' J'ai la parre (barre) du roi sur le cœur '.[2] At first he got a great reputation for patriotism, although he soon agreed with Lafayette. He was the most changeable of mortals, one day cursing vigorously an obnoxious General who attempted to give advice, and threatening to imprison him, and the next effecting a reconciliation by bursting into the tears which came so easily to him, and vowing it was all the fault of his staff. As a commander he was null: the very sight of a great army and of its long trains daunted him, and he feared to move the mass. What he would have liked

[1] Marshal Nicolas Luckner (1722–94). Commanding ' Rhin ', 14th December 1791; commanding ' Nord ', May 1792; commanding ' Centre ', July 1792; Generalissimo, 29th August 1792 to 13th September 1792; executed 4th January 1794. Sérignan, *Invasion*, 21–32, 201–3, 277; Michaud, *Biog. univ.*, xxv. 374–5; *Biog. des Cont.*, v. 421–2; Chuquet, *Invasion*, 192–4; Gay de Vernon, *Custine et Houchard*, 11–15; Dumouriez, *Vie*, i. 337, ii. 334–6, Eng. ed. iii. 11–14.

[2] Gay de Vernon, *Custine et Houchard*, 13–14.

would have been to put himself at the head of the advanced guard, which he would have led to the end of the world.[1] At the moment he was most popular in the camps, amidst which he moved continually, so that the men called him 'notre père'. Amongst civilians, who mistook his vigour of body for capacity, it was the same, and the only wish was that he might be Generalissimo. Like that of Lafayette, his appointment was unfortunate, for when in time his utter unfitness was known the prestige of the commanders was lowered. Yet the old man was no fool, witness the manner in which he either chose or accepted Berthier as his Chief of the Staff and let himself be guided in details by those skilful hands.

All this has a great importance for our subject. Had all the commanders of armies and the Generals at this stage of the Revolution been of an ordinary type such as the *ancien régime* produced in Rochambeau, they might have retained the natural and proper prestige of their rank, and the armies might have been spared much disorganization with consequent disasters and bloodshed. Not merely were they in some instances improper selections, but also their quarrels ruined them. We shall find Dumouriez, in his struggle with Lafayette and Luckner, invoking the intereference of the Assembly and so placing the foot of that body on the necks of the commanders. Worse still, they denounced one another. Dumouriez was to represent Luckner as a worthy man, misled by his staff. Custine was to denounce Kellermann and to vow that one of their heads must fall. The vile Charles de Hesse, 'Le Général Marat',[2] keeping well from the front, was to spend his time in denunciations of men who had all the heavy weight of war on their shoulders, such as Luckner[3] and Custine.[4] Civilians are always prone enough to believe in the incompetence of Generals, whose difficulties they are by nature unable to conceive. What were they to think when one General accused another of incompetence, of treason? It is possible that the Revolution might have burnt on amidst the ring of steel on the frontiers, which would have protected it against foreign foes, without biting into its armies, had the

---

[1] Dumouriez, *Vie*, ii. 335-6, Eng. ed. iii. 11-14.
[2] Chuquet, *Charles de Hesse*.   [3] Ibid., 262-5.   [4] Ibid., 245-7.

Generals behaved wisely. Then also the weak attempt at resistance, and the flight of Lafayette, and the treason and flight of Dumouriez, set free the wild tide of suspicion and fear. Lafayette had not the civic courage to march on Paris and crush the hydra: Dumouriez chose the wrong moment for his attempt to do so, and they left the armies exposed to the bitter hatreds and suspicions they had aroused.

The three commanders, who seem to have been on friendly terms with one another, had several meetings. Narbonne,[1] the War Minister, leaving Paris on the 20th December 1791, came to Metz, the head-quarters of Lafayette, to consult with them on the approaching campaign, and there he presented the *bâton* of Marshal to Rochambeau and Luckner. To Luckner the Minister paid a gracious compliment, saying that hitherto they had only known him by their reverses (when he had served against France), but now their enemies had been deprived of one of their chief defenders.[2] Then Rochambeau went to the Capital about the 18th January, and Lafayette and Luckner about the 24th or 25th February 1792,[3] for fresh consultation. The experienced Rochambeau, considering that the troops, after a long peace, were not yet fit for war, advised the occupation of a defensive position. He did not believe the enemy would attack; if they did, he would advance against their wings, between the Sambre and the Meuse, and between the Lys and the sea. Luckner on the other hand proposed war on all sides, and that *carte blanche* should be given to himself. What his plan was he would not say, but Rochambeau believed it was the raid on the unprotected states of the Ecclesiastical Electors, which was carried out by Custine from the Armée du Rhin in the autumn of this year. It is said that Lafayette supported Luckner, and the discussion became so embittered that Narbonne wished to resign, but was induced to remain by Lafayette and Luckner.[4]

The plan of Rochambeau was adopted, and, had no change been made and had these commanders remained at the head,

[1] Général Louis-Marie-Jacques-Amalric, Comte de Narbonne-Lara (1755–1813). Employed under the Empire.
[2] Sérignan, *Invasion*, 9, note 1, p. 80.
[3] Charavay, *Lafayette*, 284–5.
[4] Sérignan, *Invasion*, 81–3; Charavay, *Lafayette*, 285.

of the armies in this region, the first campaign would have been fought on ordinary lines, probably without much result. Rochambeau, a General of much experience, who, like Lafayette, had seen war in America alongside volunteer troops, understood the situation and the need for establishing the confidence of the men in themselves and in their officers. He saw that the raid over the Rhine, wished for by Luckner, would be easy, as there was no force of the enemy there, but that the troops, without instruction, officers, or discipline, must suffer loss wherever, as in Flanders, they were to find troops inured to war, trained in the tactics of the time, and disciplined.[1] Lafayette may have had some wish for an offensive towards the Rhine, but he knew how unfit his own army was for active operations.[2] Luckner was skilful and daring as a partisan. It is possible that he might have anticipated Custine's raid and have thrown the Allies into some confusion for a time, but he seems to have realized his own incompetence at the head of an army, and, talking wildly, he would probably have done nothing.

It was, however, another General, Dumouriez,[3] who ruled the situation. He had a great amount of extraordinary experience. Born in 1739, he had served in the Seven Years' War. At Klosterkamp he had been severely wounded and taken prisoner, one ball, which would have struck his heart, being stopped by a volume of Pascal's *Lettres Provinciales*, which he had carried into battle as a suitable companion. The Duke of Brunswick, whom he was to meet at Valmy, took care of him and he was released in time. Placed in retirement, he went to Corsica, which was in revolt against Genoa, but his services were refused by the Genoese, by the Corsicans, and by the party which wished to form a separate Republic. The great Minister, the Duc de Choiseul, at first reprimanded him, but later employed him, sending him to Spain and Portugal. He published a work on Portugal and composed

---

[1] Sérignan, *Invasion*, 83.   [2] Ibid., 127–31.
[3] Général Charles-François Dumouriez (1739–1832), *Vie et Méms.*, and Eng. ed.; *Lettres sur l'ouvrage intitulé la Vie du Général*; Michaud, *Biog. univ.*, lxiii. 145–77; *Biog. des Contemporains*, ii. 1480–9; Chuquet, *Valmy*, 8–23; Pouget de Saint-André, *Le Général Dumouriez*; Rose-Broadley, *Dumouriez*.

a memoir on the attack and defence of that country. Much later the Duke of Wellington described the information given him by Dumouriez on Portugal as misleading.[1] Then he was sent to Poland in 1770 to assist the Poles against Russia, but he disliked their leaders, if not the nation, and was relieved by the Baron de Vioménil.[2]

In 1772 he became one of the agents of the marvellous secret policy of Louis XV, a policy so mysterious that it is doubtful if even the King understood it. Certainly the Minister, the Duc d'Aiguillon, did not, and suspecting that Dumouriez, then at Hamburg, was engaged in some trickery, he clapped him into the Bastille. Dumouriez had understood his danger and had prophesied that the King might abandon him and that he might be hung, but he took his imprisonment gaily. Still only the death of Louis really freed him. Then for fifteen years he commanded at Cherbourg, beginning the works which made the great port there, planning the invasion of England, and satisfying his restlessness by spying in that country. As the Revolution approached he began to stir and got himself transferred to Nantes, whence he kept down disturbances in the west. Clever, active, restless, enterprising, marvellously self-confident, he was certain to rise in the Revolution. With more caution he might have dominated military matters, for in them he was wonderfully daring. Few Generals are not nervous about their communications, and a threat there recalls them from any enterprise. To such fears he was a stranger and he saw unmoved the enemy cut between him and Paris. If left to himself, he would have launched his army on Belgium (while Brunswick made for Paris), sure of recalling the Prussians by his own stroke. He knew how to exhort and encourage his troops, to rally them whilst they were in their worst state of shrieking panic. He also knew and dared to punish. One great fault of his was the failure to concentrate and to use all his forces for his strokes ; whilst trusting to indirect influences in strategy, in tactics he restricted himself too much to direct attacks. Also he

---

[1] Stanhope, *Conversations with Wellington*, p. 70.
[2] Antoine-Charles du Houx, Baron de Vioménil (1728-92). Michaud, *Biog. univ.*, xlix. 181-2.

expected too much from his troops, although he did marvels with them in their demoralized condition. One wonders what he would have accomplished with the trained, steady troops of later years.

Half of the mind of Dumouriez was devoted to politics. There he saw a great opening for distinction. At home he wished to retain the Monarchy and, although prepared to seem to act with the Jacobins, was in readiness to destroy them eventually. Abroad he pursued the policy which led Louis-Napoleon astray—the belief that it was possible to conciliate Prussia and to play her against Austria. In all this, whether war or politics, he had the advantage of the most perfect confidence in himself. Nothing overawed him. He faced Choiseul as he did the Convention, one of the three Powers (Louis XIV, itself, and Napoleon), before whom France has lain prostrate and submissive. He, a soldier, ventured to turn on and denounce an incompetent Minister for War. Even more wonderful, he got the culprit out of office. He is one of the most interesting figures of this period. It would be ludicrous to place him alongside of Napoleon whether for his military or administrative talents, but there was no one like him amongst the Marshals or the Generals of the armies. In his restless, daring, confident, ambitious nature he was of the same class as Bonaparte. Had he had the patience of the latter in matters of politics, and had he been, as he well might have been, victorious in 1793 as in 1792, he would have played a great part in the wars of the Republic and would have prevented that degradation of the armies under the Representatives which did so much harm to France. He ought to have won the *bâton*, though it is difficult to imagine him bearing the yoke of the Emperor.

With such ideas Dumouriez naturally joined the Girondins, the party which stood between the Royalists and the Jacobins; and, when a Ministry of that party was formed, he became Minister for Foreign Affairs on the 17th March 1792. The position was difficult, for he and his party were disliked both by the Court and the Jacobins.[1] A foreign war, calling off the attention of the nation, was part of the policy of Dumouriez

[1] Thiers, *Rév.*, i. 173-7.

L'ARMÉE DU NORD, 1791-2

and the Girondins. The General had already proposed his plan. Acting on the defensive on the rest of the frontiers, he proposed to attack the Austrian Netherlands and Savoy. Hitherto there had been no organized forces in the south. Only three armies, 'Nord', 'Centre', and 'Rhin', had been formed. He proposed to create a fourth, the Armée du Midi. The command of this body he asked for, and it was promised to him. Austria by her demands played into the hands of the war party, and on the 20th April 1792 war with her was declared.

Dumouriez was all powerful with the Minister for War, General de Grave, so that practically the complete management of military and political matters was in his hands. An Armée du Midi was decreed on the 15th April 1792. Whether Dumouriez was not yet ready, or whether his claim was passed by, the command of the new force was given to another General.[1] This turned his attention still more to the northern frontier. He had already in 1790 been sent to Brussels to support secretly the insurrection by which the Belgians for a time drove out the Austrian troops. This revolt had been suppressed, but Dumouriez believed the people would join a French army if one entered their country.

The change of Ministry and the consequent replacement of Narbonne by General de Grave were distasteful to the three commanders, who had wished for the retention of Narbonne: indeed, it is said that a letter written by them in his support, urging him not to resign, was published by mistake and was one of the reasons for his removal by the weak and suspicious King.[2] Lafayette especially disliked the new Ministry; he and Dumouriez were open enemies,[3] and in his communications with Roland, the new Minister for the Interior, he hardly concealed his contempt for those he considered simply as leaders of a faction.[4] The King's name was, however, all powerful with such men as Rochambeau, and, whilst the three commanders remained in the Capital, what I may call the first plan of Dumouriez was settled: Lafayette, with the

---

[1] Sérignan, *Le Duc de Lauzun*, 157, 185.
[2] Martin, *Hist. de France*, i. 257; Charavay, *Lafayette*, 285.
[3] Sérignan, *Invasion*, 289-90.   [4] Charavay, *Lafayette*, 286, 322.

'Centre', was to be the first to move and was to march on Givet, on Namur, and then on Liége, whilst the 'Nord' was to advance on Mons and, if the 'Centre' took Namur, then on Brussels.[1] On the 20th March 1792 Lafayette left Paris for Metz, Luckner probably going back to Strasbourg about the same date, but Rochambeau, who was ill, remained in the Capital for the time.[2]

So far all was plain sailing, but Dumouriez, who had a taste for intrigue, was in secret correspondence with one of Rochambeau's Generals, Biron,[3] whom we shall meet later in command, first of the Armée du Rhin,[4] then of 'Italie',[5] and lastly in La Vendée,[6] whence he went to the scaffold. Biron, thinking that Rochambeau would do nothing, had made Dumouriez believe what that General was only too ready to believe, that the Austrian Netherlands, or Belgium, were ready for a general insurrection against the Austrians and that an enormous desertion could be provoked amongst the Austrian troops. Biron sent one of his staff, Lt.-Colonel and Adjutant-General Beauharnais,[7] to Paris to treat secretly with Dumouriez. Rochambeau, it was hoped, would be unable to rejoin the 'Nord'. If Luckner could not be spared from Metz, and if General de Choisy were too ill, Biron modestly confessed that he could see no one but himself fit to replace the Marshal.[8] Then, to the discomfiture of the plotters, Rochambeau, instead of dying, began preparing to rejoin his army and had to be consulted on the plan for the campaign. He learnt with amazement that Dumouriez and the Ministers believed that 30,000 men would emigrate from Belgium and that 5,000 had already come: in reality he had received from 500 to 600. The plans for a general advance seemed to him mere madness: all that he would admit as possible was a point by Lafayette on Namur and Liége. On the 20th April 1792 the King announced in the Assembly that war was declared against

[1] Sérignan, *Invasion*, 116–17.
[2] Charavay, *Lafayette*, notes 1 and 2, p. 287.
[3] Armand-Louis de Gontaut, Duc de Biron (1747–93). Known as Duc de Lauzun till 1788. Michaud, *Biog. univ.*, iv. 522–3.
[4] Masson, *Josephine de Beauharnais*, 194–5.
[5] Sérignan, *Le Duc de Lauzun*, 198–200. [6] Sérignan, *Invasion*, 83–119.
[7] Masson, *Josephine de Beauharnais*, 194–5.
[8] Sérignan, *Le Duc de Lauzun*, 198–200.

the Emperor, and next day Rochambeau started for Valenciennes, where he arrived on the 23rd.[1]

Behind Rochambeau travelled a bearer of dispatches, sent through Maret, the future Duc de Bassano,[2] changing all that the Marshal believed to have been decided. If Rochambeau would not advance in force, there would be no opportunity for Biron to distinguish himself or to win the *bâton* which Dumouriez dangled before his eyes. It was difficult to remove Rochambeau or to force him to advance, but he might be left with his reserves whilst Biron and others were entrusted with fighting divisions.[3] Just as the Marshal had concluded a friendly and sensible agreement with the Austrians in his front that neither side should at present undertake any small and useless affairs, he learnt that Lafayette was to move on Namur about the 30th April 1792 and that he himself was to place certain bodies, whose composition was fully detailed, under Biron and other officers named, who were to advance against the enemy. To ensure obedience the plan was attributed to the King, and once more the general insurrection, which was sure to take place amongst the Belgians, was given as a reason for the movement. This was taking command of his army over Rochambeau's head, and, sending for Biron, the old Marshal showed openly that he believed that the plan had been concealed from him in Paris and that Biron, who was in the secret, was at the head of a petty intrigue. However, there was the King's name, and Rochambeau, whilst openly disapproving the plan, said he would do all in his power for success.[4] The result was that at least one future Marshal began his career by a disaster. Two disgraceful panics occurred, for not only were the men shaken, as Rochambeau had feared, but the very Generals that had been in league with Dumouriez to pass over Rochambeau for active operations showed the greatest incompetence and timidity in the field.

In compliance with what were really the orders of Dumouriez, three columns were set in motion. On the 30th April 1792

---

[1] Sérignan, *Invasion*, 83–119. [2] Ibid., 123; *Le Duc de Lauzun*, 247.
[3] Dumouriez, *Vie*, ii. 229–32, Eng. ed. ii. 294–8; Sérignan, *Invasion*, 107.
[4] Sérignan, *Invasion*, 118–26; *Le Duc de Lauzun*, 247–8. 'A la vérité on ne le consultait pas.' Dumouriez, *Vie*, ii. 232.

one advanced from Dunkirk to Furnes where it found no enemy and, after being complimented by all the magistrates and the corporations, returned home safely. The other columns were less fortunate. On the evening of the 28th April General Théobald Dillon [1] with some 2,300 men, guided by Dupont, the brother of the Dupont who was to surrender at Baylen,[2] advanced from Lille on Tournai and, after passing through Baisieux, met a small force of the enemy, whereupon he determined to retire. While doing this, on the 29th April, his men broke and fled for Lille, which they re-entered in wild confusion, crying out, 'Treason', wounding Dupont, and not only killing their General, Théobald Dillon, but venting their fury on his corpse, which they hung up by its heels. On their side the Austrians brought into Brussels a long convoy of captured guns and French prisoners.[3]

Meantime Biron with some 15,000 men moved from Valenciennes on Mons. Accompanying him as part of his staff were Colonel Berthier, Alexandre Beauharnais (separated from his wife Joséphine, the future Empress), and two sons of Philippe-Égalité—the Duc de Chartres (the future King Louis-Philippe) and the Duc de Montpensier, both A.D.C. to Biron. Captain Mortier also belonged to the force. A successful action was fought at Quiévrain on the 28th April, where Mortier saw his first engagement and had his horse shot under him. Berthier and Mortier were thus the first of the future Marshals to be engaged on this frontier.

Berthier was a good type of the staff officer of the *ancien régime*. Born at Versailles on the 20th February [4] 1753, he had entered the corps of *Ingénieurs Géographes* (in which his father

---

[1] Comte Théobald Dillon, brother of the Lieut.-Général Comte Arthur Dillon (1750-94), whom we shall find serving under Dumouriez in the Argonne. These Dillons were of an Irish family. Madame Bertrand, who was at St. Helena, was a Dillon.

[2] Général Comte Pierre-Antoine Dupont-Chaumont (1759-1838). His brother, the Baylen General, was Comte Pierre Dupont de l'Étang (1765-1840), who at this time was A.D.C. to Théobald Dillon. The brothers are generally distinguished, the elder as Antoine, and the Baylen one as Pierre. Sérignan calls them both Dupont-Chaumont, but gives the rank, the elder at this time being Colonel, and the other Captain. *Fastes*, iii. 195-9.

[3] Sérignan, *Invasion*, 133-55; Chuquet, *Invasion*, 46-7; Thiers, *Rév.*, i. 183-4; Dumouriez, *Vie*, ii. 235-6, Eng. ed. ii. 302-3; Desbrière, *La Cav. pendant la Rév. : La crise*, 103-16.

[4] In most accounts this is in November, but I follow Révérend.

had served) in 1766 or, according to another account, in 1769, but became Lieutenant of infantry in the *Légion de Flandre* on the application of the officer commanding that corps, the Vicomte d'Harembures, who considered that Berthier's good character and talent for designing would make the young officers work.

In 1776 the Prince de Lambesc got him transferred to the cavalry regiment *Royal-Lorraine* [1] on account of his skill in managing his horse and arms. He next served on the staff, first as A.D.C. to the Comte de Metfort, who commanded the 'Armée de Normandie', then in the war in America on Rochambeau's staff, and then on that of the General Baron de Vioménil in Jamaica.

On his return to France he was employed on various military works and accompanied Custine to Prussia to study the organization of the Prussian army. In 1786 he was appointed to the Staff Corps.

We find him in 1789 as Lt.-Colonel and Chief of the Staff to the Baron de Besenval, commanding the army assembled round Paris. On the 14th July, when the mob was beginning the attack on the Bastille, these troops were ordered to withdraw from the Capital, and, when the staff dispersed, Berthier, who was with another staff officer, Mathieu Dumas, troubled about his portfolio, buried it in a thicket in the garden of the Baron de Besenval's hotel.

The National Guard was now formed, and its commander, Lafayette, having known Berthier in America, had him brought on the staff of the new body on the 25th December 1789, he then having the rank of Lt.-Colonel and being *Aide-maréchal général des logis*, say Assistant Quartermaster-General. Two days later Berthier was appointed to command at Versailles and to be Second in Command of the National Guard there. We know nothing of the part played by him in the extraordinary scene at Versailles on the 5th and 6th October, when the mob came to force the King to go to Paris, but it is certain that Lafayette was there in person, and the Court, with habitual folly, instead of entrusting him

---

[1] See for Lorraine Susane, *Cav. franç.*, ii. 115-22. Lambesc does not appear as Colonel.

with the custody of the *Château*, left this to be undertaken by the *Maison* : it was due to some failure on the part of the troops of the latter, apparently, that the mob eventually invaded the *Château*, the National Guard occupying only the exterior posts formerly held by the Gardes Françaises.[1] All we know is that Lafayette, in applying for Berthier's promotion and praising his conduct as *Commandant pour le Roi* at Versailles, said that the King and Queen had signified to Berthier their satisfaction at the state of Versailles.[2] This praise was the more remarkable because Louis wrote later that of all the National Guard only the Baron de Gouvernet and Berthier could be named with praise.[3] It must also be counted to Berthier for righteousness that his conduct brought down on him the wrath of Marat, who styled him ' l'odieux Berthier '.[4]

Anyhow Berthier was promoted Adjutant-General with the rank of Colonel on the 1st April 1791, and was appointed in succession to the staff of several military divisions. After being entrusted with the raising of the volunteers of the departments of Loire and Seine-et-Oise, he was appointed to the *Dépôt de la Guerre*, but immediately afterwards nominated Chief of the Staff to Rochambeau, where we now find him.

The other future Marshal whom we now meet and whom I have classed amongst those that were civilians at the time of the Revolution was the tallest of all those that won the *bâton*. Édouard-Adolphe-Casimir Mortier was born on the 13th February 1768 at Cateau-Cambrésis in Flanders. His father, a *marchand mulquinier*,[5] that is to say a linen manufacturer, was sent as deputy to the National Assembly by the town of Cambrésis. Mortier was educated at the *Collége des Anglais* at Douai, where he learnt to speak English. Long afterwards, talking to an English officer, a prisoner, who said the Marshal spoke the language like an Englishman, he replied, ' I could have spoken it tolerably : I resided in England a good deal while, when very young, I went there only to spend money for my father '. In 1791, when twenty-

---

[1] Mathieu Dumas, *Souvenirs*, i. 456–7. Cf., however, Thiébault, i. 248.
[2] Derrecagaix, *Berthier*, i. 19–20. [3] Daudet, *Hist. de l'émig.*, ii. 125.
[4] *L'Ami du Peuple*, 9th January 1790, quoted in Furgest's *Marquis de Saint-Haruge*, 310.
[5] Foucart et Finot, *Déf. nat.*, ii. 244.

three years old, he obtained a commission as *sous-lieutenant* in the fine cavalry corps, the *Carabiniers de Monsieur*.[1] This would have brought him on my list of officers, but, instead of taking the commission, he preferred to join the first battalion of volunteers of his department, the ' Nord ', raised on the 1st September[2] 1791, where he was elected by the men as Captain. The corps joined the Armée du Nord where we now find him, but he was to do most of his service under the Republic in the ' Sambre-et-Meuse ' under Jourdan.

Stopping short of Mons, Biron determined to retire. This was partly on the advice of Berthier, who was sent back to explain matters to Rochambeau in Valenciennes. Then a panic occurred amongst Biron's cavalry and on the 30th April at Quiévrain his troops broke and fled for Valenciennes. In neither his case nor in that of Dillon had the enemy been in presence of the affrighted troops.[3] Thus in 1792 Berthier and Mortier saw a war begin in disaster on the northern frontier which they were to see end even more gloomily in 1814 under the walls of Paris. The experienced and sensible Rochambeau had been thoroughly disgusted with the calamitous interference to which he was subjected from Paris, and had wished to resign. Now that the weakness of the Generals who had intrigued against him was manifest and his opinion of the state of his men fully justified, he insisted on being replaced. Berthier was sent to Paris with his dispatches and his resignation. The army did him justice. In 1805 Napoleon presented to him several officers, amongst whom was Berthier, saying, ' Marshal, here are your pupils '. ' They have far surpassed their master,' replied the old man.

Berthier's mission to Paris with Rochambeau's resignation did him much harm. The disasters were of course most annoying to Dumouriez and to all who had been clamouring for a general advance, and naturally they tried to throw the blame on Rochambeau.[4] No doubt Berthier had to defend the

---

[1] Susane, *Cav. franç.*, ii. 187–207.
[2] Susane, *Inf. franç.*, i. 336. 7th September, Duprez, *Vol. Nat.*, 460.
[3] Sérignan, *Invasion*, 156–85 ; Sérignan, *Le Duc de Lauzun*, 251–60 ; Dumouriez, *Vie*, ii. 234–5, Eng. ed. ii. 301–3 ; Desbrière, *La Cav. pendant la Rév. : La crise*, 116–18.
[4] Sérignan, *Invasion*, 195–6.

Marshal, and the plain statement that it was the cowardice of the men which had been the immediate cause of the rout was most unpleasing to patriots who were already believing in the virtues of Freedom. Roland, then Minister for the Interior, alleged on the 23rd May that both Berthier and La Colombe, the A.D.C. of Lafayette, had said, ' The French soldiers being cowards, the numerical superiority of the army could not be too great '. La Colombe, and no doubt Berthier, denied this, declaring that the word ' lâches ' which they had uttered only referred to the men who had fled instead of fighting under Biron ; Lafayette supported his A.D.C.[1] Officially, of course, there could be no complaint against Berthier, and the new Minister for War, Servan, seems to have sent him to meet Lafayette on his way back to the ' Nord ',[2] where, as we shall see, Berthier soon became Chief of the Staff to Luckner, who replaced Rochambeau.

It is strange to find Dumouriez asserting in his Memoirs that these routs, which he had seen repeated by the troops of the ' Nord ' under himself in the march for Valmy, were ' le résultat d'un complot très noir ' of, he hints, the Jacobins.[3]

Dumouriez offered the succession to Biron, but that General was disgusted with his experience and declared he would rather be killed as a soldier than be hung as a General. Then Dumouriez chose Marshal Luckner, commanding the ' Rhin ' at Strasbourg, who had extraordinary credit at the moment. Even Biron had assumed that he would be the man, if he could be spared, and Dumouriez announced his nomination amidst the applause of the Assembly, even before Luckner had accepted. At first the old Marshal declined the command for several reasons, and it was only after some correspondence that he agreed to go to Paris to see Dumouriez. Leaving Strasbourg on the 9th May 1792,[4] he reached the capital and at first, professing to prefer the role of subaltern, offered to serve as Second in Command under Rochambeau and to help to restore discipline in the ' Nord '. Rochambeau declined this arrangement, saying his health made it necessary for him to retire. Oddly enough, whilst Lafayette in January

---

[1] Charavay, *Lafayette*, 299–300. [2] Ibid., 298.
[3] Dumouriez, *Vie*, ii. 236–7, Eng. ed. ii. 303–5. [4] Pajol, i. 20.

L'ARMÉE DU NORD, 1791-2

of that year had said that one-third of the officers of the 'Centre' had already left the army and that he hoped another disaffected third would also go,[1] Rochambeau now in May reassured Luckner on the spirit of the officers of the 'Nord'. 'Do not believe in exaggerated rumours as to continued resignations; several have reached me, I have refused them, and I have succeeded in getting the greater part withdrawn.'[2] Luckner was forced to accept the command, and all the more as he had professed to be so anxious for active operations. Leaving Paris on the 14th May 1792, he reached Valenciennes on the evening of the next day.[3]

[1] Charavay, *Lafayette*, 283.
[2] Sérignan, *Invasion*, 207.
[3] Ibid., 199-207.

VI

L'ARMÉE DU NORD (*continued*), 1792

Conference of Luckner with Lafayette and Rochambeau. He advances on Menin and Courtrai but withdraws. Dumouriez, having resigned the Ministry of War, joins the 'Nord'. Cold reception by Luckner and Berthier. Dumouriez takes Macdonald as A.D.C. Conference of Luckner, Lafayette, and Dumouriez. Adoption of the *Chassé-croisé*. Dumouriez's anger with Lafayette. Left in command at the Camp de Maulde, Dumouriez refuses to follow Luckner to Metz and, appealing to the Assembly, succeeds in remaining in the North. Adoption of horse artillery. Position of future Marshals on the completion of the *Chassé-croisé*. Attack on the Tuileries by the mob on the 10th of August 1793. Lafayette opposes the Assembly, but has to fly and is imprisoned by the Allies. Shock to the army.

ONCE arrived, Luckner showed a curious timidity for a General who on the 24th April had written on the necessity for satisfying his demands and for abandoning the defensive role, as ruinous as it was unsuited to the character of the French and to the true national interests.[1] Also he knew how anxious Dumouriez was for the invasion of Belgium. His first act was to try to get Rochambeau to remain, if it were only to stay at Valenciennes and to command part of the troops, this being obviously not a mere piece of presumption, but the wish to have the support of the senior Marshal. Then he got Rochambeau to call up Lafayette, the commander of the ' Centre ', to join them for a consultation, and Rochambeau offered to remain until Lafayette arrived. Next, on the 16th May the two Marshals visited the Camp de Famars,[2] their inspection being interrupted by an incursion of the enemy on Bavai, whereupon they advanced with 3,000 men, only to find the foe had retired again.[3]

Lafayette arrived, apparently from about Givet, on the 19th May 1792, and the result of the conference of the three Generals, as far as it is known, was the adoption of a foolish

[1] Sérignan, *Invasion*, 203. [2] South of Valenciennes.
[3] Sérignan, *Invasion*, 207–10.

plan by which all the forces of the 'Nord' were to be moved to between the Lys river and the sea, and were to fall on the Austrian right, forcing it back on the Rhine and taking the fortresses as they came on them. Meanwhile Lafayette with the 'Centre', now round Givet, was to threaten the Austrian left, in order to prevent them from reinforcing their right against Luckner. If they did weaken their left, then Lafayette was to take the principal role and was to advance resolutely on Mons. This wonderful plan by which Luckner, placing himself with his back to the sea and leaving the enemy between him and Lafayette, was at best to drive the Austrians back on their communications, must have been the conception of Luckner, who, a good partisan, was helpless as a commander. Lafayette was by many years junior to the two Marshals and perhaps saw an opening for himself, whilst Rochambeau, ill and just leaving, probably did not care to dispute with his successor.[1]

Jomini calls this proposal a monstrosity in strategy and blames the Government for not realizing the difference between a Hanoverian Hussar and a Marshal entrusted with the destiny of France;[2] but the presence of Rochambeau takes much of the sting from this criticism, even if the plan were not much the same as Rochambeau himself had proposed at first. Rochambeau now retired, despising the offer of Dumouriez to give him the command of the Interior, to live at Paris and give advice to the Minister for War.[3]

Luckner was unhappy about his army; he had not got tents, then thought indispensable; he had not enough Generals; for staff he only had Beauharnais; and, above all, he had wanted Berthier, who was still absent. General Valence was also writing to the Minister in fear lest Berthier might be allowed to go to another army. Berthier and Jarry, Valence wrote, were indispensable to Luckner: one or both wished to go to the army of Lafayette, but it was of the greatest importance to retain them with the 'Nord'. If Jarry, the actual Chief of the Staff, were put in his proper place as General Commanding the *avant-garde*, and Berthier were

---

[1] Sérignan, *Invasion*, 210–12.   [2] Jomini, *Rév.*, ii. 18–19, 20.
[3] Dumouriez, *Vie*, ii. 239, Eng. ed. ii. 308.

made Chief of the Staff, then the staff could be organized to work : never had Valence seen such confusion. Berthier had, as we have seen, been sent to the army of Lafayette, whence probably came the belief that he was to be transferred to that force. Now on the 21st May the Minister ordered him to rejoin the ' Nord ', telling Luckner that he could be employed as *Maréchal de camp*, that is, as General of Brigade, for he would be the first to be promoted and there was a vacant place : indeed on the 22nd May 1792 he was promoted. On the 28th or 29th May he was at Valenciennes and at once was put in the post of Chief of the Staff. He himself was ' véritablement effrayé ' at the confusion in which he found everything. Staff officers above all things he wanted ; indeed everything was wanting, and the Minister could only give Luckner the cold comfort that the commanders had made similar complaints in 1742-4, and yet Marshal Saxe had managed to beat every one. But Luckner was not a Saxe.[1] The striking thing here, however, is the value attached to the services of Berthier, then only a Colonel.

The fates of these two, the best staff officers that at first had been with the ' Nord ', were very different. Berthier was to become the type of the staff officer of the Empire. Jarry,[2] who had lived forty years in Prussia as M. de Villette and, after organizing the Academy of War at Potsdam, had returned to France with the Prussian rank of Colonel, was to emigrate and was to train officers for the English staff as Superintendent of the Senior Department, then at High Wycombe, of the Staff College from 1799 till he resigned in October 1806.[3] His former comrade was then a Marshal and a Prince.

By this time Luckner was suggesting to the Minister that it might be wise to adopt the defensive role he had thought so ruinous, but, spurred by the Minister, at last he moved and, reinforced by 6,000 men sent from the ' Centre ' by Lafayette, left the camp of Famars on the 9th June 1792 with 20,000 men. Marching north-west to Lille, and then

---

[1] Sérignan, *Invasion*, 212-31.
[2] For Ségur-Jarry see Sérignan, *Le Duc de Lauzun*, note 2, pp. 71-2, 100 ; Griffiths, *A Pioneer in Military Education*.
[3] Mockler-Ferryman, *Annals of Sandhurst*, pp. 87-8.

passing over ground on which the 'Nord' was to fight later, he reached Menin, which was easily captured, as was Courtrai on the 19th June. Here the ardour of Luckner ended. The Austrians under Beaulieu, a General to become known in Italy, attacked Courtrai, part of which was burnt by the French. For some extraordinary reason Luckner determined to retire; on the 30th June Courtrai was evacuated and that night the troops were again under Lille. The long projected invasion of Belgium was ended.[1]

Berthier of course had gone as Chief of the Staff. The volunteer battalion, the 1st Ille-et-Vilaine, which Lt.-Colonel Moreau commanded, formed part of Luckner's force.[2] I presume that the volunteer battalion in which Captain Mortier served remained at Quérenaing or Ruesnes,[3] and that the 87th Regiment, in which Macdonald was *sous-lieutenant*, was left at St. Omer; he himself may have already been taken as A.D.C. by General Beurnonville, who commanded the 2nd Division,[4] and so may have marched with this force. Sérignan makes the volunteer battalions of Davout and Saint-Cyr serve with this force, but Davout's battalion, the 3rd, not the 1st, of the Yonne, was at Sedan as a part of Lafayette's army,[5] and Saint-Cyr, who belonged to the 1st Chasseurs de Paris, had not yet entered the volunteers and was a simple citizen.[6]

The retreat of Luckner was a heavy blow to Dumouriez, who believed the Marshal was in earnest in the support of his favourite scheme for the invasion of Belgium. The Girondist Ministry, in which Dumouriez was Minister for Foreign Affairs, had been dismissed by the King at his instance on the 13th June 1792, but, though he became Minister for War in the new Ministry, he failed to get the King's support and on the 16th June he also resigned.[7] Now he sought military distinction. He had his choice of being posted to one or other of the

---

[1] Sérignan, *Invasion*, 232-78; Jomini, *Rév.*, ii. 20-3. For map see Jomini, *Rév.*, Atlas, i and viii.
[2] Sérignan, *Invasion*, 215.   [3] Ibid., 214.
[4] Macdonald, *Souvenirs*, 11; Sérignan, *Invasion*, 216.
[5] Ibid., 217; Vigier, *Davout*, i. 23-5.
[6] Gay de Vernon, *Saint-Cyr*, 1.
[7] Dumouriez, *Vie*, ii. 255-316, Eng. ed. ii. 331-422; Thiers, *Rév.*, i. 189-97; Martin, *Hist. de France*, i. 276-9.

three armies in the north and east, and naturally he chose the 'Nord' where he believed he had influence over Luckner and where he could encourage the Marshal in his schemes on Belgium. Horrified when he heard of Luckner's intention to retreat, he was detained in the Capital until the 27th June and, hurry as he might, when he got to Lille on the 1st July [1] it was too late: Courtrai had been abandoned and it was no longer possible, as he had hoped, for him to induce the Marshal to carry out his plans.[2]

More disappointment was to befall him. He found himself rudely received and ignored as far as possible, not only by the General Officers and the staff, but by the Marshal himself. Berthier, the Chief of the Staff, did not make the usual notification in orders of his arrival. Although he was the senior General next to Biron, no post was given him and he was kept idle at head-quarters, as if he had merely come as a spectator. When he suggested to the Marshal that it would be better to encamp at Quiévrain, Luckner got angry and declared with oaths that he did not want advice and would imprison in the citadel every General Officer who argued. As many officers do in such cases, Dumouriez put all this down to the Marshal's staff and especially to Berthier, its head. It must have been true that Berthier disliked Dumouriez, for he never paid the usual visit to him and did not allot to him the guards, sentries, orderlies, &c., which it was customary to post for Generals without special commands of their own: how indeed could the orderly Berthier, a lover of routine and a supporter of the *ancien régime*, do ought but distrust the scheming would-be demagogue, the political General he saw in Dumouriez?[3]

In reality, however, Dumouriez's arrival was not very welcome to Luckner, for the old Marshal, probably rather ashamed of what had been the end of all his brave speeches and proposals, did not care to have by his side the man he had professed to agree with and to second. Also he wished to be left alone in quiet, and no doubt knew that Dumouriez

---

[1] Sérignan, *Invasion*, 269–70, 280.
[2] Ibid., 278–80; Dumouriez, *Vie*, ii. 324–31, Eng. ed. iii. 1–9.
[3] Dumouriez, *Vie*, ii. 331–4, Eng. ed. iii. 9–14; Chuquet, *Invasion*, 48–9; Sérignan, *Invasion*, 280–1.

had not abandoned his plans for the offensive. Consequently if, as Dumouriez suspected, Berthier and the staff tried to keep him from having a private interview (for they knew how changeable their chief was), the Marshal may have been a very willing accomplice in the matter. At last Dumouriez succeeded in getting Luckner alone and reproached him with being led by others, Charles Lameth, Noailles, and Mathieu de Montmorency,[1] and by the Lafayette party, and for signing the letters submitted by Berthier, without reading them. Luckner, as often happened, veered round, burst into tears, denounced his advisers, and kept Dumouriez to dinner, during which he reprimanded Lameth and de Montmorency and blamed Berthier, who next morning paid the General the long-due visit. We are not told what was Berthier's answer when Dumouriez, who says that he owed his promotion to him, told him that it was time to finish this comedy and to think of making war in earnest.[2]

Not much permanent impression had been made on Luckner, who on the 8th July 1792 sent the General to command the left of his army at Saint-Amand, with the Camp de Maulde.[3] This did not seem to Dumouriez to be his right position, but he went there on the 9th July, and, as large works were being carried out at Maulde, he shifted his quarters to that camp. Here Beurnonville was commanding eight battalions and ten squadrons and on the 17th June 1792 had taken as A.D.C. his protégé, the young Macdonald, only promoted Lieutenant on the 10th October 1791, whose regiment, the 87th, seems all this time to have been left at Boulogne or at the camp of Saint-Omer.[4] With the approval of Beurnonville, Macdonald had married the first of his series of wives.

The Revolution had found this officer twenty-six years old, with more than a year's service in the *Légion de Maillebois* (raised in Holland for the service of the Dutch), and with four

---

[1] Lieut.-Général Charles-Malo-François de Lameth ; Louis-Marie, Vicomte de Noailles (1766–1804), brother-in-law of Lafayette ; Mathieu-Jean-Félicité Laval, Duc de Montmorency (1760–1826), A.D.C. to Luckner. All three had served in America with Rochambeau and Lafayette, and all soon emigrated.
[2] Dumouriez, *Vie*, ii. 338, Eng. ed. iii. 16–17 ; Sérignan, *Invasion*, 282–3.
[3] South of Tournai, north of Saint-Amand. For the camp see Sérignan, *Invasion*, 232–3 ; Dumouriez, *Vie*, ii. 340–1, Eng. ed. iii. 19–21.
[4] Susane, *Inf. franç.*, v. 64 ; Macdonald, *Souvenirs*, 11.

years' service in the French army. Both his father and mother were Scotch : his father had followed the fortunes of Prince Charles in 1745. Dumouriez apparently had not brought any staff with him, and, having employed the young A.D.C. on several missions, and being pleased with his work, offered to take him as his own A.D.C. with the rank of Captain. Macdonald at first declined, but, as Beurnonville himself urged him not to miss such a chance, he at last accepted and, to anticipate a little, when Dumouriez received the command of the ' Nord ', Macdonald became his A.D.C. as Captain on the 29th August 1792.[1]

Macdonald had many personal advantages. Tall, well-shaped, proud and frank in look and speech, he carried his head high, but this was tempered, says Philippe de Ségur, by ' le fin sourire d'une gaieté doucement railleuse '.[2] Unfortunately this ' fin sourire ' appeared to some persons as ' son air moqueur ' and caused suspicions of his earnestness and of his patriotism at a time when it was not sufficient to be a Republican, unless you had the outward appearance of one also. A master of jeers, his tongue did him much harm, though he seems never to have realized this. How much of interest the young staff officer must have seen under Dumouriez, but his memoirs of the period are as arid as if it had been a question of peace manœuvres !

If Luckner was not willing to listen to advice from Dumouriez, it was different when Lafayette was in question. On the 5th July 1792 the commander of the ' Centre ' arrived at Valenciennes from Maubeuge, and next day the two commanders had settled the extraordinary plan which is called the *Chassé-croisé*. In the first place they recommended the King to make peace, as the means entrusted to them to defend the Kingdom were insufficient compared to those possessed by the Allies. Then they believed that the enemy would attack, not in the north, but by the middle Rhine and the Meuse district, so that a mere retaining force or *corps d'observation* would be sufficient in the north, whilst the mass of the troops was drawn more to the south, where Brunswick's Prussian and Austrian army might be expected. As for the commanders

---

[1] Macdonald, *Souvenirs* 11–12.   [2] Ségur, *Mélanges*, 206.

L'ARMÉE DU NORD, 1792

themselves, they proposed to change their role, Luckner undertaking the defence of Lorraine and Alsace, and Lafayette the country from Montmédy to Dunkirk. All this was simple enough: Luckner went back to the Rhine country and was to control the Armée du Rhin as well as his own force, now the Armée du Centre, so that he had the district he had come from. He, the senior of the commanders, would have the most important post, that on which the first shock of the enemy was to fall, whilst Lafayette, the junior, had what was now the less important district of the 'Nord'.[1]

The real reason for the change was, however, a political one. Lafayette, who once had swayed Paris as the Commander of the National Guard, had his eyes fixed on the Capital, where the extreme Jacobin party was daily becoming more menacing to the Crown and was intimidating the Assembly. He wished to use his army against the turbulent factions of Paris; his troops had already voted addresses in the sense he wished; he had written to the Assembly denouncing the outbreak of the 20th June 1792 (when the mob had first invaded the Tuileries) and he had appeared at the bar of the Assembly itself to urge the punishment of the leaders of that insurrection. The Jacobins had taken up his challenge and had demanded his trial, which the Assembly only refused on the 8th August.[2] Ready, apparently, to use his troops in the Capital, or to receive the King if the latter would escape, he wished to be within easy striking distance of Paris, and the proposed change gave him this advantage.[3] As for Luckner, it is difficult to say how far he was acquainted with the plans of his comrade: he must have known much of them and in all probability would have sympathized if they had been successful. Meanwhile his removal to Metz freed him from the necessity for taking any decided part in the question between Lafayette and the Assembly, and his control over the 'Armée du Rhin' may have been the more welcome if he really cherished plans for the raid into the district of the Ecclesiastical Electors, of which he had thought and which Custine was to carry out later.

[1] Sérignan, *Invasion*, 284–6; Chuquet, *Invasion*, 29; Jomini, *Rév.*, ii. 24–5; Charavay, *Lafayette*, 317–18.
[2] Ibid., 324; Thiers, *Rév.*, i. 256; Mathieu Dumas, *Souvenirs*, ii. 442–51.
[3] Ibid., 360–1, 378, 396–7.

For the success of Lafayette's plan he had to carry his own troops to the north with him. He believed he had won over enough officers and men to be able to trust they would follow him against the Assembly, or at least obey if the King should reach them. In consequence it was arranged that the troops of the 'Nord' and 'Centre' were to change, as well as the two commanders: that is, just as the enemy was expected to appear on the frontier, the two armies that were to meet him were to begin a counter-march along their front, Luckner's troops moving south-east and those of Lafayette north-west. The most extraordinary thing about this *Chassé-croisé* is that the new War Minister, Lajard, approved it, and, after another visit of Lafayette to Valenciennes, the movement was at once begun, on the 12th July 1792.[1] Biron was to go and command the 'Rhin' under Luckner. Arthur Dillon, the brother of the murdered Théobald Dillon, was to command under Lafayette from Valenciennes to Dunkirk, Lafayette himself going to Montmédy. As a temporary measure Dumouriez was to remain in the Camp de Maulde with six battalions and five squadrons until the 20th July, when Chazot with 5,000 men of Lafayette's would arrive and Dumouriez would join Luckner in Metz.[2]

Inexcusable as a military operation, still the *Chassé-croisé* was not quite so dangerous as it is generally represented to have been. In the first place the two commanders were right in believing that there was no probability of the enemy attacking in force in the district of the 'Nord', so that a mere *corps d'observation*, with the garrisons, would suffice to hold the frontier till the change should be effected.[3] Then a large, and probably the best part of the troops of the 'Centre' was already in the district of the 'Nord', pushing as far as Maubeuge: indeed the two armies were so intermingled that, as Lafayette said, it would certainly have taken more than two days to reorganize, or rather to disentangle them.[4] Also the change of troops, I take it, only applied to the active part of each army; the garrisons and depots seem not to have been affected. Counting the troops left temporarily under Dumou-

---

[1] Lajard was Minister for War 16th June–24th July.
[2] Sérignan, *Invasion*, 285–90; Chuquet, *Invasion*, 49.
[3] Sérignan, *Invasion*, 285. [4] Ibid., 289.

riez, Luckner reported that he was taking twenty-three battalions and twenty-two squadrons, and was leaving sixty-one battalions and twenty-one squadrons.[1] Many of the volunteer battalions must have remained where they were, for instance that of Captain Mortier did not go south with Luckner, nor did that of Lt.-Colonel Oudinot go north with Lafayette. As we shall see, owing to the disobedience of Dumouriez the whole movement was not carried out as proposed. Luckner, at least, made the most impossible arrangements, for he took away with him the battalions formed of the grenadier companies of different regiments, depriving corps of their picked men and thus causing much dissatisfaction; witness, for instance, the anger of Labourdonnaye, who was commanding at Lille.[2] Also, had Luckner not been so careless, nor Lafayette so absorbed in politics, they would have seen the necessity for the latter's either being at Valenciennes or else having some trusted Lieutenant there until the transfer should be completed. We shall find what happened from want of this precaution.

As Dumouriez was to be left in temporary command of the troops and fortresses in the Department of the Nord, he was sent for and, on arriving from the Camp de Maulde, probably accompanied by his A.D.C., Captain Macdonaid, he was informed of the arrangements and was told to report to Lafayette if anything unexpected happened before he marched. The Generals of the *ancien régime* were not extremely subordinate, and Dumouriez gave his opinion that the movement was very imprudent and very ill timed. Then, turning to Lafayette, who was looking at a map, he told him that they must both be sorry he should be under Lafayette's orders for a few days. 'I promise you, before the Marshal, to serve faithfully for your own glory, provided that you work for the good of your country.' This was strange language to use to a commander of an army to which Dumouriez was to belong for a time. Still he went on, 'But you will judge that I cannot forget your proceedings, and I swear to you that after the war we shall settle our quarrel together'. This referred to Lafayette's opposition to the Girondin Ministry and to Dumouriez.

[1] Sérignan, *Invasion*, 287-8.   [2] Ibid., 302, 326.

Lafayette would have replied, but Luckner stepped in between the two and they all three left the room, Luckner saying to his staff outside that Dumouriez was very generous and had put off his quarrel till the end of the war. A rumour at once spread that the two had fought and Lafayette had been wounded, a good commentary on the state of discipline at the time.[1]

Dumouriez at once returned to the Camp de Maulde. Next day, the 12th July 1792,[2] Luckner started for Landrecies on his way to Metz. Before reaching Landrecies he received an order calling him to Paris to give information to the Council of the King, and so, while Berthier presumably went on for Metz, Luckner turned off for the Capital, where he was heard by the Ministers, by the *Commission des Douze* of the Assembly, and by the Assembly itself.[3] The Assembly had decreed that the Marshal should be invited to come and give it an account of the orders he had issued and received for the operations of the campaign, and to represent what was necessary for the success of further operations. It was early days for such interference, and Luckner replied that he was ready to conform to their decree, but that, as General of an army, he had only to report to the King, his supreme chief, and to the Minister: the account wanted was contained in the correspondence with the Ministers and in the registers of his staff. All this, he said, had much connexion with future operations, and prudence and his duty commanded secrecy. He did send them notes on what they might do for recruiting, and offered to communicate to them in the manner they might consider constitutional, and with proper reserve, the more special details he had already submitted to the King.[4]

Finally the Marshal appeared before the *Commission des Douze*, joined to the *Comité militaire*, to confer on matters whose public communication had seemed to him improper.[5]

---

[1] Dumouriez, *Vie*, ii. 348–50, Eng. ed. iii. 30–2 ; Sérignan, *Invasion*, 289–91.   [2] Ibid., 320.   [3] Ibid.
[4] Mathieu Dumas, *Souvenirs*, ii. 376–80.
[5] Mathieu Dumas, ibid., 378, says on the 18th July, whilst Sérignan, *Invasion*, 320, makes him leave Paris that day. For the *Commission des Douze* see Aulard, *Recueil*, i. xlvi–liv. Sérignan, quoted above, calls it the *Conseil des Douze*. Not to be confused with the *Commission des Douze* which the Girondins tried to establish, 18 to 27 May 1793.

He was questioned on the operations concerted with Lafayette and then was asked if he knew of the resolution taken by Lafayette to march on the Capital, whether this step had his approval, and if the movements proposed for his army as well as for that of Lafayette were not combined with the plan for carrying off the King and protecting his retreat. Indeed, according to Dumouriez, the plan brought a mass of both armies together for two days by La Capelle, only about a hundred and twenty miles from Paris.[1] The old Marshal was as weak and as changeable as a child; for instance, before leaving Valenciennes, he had agreed with Dumouriez that the *Chassé-croisé*, which he had just approved, was imprudent.[2] He must have known much, if not all of the political plans of Lafayette, but before the Commission he became timid, embarrassed, and answered vaguely in a German jargon hard to be understood. Finally, when pressed by those members who wished to compromise Lafayette, he replied that he did not meddle with all these intrigues. Nothing more could be got from him on this point, but it was as injurious as possible to Lafayette and so disgusted the friends of that General that the Marshal's A.D.C., Mathieu de Montmorency,[3] told him before Mathieu Dumas that, after what had happened, he would request the Marshal to dispense with his services as A.D.C.[4] During the time Luckner passed at the Capital after this he was surrounded by the Girondins, who tried to get matter from him for accusing Lafayette and either succeeded or else asserted they had done so. The Marshal may have committed himself, but when he reached Metz he wrote in warm terms of friendship to Lafayette, denying the reports of what he had said and assuring him of his loyalty and support.[5] Leaving Paris on the 18th July 1792, Luckner, anxious for news of his army, reached Châlons on the 19th,[6] to find matters in confusion, although he did not realize the full state of affairs until he got to his new head-quarters at Metz, where he found Berthier fully informed.

---

[1] Dumouriez, *Vie*, ii. 347-8, Eng. ed. iii. 29.
[2] Ibid., 350-1, Eng. ed. iii. 33.
[3] Mathieu Dumas, *Souvenirs*, ii. 380.
[4] Ibid., 376-80.   [5] Charavay, *Lafayette*, 320-2.
[6] Sérignan, *Invasion*, 320.

Meanwhile Dumouriez had not joined the 'Nord' merely to do the ordinary work of a Lieut.-General, but to carry out his plan for the invasion of Belgium. He now realized the ineffectiveness of Luckner and had no wish to accompany him to Metz. Disliking Lafayette and unwilling to serve under him, he yet clung to his post in the north, since it kept open possibilities. Fortune now threw him cards which he played with much skill, greater boldness, and complete success. The completion of the *Chassé-croisé* depended on the enemy's making no attack whilst the troops of the two armies trailed along the frontier in opposite directions. But the enemy did attack, and on the 15th July took the small town of Orchies, between Lille and Valenciennes, and on the night of the 17th July Bavai, between Valenciennes and Maubeuge.[1]

In reality the enemy wished merely to harass, not to attack seriously; but there was some actual danger. No one was formally in command in the north, and La Noue, who was at Maubeuge, and Carle at Dunkirk, said they would only execute orders from the Commander-in-Chief:[2] Labourdonnaye at Lille was averse to obeying any one, but all were alarmed at the departure of the mass of the army. When the Minister had tried to calm Labourdonnaye by speaking to him of the Armée du Nord's moving to his support, 'The Armée du Nord,' replied Labourdonnaye, 'What Armée du Nord? There is no more an Armée du Nord. We have garrisons of the first line, like the Camp de Maubeuge or de Maulde, but we have no more an army since the extraordinary movement of the two armies which you have authorized.'[3] While the Generals left in the north were alarmed at their position, the two Commanders-in-Chief were roaming the country, so that communication with them was slow and difficult. Then also it was known that the Minister was about to be changed, and on the 24th July Lajard was succeeded by d'Abancourt.[4]

Dumouriez 'grasped the skirts of happy Chance'. Styling himself the 'Lieut.-General Commanding the Armée du Nord', he called up troops from Carle at Dunkirk. Then he wrote both

---

[1] Serignan, *Invasion*, 291–305; Dumouriez, *Vie*, ii. 331–5, Eng. ed. iii. 34–6.
[2] Ibid., 351, Eng. ed. iii. 34.   [3] Sérignan, *Invasion*, 301–2.
[4] Ibid., 310–12; Bajot, *Chronologie*, 4th ed., 32.

to Lafayette and to Luckner, showing how impossible it was for him to start for the south, or for La Noue to move from Maubeuge to relieve him: he would only leave the north when he could do so without danger to the country. The fears of the Assembly might be a good card to play and, taking advantage of the possibility that Lajard's place might not be filled up, he wrote to the President, then Aubert du Bayet, whom we shall meet in La Vendée in command of an army. He also wrote to the King with superb self-confidence. He, Dumouriez, who had as Minister been directing the armies, who before becoming Minister had been intended for the command of an army, would be but third or fourth in Luckner's army, if imperious necessity had not made him the chief in the north. It was absurd that Lafayette, occupied as he was on the Meuse and the Moselle, should dictate orders for the north, of which he knew nothing. Arthur Dillon was coming with part of Lafayette's army and was senior to Dumouriez. If Dillon were put in the Armée du Centre and the modest Dumouriez given the command of the Armée du Nord, he ventured to believe that he could serve the Nation and the King there usefully. It is to be presumed that Lafayette was not to be left in the cold, but was to command the southern part, or right wing, of the 'Nord' as a separate body, a plan which had much in its favour, for the front of the 'Nord' was too long. Anyhow, he, Dumouriez, must be authorized to remain in the north.[1]

He used his tongue as skilfully as his pen. Arthur Dillon arrived, so that the need that Dumouriez's troops should remain was past, but he dwelt on the dangers of the situation and on the responsibility which would fall on any General who allowed an invasion of the territory. The Generals were not yet under the iron yoke of the Assembly, but they knew how loud was the cry if any of the enemy penetrated into France. Also every General, as Napoleon was to complain, believes that it is his own post that is in the greatest danger, and never thinks he can have enough troops. Dillon assembled a council of war at Valenciennes on the 23rd July 1792, which agreed unanimously that it would be the greatest imprudence

[1] Sérignan, *Invasion*, 304–16.

to let Dumouriez's troops go.¹ Meantime the Assembly debated on the General's letter. Many deputies took umbrage at the way in which Dumouriez, as they believed, feigned to ignore the existence of a Minister for War. Mathieu Dumas and Lacuée (a future Minister of the *Administration de la Guerre* under Napoleon) argued that the matter should be left to the *pouvoir exécutif*, which alone ought to decide such a point. The Assembly argued and came to no conclusion, and, as the matter had been laid before it, the Minister was paralysed. So far Dumouriez had won the day : his troops were to stay ; but it did not follow that he himself was to do so.²

The anger of the two commanders at this insubordination can be imagined. At first they did not realize the extent of Dumouriez's audacity. Lafayette, surprised at the movements of troops which the General was making, simply forwarded his letter to Luckner, saying that it seemed the Lieut.-General was arranging a campaign after his own fashion, and that he supposed that Luckner would have sent him orders. Then he received a letter from Carle, commanding at Dunkirk, explaining his astonishment at receiving orders from Dumouriez. Considering the situation urgent he had complied and had sent troops to Valenciennes, but this left him weak. If the King had changed the superior command of the 'Nord', he ought to be informed, but he hoped he would remain under the orders of Lafayette and 'it would be with much regret that he should learn the contrary'. On arrival at Metz Luckner received both these letters, forwarded by Lafayette. The two commanders were furious, for not merely was Dumouriez disobeying orders, but obviously he was usurping over other Generals an authority that had never been given to him. Luckner wrote to the Minister, complaining bitterly of Dumouriez's conduct and requesting that he should be forced to bring his division to Metz. The Minister, Lajard, was about to leave office and was uncertain what would be the decision of the Assembly, so he 'hung in the wind'.³ Luckner now took a serious step : on the 28th July 1792 he wrote to Dumouriez

---

¹ Dumouriez, *Vie*, ii. 354–6, Eng. ed. iii. 38–42 ; Sérignan, *Invasion*, 322–32.
² Ibid., 316–18 ; Mathieu Dumas, *Souvenirs*, ii. 380–5.
³ Sérignan, *Invasion*, 319–23.

that he had asked the King to give him another destination which would not leave him under his orders. If Dumouriez had not received fresh instructions in consequence from the Minister, he was to put his division in movement on the 2nd August on the route already settled and to come south. Then, foreseeing that Dumouriez might still disobey, he informed him that he had given orders to Beurnonville in that case to take command of the division. This stroke is said to have come from Berthier; no proof seems to be given, except the inference that, as Luckner did not show his wrath till he reached Berthier at Metz, it must have been his Chief of the Staff who was urging him on this extreme course. This argument is of little weight : a Commander-in-Chief, travelling without his staff, seldom troubles with dispatches when he can spare himself, and it was not till he got to Metz that Luckner understood the whole situation. A 'lettre insolente' from Berthier referred to the concentration at the Camp de Maulde. However, Dumouriez had been warned by Biron, who was at Metz, of the coming blow, and he met it boldly. Getting Dillon to write in his support to the Marshal and to plead the impossibility of sparing the troops or Beurnonville, he himself wrote to the King, daring to complain of Luckner's letter, but not of the Marshal himself. 'It is not against him, but against his staff and especially against *le sieur Berthier*, who leads him astray and will end by ruining him.' He had not disobeyed the Marshal; if Luckner had been with him, he would have ordered what had been done. Luckner had asked that Dumouriez should be given another post. The General on his side pressed for an answer to his request for the command of the 'Nord'.[1]

That a General of Division should venture to complain direct to the King of an order given by his commander, a Marshal, is almost beyond the bounds of credibility, but Dumouriez was fighting for what he valued more than anything, the invasion of Belgium : could he but remain, he would try to carry out that darling plan. He wrote to the Minister, saying he had complained to the King of the harshness of the Marshal's letter and repeating his accusation against Berthier.

[1] Sérignan, *Invasion*, 336-42 ; Dumouriez, *Vie*, ii. 357-60, Eng. ed. iii. 43-8.

He even ventured to tell Luckner himself that he considered he was fulfilling his instructions, it was for Dillon to confirm or counter-order the directions of the Marshal; Dumouriez himself must remain, but, as the matter was in the hands of the King and of the Assembly, no change could be made till orders should come from Paris.[1] In fact the placing of the matter before the Assembly was the strongest card played by Dumouriez; yet it was this precedent that made the hands of his successors very weak in later times.

Dumouriez triumphed: the Minister informed Luckner that, conformably to the opinion of the council of war at Valenciennes, and on the representation of the Assembly, the *Conseil du Roi* had recognized the insufficiency of the force on the northern frontier, and that in consequence the 2nd Division was to remain at Maulde and to form part of Lafayette's Armée du Nord.[2] This settled the fate of the troops, but what about Dumouriez? Was he himself to remain or to go to Metz? Lafayette refused to have him at any price. On the 30th July 1792 he wrote to Dillon that neither Luckner nor he wished Dumouriez to remain in the 'Nord'; he was not employed in Lafayette's army and, as Lafayette had no command to offer him, he was to be ordered to leave.[3] Later, on the 4th August, he wrote to the Minister that he did not believe, and considered as a joke, the report that Dumouriez was to be sent to his army. He had accused Dumouriez publicly of madness or treason in public matters; could a commander who had expressed such opinion on a General be able to entrust him with the destiny of a part of the men and fortresses confided to the army?[4] Dumouriez asserts that Lafayette even gave Dillon orders to arrest him and to send him to the citadel of Metz, a thing Dillon did not do, only informing Dumouriez after Lafayette had emigrated; but this seems to want corroboration.[5] Luckner had said that Dumouriez forgot the duties of a Lieut.-General towards a Marshal of France; he thought it was necessary that he should be punished; if his disobedience remained unchastised the

---

[1] Sérignan, *Invasion*, 342–4.   [2] Ibid. 345.   [3] Ibid. 345–6.
[4] Charavay, *Lafayette*, 322–3.
[5] Dumouriez, *Vie*, ii. 360, Eng. ed. iii. 48; cf. Sérignan, *Invasion*, 346.

army would be lost.¹ He was right, for there were other Generals as unwilling to obey. Labourdonnaye, for instance, a man who was to command the 'Nord' and with whom Dumouriez was to have difficulties, was wanted by Luckner at Metz, but told the Minister that his health would not permit him to change residence or army at this time. Then when Luckner, not knowing why he did not appear at Metz, wrote to him, he replied angrily that, if the Minister had done his duty, he would have told the Marshal about his peculiar health, adding a sneer that, if the armies and General were all on the high roads, there would be no one left to watch the frontier.² When the decision of the Minister was known, Luckner may have been glad enough to get rid of Dumouriez, but he complained that he was made a laughing-stock, that his plans were changed without consulting him, that his troops were reduced to two-thirds, and that he would not be responsible for the defence of Alsace.³

Lafayette, now commander of the 'Nord', was at Sedan. So large a part of the 'Nord' now consisted of troops which had been under him in the 'Centre', that his organization of them in the latter force comes properly here. Perhaps his service in America amidst the Colonials in their rebellion against England had prepared him for the use of volunteers and of raw troops, and he stiffened his volunteer battalions by brigading them with the regulars, joining two of them to one of the line,⁴ an admirable arrangement adhered to by his successor with the 'Nord', Dumouriez, and a precursor of the *Amalgame*. Also he realized the advantage of having horse artillery. General Mathieu Dumas had already formed two batteries at Metz under Barrois and the future brother-in-law of Hoche, Debelle; these batteries had their gunners mounted, but at Strasbourg they were experimenting on the Wurtz system, in which the gunners were carried on light carriages and on the wagons and gun-carriages. By the decree of the 17th April 1792 nine such

---
[1] Chuquet, *Invasion*, 51.   [2] Sérignan, *Invasion*, 348-9.
[3] Chuquet, *Invasion*, 51.
[4] Charavay, *Lafayette*, 283; Chuquet, *Invasion*, 76-7. The regular battalions detailed by Chuquet belonged, I take it, originally to the 'Centre' and went with Lafayette to the 'Nord'. None of them are given as with the 'Nord' in May or June 1792.

batteries were formed, three of them to be attached to each of the great armies, 'Nord', 'Centre', and 'Rhin'; but from want of horses at first only one of each group had mounted detachments, the others having the Wurtz carriages.[1] In all the armies at this time a detestable system was adopted of forming battalions with the grenadier companies of different regiments, with the result that these bodies, composed of picked men, behaved worse than ordinary regiments.

When the *Chassé-croisé* was completed the future members of the Marshalate, as far as the 'Nord' was concerned, stood as follows. Lt.-Colonel Jourdan and Captain Mortier with their volunteer battalions, and Captain Macdonald, A.D.C. to Dumouriez, remained as before with the 'Nord', but General Berthier, Chief of the Staff to Luckner when the Marshal commanded the 'Nord', accompanied him to the 'Centre' at Metz in the same capacity. Then Lafayette had brought the 6th Hussars, to which Colonel Grouchy had just been transferred, the Chasseur regiment in which Murat was Sergeant, and the volunteer battalion of Lt.-Colonel Davout. Grouchy and Davout, who now marched from Sedan to the Camp de Maulde, had already been brought into the district of the 'Nord', but I think it was only now that Murat and Ney[2] came north. As for other men who have an interest for us the volunteer battalions of Lt.-Colonels Moreau and Souham remained in the 'Nord'. General Biron had left the 'Nord' to command the Armée du Rhin at Strasbourg, under the control of Luckner. Colonel Beauharnais had gone with Luckner's staff to Metz. In the Memoirs of General Pouget we get a glimpse of Grouchy at this moment, when, still with the Dragoons, he showed a volunteer battalion, which with his own regiment formed an advanced post on the Sambre before Maubeuge, how to act with the cavalry in mutual support if attacked.[3]

A word may be said here as to his early life. Emmanuel de Grouchy, born on the 23rd October 1766, began his military

---

[1] Mathieu Dumas, *Souvenirs*, i. 514-17; Susane, *Art. franç.*, 351-7; Chuquet, *Invasion*, 86; Charavay, *Lafayette*, 283; Coutanceau, *Nord*, 1ᵉ Partie, ii. 129-77.   [2] For Ney see p. 63.

[3] Pouget, *Souvenirs* (wrong in date), 11-12.

career in the artillery, but in 1784 became Captain in the cavalry regiment *Royal-Étranger*, which was then at Belfort.[1]

On the 25th December 1786 he was appointed to the *Compagnie écossaise* of the Gardes du Corps. His rank in it was only *sous-lieutenant*, but it carried that of Lt.-Colonel in the army. This was an important appointment, as the Gardes du Corps du Roi, part of the cavalry of the *Maison du Roi*, formed with the *Cent-Suisses* the inner guard of the Louvre, and Grouchy's was the first and privileged company of the four, specially surrounding the King. We may call it the crack corps of the French army.[2]

Good as was his position in the *Maison*, it was hardly a pleasant one for Grouchy, who had become imbued with the new spirit of the time. It is significant that his elder sister, Marie-Louise,[3] married the Marquis de Condorcet, one of the bright lights of the first days of the Revolution, who poisoned himself in 1794 to avoid the scaffold. By that time, of the sixty signatories to the marriage contract all except Danton and Robespierre had fled from France or been guillotined by one another.[4]

On the 17th January 1787 Grouchy was placed in retirement. Wishing to return to the line, on the 18th December 1791 he was appointed Lt.-Colonel to the 12th Chasseurs à cheval or Chasseurs de Champagne,[5] and commanded this regiment, the titular Colonel being Menou, the future ' Abdallah Menou '.

As far as the troops were concerned the *Chassé-croisé* was completed : the fate of Dumouriez himself was soon settled by a dramatic change in the command of the ' Nord ' caused by the action of Lafayette. The dispute, the history of which I have given rather fully, was of an importance which seems not to be realized by civilian writers. Hitherto the interference of the Assembly with the armies appears to have been intended for political ends : when, for instance, Luckner was examined by its committees, the object would seem to have been more to extract matter for accusation against Lafayette

---

[1] Grouchy, *Méms.*, i. 3. [2] Susane, *Cav. franç.*, i. 209-15.
[3] Grouchy, *Méms.*, i, x. [4] Martin, *Hist. de France*, ii. 163.
[5] Susane, *Cav. franç.*, iii. 124-7. The *Memoirs* make him pass at once from the *Maison* to this regiment.

than to meddle with the military operations. Something of
the same hostility to Lafayette affected the debate on the
appeal of Dumouriez to them, but the example was set of the
Assembly undertaking the supervision of the actual operations
in the field, and this too at the instance of a General. Also
not merely the good faith but the skill of the commanders
had been in question. No doubt Dumouriez had exaggerated
the danger of the shift of the armies : in a short time he, who
had been complaining of the draining of troops from the north,
was himself to draw forces from this very Camp de Maulde to
the Argonne. But his representation of the peril to the district
was exactly one to tell on civilian minds, almost always intent
on the guarding of every point of a frontier. Further, any
members who had seen the puzzled and confused Luckner were
not likely to form a high estimation of the talent of that
commander. Putting aside for the moment all question of
the fidelity of Lafayette, the net result of this incident was to
place the hand of the Assembly on the neck of the army.
Dumouriez's appeal to the Assembly was clever: it was not
wise, and he himself had cause to rue what he had done.

As for Lafayette, after settling the movement for the
Chassé-croisé with Luckner, he had remained forty-eight hours
at Valenciennes, arranging the march of his own troops, then
going to the camp at Villers-le-Rond, or Rimogne, between
Rocroi and Mézières.[1] It was here that he had received the first
information from Dumouriez, showing that that General was
altering the arrangements made with Luckner. On the
29th July Lafayette was at Longwy, whence he returned to
Rimogne, and on the 2nd August he was at Brouelle, near
Sedan.[2] His choice of head-quarters here instead of at Valenciennes, so much farther from Paris, was significant. The state
of Paris was becoming more and more alarming. Luckner's
doubtful utterances during his visit to the Capital about this
time injured Lafayette, and it was only on the 8th August
that the Assembly by 406 votes against 224 had pronounced
against his formal accusation for treason. All this time he had
been offering the King an asylum in his army. He did not

[1] Sérignan, *Invasion*, 291, and note 1, p. 319.
[2] Charavay, *Lafayette*, 317-22.

intend to march on the Capital, but had placed two regiments of Hussars, under Alexandre Lameth, at Compiègne and was ready to move troops forward by forced marches to receive the Monarch, who was, he hoped, to take command of the army and march against the enemy, whilst order was restored in the Capital.[1] Unfortunately the distrust of the Court was too great, and the King, disbelieving his own danger, would not make the attempt to escape, his last hope of safety. Now came news which Lafayette might well have expected. On the 10th August 1792 the mob of Paris had invaded the Tuileries, care first having been taken to strip the Capital of almost all the regular troops. Adjutant-Major Brune, called up recently from his battalion in the Armée du Rhin, doubtless was amongst the assailants: Lefebvre, Captain in a regular battalion, was probably in the Capital, but was not the man to be mixed in any vile work. Even the two battalions of the Swiss Guard, weakened by a detachment of 300 men and deprived of the artillery, would, with the other few defenders of the Tuileries, probably have repulsed the assailants, but the wretched King, too feeble to head or even to address his protectors,[2] ordered their fire to cease. The Royal Family was imprisoned in the Temple, the Swiss, made prominent by their red coats, were massacred, the Monarchy was suppressed, and a convention was summoned. Commissioners were at once sent to the armies to secure the adhesion of the troops.[3]

Lafayette immediately declared that the Assembly was not free, which was true; when not over-awed by the mob or by the shouting crowd in the galleries, the majority was sane enough, for whilst, as Mathieu Dumas points out, the Jacobins could only muster 224 votes against Lafayette two days before the revolt, the majority of 406 consisted of 160 adherents to the Constitutional Monarchy and 246 of so-called independents of various opinions.[4] The mass of the country would have been quite satisfied with any workable constitution: the main point

---

[1] Mathieu Dumas, *Souvenirs*, ii. 360 1, 379, 396–7; Thiers, *Rév.*, i. 233–4, 244–5, 255–6.   [2] Campan, ii. 250–60; Lavalette, i. 65–76.
[3] Thiers, *Rév.*, i. 248–81; Martin, *Hist.*, i. 310–22; Mathieu Dumas, *Souvenirs*, ii. 438–40, 459–66; Susane, *Inf. franç.*, ii. 160–4; Journal d'un Garde-Suisse, *Revue de Paris*, 1st October 1908; Thiébault, i. 298–309; Frénilly, 164–71.   [4] Mathieu Dumas, *Souvenirs*, ii. 450–1.

was to prick the bladder at the Capital, crush the mob, and so give heart to the ' dastardly honnêtes gens '. Here came in the flabbiness of Lafayette: everything called for a march on Paris, but that would have been contrary to the Constitution, and the General was struck with the strange helplessness of many such men in similar situations. He committed himself boldly enough by getting the Ardennes' authorities to arrest the Commissioners sent to his army, using a party of heavy cavalry, the arm least inclined to the new doctrines, but he trusted to the formation of a sort of local protest against the Revolution at Paris, in which he hoped the rest of the country would join. Possible enough in other countries, this policy was hopeless in France, accustomed to a centralized government and ready to obey the rein, no matter what hand grasped it. In any case such action must have been slow, and time was precious.

It was the misfortune of France that the extreme party always acted with a vigour unknown to their opponents. The Assembly sent fresh Commissioners and poured newspapers and appeals on the army, whilst the General most foolishly suffered his men to read the Parisian literature, which he despised, but which told on the troops. He had believed that he had won over most of his Generals and could depend on his men, but his only chance had been to hurl his troops on the Capital without giving them time to consider. On the 15th August he reviewed the Sedan troops, amongst whom may have been Lt.-Colonel Jourdan and Sergeant Murat; Lt.-Colonel Davout's battalion had left the town for the Camp de Maulde.[1] The General attempted to make his men take the oath to the Nation, the Law, and the King. Only a few days back, and he had succeeded in having addresses of fidelity and devotion sent by many regiments to the Capital, but now the men had been worked on in the opposite sense, and his invitation to the oath was met by the murmurs of men and officers: he had lost his hold on the army. On the 17th August 1792 the *Conseil exécutif*[2] decreed that Lafayette

[1] Vigier, *Davout*, i. 25.
[2] The *Conseil exécutif provisoire*, or Council of the Ministers. Thiers, *Rév.*, i. 271; Aulard, *Recueil*, i, pp. xi-xiii. Abolished by decree of 1st April 1794. Wallon, *Rep.*, iv, note 2, p. 224.

L'ARMÉE DU NORD, 1792

was to hand over the command of the 'Nord' to Dumouriez, or, in his absence, to the senior General present, and was to come to Paris to account for his conduct. Two days later the Assembly decreed that Lafayette should be accused of treason, ordered his person to be seized, and forbade the army to obey him.[1] This was unnecessary, for the General had already abandoned the contest. On the 19th August 1792 he left Bouillon with Alexandre Lameth and twenty-one officers of his staff, amongst them Victor La Tour-Maubourg, the future cavalry General of the Empire,[2] and entered the territory of the enemy. His reception must have astonished him, coming, as he believed, as one who had sacrificed so much for the King. To the Allies, however, he was the arch-fiend of the Revolution, and he was kept in the strictest, harshest, and most unjustifiable imprisonment, first by Prussia and then by Austria, who did not realize how gladly the Jacobins would have received and guillotined him. He was only released in consequence of the negotiations after the victories of Bonaparte in 1797, and did not re-enter France till that General had seized power. Disliked by Napoleon and distrusted by the Restoration, he remained in obscurity until the Revolution of 1830 gave him another opportunity for constitution-making.[3]

The flight of Lafayette, who, poor man, was believed to have joined the Allies in order to serve against France, was a shock to the army, and not only a triumph for the Jacobins but apparently a justification of their hatred for the General. They had denounced him as a traitor, and, lo, he was in the ranks of the enemy! From this time suspicion of the Generals became a mania amongst the Jacobins.

Also this emigration shook the confidence of the troops in their leaders, and one can fancy the feelings with which Davout, arriving at Condé, learnt that his commander had passed over to the enemy. The oath of fidelity to the

[1] Charavay, *Lafayette*, 325–8 ; Aulard, *Recueil*, i. 16, 24–5 ; Wallon, *Représentants*, iv. 10–12 ; Jules Thomas, *Lafayette*, 101–2.
[2] Two La Tour-Maubourgs went over, Marie-Charles-César de Fay, Marquis de La Tour-Maubourg (1758–1831), who became Count and Senator under the Empire ; and the future cavalry commander, Marie-Victor-Nicolas de Fay, Marquis de La Tour-Maubourg (1768–1850), younger brother of the Senator ; he lost a leg at Leipzig.
[3] Charavay, *Lafayette*, 328–31 ; Jules Thomas, *Lafayette*, p. 111.

Nation, the Law, and the King had been taken by the troops of the 'Nord' at Maubeuge and Pont-sur-Sambre, who had come with Lafayette and were devoted to him. Dillon was so secure in his faith in Lafayette that he published his own oath in the newspapers. Dumouriez, at Maulde, was more cautious and refused to administer the oath to his men, troops of the original Nord', knowing nothing of Lafayette. Then, when the triumph of the Assembly was certain, Dillon had to explain his conduct to the Commissioners and repeat that explanation in the papers. All this must have told with lamentable results on the troops. If Generals could be traitors in camp, why not when leading their men in the field ? ' The soldiers ', says Dumouriez, ' considered all their officers as traitors, and this was made a pretext to neglect all discipline and subordination.'[1]

[1] Dumouriez, *Vie*, ii. 382, Eng. ed. iii. 76.

OPERATIONS IN ARGONNE

To Givet

SEDAN

R. Meuse

hémery

Mouzon

Stonne

oLa Berlière

MONTMEDY — To Longuyon
To Longwy

Stenay

Buzancy

Dun-sur-Meuse

R. Aire

R. Meuse

ry

Vienne-Ville

La Chalade

tin-
ns.   Les Islettes

Clermont-en-Argonne

VERDUN — To Fresnes & Metz

Ste. Menehould

erre
eau

R. Aire

Bar-le-Duc
and Toul

VII

L'ARMÉE DU NORD (*continued*), 1792

Dumouriez in command of the ' Nord '. Brunswick advances, but Dumouriez prepares to advance into Belgium. The fall of Longwy forces him to go to Sedan. Council of war advocates the expedition to Belgium. The Minister urges him to march south. Position of Dumouriez, and creation of the Armée des Ardennes. Luckner Generalissimo. End of Luckner. Disbelief of French Generals as to Brunswick's march on Paris. Brunswick takes Verdun. Dumouriez marches for the Argonne, the Thermopylae of France ; arrives at Grand-Pré. He still disbelieves in the march on Paris. Brunswick seizes the defile of La Croix-aux-Bois. Dumouriez marches to Dommartin. Panic of his troops. The delays of Beurnonville. The raw troops at Châlons. Confidence of Dumouriez. Arrival of Kellermann's Armée du Centre. Fine state of his army compared with that of Dumouriez. The old army prepares for battle at Valmy. The troops of the Nord sandwiched with those of Kellermann at Valmy. Comparative strength of regulars and volunteers on the field of Valmy. Position of the future Marshals at the battle. Paris in panic, and pressure brought on Dumouriez to retire. He refuses, and still dreams of Belgium. Napoleon considers him too audacious.

DUMOURIEZ was the natural, if not the inevitable successor of Lafayette, for Arthur Dillon, the senior General, was ' suspect ' from his conduct. Dumouriez had understood the situation from the first moment he heard of the 10th August ; the Jacobins were triumphant, and, much as he disliked them, to declare for the King was to begin a civil war at the moment when a mass of enemies was gathering on the frontier. We shall find him next year in a different mind on that point. He blames Lafayette for not consulting him as to the plan for opposing the Jacobins, saying he would have instantly acceded,[1] but Lafayette could hardly be expected to entrust such a dangerous confidence to a man who was only waiting for peace to challenge him to a duel. Anyhow, all this was too late now ; he refused, as I have said, to administer to his own

[1] Dumouriez, *Vie*, ii. 359, Eng. ed. iii. 46–7.

troops the oath of fidelity to the King, he received the Commissioners from the Assembly well, and he wrote to the Assembly assuring them of his devotion and adhesion and vowing he would crush the rebellion of ' this little Sulla '.[1] To his annoyance the Commissioners had accepted the explanation of Dillon and had retained that General in command, but he hoped that Lafayette would be dismissed and that Dillon, going to Sedan, would leave him free for his expedition into Belgium. Then came the news of his own appointment to command, when at once he wrote to the authorities, civil and military, in the Ardennes and Sedan to set at liberty the Commissioners imprisoned by Lafayette and to arrest Lafayette himself, but the news of the flight of his predecessor cleared the situation.[2] One fact he may have stored in his memory for possible use; instead of pressing on, the enemy in his front had withdrawn. They had never really intended to take the offensive, but he seems to have thought it possible that the withdrawal was arranged in combination with Lafayette.[3] It would have been difficult for any commander to march on Paris if the enemy had been pressing on him. How if, in such a case, a compact were made with the enemy, setting free the army for a march on Paris ? This idea probably remained in his brain and was certainly acted on in 1793. The essential difference between him and Lafayette will be seen. To his quick brain either a march on Paris must be undertaken or the Jacobins must be allowed to triumph, whilst Lafayette sought to over-awe the Capital by the provinces. We shall, however, find Dumouriez, when his turn came, failing from want of rapidity in his stroke.

Arthur Dillon showed some resentment at his supersession, but Dumouriez smoothed matters by proposing to give him the command at Sedan, reserving himself for the expedition into Belgium. With much truth he told the *Conseil exécutif* that the frontier entrusted to Lafayette, or the ' Nord ', was too far extended and should be divided into two, a plan carried out later by the creation of the Armée des Ardennes,

---

[1] Sérignan, *Invasion*, 351–2 ; Chuquet, *Valmy*, 233 ; *Revue de Paris*, 15th September 1908, 226–7.
[2] Dumouriez, Eng. ed. iii. 56–71.
[3] Aulard, *Recueil*, i. 25–6 ; Dumouriez, *Vie*, ii. 377, Eng. ed. iii. 70–1.

L'ARMÉE DU NORD, 1792

intermediate between the 'Nord' and the 'Centre', or 'Moselle'. He dispatched Dillon to Sedan to relieve d'Hangest of the artillery, who, as senior General, had taken Lafayette's place temporarily. Dillon was to command, under Dumouriez, 'the *corps d'armée* from the Sambre to the Meuse': Dillon, however, was too unpopular, the *Conseil exécutif* objected to him from the first, the Assembly decreed that he had lost their confidence, and, much to the annoyance of Dumouriez, the Minister removed him from employment, so that d'Hangest remained in command at Sedan.[1]

Whoever commanded at Sedan Dumouriez was determined not to go there, and began his preparations for the march into Belgium. Let the Sedan forces and the 'Centre' from Metz deal with any advance of the enemy.

On the 19th August, whilst Lafayette was leaving France, Brunswick, having passed the Rhine at Koblenz, crossed the frontier at Longwy, and, brushing by the head of Luckner's Armée du Centre, attacked Longwy. Dumouriez did not care. What matter if the Allies took Longwy, Montmédy, or Verdun? Let d'Hangest attack one of their flanks, and the 'Centre' the other: his dash into Belgium would call them off. On the night of the 24th August, however, Westermann, a friend of Danton's, the Minister of Justice, arrived from Sedan. Longwy had surrendered on the 23rd after two days' defence instead of three weeks; shaken by Lafayette's flight, the Sedan force was in despair and was on the point of disbanding. Dillon had not dared to take command, but had stopped at Givet; d'Hangest could only groan; Chazot, who had gone south with Dillon, commanded temporarily, but did not inspire confidence. All was lost if Dumouriez did not arrive. The Minister wrote to the same effect. Influenced only, he said, by the fall of Longwy,[2] Dumouriez gave way so far as to postpone the expedition to Belgium, which he swore he would undertake that very year, and on the 27th August 1792 he started for Sedan with one A.D.C., probably Captain Macdonald, and Westermann, General Labourdonnaye being

---

[1] Dumouriez, *Vie*, ii. 373-5, Eng. ed. iii. 65-7; Chuquet, *Valmy* 25-7; Aulard, *Recueil*, i. 25-8.
[2] *Revue de Paris*, 15th Sept. 1908, 236.

brought from Lille to Valenciennes to command the northern part of the Armée du Nord, under the direction of Dumouriez.[1] Believing Sedan and Mézières would not be attacked, he abandoned them, he said, to their own forces. ' Il s'agit d'ailleurs de sauver le tronc sans s'attacher aux branches.'[2]

It will give an idea of the stress of the moment to say that on the 2nd September 1792 the Minister was informing Dumouriez that the Assembly had decreed the withdrawal from the Dragoons of their muskets, and the Minister thought the same could be done with the artillery and with the Sergeants and the Corporal-Quartermasters, which would give some 2,500 muskets, besides relieving the Dragoons, the artillery, and the Sergeants.[3] (It would be interesting to know what the Dragoons thought of this method of lightening them.) Even then it would be well not to fire the muskets, for powder was scarce, and the Minister suggested that they should recur to the manner of fighting of ' peuples valeureux et libres, c'est-à-dire, corps à corps '. Frederick the Great, said Servan, had only imagined his fires to alarm or seduce the French, but, if Dumouriez's troops advanced intrepidly with the bayonet, the enemy would fly like children.[4] This is interesting to those who believe it was to their fire that the first French victories were due.

Arriving at Sedan on the 28th August 1792 Dumouriez did his best to encourage his troops, but he himself did not consider them fit to face Brunswick, and on the 29th August he held a council of war,[5] the decision of which is entirely misrepresented in his own Memoirs. His statement of the situation is remarkable. Brunswick with 55,000 men, supported by 16,000 Austrians, with other columns in rear,[6] had taken Longwy and it was impossible to stop his marching on Verdun

---

[1] *Revue de Paris*, 15th Sept. 1908, 230-43 ; Chuquet, *Valmy*, 27-30 ; Foucart et Finot, *Déf. nat.*, i. 149-53 ; Dumouriez, *Vie*, ii. 381-2, Eng. ed. iii. 73-5.
[2] Ibid., 243. [3] Ibid., 248. [4] Ibid., 250.
[5] On the 28th August, Dumouriez, *Vie*, ii. 386, Eng. ed. iii. 81 ; on the 29th, Article on Dumouriez in *Revue de Paris*, 15th Sept. 1908 ; and Chuquet, *Valmy*, note 2, p. 32 ; on the 30th, Dillon in Foucart et Finot, *Déf. nat.*, i. 154.
[6] This calculation is near enough ; altogether the Allies had 81,000 men. Chuquet, *Invasion*, 145.

or Montmédy. Dumouriez himself could only bring into the field 17,000 men, and Luckner at Metz had but 15,000. If a prudent defensive were adopted and the troops found themselves always drawing back on the Capital, followed by the enemy, they would distrust their leaders, agitated as they were by the flight of Lafayette, and a single check would cause them to disband. Considering their behaviour later, this cannot be considered too highly coloured a statement, but then came the marvellous decision, no doubt suggested by Dumouriez and agreed to under his influence. Let good garrisons be placed in the fortresses from Sedan to Maubeuge and the Sedan force be sent north on Brussels, whilst those left in the Camp de Maulde by Dumouriez, reinforced by all the volunteer battalions of the ' Nord ', should move west of Tournai. Then the Austrians would abandon their allies, to fly to the rescue of the Netherlands, and the Prussians would not dare to penetrate into the interior by themselves. ' It is in Belgium that we unanimously think the safety of France lies. This is our final opinion.' [1]

The real opinions of men are seldom represented accurately by their votes in a council or committee held under a vigorous personality. One suspects that Dillon in his opinion, which was strongly in favour of the decision, may have been influenced by the hope of being left at Sedan in an independent command. Others, like Money,[2] probably signed believing that the plan would never be sanctioned by the Government, and some of the leading Generals mentioned by Dumouriez as present were not in attendance. Gradually Dumouriez found that several of the Generals regretted their vote, whilst the army was indignant at what seemed the abandonment of its own district.[3] Also Servan, the Minister, wrote opposing the Belgian expedition and advising Dumouriez to march on the Argonne and the Clermontais : Kellermann, now at the

---

[1] Foucart et Finot, Déf. nat., i. 153–4 ; Chuquet, Valmy, 32–4 ; Money, 37–9 ; Revue de Paris, 15th Sept. 1908, 231–3. Compare the erroneous account given by Dumouriez, Vie, ii. 386–90, Eng. ed. iii. 81–6.

[2] General John Money (1740–1817) was an Englishman ; see Alger, An Englishman in the French Revolution, 132–4.

[3] Foucart et Finot, Déf. nat., i. 154 ; Chuquet, Valmy, 36–7, and note 2, p. 32 ; Money, 39–41.

head of the 'Centre' instead of Luckner, was marching to meet and second him. Finally, learning that Verdun was invested, the Minister appealed to Dumouriez in the name of the country to march direct between the Meuse and the Marne on Sainte-Menehould or even on Châlons. To tempt him south the Minister said that, once behind the Marne, he could hand over the army to a Lieut.-General, who would be guided by the advice of Luckner, now at Châlons, as Generalissimo, and go north himself for Belgium.[1]

Two points, on which mistakes are often made, must be mentioned here. Dumouriez, when he arrived at Sedan, was simply the commander of the 'Nord' and in that capacity ordered large reinforcements to be sent south to him from that very district which he had been declaring ought not to be weakened. As soon as he got to Sedan, he chose to consider the troops there, really part of the 'Nord', to be a distinct force, which he called the Armée des Ardennes,[2] a title only used by the *Conseil exécutif* on the 14th September, apparently by accident, and not made official until after Valmy, on the 1st October 1792.[3] The *Conseil* seems to have meant this term for all the troops from the 'Nord' which Dumouriez had in the Argonne, but the General chose to apply it only to the part of his force, 'l'élite de l'Armée des Ardennes', as he said,[4] which he sent in pursuit of the Allies in conjunction with Kellermann's Armée du Centre. The rest of his force in the Argonne, which we shall find him sending back north under Beurnonville and which in 1793 became the Armée de la Belgique, either had no name until then, or may have been considered by him as still part of the Armée des Ardennes. As for the troops he had left in the north, these he had handed over to Labourdonnaye, brought from Lille to Valenciennes,[5] but that General was sent to Châlons to organize the raw troops there. On the 11th September Dumouriez asked the Minister to give Labourdonnaye the command of the troops in Flanders,[6] but it was not till the 28th September that the

---

[1] *Revue de Paris*, 15th Sept. 1908, 247–8 ; Chuquet, *Valmy*, 34–6.
[2] *Revue de Paris*, 15th Sept. 1908, 231.
[3] Aulard, *Recueil*, i. 56, 82.
[4] La Jonquière, *Jemappes*, 41.
[5] Chuquet, *Valmy*, 30.
[6] Chuquet, *Retraite*, 157.

General arrived at Denain.[1] All this time the troops in the north, and those in the Argonne not belonging to Kellermann, officially formed part of the ' Nord ', but on the 1st October 1792 the *Conseil exécutif* placed Labourdonnaye in command of the Nord and created a new force, the Armée des Ardennes, under Dumouriez, probably meaning, as I have said, all the former troops of the ' Nord ' in the Argonne.[2] Then, when Dumouriez arrived in the Argonne, nominally he was not independent, for the old Marshal Luckner, relieved in the command of the Armée du Centre by Kellermann, had been made Generalissimo of the three armies, ' Nord ', ' Centre ', and ' Rhin ', on the 29th August 1792, and, after nearly falling into the hands of the enemy, had arrived at Châlons, where troops were assembling, on the 4th September 1792.[3] This appointment was not quite a serious one, and the Minister, warning him that he could only give advice to the commanders, even informed Dumouriez that Luckner had been sent to Châlons, ' where he can be useful without injury to public matters or to the Generals, if unfortunately he be again assailed by bad counsels ',[4] which were believed to have come from such men as his late Chief of the Staff, Berthier. However, Luckner took his position seriously enough,[5] and as the time had not yet come for giving orders to the commanders from Paris, even the Minister found him to be a convenient channel, and when there was a question of Dumouriez appointing a General to command in the north and to attack Belgium, that officer was to be directed by the advice of the Marshal.[6] When the Minister wanted Kellermann's Armée du Centre to join Dumouriez in the Argonne, he told the latter General to get Luckner to have this done.[7]

Dumouriez himself, little as he had made of the Marshal's authority in the north, now treated him as really having a control over him and on the 5th September 1792, writing from Grand-Pré in acknowledgement of the receipt of the Marshal's notification of his appointment and describing it as made by

---

[1] Chassin, *La Vendée patriote*, i. 83.   [2] Aulard, *Recueil*, 81–2.
[3] *Revue de Paris*, 15th Sept. 1908, note 3, p. 229, and note 2, p. 251.
[4] Ibid., 229 ; Aulard, *Recueil*, i. 39–40.   [5] Chuquet, *Retraite*, 38.
[6] *Revue de Paris*, 15th Sept. 1908, 247.   [7] Ibid., 257.

'juste titre', he went on, 'No one renders more justice than I do to your military talents and long experience: thus you can be sure that I shall furnish you with the most exact account of all which concerns the Armée du Nord', and he gave a full account of all his proceedings. Then, referring to their former dispute caused by his remaining in the north when Luckner went south, Dumouriez went on, 'You have been very angry with me, M. le Maréchal, and that from want of explanation. Be sure that no one respects you more than I do, or is more satisfied to find himself once again under your orders.'[1] Dumouriez was probably clever enough to see that use could be made of the Marshal, and indeed it was due to Luckner that the uncertainties of Kellermann were ended and the Armée du Centre joined in time for Valmy.

The *Conseil* had never really trusted Luckner and had ordered him to send to them every day copies of all his orders and of all his deliberations, as well as of the letters and reports which he might receive from the armies: indeed not even in England had such a 'Generalissimo-in-partibus' been dreamt of. He lived at Châlons in a sea of confusion, as will be seen when I describe the force there, and 'le triste Maréchal Luckner', as once he described himself, was not the man to make head against the difficulties with which he now met at the end of a long and honourable career. Still his order which brought up Kellermann for Valmy tempts one to believe that he was not the mere ignorant trooper historians represent him as being. Also he had the wisdom to approve of the plan of his Chief of the Staff, Laclos,[2] by which the mass of the forces in Alsace would have been thrown on Koblenz and on the rear of Brunswick, a plan successfully objected to by Custine and Biron, but far superior to that actually carried out by Custine. Probably no one was more glad than the old Marshal when on the 13th September he was called to Paris, nominally to confer with the *Conseil exécutif*. He reached the Capital on the 22nd September 1792[3] and from that time ceased all command.

---

[1] *Revue de Paris*, 15th Sept. 1908, 252-6.
[2] Pierre-Ambroise-François Choderlos de Laclos (1741-1805), author of *Les Liaisons dangereuses*. Michaud, *Biog. univ.*, xxiii. 54-6.
[3] Aulard, *Recueil*, i. 54-5, 59.

On the 8th January 1793 the Convention decreed that he might retire where he liked, and he went to the Department of the Meurthe. He might have passed through the Revolutionary period, but unfortunately he reminded the butchers of his existence by making a claim for his pension, and he was denounced by Prince Charles de Hesse, ' le Général Marat '.[1] Brought before the Revolutionary Tribunal, he was convicted of being ' le vil courtisan et l'esclave titré d'un tyran conspirateur ', and was guillotined on the 4th January 1794, no doubt dying as much surprised at the axe of the Republic as at the ' parre ' of the Monarchy. He died with some spirit, for when the mob cried, ' A la guillotine ', he replied, ' On y va, canaille '.[2] Probably some of the last sounds he heard were the strains of the *Marseillaise*, the ' Chant de guerre pour l'Armée du Rhin, dédié au Maréchal Luckner '. When commanding that army he was loved and honoured as devoted to the country which now slew him as a traitor.[3] The patriots, for their part, saw with regret that he expressed no sympathy for the Republic which sent him to the guillotine.[4]

The French Generals on the Rhine—Luckner, Biron, Kellermann, and Custine—had hitherto believed as little as Dumouriez in the march of Brunswick on Paris. The left wing of the Duke under Hohenlohe-Kirchberg had crossed at Speyer and a threat was made on Strasbourg. The advance was taken to be intended for an invasion of Alsace and the main struggle was expected on the Rhine. Brunswick, indeed, had never meant to march on Paris as he was now doing. His own army of 42,000 Prussians was to have been joined by 15,000 Austrians under Clairfayt from the Austrian Netherlands, while some 40,000 to 50,000 Austrians covered his right and another 23,000 his left. Austria had been unable to bring up her whole contingent, and Hohenlohe had only 14,000 men on the left. The cautious Duke was left with a force far inferior to that for which he had hoped. Still on he came, halting till six days' bread was baked and then, when his wagons were full, going on till a fresh baking was required. Following a system which would be cruel if adopted by other nations against

---

[1] Chuquet, *Charles de Hesse*, 264–5.
[2] Greville, *Mems.*, 1st Series, ii. 219.
[3] Tiersot, *Rouget de Lisle*, 101.
[4] Wallon, *Trib. rév.*, ii. 324, 327.

Prussians, his guns were laid, not so much on the fortifications, as on the houses of Longwy, and the garrison, pressed by the civilian population, surrendered on the 24th August. Turning south, the same style of bombardment made the population of Verdun force the garrison to evacuate the fortress on the 2nd September, Lt.-Colonel Marceau of the volunteers going out with the flag of truce.[1] Brunswick had cut his way through the fortresses and had placed himself between the Armée du Centre of Kellermann and that of the 'Nord' under Dumouriez. Nothing lay between him and Paris but the mass of *Fédérés* collecting at Châlons. On the 31st August Dumouriez had heard the sound of the guns which were firing on Verdun, an appeal to which few Generals are deaf. Also the corps of Austrians under Clairfayt, which he believed would be drawn on Belgium if he marched there, was advancing by Longuyon, passing to the south of Montmédy to cross the Meuse at Stenay and either to attack or to observe him. Now he partly realized that the advance of Brunswick, slow and spasmodic though it was, still might be meant for Paris. Might he not find himself between two fires? Sedan, he said, with a curious anticipation of 1870, was detestable as a camp, and he might be taken with his whole army.[2] Suddenly he abandoned the cherished dream of Belgium and on the 1st September 1792 left Sedan with all his troops, except four battalions, to seize the defiles of the Argonne, whilst the skilful but cautious Brunswick was absorbed in the attack on Verdun and had no thought of the passes of the Argonne in front of him. 'There,' said Dumouriez to one of his staff, Thouvenot, pointing on the map to the Argonne, 'there is the Thermopylae of France.'[3]

The Minister had assumed that he would move behind the Argonne, of which Servan seems to have thought more as a screen than as a post; but Dumouriez calculated that this would expose his object and would enable Clairfayt from Stenay, if not Brunswick from Verdun, to forestall him.[4] The road in front, or to the east of the Argonne, was the nearest:

[1] Parfait, *Marceau*, 58–64 ; Maze, *Marceau*, 9–10.
[2] Chuquet, *Valmy*, 38–9 ; *Revue de Paris*, 15th Sept. 1908, 234.
[3] Dumouriez, *Vie*, ii. 390–9, Eng. ed. iii. 86–99 ; Chuquet, *Valmy*, 38–60, each passage giving a description of the Argonne.
[4] Chuquet, *Valmy*, 36, 40–1 ; *Revue de Paris*, 15th Sept. 1908, 240–1, 247.

Dillon with the advanced guard (a force which included Colonel Grouchy's 6th Hussars and the 12th Chasseurs, where Murat was Sergeant [1]) was to make a false attack on Stenay, when Clairfayt would draw back, and behind this screen the army would reach Grand-Pré. Dillon, who started from Mouzon, did not throw much weight into his attack on Stenay, but the whole daring march succeeded. On the 1st September 1792 Dumouriez encamped near Mouzon, next day he was at La Berlière, and on the 3rd September he reached Grand-Pré, Dillon going on to the Islettes,[2] whilst the Allies were licking their lips over captured Verdun, not dreaming of the bar which was being drawn across their front. 'If I had to do with Frederick the Great,' wrote Dumouriez, 'I should have been pushed back as far as Châlons, but ... the Prussians no longer know how to make war.'[3] He had brought some 19,000 men, Grouchy and Murat being, as I have said, with Dillon, and Captain and A.D.C. Macdonald with Dumouriez himself. He had sent for reinforcements from the north, Duval was to bring 3,050 men from Pont-sur-Sambre, including the volunteer battalion of Lt.-Colonel Jourdan,[4] and Beurnonville was to join with 10,000 men from the Camp de Maulde, a large draft on the Armée du Nord, but one which the influence of Dumouriez was strong enough to get carried out.[5] It is one of the curiosities of military history that, even when he reached Grand-Pré, Dumouriez disbelieved in any march on Paris. On the 7th September 1792 he wrote to the Minister from Grand-Pré, ' Your letter of 5th, which I receive at this moment, in no way changes my opinion on the march of the Prussians. I will tell you more: that is, that I believe that their actual plan is not to march on Paris, but rather to take Metz and Nancy and to winter in Lorraine and the Bishoprics.'[6] He was happier when he went on to say that he hoped 'la lenteur allemande' would give him time to assemble 50,000 to

---

[1] Money, 46-63.
[2] Ibid., 41-66; Chuquet, *Valmy*, 58-61; Dumouriez, Eng. ed. iii. 91-102.
[3] *Revue de Paris*, 15th Sept. 1908, note 1, p. 254.
[4] Chuquet, *Valmy*, 98.
[5] Ibid., 154; Foucart et Finot, *Déf. nat.*, i. 155, 160-1; *Revue de Paris*, 15th Sept. 1908, 252-8.
[6] Ibid., 15th Oct. 1908, 790. This seems inconsistent with his movements.

60,000 men between then and the 24th, ' et qu'alors je pourrai suivre mon génie, et prendre une marche moins prudent '.[1] What he most desired was to have news of Kellermann and to be able to concert operations with him. All the dispatches of Dumouriez at this period are worth study.[2] In reality, he was only just in time. The small force which he had sent on to try to enter Verdun, unable to do so, had fallen back on the Islettes pass through the hills, and on Sainte-Menehould. Then, disorganized by the arrival of the demoralized former garrison of Verdun, this body was just abandoning its hold, when Galbaud, its commander, heard that Arthur Dillon with the advanced guard of Dumouriez (in which Grouchy and Murat served) was close to him. Galbaud reoccupied the Islettes just as Dillon, believing him in retreat, drew back northwards. For a whole day, on the 4th September, the most important pass of the Argonne lay open to the enemy. Still, Dumouriez now held the passes in front of Brunswick. They, he declared, should be the Thermopylae of France; but, always confident, he would be more fortunate than Leonidas. Indeed, he considered his position so strong that the Duke would not attempt to attack it, but would try to pass round his right by Bar-le-Duc. At one time he planned a movement by which he, issuing from the Argonne, and Kellermann, whom he knew to be moving from Metz by Toul, should join in crushing the Duke. In the end he intended to hold in the Argonne. It was in this frame of mind on the afternoon of the 12th September that he learnt that Brunswick had seized the defile of La Croix-aux-Bois on his left. An attempt to retake the pass was defeated. The skilful Duke had pierced the Argonne, cutting Dumouriez from the 'Nord' and from the reinforcements he expected thence. The resemblance to Thermopylae was getting closer than the General had intended.

An ordinary General would have at once fallen back on Châlons, there to meet the reinforcements of trained troops from the north, besides any sound material amongst Luckner's *Fédérés*, but, had the Prussians caught him in the open, his men would probably have broken. Instead, Dumouriez deter-

---

[1] *Revue de Paris*, 15th Oct. 1908, 792.
[2] Ibid., 15th Sept. and 15th Oct. 1908.

mined to cling to the Argonne and to draw in his centre and left on his right at Sainte-Menehould. Before daybreak on the 15th September the centre had crossed the Aisne, covered by a rear-guard partly formed of Duval's troops, in which Lt.-Colonel Jourdan served. These had been chosen as some of the best troops and drew off in good order, but to the north was the division of Chazot, which had retired on Vouziers after failing to retake the Croix-aux-Bois. Starting late, Chazot's division, reaching the plain of Montcheutin, came on a small body of Prussian cavalry which was following the rest of the army and which fell on Chazot, whose men became panic-stricken. The Chasseur regiment in which Murat served held for a moment, preparing to fire its pistols, but it was crushed by the Prussian Hussars[1] and the whole mass broke and, rushing after the main body, threw it also into confusion. The whole force poured into the camp at Dommartin-sous-Hans, where Dumouriez was preparing the encampment. Shouting ' Treason ', and that ' all was lost ', on they went. Some even got as far westwards as Châlons, where they threw terror into the body of recruits poor Luckner was collecting, and stopped the dispatch of the reinforcements he was sending on to Dumouriez.

Mounting with his staff, amongst whom was Macdonald, Dumouriez at last got the army into some state of order in the encampment at Dommartin-sous-Hans. Then, having been twenty hours in the saddle, he dismounted for rest. Hardly had he and his staff sat down to dinner than the whole army was in flight again, this time from simple terror. Again the soldiers shouted ' Treason ', and now they accused Dumouriez of desertion. Taking his life in his hands, Dumouriez rode into the mass of fugitives with his staff, and by word of mouth and slash of sabre at last got the mob to halt. The confused mass of troops passed that night all mingled together. Next day, the 16th September, he got it into camp close to

---

[1] ' Le 12me régiment de Chasseurs à cheval, au lieu de charger les ennemis, est venu fouler aux pieds l'infanterie. Je renverrai ce régiment sur les derrières.' Dumouriez to the Minister, *Revue de Paris*, 15th Oct. 1908, 808. Chuquet, *Valmy*, describes them as making a good front at first till panic-stricken. I follow Desbrière, *La Cav. pendant la Rév. : La crise*, 322.

Sainte-Menehould. How Dumouriez could have the nerve to do this is astonishing. Not another General but would have headed for Châlons and would have refused to keep such men near the enemy until they had shown real confidence in themselves. Far from doing so, Dumouriez calmly drew up to meet any attack, not only from his original front, to the east, but also on the west, his former rear. Of the future Marshals with him, Grouchy, promoted Major-General, had left for the south about the 7th September, but it is amusing to think of the stolid Jourdan and the excitable Murat being dragged along by the body of fugitives, whilst Macdonald, alongside of Dumouriez, tried to stop them.[1]

Nothing can better give an idea of the nervous state in which were the troops of Dumouriez than the fact (to anticipate a little) that the moment Kellermann arrived on the 18th September near Sainte-Menehould, Dumouriez got him to send some of his troops into his own camp, so that the force there might be sure that the Armée du Centre was really close to it.[2] These detachments indeed were meant to play the same part as the tiny body of English soldiers hurried up in the Nile steamers in an attempt to reassure the garrison of Khartoum, but, more fortunate than Wolseley, Kellermann arrived in time. Still, knowing the state of his men, the man of iron clung to the Argonne. Confident in his future, he was even promising Labourdonnaye, now commanding in the north, to send ten thousand men soon to him. The immediate danger in which he stood never took his mind off the longed-for expedition to Belgium.

One circumstance, which seemed to spell ruin, did not affect his determination. He himself had brought to the Argonne some 19,000 men, amongst whom was the Chasseur regiment in which Sergeant Murat was serving. On the 9th September he had been joined by Duval from Pont-sur-Sambre, bringing 3,050 more troops of the 'Nord', including the volunteer

---

[1] ' Il semble que Dumouriez avait autre chose à faire que de distribuer des coups aux fuyards, il eût rassuré ses troupes en cédant à leur désir de repasser la Bionne, . . . elles avaient raison. Dans plus d'une occasion l'intelligence bien connue du soldat français a donné des leçons aux généraux.' Saint-Cyr, *Rhin*, vol. i, p. lxxi. I give the criticism as characteristic of Saint-Cyr.

[2] Chuquet, *Valmy*, 186.

L'ARMÉE DU NORD, 1792

battalion of Lt.-Colonel Jourdan. He counted much on the support of Beurnonville, who was to bring two divisions, his own and that of Dampierre, the last troops which could be drained from the Armée du Nord, which now was left with but a few battalions.

On the 13th September Beurnonville reached Rethel, where he was met by Captain Macdonald, A.D.C. to Dumouriez, with orders to move to Suippes, west of Sainte-Menehould, so as to keep clear of Brunswick, and then, moving east, to join the army.[1] Coming down the River Suippe, on the 16th September Beurnonville got to the village of Auve, not far from Sainte-Menehould, and saw the columns of Dumouriez marching on that town. 'The enemy!' said he, and swung round westwards for Châlons, making no use of the seven squadrons which he had for reconnoitring.[2] That night he was with the old Luckner, whom he told that he had seen Brunswick between himself and Dumouriez. Even when reassured by Dumouriez (for Brunswick moved slowly and was still north of the French position in the Argonne), and urged to advance, Beurnonville remained at Châlons till the 18th September and only joined Dumouriez on the 19th September, the day before Valmy, when Brunswick was actually coming down south. Indeed Goethe, with the Prussians, saw Beurnonville's columns as they marched in. Labourdonnaye had added seven battalions of *Fédérés*, troublesome troops, to this column from the 'Nord'; these only went, not to fight, but to get accustomed to an army.[3] Dumouriez now had altogether some 35,000 men, a force we may call the 'Armée des Ardennes', although it all really belonged to the 'Nord'. A little more hesitation on the part of Beurnonville, and he would have been cut off from the army.[4]

The only force in rear between Dumouriez and Paris was that at Châlons, an enormous depot, where a mass of young troops was assembling, raw levies more dreaded by their Generals than Brunswick was. Once they were bringing their artillery to

---
[1] Chuquet, *Valmy*, 128, 159; Dumouriez, *Vie*, iii. 36–7.
[2] Desbrière, *La Cav. pendant la Rév.: La crise*, 323.
[3] Chuquet, *Retraite*, 49–50.
[4] Dumouriez, *Vie*, iii. 36–8, Eng. ed. iii. 154–6.

bear on the prison, where they proposed to massacre all the aristocrats and were only stopped by the old Marshal Luckner, who threw himself in front of the muzzles of the guns, crying out, ' Kill your General, if you dare ! ' On another occasion, when Luckner tried to stop the confusion caused by fugitives from the army of Dumouriez, they wanted to arrest him. As for sending them to the front, one moment they were willing to start, the next they refused, unless, indeed, all the battalions from Paris went together.[1]

Luckner, as we have seen, was called to Paris, and the command passed to Labourdonnaye, brought from Valenciennes, who was given the command of an imaginary ' Armée de l'Intérieur '. This he was too wise to attempt to organize and he entreated to be allowed to leave ; his troops had already killed a Lt.-Colonel, and it was as much as his life was worth to remain.[2]

In February 1793 General Casabianca landed a mixed force in Corsica, when his volunteers, roused by a night alarm, forced him to re-embark them on pain of being hanged. ' If I had had enough regular troops ', explained the poor General, ' of course I would have used force and thus would have repulsed the rope they showed me.' [3]

Marceau, himself a Lt.-Colonel of a volunteer battalion of the 1791 levy, describes them as ' thirty-two thousand *Fédérés*, or rather thirty-two thousand scoundrels, who are only men in name and who, if not brought into order, will ruin us. They pillage, and assassinate every one not to their mind.' [4] Indeed, when the volunteer battalion to which Thiébault belonged passed through Soissons, the *Fédérés* there formed a plan for attacking and plundering them. The battalion had to be called under arms and to be marched out of the camp. These men later ' made themselves remarked in the army by their indiscipline, their pillaging, and even by their cowardice '.[5] Labourdonnaye escaped with his life at the end of September 1792, going to command the ' Nord ', and these troops at last were got into some order. Still a mass of irregular troops

---

[1] Chuquet, *Retraite*, 36-50. [2] Rousset, *Volontaires*, 84-5.
[3] Krebs et Moris, *Alpes*, Appendix No. 37.
[4] Parfait, *Marceau*, 332. [5] Thiébault, i. 332-3.

is always dangerous, and in 1870 a similar gathering at Châlons insulted the gallant and chivalrous Marshal Canrobert on parade.[1]

All through this time of anxious expectation Dumouriez stood confident and determined. I know of no such resolution as his. He seems to have been the only man in favour of his own plan. Generals and Ministers all assumed that a retreat westwards was the only course. Although till the *Fédérés* joined he had no troops of the new levy, the ranks of his volunteer battalions had been largely filled by raw recruits. He knew that a shriek from one of these men might set his whole force in flight, when he would be lucky if he were not massacred by them as Théobald Dillon had been. The flying mass, once in motion, would have swept away Beurnonville, and the Châlons mob would but have added fresh confusion. For none of these things cared Dumouriez. Firm-fixed at Sainte-Menehould, he looked south for Kellermann and the Armée du Centre.

Kellermann came, and with him came the safety of France.

The man who was to be the first or senior Marshal of the Empire, who won the first victory for the Republic with troops of the *ancien régime*, was a good specimen of the Generals of the Monarchy. François-Christophe Kellermann was born at Strasbourg in Alsace on the 28th May 1735, and he always retained the accent of his country, an accent then disagreeable to the French. His career before the Revolution forms a striking contrast to those of many of the Marshals. Starting from Cadet, he had worked his way up, inch by inch, passing through every grade and gaining the inestimable experience of long regimental service. Although he owed his rise to no sudden favour, he had served in close connexion with some of the higher nobility and had been employed by them when a good organizer and drill was required. He was to show that he could command an army well enough : there were men who could do that, but who could not prepare the troops they had to wield. Just as Napoleon used Berthier for his staff work, so he seized on Kellermann for his reserves.

Kellermann had entered the army in 1752, when only seven-

[1] Bapst, *Canrobert*, iv. 149-61.

teen, in the infantry regiment of Lowendhal,[1] a German regiment in the service of France. He served in two infantry regiments and then in some of the curious corps of mixed infantry and Dragoons, *Volontaires d'Alsace*, *Volontaires de Dauphiné*, &c. These *Volontaires* were composed of picked officers and men from ordinary regiments, and carried on partisan warfare: they were high in favour.[2] He became Captain in 1769, Brevet Lt.-Colonel in 1772, Major in 1779, and Lt.-Colonel in 1780. He served in the Seven Years' War and was present at the battle of Bergen. He distinguished himself in the campaigns of 1761 and 1762, obtaining the Cross of Saint-Louis. In 1765 he was sent to Poland with other officers and charged with the organization of cavalry in the Palatinate of Cracow.

In 1783 he organized the crack Hussar regiment *Colonel général des Hussards*,[3] was promoted *Brigadier général des Armées* on the 1st January 1784, and on the 9th March 1788 *Maréchal de camp*, say Major-General, or rather a staff officer whose business it was to place troops in quarters and in the field. In his thirty-nine years' service he had had six campaigns. One of the last marks of royal favour fell to him, for in 1790 he was made Commander of the Order of Saint-Louis, which brought him a pension of 800 livres. This he lost under the Revolution but retook on the Restoration, with what feelings one can imagine.

Taking command of the Armée du Centre at Metz on the 2nd September, as will be told under the history of that army, he had arrived at Vitry on the 15th by a curiously devious route, which partly had the approval of Dumouriez, who, like all the Generals, was not sure whether Brunswick was not really aiming for Metz and then for Alsace. On the 12th September Dumouriez had at last called on Kellermann to join him,[4] but even then this was put more as a precaution than as essential and it had only got Kellermann as far as Vitry. Then at last, when he had determined to leave Grand-Pré for Sainte-Menehould, in a dispatch which reached Keller-

---

[1] Susane, *Inf. franç.*, v. 364, No. 1437.   [2] Ibid., i. 240-2.
[3] Susane, *Cav. franç.*, ii. 242-3.
[4] The letter reached Kellermann on the 13th. Chuquet, *Valmy*, 164.

mann on the 15th, he begged his comrade to come to his help without losing an instant.

Luckner, apparently writing in advance, had ordered Kellermann to march on Sainte-Menehould and to join Dumouriez as quickly as possible. On the 18th September he was two leagues off at Dampierre-le-Château and on the 19th he reached Dumouriez.[1]

The Armée du Centre was sixteen thousand strong,[2] but this does not represent the real acquisition made by its junction. It was the finest and most trustworthy force which France had in the field, the original Armée du Nord, brought south by the *Chassé-croisé* and reinforced by some of the best troops of the Armée du Rhin. Whilst Dumouriez's force, the Armée de l'Argonne or the Armée des Ardennes, was so largely composed of volunteers, Kellermann brought hardly any. Whilst Dumouriez's men were in a nervous state, ready for a panic and much demoralized by the wild flights through which they had already gone, Kellermann's men came up unbroken, untouched; the indiscipline which had existed for a time had ceased, their leaders were obeyed, and, whilst the other troops had been scurrying along the Argonne, their march had been a triumphal one through an enthusiastic population.[3] At the moment when the fate of France was to be decided, instead of the new, nervous army which Brunswick had been hunting, an old army, such as the Monarchy was wont to put in the field, stepped forward to receive the enemy.

Here I have to break my account of Valmy, which I shall give in the history of the Armée du Centre, where the main incidents are described. I acknowledge that this is one of the inconveniences, not many I hope, of my system of following the history of each army separately, but here a break is inevitable. However much Kellermann and his Armée du Centre were helped by Dumouriez and by part of the troops of the 'Nord', it was the Armée du Centre which came to receive the blow of the Prussians. To give the account of this day of the 20th September 1792 under Dumouriez would be to describe Ligny under the history of the Duke of Wellington, breaking

---

[1] Chuquet, *Valmy*, 165-6, 186. [2] Ibid., 186.
[3] Le Grand, 95.

it off from its real sequence, the history of the army of Blücher. Also in reality the loss to the reader here is not great. Valmy was much more a question of nerves than of fighting. Would the French troops stand the steady approach of the disciplined army of Brunswick ? ' Vos soldats continuent-ils à refuser toute discipline ? ' the King of Prussia had asked of the French Minister, Comte Louis-Philippe de Ségur. ' Sire, nos ennemis en jugeront,' was the reply,[1] and this day the enemy could judge. All that the reader here need keep in his mind is that, in the midst of the troops of the ' Nord ', so apt to shriek and fly, the old troops of Kellermann, crammed on the bad position to which they had been guided by Dumouriez, stood so firmly and presented such a formidable front that Brunswick drew off his men, without delivering a decisive onslaught.

Although Kellermann played the principal part on the actual field, very much of the credit for the victory must be allowed to the aid so skilfully given by Dumouriez. Actually a mere spectator, Dumouriez had nevertheless intended to lead the sweep round the Prussian left himself. One doubts whether this might not have ended in another rout had it been pressed home, but, as Kellermann sent to request him to come and see him, Dumouriez assigned the command of this detachment to others, who were too timid to do more than catch a few stragglers, missing all the Prussian baggage.[2] About noon Dumouriez himself appeared on the mound of Valmy, and we get a glimpse of him, doubtless followed by Macdonald, discussing the situation with the leaders of the ' Centre ' (Kellermann, Senarmont, Muratel, the Duc de Chartres, &c.), walking his horse, as if on parade, seeming neither to hear nor to see the bullets which sang round him and some of which fell close.[3] Finally he judged that Brunswick would not assault and, with his usual indifference to events which would have stirred the blood of most men, he returned to his own camp to await results.

Except for two battalions, all the troops of the ' Centre '

---

[1] *Revue des Deux Mondes*, 15th January 1908, 260.
[2] Dumouriez, *Vie*, iii. 41–6, Eng. ed. iii. 162–5 ; Chuquet, *Valmy*, 197–8, 224–5.
[3] Le Grand, 112.

that Kellermann massed on the mound of Valmy were regulars. It is not quite easy to speak certainly of those troops of Dumouriez that were used to support Kellermann on either flank. Stengel, who fought well on the right, had only regular troops.[1] Beurnonville, who was in support of Stengel, had, I presume, the troops he had brought with him from the north, four regular battalions, the *Légion germanique*, and ten battalions of volunteers,[2] but I doubt these being engaged. Chazot, who was on the left, had originally four regular battalions and eight of volunteers of the 1791 levy, but he was sent with nine battalions only, presumably three of regulars and six of volunteers, as the regular battalions were each linked with two of volunteers in this army.[3] However, there is nothing to show the exact composition of the divisions of Beurnonville and Chazot on this day.[4] In both armies all the cavalry and artillery were regulars and all the volunteers were of the 1791 levy, except the seven battalions of *Fédérés* sent up from Châlons, who took no part in the day.[5] Altogether Dumouriez had twenty-one battalions of regulars and thirty-six of volunteers and *Fédérés*. As for the comparative strength of the forces brought on the actual field by the two commanders and not including those assigned to the flanking movement, it will be seen by the detail which will be given under the Armée du Centre that Dumouriez had twenty-nine battalions and thirty squadrons, sandwiched with the sixteen battalions and thirty squadrons of Kellermann.

If we treat the force in the Argonne under Dumouriez as what it really was, a part of the Armée du Nord, we get the position on this day of the men in whom we are interested, belonging to that body, as follows : Captain Macdonald we are certain was on the field with Dumouriez, to whom he was A.D.C., and in all probability the 5th Hussars, in which Ney was Adjutant, and the 12th Chasseurs, in which Murat was Sergeant, were also employed, one would have thought under Stengel, as they were part of the *avant garde*,[6] although Susane, mentioning the 12th Chasseurs as

---

[1] Chuquet, *Valmy*, note 2, p. 249. [2] Ibid., note 3, pp. 184, 197.
[3] Ibid., 55–6, 197. [4] Ibid., 249.
[5] Chuquet, *Retraite*, 49–50. [6] Chuquet, *Valmy*, note 2, pp. 55–6.

distinguishing itself at Grand-Pré, omits all reference to Valmy,[1] so that it may have been kept in reserve. As Lt.-Colonel Jourdan's volunteer battalion was part of the reinforcement brought by General Duval, I presume he was some seven miles off at Vienne-le-Château, where Duval had been detached and whence his column was to have made a foray on the enemy's baggage.[2] The volunteer battalion of Lt.-Colonel Marceau formed part of the force under Dillon, guarding the Islettes, to the east of Sainte-Menehould, where he was slightly engaged with the Hessians.[3] As for the others belonging to the 'Nord', Grouchy, promoted *Maréchal de camp* or General of Brigade on the 7th September 1792, had gone to the Armée des Alpes; the volunteer battalion of Lt.-Colonel Davout had been left in Condé;[4] and that of Captain Mortier had also, I think, been left in the north when the reinforcements had marched for the Argonne. The Armée du Centre had at most two future Marshals on the field this day, Kellermann and perhaps Adjutant Ney.

Next day Kellermann retired from what he called his 'désagréable' position to a stronger one, behind the Auve; while Brunswick later moved to Hans, occupying both Valmy and Mont Yvron.

All this time the Capital had been in a state of shrieking terror, and the cruel massacres of the first days of September in Paris were as much due to vile cowardice as to hatred of the victims. The Government also had been in great alarm at the advance of Brunswick, and Danton, then Minister of Justice, with Servan, the Minister for War, had been almost alone in withstanding the proposal to abandon Paris. Even Servan believed Dumouriez to be wrong in clinging to the Argonne, and advised retreat on Châlons. Kellermann had proposed this course from the first. How Dumouriez could resist the pressure brought on him to retire is impossible to conceive. A civilian government (and governments are almost always composed of civilians) inevitably loses its head if an enemy chances to

---

[1] Susane, *Cav. franç.*, iii. 126.
[2] Chuquet, *Valmy*, 98, 198; Belliard, i. 74.
[3] Chuquet, *Valmy*, 254–7; Maze, *Marceau*, 11–12; Parfait, *Marceau*, 67–72.   [4] Vigier, *Davout*, i. 27.

be nearer to the Capital than its own army. President Lincoln in 1865 ruined McClellan's campaign by insisting on withdrawing McDowell's Corps from him to cover Washington. He could not realize that a town might be fully protected by a force not actually covering it. Dumouriez knew better. He brought up every man he could to the Argonne and turned an indifferent ear to the clamours of the Capital. Was Paris threatened? Let every available man from the rear, from the Armée du Nord, even from the Armée du Rhin, be sent to his camp. If Brunswick marched on Paris, let the Duke find a desert on his route. Let anything or everything happen, he would stand with his back to the Argonne. He might have used the boast of Roderick Dhu; but, unlike that misguided chief, he had no idea of losing a single advantage and his pen well helped his sword. If only he were trusted, on the 15th November he would be in Brussels.[1]

Napoleon, at the end of his career, with all his vast experience to look back on, gave an opinion which shows better than any words of mine the extraordinary daring of Dumouriez. He considered the General had been too audacious. 'And that from me should count for much, for I consider myself as the most audacious man in war who perhaps has ever existed; and most certainly I should not have remained in the position of Dumouriez, so dangerous would it have seemed to me. I could only explain his manœuvre to myself by saying that he did not dare to retreat. He must have considered there was more peril in retreating than in remaining. Wellington had placed himself in this position with reference to me on the day of Waterloo.'[2]

Although Chuquet disagrees,[3] I must believe the great master of war to be right, but he may have underrated the marvellous confidence of Dumouriez. Brunswick had wished to get the French into the open plain and, if he had caught the two armies away from the Argonne, another such panic as that of Montcheutin might well have been fatal to them. Napoleon did not say whether he considered the shaky state

---

[1] Dumouriez, *Vie*, iii. 51, Eng. ed. iii. 176.
[2] Las Casas, *Mémorial*, 10th Nov. 1816.
[3] Chuquet, *Valmy*, 121.

of the troops an element in the question. None of the later commanders could have taken such a risky course; for them this would have led to the scaffold. Whatever the reasons of Dumouriez, his courage in standing in such a position in defiance of the Government and of Kellermann should place him high amongst commanders. It would be a curious question for military critics whether his success now had anything to do with Napoleon's attempt in 1814 to halt the Allies by throwing himself in their rear.

VIII

L'ARMÉE DU NORD (*continued*), 1792

Kellermann wishes to retire, but is placed under Dumouriez, who negotiates with Brunswick. Brunswick retires, followed by Kellermann with the Armée du Centre and the Armée des Ardennes, which is now formed officially. Its history. Beurnonville marches north with the rest of the troops of Dumouriez for Belgium. Dislocation of the forces in the Argonne and new distribution of the future Marshals, &c. Promotion of Murat to Lieutenant. Dumouriez and Macdonald go to Paris. Dumouriez has a hostile interview with Murat in the house of Talma. Luckner refuses to see him. Dumouriez invades Belgium. Part taken by future Marshals and Moreau in the campaign. Battle of Jemappes, 6th November 1792. Contrasts between old and new troops. Bravery of Louis-Philippe. Preponderating fire of French artillery. Action of future Marshals in the battle. Dampierre and Dumouriez. The valet of Dumouriez. Belgium occupied and the troops placed in cantonments. Murat at Paris.

KELLERMANN had from the first longed to march on Châlons and now, alarmed at having the enemy between him and Paris, he tried to force the hand of Dumouriez by declaring, what of course was true, that he was independent, and that, if Dumouriez would not retire on Châlons, he himself would do so with his own Armée du Centre. Dumouriez had to appeal to the Government, which placed Kellermann under him. Gradually, however, Kellermann was drawn into Dumouriez's scheme. True to his character, that General had begun a system of negotiations with the Prussians, which, carried out with much doubtful faith on both sides, ended only when the Prussians recrossed the frontier. He had long formed the project of separating the Prussians from Austria. He had begun this policy when Foreign Minister, and his emissary, Benoît, when ordered to leave Berlin in April 1791, replied that what the Prussians would not then hear, they might listen to on French soil. On the other hand, the Prussians had many reasons for now attending to him. Their army was fast fading away from sickness, and they believed they might gain by diplomacy what it seemed hopeless to expect from battle. If only the safety of Louis XVI were assured and a position provided for Royalty in the new state of affairs in France, they were willing to withdraw. Dumouriez tempted them on in this path, and, by the time the finality of the declaration of the 21st September 1792 of the Convention, establishing the Republic, was fully realized by Brunswick, the Duke had become too weak to attack.[1]

Dumouriez acted with a curious mixture of good and bad faith. The system he was urging on the Prussians was his own policy. He really did want the friendship of Prussia, but he also wished to get its troops out of France without the risk of a battle, as he considered them too formidable for him. Once he were free from them, he could turn to his daring plan of an invasion of Belgium. He skilfully concealed from them the hopelessness of their demand for the restoration of Louis XVI. At last he was glad to finish by an assurance to Brunswick that the Allies could retreat unmolested. All the time he was collecting forces in case his craft failed. d'Harville, with a Corps which we shall soon find in Belgium, 10,000 strong, was brought from Rheims to the Suippe, to the camp of Auberive. On the 1st October Dubouquet joined Dumouriez from Fresne with 15,000 men.[2] Brunswick, however, was already off. On the 30th September 1792 he had left his camp and had marched north for Grand-Pré and then for Verdun. Kellermann was not quite in the secret, and Dumouriez had to delay him curiously in order to prevent his taking the pursuit too seriously. Finally, Kellermann saw the Prussians over the frontier, and on the 23rd October 1792 three salvos from his guns told France that her soil was free from the footsteps of the invaders.

Even now it is impossible to say who really had been befooled in these negotiations. Dumouriez had lost an opportunity of maiming the Allies during their retreat but he had got rid of the sword pointing at Paris and was now free to attack Belgium. Brunswick had got his troops out of France without difficulty

---

[1] Chuquet *Retraite*, 70–107, 148–77; Foucart et Finot, *Déf. nat.*, i. 178–81; Dumouriez, *Vie*, iii. 61–72, Eng. ed. iii. 189–202.

[2] Chuquet, *Retraite*, 124–5.

and was now able to deal with Custine and the French forces on the Rhine. Still, some distrust had been sown between the Allies, and all this negotiation may have helped on the peace with Prussia which was to come in 1795.

The proper course for Dumouriez would have been to pursue the Allies with the 72,000 men whom he had under his hand, but he had never lost sight of the beatific vision of the invasion of Belgium and preferred to let Brunswick draw off unpressed, whilst he sent the greater part of his own force northwards. Kellermann with his Armée du Centre, that is to say, the troops he had brought from Metz and those that had joined from the Armée du Rhin, some 16,000 strong, was to escort, rather than pursue, the Allies to the frontier. With Kellermann and under his control, Dumouriez sent those troops of his own army who, under Arthur Dillon, had guarded the Islettes and had formed his southern wing. This body was now reinforced to 16,000, a strength increased later from garrisons.[1] To it he transferred the title of 'Armée des Ardennes', by which he had hitherto designated the whole of the force belonging to the Nord but now in the Argonne. As I have already said, the *Conseil exécutif* had used this title, as if by chance, on the 14th September 1792,[2] but now, on the 1st October 1792, on the recommendation of the Minister it formally acknowledged the separation of the two bodies, the Armée du Nord, under Labourdonnaye, that is to say, the troops whom Dumouriez had left in the north when he came to Sedan; and the Armée des Ardennes under Dumouriez, by which apparently they meant all the troops of the Nord in the Argonne.[3]

Whether or not Dumouriez, by using this title for the force which he sent eastwards, meant to conceal the dispatch of the mass of his own force northwards, this Armée des Ardennes, put under Arthur Dillon, became one of the eight, and later one of the eleven armies of the Republic.[4]

[1] It was 18,000 when it got to the frontier (Money, 144), but Kellermann, including his own Armée du Centre, said he only had 28,000 (Chuquet, *Retraite*, 204). Just before the Belgian campaign the 'Ardennes' had 20,000 (Chuquet, *Jemappes*, 73). Dumouriez, *Vie*, iii. 81, Eng. ed. iii. 214–15, gives Kellermann and Dillon each 25,000, and Chazot 7,000 to 8,000, and garrisons 10,000.   [2] Aulard, *Recueil*, i. 56.   [3] Ibid., 81–2.
[4] Ibid., 82, iii. 533–4; Jomini, *Rév.*, iii. 430–1.

Marching alongside of the Armée du Centre, under the control of the commander of that army, Kellermann, it saw the Allies over the frontier on the 22nd October 1792 and then swung round northwards, by Montmédy, Sedan, Mezières, and Rocroi, for Givet on the Belgian frontier, to take part in the invasion of Belgium, although it was not at the battle of Jemappes. Acting as one of the bodies in the north under Dumouriez, after the defeat of Neerwinden it remained nominally an independent army, but in reality it was almost always under the orders of the commander of the Nord and hardly had a separate existence. Most of its strength was taken up by garrisons, and the few troops it could bring in the field acted with the Nord.

The rest of his own force, the remainder of the troops he had brought or had received from the north, and the reinforcements from Châlons, some 40,000 men,[1] Dumouriez put under Beurnonville and sent north from Vouziers to Valenciennes for the Belgian frontier, where we shall find it. This body, which was to be the force which fought at Jemappes, at present was nameless and was not included in the official list of armies. On the 6th October 1792 the *Conseil exécutif* had entrusted Dumouriez with the chief direction (say command) of the projected expedition into Belgium. He was to continue to command the 'Ardennes', but that was to be reinforced by such armies and divisions as were considered necessary, and the generals of such forces were to be under him.[2] This does not look as if they quite understood what he was doing. After Dumouriez had rejoined Beurnonville's army he styled it the 'Armée de la Belgique', or, as he himself liked to put it, the 'Grande Armée'.[3]

This dislocation of the forces in the Argonne altered the distribution of the armies and of the future Marshals with them. The 'Centre', at first marching to the frontier with the Armée des Ardennes, then returned to its own district by the Rhine as the Armée de la Moselle, and ceased to have any direct connexion with the 'Nord'. With the 'Ardennes',

---

[1] Dumouriez, *Vie*, iii. 83, Eng. ed. iii. 216-17, gives Beurnonville only 22,000; he had 40,000 in Belgium. Chuquet, *Jemappes*, 72.
[2] Aulard, *Recueil*, i. 100.   [3] Chuquet, *Jemappes*, 72.

which now interposed between the two bodies, it had some connexion, the inner wings of the two armies sometimes acting together for a stroke. With the 'Centre' went its Commander, Kellermann. The battalion of regulars in which Captain Lefebvre served, leaving Thionville, the siege of which was now raised, joined the ' Centre ',[1] whilst the volunteer battalion of Lt.-Colonel Oudinot, which had been left in rear, now came up to Thionville.[2] All these men ceased any further connexion with the Nord.

With the Armée des Ardennes, first under Arthur Dillon, and then from the 15th October 1792 under Valence, went Ney, promoted *sous-lieutenant* on the 29th October 1792 and almost immediately taken as A.D.C. by the old General Lamarche, formerly Colonel of his Hussar regiment and now leading a brigade in this army. His regiment, 5th Hussars, joined the Ardennes.[3] The regiment of regulars in which Hoche was Captain, the 58th, leaving Thionville, joined this force.[4] The volunteer battalion of Lt.-Colonel Moreau, 1st Ille-et-Vilaine, is shown by Money, who had a brigade here, as part of the force,[5] but, as I shall explain later, this is a mistake; the battalion remained in the north and had not been at Valmy. Lt.-Colonel Marceau of the volunteers was on the staff of General Dillon, and, when Dillon became 'suspect' and was called to Paris on the 15th October, Marceau accompanied him and did all he could to defend him. Dillon, a Royalist at heart, had better have emigrated, as once at least he wished to do.[6] Arrested on the 1st July 1793, he was included amongst the victims of the alleged 'conspiration des prisons' and was guillotined on the 13th April 1794, shouting vigorously, ' Vive le roi ', as he mounted the scaffold.[7] As for Marceau, he had no further connexion with this army, becoming Captain in the *Cuirassiers légers* of the German Legion,[8] with which he served in La Vendée. Although, as I have said, first Dillon,

---

[1] Wirth, *Lefebvre*, 63-4.
[2] Nollet, *Oudinot*, 5 ; Déprez, *Vol. nat.*, 457.
[3] Money, 134, 173 ; Desbrière, *La Cav. pendant la Rév.* : *La crise*, 156.
[4] Cuneo d'Ornano, *Hoche*, i. 29.
[5] Money, 164.   [6] Ibid., note, p. 138.
[7] Wallon, *Trib. rév.*, iii. 196-8 ; *Biog. des Cont.*, ii. 1381 ; Michaud, *Biog. univ.*, xi. 368.   [8] Parfait, *Marceau*, 72-4.

and then Valence led this army, Dumouriez remained officially its commander until January 1793, when its real leader, Valence, was formally appointed.[1]

It will be convenient to summarize here the effect which the breaking up of what I may call the Argonne group of future Marshals and other men in whom we are interested had on their personal fortunes. Lt.-Colonel Marceau went to La Vendée, and then to join the ' Ardennes ' in April 1794, thence passing to the ' Sambre-et-Meuse '. Kellermann, Lefebvre, and Oudinot went east, Kellermann soon going south to join the group of future Marshals connected with the armies of the Alpes and of ' Italie ', but the others joining the eastern group of future Marshals, where they met Bernadotte, Saint-Cyr, and Soult. The march of the rest of the troops, the Armée des Ardennes and the force under Beurnonville, took to the north Dumouriez, Jourdan, Macdonald, Murat, and Ney, with Hoche, and these went into the region where Davout and Mortier and, I think, Moreau, had been left. The fortunes of these men were now linked with that of the Armée du Nord, under which I will recount them, always remembering that the ' Nord ', at this moment but a weak body, had detached from itself almost all the troops forming the Ardennes and the force of Beurnonville, and was again to absorb all except the ' Ardennes ', which was hardly a separate body.

With the future Armée de la Belgique, the force which Beurnonville took north, went the 12th Chasseurs,[2] in which Murat was promoted *sous-lieutenant* on the 15th, and Lieutenant on the 31st October 1792. I presume that the volunteer battalion of Lt.-Colonel Jourdan marched with this force: it is not included in the ' Ardennes ',[3] but it is not named in this body by Chuquet.[4] It was while belonging to the Armée de la Belgique in December 1792 [5] that Captain and A.D.C. Macdonald went with his General to Paris and then accompanied him to the north. The volunteer battalion of

---

[1] La Jonquière, *Jemappes*, 23–6.
[2] Chuquet, *Jemappes*, note 2, p. 72 ; Desbrière, *La Cav. pendant la Rév. : La crise*, 328.
[3] Money, 164, names the 1st Haute-Vienne ; Jourdan was in the 2nd.
[4] Chuquet, *Jemappes*, note 2, p. 72.
[5] Déprez, *Volontaires nationaux*, 501.

L'ARMÉE DU NORD, 1792

Lt.-Colonel Davout, 3rd Yonne, is shown by Chuquet as in this force, but that seems impossible, and Vigier's account, which makes it part of the garrison of Condé, must be right, for, to take one incident only, on 1st September it was engaged, apparently near that fortress.[1]

As for Dumouriez himself, he went off to Paris, which he reached on the 11th October [2] with his A.D.C. Macdonald, in order to consult with the Government. At that time the great actor, Talma, was living in the Rue Chantereine in a house bought later by General Bonaparte, in whose honour the Municipality renamed the street ' Rue des Victoires '. Talma gave an entertainment in honour of Dumouriez. Suddenly an uninvited and unwelcome guest appeared in the person of Marat with two friends of his. Marat was coldly received by Dumouriez, and he withdrew to denounce in his paper and at the Jacobins what he described as the ' son of Thalia feasting the son of Mars '.[3] Dumouriez was indeed treading on the thinnest crust over the fiery lava ready to receive him. He was pleading for the life of the King and could hardly have concealed his dislike of much that was done at Paris. He required victory, and repeated victory, to retain his post and his life. He had one warning before him. Luckner, who but a short time before had been the favourite commander of the Nation, now, superseded by Kellermann in the command of the Armée du Centre, and in the command at Châlons by Labourdonnaye, had got as far as Paris on his way to the scaffold. Dumouriez tried to see him, but the old Marshal, remembering their disputes in the Armée du Nord, declared he was not at home.[4]

Having settled matters with the Government, Dumouriez left Paris on the night of the 15th October [5] and arrived at Valenciennes on the 20th October, with his A.D.C., Captain Macdonald, to take general command of the four bodies with

---

[1] Vigier, *Davout*, i. 27-9.

[2] La Jonquière, *Jemappes*, 20, correcting the *Méms.* of Dumouriez, *Vie*, iii. 108, Eng. ed. iii. 254. See also Foucart et Finot, *Déf. nat.*, i. 260.

[3] Dumouriez, *Vie*, iii. 114-15, Eng. ed. iii. 260-1.

[4] Grouchy et Guillois, *La Rév. franç.*, 388.

[5] La Jonquière, *Jemappes*, 22, correcting Dumouriez, *Vie*, iii. 138, Eng. ed. iii. 291.

which he intended to invade the Austrian Netherlands. Under his own immediate command was the so-called Armée de la Belgique, which, as Beurnonville described it, had flown or swum northwards to Valenciennes from the Argonne. Next, on the right at Maubeuge, was a Corps of some 10,000 raw troops under d'Harville. This represented the reserve which poor Luckner had commanded at Châlons. Brought up to Suippes to support Dumouriez, it had been sent north when Brunswick retired. As it turned out, these two were the only bodies used at the battle which decided the fate of Belgium for the moment. On the extreme right (or east) was the Armée des Ardennes under Valence. On the extreme left (or west) was the so-called Armée du Nord under Labourdonnaye, who after all had escaped with his life from the *Fédérés* at Châlons. The 'Nord', once a large army, had been drained of almost all its troops and it now consisted of battalions left behind in Flanders and some volunteers of the new levy.[1]

Although the troops had seen the enemy retire from before them at Valmy, they were far from having full confidence in themselves, and, when Dumouriez sent his A.D.C., Macdonald, to accompany a reconnaissance from Lille on Tournai, that officer returned to report that he had seen the whole detachment break, panic-stricken, and fly back to Lille. This was but one of the trifles which did not affect the marvellous confidence of Dumouriez, and he planned his advance as if he were leading the finest troops in the world. He himself led the Armée de la Belgique, the 'Grande Armée', 40,000,[2] supported on his right by d'Harville's Corps of 10,000 men, on Mons, where the Duke of Saxe-Teschen had collected 12,000 men. Far on the left (or the north), Labourdonnaye with the Nord, 18,000 to 20,000 men, was to threaten the enemy's right and rear by Ath, O'Moran's or Berneron's force acting between him and Dumouriez.[3] On the right Valence with the Armée

---

[1] For its probable composition see Desbrière, *La Cav. pendant la Rév.: La crise*, 327–8.

[2] For an approximation to the composition of this force see La Jonquière, *Jemappes*, 49–51, containing, however, errors, e. g. the inclusion of the 3rd Yonne (Davout), p. 51. See also Chuquet, *Jemappes*, note 2, pp. 72–3, with the same caution.

[3] For O'Moran and Berneron see p. 144.

des Ardennes, 20,000 men, moved separately,[1] marching on Namur by Givet.

To us the whole interest of this campaign lies in the battle of Jemappes, fought on the 6th November 1792, which gave the French Belgium. Dumouriez had not conducted the campaign on the best strategic lines, but the Austrians had been threatening Lille, and it may have seemed wiser to stop them by a direct attack than, by a more telling movement on their communications, to run the risk of losing any town and so causing dismay in France. He found the Austrians occupying a strong position on the heights of Cuesmes and Jemappes, to the west of Mons and north of Quiévrain, where Captain Mortier, now with d'Harville advancing from Maubeuge, had seen a rout of the French in April. The enemy, strongly posted and entrenched, had probably some 13,796 men on their front, not counting the garrison of Mons.[2] The French were far stronger, for Dumouriez had some 30,000 and d'Harville 10,000.[3] The intention of Dumouriez had been to attack himself in front, whilst d'Harville on his right turned the left of the enemy, but the orders he gave d'Harville, rather tying him to keep abreast of the right, delayed the movement, and that General, having many raw troops, moved very cautiously and slowly, so that the battle became a direct attack, in which the French, covered by their guns, drove the Austrians from their positions with heavy loss. Mons surrendered next day and the Austrians abandoned Belgium.[4]

Dumouriez had won the second, really the first battle of the Revolution. Almost all the fighting had been done by his own

[1] For Belgique, Ardennes, and d'Harville, see Chuquet, *Jemappes*, 72–3, and Desbrière, *La Cav. pendant la Rév. : La crise*, 326–31. The detachment of Berneron before Jemappes (Chuquet, *Jemappes*, 89) would make the strength of the Armée de la Belgique at the battle pretty near the 30,000 given by La Jonquière, 89. The strength of the 'Nord' I take from Dumouriez in La Jonquière, *Jemappes*, 104. Probably it was less. Dumouriez, *Vie*, iii. 143, Eng. ed. iii. 298, gives it 18,000.

[2] La Jonquière, *Jemappes*, 124, 143 ; Desbrière, *La Cav. pendant la Rév. : La crise*, 336.

[3] La Jonquière, *Jemappes*, 146.

[4] Ibid., 125–221 ; Chuquet, *Jemappes*, 84–101 ; Jomini, *Rév.*, ii. 216–36 ; Belliard, i. 85–90 ; Foucart et Finot, *Déf. nat.*, i. 272–9 ; Dumouriez, *Vie*, iii. 158–81, Eng. ed. iii. 318–47 ; Desbrière, *La Cav. pendant la Rév. : La crise*, 332–6 ; Plan in Jomini, Atlas, vi ; Thiers, *Rév.*, Atlas, iii ; Alison, Atlas, v ; La Jonquière, *Jemappes* (end of volume) ; Rose and Broadley, *Dumouriez*, 136.

immediate command, the Armée de la Belgique, d'Harville's fire towards the end of the day having done harm to the French. He himself had been everywhere, exciting his men. The volunteers of the first formation had fought well, and General Dampierre, who was to have a very different experience of them, burst into enthusiasm about their conduct.[1] Still, the French had a great superiority in numbers and their artillery, much used this day, had a preponderating fire. 'General Dumouriez', he wrote, 'observed at this combat that the French soldier counts infinitely on the superiority of his artillery; that on the success of this arm depends the greater or the less confidence and impetuosity of the troops, and that his courage sensibly cools if he sees his artillery receive a check or draw back.'[2] Throughout these wars of the Republic the excellent French artillery, always a fine body, made up for many deficiencies in the armies. Here several batteries of the new arm, horse artillery, were used: newly formed, the men did not yet ride well, 'mais ils avaient le diable au corps',[3] and their effect was so good that every General wanted them.[4]

The battle was very different from that of Valmy, which was one of simple resistance by regular troops, the only question being the trial of the spirit of the men. Jemappes was one of those attacks in which French Generals believe their men most excel. Also it was an attack delivered by volunteers mixed with regulars. It was a better test of the new army than Valmy had been and it presented curious instances of the contrasts between the troops of the old and the new model. The regular regiments went forward shouting their ancient cries, 'En avant, Navarre sans peur!' and 'Toujours Auvergne sans tache!' while the volunteers were inspirited by the chant of 'Amour sacré de la patrie', which they took up.

'M. de Chartres', the future Louis-Philippe, who had left Kellermann and had joined Dumouriez, was commanding the Centre, with Dampierre. The Prince of the House of Orleans led the revolutionary levies with great spirit. When one brigade was shattered, he formed the wreck into what he

---

[1] La Jonquière, *Jemappes*, 167–8.
[2] Ibid., note 1, pp. 201–2; Dumouriez, *Vie*, iii. 246, Eng. ed. iii. 436.
[3] Susane, *Art. franç.*, 216.   [4] Foucart et Finot, *Déf. nat.*, i. 279.

laughingly called the 'battalion of Jemappes'. On this he directed all the stragglers and sent it again on Mons. This shows that, had the Revolution kept within ordinary limits, the officers that sympathized with it would have remained in the service, and the army would have rapidly become an homogeneous and formidable force, without passing through the nightmare of distrust, suspicion, and the judicial murder of so many Generals.

As for the men with whom we are concerned, Captain and A.D.C. Macdonald and, it is said, Colonel Brune, an Adjutant-General,[1] were on the staff of Dumouriez. Macdonald says that he himself led a Dragoon regiment at a gallop on to the heights.[2] This would seem to have been on the final advance of the Centre under the Duc de Chartres.[3] For his conduct this day he was promoted on the 12th November 1792 to be Colonel of the 94th regiment,[4] but, remaining on the staff, he never joined that corps. As for Brune, who had been sent to this army in December, Dumouriez was complaining to the Minister that the army had been stuffed with staff officers who knew nothing of their work, one being a dancer.[5] The 12th Chasseurs, or 'Champagne', in which Murat had been promoted Lieutenant on the 31st October 1792, belonged to the *avant-garde*, under Beurnonville.[6] It is said to have distinguished itself,[7] but is not mentioned in the accounts. Captain Mortier's volunteer battalion, 1st Nord, was in the Corps of d'Harville,[8] which did little this day. Lt.-Colonel Jourdan's battalion, 2nd Haute-Vienne, probably also was with d'Harville, in whose Corps it was at the end of December.[9] Amongst others present at this battle were Belliard, the future cavalry General of the Empire and Chief of the Staff to Murat; César Berthier, the brother of the Marshal; Colonel Souham; and de Flers, now leading a brigade, but soon to command the Armée des Pyrénées-Orientales.

---

[1] Aulard, *Recueil*, i, note 1, p. 281; *Fastes*, ii. 251.
[2] Macdonald, *Souvenirs*, 16.
[3] Chuquet, *Jemappes*, 95.
[4] Ibid., 51.
[5] La Jonquière, *Jemappes*, note 3, p. 77.
[6] Ibid., 49-50.
[7] Susane, *Cav. franç.*, iii. 126.
[8] Desbrière, *La Cav. pendant la Rév.: La crise*, 329. d'Harville reports the punishment of a Captain of the 1st Nord. La Jonquière, *Jemappes*, note 1, p. 85.
[9] Desbrière, *La Cav. pendant la Rév.; La crise*, 358.

The volunteer battalion, 3rd Yonne, of Lt.-Colonel Davout, shown as in the 4th brigade of the *division de gauche* (under Miranda) of the Armée de la Belgique,[1] really formed part of the garrison of Condé, which advanced northwards for Blaton and Ath, first under O'Moran and then under Berneron, moving between the left of Dumouriez and the right of the 'Nord', which, under Labourdonnaye, was advancing through Flanders for Antwerp. This column made little way and the Austrians held their ground at Bury, but it was partly composed of troops of the new levy and was destitute of supplies, so that Dumouriez acknowledged that Berneron had shown much zeal and courage; indeed he had held the body of the enemy in his front. Lt.-Colonel Davout, specially entrusted with 300 men of his battalion for the attack on the Hermitage of Péruwelz,[2] on the 24th October 1792, distinguished himself by his success.[3] The future General Thiébault served in a volunteer battalion in this column.[4] The volunteer battalion, 1st Ille-et-Vilaine, of Lt.-Colonel Moreau served with the 'Nord' under Labourdonnaye.[5] Lieutenant and A.D.C. Ney, promoted Captain the day before the battle, no doubt was with his General, Lamarche, in the Armée des Ardennes, where also Captain Hoche served in the 58th regiment.[6]

One thing may have had consequences later. On the day before the battle Dumouriez had halted General Dampierre, who was pressing on for positions which Dumouriez meant to be attacked next day, and he had received what he styles an 'algarade indécente', an 'improper outburst', from his subordinate. On the day of the fight, going to where 'the famous Dampierre' should have been, he could not find him.[7] Dampierre himself, knowing nothing of this, was loud in praise of his commander, whom he urged to continue to unite in a supreme degree the prudence and method of Turenne to the bravery and audacity of Condé, above whom his place was marked for posterity. He praises the perspicuity with which

---

[1] La Jonquière, *Jemappes*, 51.　　[2] North of Condé.
[3] La Jonquière, *Jemappes*, 54-62, 99, 103-12; Vigier, *Davout*, i. 29-31; Dumouriez, *Vie*, iii. 182-3, Eng. ed. iii. 315, 348-9.
[4] Thiébault, i. 340-4.
[5] Desbrière, *La Cav. pendant la Rév.: La crise*, 327.
[6] Money, 164; Cuneo d'Ornano, *Hoche*, i. 29, 36.
[7] Dumouriez, *Vie*, iii. 173, Eng. ed. iii. 339; La Jonquière, *Jemappes*, 162.

Dumouriez had halted him.¹ Indeed, Dampierre was in a very lyric state, thanking the ' Dieu plébéien ' for allowing him to have helped his comrades to humiliate the great ones of the earth.² If he ever knew in time of what Dumouriez really thought of him, this may help to explain his readiness to replace Dumouriez in command of the ' Nord ', when that General tried to upset the Republic. The most curious thing about the battle is the praise given by Dumouriez to his *valet de chambre* Baptiste Renard, who rallied a brigade and seven squadrons, and who for recompense only asked to be allowed to wear the uniform of the National Guard. Baptiste was presented to the Assembly and was declared to have raised himself to the quality of first defender of the Republic. Embraced by the President, he was ordered to be armed, clothed, and mounted at the expense of the Nation.³

All Belgium, except Luxembourg, was easily overrun in a month ; the armies advanced, swinging round on their right. The ' Ardennes ' on the right, under Valence, reinforced by d'Harville's corps, moved down the Meuse (Ney, if with Valence, now getting his first sight of Charleroi), for Huy and Saint-Trond, leaving d'Harville and Captain Mortier before Namur. Dumouriez's own Armée de la Belgique occupied Liége. The corps of Berneron, late O'Moran, in which Lt.-Colonel Davout served, marched through Ath for Louvain, the column of Davout, at least, joining in the siege of Antwerp made by the Armée du Nord, now under the Peruvian, Miranda,⁴ for Labourdonnaye, always resisting Dumouriez, the supreme commander of all these forces, had been removed on the 21st November 1792.⁵ Antwerp taken, the ' Nord ' moved on for Tongres and Roermond, so that the French now lined the Meuse. Very little more advance would have thrown the Austrians over the Rhine and have altered the war, but the

---

¹ La Jonquière, *Jemappes*, 136-41. ² Ibid., 168.
³ Ibid., 160, 225-8 ; Dumouriez, Eng. ed. iii. 336.
⁴ General François Miranda (17 ?-1816). Born in Peru, made General by the Girondins, tried but acquitted after Neerwinden, fought in South America in 1811-12 against the Spaniards, who captured him. Michaud, *Biog. univ.*, xxix. 121-2.
⁵ Aulard, *Recueil*, i. 254. He seems still to have commanded in Flanders till the 9th Jan. 1793 : ibid., 440-441. Miranda seems to have taken command of the ' Nord ' on the 27th Nov. 1792. La Jonquière, *Jemappes*, 204.

troops of Dumouriez were not only exhausted but ill supplied, and enormous desertion set in. The volunteers considered themselves now free, and whole battalions set off for their homes. In October 1792 there had been 100,000 French in Belgium; in December only 45,000 remained. Dumouriez himself thought of attacking Holland, but the *Conseil exécutif* was then unwilling for war there, and on his right Custine and Kellermann were quarrelling. In consequence Kellermann was sent to command the Armée des Alpes, and the great Beurnonville on the day after the battle, when he entered Mons, went to replace him.[1] Then, however, both Custine and Beurnonville were defeated and Dumouriez placed his troops in cantonments.[2] The Armée des Ardennes (where Lieutenant Ney was A.D.C. to Lamarche), under Valence, reinforced by the Corps of d'Harville, had taken Namur after a brief siege on the 2nd December 1792.[3]

Here we begin to get some idea of Murat. Joachim Murat had been born on the 25th March 1767[4] at La Bastide-Fortonière-en-Quercy, near Cahors. His father was a farmer who also kept an inn, and here Joachim learned the care and love of horses. His parents were well off and intended him for the Church: after being taught by the *curé* of the parish, he won a *bourse* at the College of Saint-Michel at Cahors, which he entered when ten years old. Thence he passed to the seminary of the Lazarists at Toulouse, where he already wore a clerical dress. But in reality his tastes lay elsewhere and, when a regiment of cavalry passed through Toulouse, he escaped and enlisted on the 23rd February 1787 in what was then the *Chasseurs des Ardennes*, but which had borne the title of *Niel* and which next year became the *Chasseurs de Champagne* or 12th Chasseurs.[5]

In 1789 an affair whose character is unknown forced him to leave, and he returned crestfallen to his family. To support himself he became clerk to a haberdasher of Saint-Ceré, and frequently brought goods to Marbot's mother, according to that officer.[6]

---

[1] Belliard, i. 90.
[2] Chuquet, *Jemappes*, 119–33.
[3] La Jonquière, *Jemappes*, 205–6.
[4] Murat, *Lettres*, i. 2.
[5] Susane, *Cav. franç.*, 124–7, 307, No. 636.
[6] Marbot, i. 48.

When the *fête* of the Federation was to be held at Paris on the 14th July 1790, the canton of Montfaucon chose Murat as their delegate, so presumably he had entered the local National Guard. Then he managed in some way to get reinstated in his old regiment.[1]

The spirit of the Revolution was now in full work on the army, and, as a party of the 12th Chasseurs had been placed at Montmédy to receive the royal family in its flight to Varennes, the regiment was anxious to disavow any knowledge of the object of this detachment. It fell to Murat to be sent by his comrades, apparently with the Adjutant, to address the municipality of Toul. On the 5th July 1791 we find Murat writing to his brother from Toul and sending his speech: he was 'très occupé dans ce moment où tous les esprits fermentent': he wanted news of the 'charmante Mion': one brother had promised him a louis and Murat thought that an honest man, a brother, must be a man of his word. As for himself, he would die rather than cease to be a patriot: he was working for promotion and was about to be made Corporal (a grade that does not appear in his records).[2] In 1792 a new body, the *Garde constitutionnelle*, was to be formed to take the place of the military part of the *Maison du Roi*, and Murat, apparently by the influence of S. B. Cavaignac, one of the Directors of the Department of Lot,[3] obtained appointment to the new Guard—obviously a matter of difficulty, as it was to be chosen, one-third from the army, the rest from the National Guards of Departments, and how did the Department come to choose a Chasseur?

However, after a month's service in it, Murat left the *Garde constitutionnelle*, dismissed, according to some, for his quarrels and duels, but by his own account because he resigned rather than take his punishment for absence without leave. He declared to the *Comité de surveillance* of the Assembly and to the administrators of his Department that the Guard was guilty of *incivisme* and that his Lt.-Colonel, Descours, had attempted to get him to serve in the army of Condé at Koblenz.[4] True or not, this accusation must have got him the support

[1] Murat, *Lettres*, i. 2–4.
[2] Ibid., 4–5.
[3] *Fastes*, i. 411.
[4] Murat, *Lettres*, i. 2–5.

of the *patriots*, for he was allowed to rejoin his former regiment and promoted Corporal in April and Sergeant in May. His further steps we have already traced.

During the pause in the operations we find him as Lieutenant, then 25 years old, in Paris on the 19th November 1792. His promotions had elated him. In October 1792 he had written to a friend, ' At last I am *sous-lieutenant* ', and his family would see by this great rise that he had had no great disposition to be a priest, but hoped soon to prove more positively that he had not been wrong in wishing to be a soldier. ' I shall make my way, if God and the balls permit,' the Deity, be it remarked, being still considered in the matter.[1] Now in the Capital, where he had been sent by the *Conseil d'administration* of his regiment to make some purchases, and where he was trying to get a horse from the ' brewer-general ', Santerre, he wrote even more cheerfully about his future. ' I am Lieutenant, and if the Colonel [2] is nominated General, about which there is no doubt, I am his A.D.C. and Captain. At my age, with my courage and my military talents, I can go a little further. God will that I may not be frustrated in my attempt.' The Deputies from his Department had received him most cordially in Paris, and he had even been told that, had there not been doubts in the Department about his age, he would have received votes to be a Representative. ' Je me suis excusé sur la faiblesse de mes connaissances.' There is something touching in his anxiety to be remembered to his fellow citizens of the Department. When he had helped to crown the felicity of all, he would return home to enjoy with them the fruits of their happy Revolution.[3] Allowing for a little southern brag, the letter gives rather a pleasant idea of Murat at a time when patriotism had not run sour. He wanted a copy of his baptismal certificate, perhaps on account of the charges said to have been brought against him by the Minister, Pache, who believed he belonged to the family of Murat d'Auvergne and who taxed him with being an aristocrat, an accusation which gave him much trouble later.[4]

---

[1] Lumbroso, *Murat*, 6. Note corrected by Murat, *Lettres*, i. 5, note 1.
[2] General Joseph-François-Jean-Baptiste d'Urre de Molans.
[3] Murat, *Lettres*, i. 5–6 ; Lumbroso, *Murat*, 6–7.   [4] Landrieux, 93.

L'ARMÉE DU NORD, 1792

Lieutenant Murat was in Paris again on the 15th February 1793. He had been sent by his chiefs from Arras, where the 12th Chasseurs were, probably to make purchases, as in November 1792. He had lost a brother and in true revolutionary style urged his father not to weep for him if he fell. If the war did not claim him amongst its victims, he would return covered with laurels and bearing the esteem of his fellow citizens. 'If my grateful country grants rewards, do not fear poverty, my father,' which was rather an optimistic view to take of national gratitude. The decree for the levy of 300,000 men had been issued, and Murat sent an address to the municipal officers of La Bastide-Fortinière, to awaken the courage of young men and to get them to abandon their mistresses for the camps. Knowing what was coming as to the Church, it is odd to find him asking that his address might be read after Mass. He complained that, as indeed sometimes happened to very zealous patriots, he himself had been accused of being an *émigré*, an accusation which it was sometimes troublesome to disprove. He had written to the municipality and had got no answer. He left Paris, probably about the end of February 1793, saying he was going to Holland, but he can hardly have taken part in the campaign there.[1]

---

[1] Murat, *Lettres*, i. 7, 9-10. The letter given as of the 25th February, No. 7, must be of April, as explained farther on.

IX

L'ARMEE DU NORD (*continued*), 1793

Gloom of Dumouriez, he goes to Paris and displaces the Minister, Pache. He invades Holland. Beaver Camp. Murat again in Paris. Plans of Dumouriez upset by advance of Allies, who raise the siege of Maestricht. Rejoins the main army. Dispute with Commissioners. ' I am not Caesar.' Is beaten at Neerwinden. Future Marshals engaged, Moreau and the Archduke Charles. Mack the winner. Dumouriez retreats. Macdonald returns to the army. Dumouriez intends to overthrow the Convention, enters into treasonable correspondence with the enemy. His bad arrangements. Arrests the Commissioners sent to him by the Convention, with Beurnonville, and hands them over to the Austrians. Is fired on by the battalion of Lt.-Colonel Davout and takes refuge with the enemy. His future life. Estimation of him by the Duke of Wellington. His former position in France. Sympathies of the future Marshals present. Conduct of Macdonald. Disastrous effect on the commanders of the conduct of Dumouriez. Convention seizes all power over the armies. The predicament of Macdonald.

DUMOURIEZ himself, although successful, was melancholy enough. All December, he says, he seldom left his quarters and remained plunged in the bitterest reflections. The trial of the King had begun, and all the difficulties of the situation, political and military, must have been apparent to the General, who already meditated on the saying of Plutarch, ' When a thing ceases to be honourable, it is time to see its turpitude and renounce it '.[1] Was the cause of the Revolution an honourable one ? He himself on the 1st January 1793 arrived at Paris [2] with his A.D.C., Macdonald, who, it will be remembered, in November 1792 had been promoted Lt.-Colonel. While trying to save the life of the King, Dumouriez entered into an arduous struggle with the War Department, the natural and eternal enemy of every officer. His charges against it of wild incapacity were supported by other commanders, and, marvellous man that he was, he actually

[1] Dumouriez, *Vie*, iii. 240, Eng. ed. iii. 428.   [2] Chuquet, *Trahison*, i.

succeeded in getting the Minister, Pache,[1] replaced by his own friend, General Beurnonville, the first patron of Macdonald. A swaggering, self-seeking boaster, Beurnonville had plenty of good sense and at this time was active enough. He set himself to purge his administration, which rapidly improved. Such work is never done with impunity, and it was probably now that much of that bitterness was caused amongst the civilian functionaries which was vented later on the Generals, when the men that Beurnonville ejected had crept back again to their inheritance.

It is strange that Macdonald tells us nothing of his General's stay in Paris during this momentous time. All was in flux, and there was a wild dance of confusion amongst the Ministers and the different Committees. The King's head fell on the 20th January 1793, so one object of Dumouriez's journey failed. Also he could not get the revocation of the decree of the 15th December 1792, by which the Convention, preparing the union of Belgium to France, intended first to plunder Belgium.[2] On the other hand he did, as I have said, succeed against Pache, the Minister. Then, before Beurnonville took the War Office, Dumouriez, leaving Macdonald in the Capital, started from Paris for his army on the 26th January 1793, no more advanced for a plan of campaign than the first day, he said. One scheme, however, he had. Dutch emissaries had come to him, suggesting the invasion of Holland, a plan he liked; but, believing that France was not sufficiently prepared for a great war and that the invasion of Holland would bring England into the field, he proposed to go to London as special ambassador to explain, 'avec force, mais sans jactance', the motives of France's conduct and to attempt to detach England and, his favourite hobby, Prussia, from Austria. Maret, the future Minister of Napoleon, was already applying to London for the reception of the General, when on the 1st February 1793 the Convention declared war on England and ordered Dumouriez to march on Holland.[3]

---

[1] Jean-Nicolas Pache (1740–1823). For his misdeeds see Chuquet, *Jemappes*, 134–78, and id., *Trahison*, 1–14; Dumouriez, *Vie*, iii. 355–6.
[2] Chuquet, *Jemappes*, 194–200; Delhaize, *La Domination française*, vol. i.
[3] Chuquet, *Trahison*, 1–23.

Instead of pushing the Allies over the Rhine, Dumouriez left Miranda to besiege Maestricht, covered by the Armée de la Belgique, by the ' Ardennes ' under Valence, and by d'Harville at Namur,[1] whilst he himself invaded Holland with a scratch force of 1,000 horse and 15,000 infantry [2] (mere lads, most of them of the last levy),[3] increased later by 5,000 men. The plan was an extraordinary one, for it was obvious that Dumouriez should have acted with the Armée du Centre and have won the line of the Rhine. The siege work round Maestricht and the severity of the winter were too much for the bodies and minds of the new troops, and the roads to France were covered with volunteers going home.[4]

It is worth giving the strength of the armies at this moment.

'Nord '	18,322
' Belgique '	30,197
' Ardennes '	23,479
d'Harville	12,051
Garrisons in Belgium	15,000
Total	99,049
' Hollande '	23,244 [5]
	122,293

As for the men with whom we are concerned ; Lieutenant Ney, promoted to that rank on the 5th November 1792, was probably with General Lamarche in the Ardennes as A.D.C. ; his regiment was with the ' Nord '. Captain Hoche's regiment was with the ' Ardennes ', as also was the volunteer battalion, 1st Ille-et-Vilaine, of Lt.-Colonel Moreau. Lieutenant Murat's Chasseur regiment was in the Armée de la Belgique. The volunteer battalion of Lt.-Colonel Davout, 3rd Yonne, is shown as with the Armée de la Belgique. Lt.-Colonel Jourdan and Captain Mortier both were with d'Harville. For all practical purposes the armies, ' Nord ', ' Belgique ', ' Ardennes ', and the Corps of d'Harville, can now be considered as one body.[6]

---

[1] Chuquet, *Trahison*, 29–30.
[2] Dumouriez, *Vie*, iv. 31–2, says 13,700 combatants.
[3] Lieutenant Dellard marched in a volunteer battalion (3rd Lot), only raised on the 18th Sept. 1792. Dellard, 2–8 ; Déprez, *Vol. nat.*, 446–7 ; Susane, *Inf. franç.*, i. 332.
[4] Du Casse, *Vandamme*, i. 34, 39–40.
[5] Desbrière, *La Cav. pendant la Rév. : La crise*, 361. [6] Ibid., 350–61.

The dash of Dumouriez into Holland does not concern us, as, except perhaps Brune, no future Marshal went with the expedition. Even Macdonald, A.D.C. to the commander, for some unexplained reason remained in Paris when Dumouriez left it on the 26th January 1793. Still the expedition is a specimen of the faulty strategy and wild dreams of the period. On the 16th February 1793 Dumouriez commenced his advance. Lt.-Colonel Moreau had begun his successes against fortresses by seizing the forts of Saint-Michel and Stevensweert, on the Meuse above Venlo.[1] Dumouriez struck north for Antwerp, and d'Arcon, the engineer who had planned the floating batteries to attack Gibraltar, now bullied Breda and Gertruydenberg into surrender. Reaching the Holland Deep, Dumouriez's reserve was lodged in reed-thatched huts by the edge of the sea, where the men called their quarters the *Camp des Castors*, or 'Beaver Camp'.[2] He meant to cross the Holland Deep and, turning the Dutch defences, to march by Rotterdam, Delft, Haarlem, The Hague, and Leyden on Amsterdam. Miranda, taking Maestricht, was to march north by Grave and Nijmegen to meet Dumouriez from Utrecht, and the two would then take the force of Brunswick-Oels between two fires. It was assumed that the Austrians would remain quiescent all this time. This grand scheme was nothing to the visions of the *Conseil exécutif* and the Minister, Beurnonville, at Paris. He was prepared to send the worthy Valence with the regular troops, a cavalry regiment, and some volunteers, of the Armée des Ardennes, among whom I think Ney would have been included, on a voyage of three years to conquer India, touching at Rio de Janeiro and the Cape. The French at this period had a mania for expeditions, and those to Egypt and to San Domingo showed that Bonaparte sympathized with the idea.[3]

Suddenly all the plans of Dumouriez came to the ground with a crash. Using the breathing time he had given them, the Allies had formed an army of 40,000 men on the left bank

---

[1] On the Meuse, not far from the frontier of Holland. Chuquet, *Trahison*, 24–5.
[2] Near Moerdyk, west of Gertruydenberg, on the Holland Deep.
[3] Chuquet, *Trahison*, 23.

of the Rhine. In command was the Prince of Coburg, whose talents were held in high respect by both sides, and whose name, linked with that of Pitt, long formed the typical arch-enemy for all patriots. Coburg had that excellent staff officer Mack to assist him. Such a conjunction was most favourable. Little may, however, have been expected from one of the Generals, the Archduke Charles.

The gathering storm had not been unnoticed by the French round Maestricht. Miranda's forces had been much reduced by desertion, and, if he himself were sanguine, his best Generals saw the danger of their situation. Danton and another Representative, Delacroix, were on the spot, but they found it amusing to make a revolution at Aix-la-Chapelle, and to get the capital of Charlemagne to demand its union with France. At last the storm burst. On the 1st March 1793 Coburg crossed the Roer and easily rolled up the French forces, which retreated in confusion on Louvain. So great was the dispersion of Miranda's troops that Stengel, the future cavalry leader in Italy, was lost for three days, and it was reported that he had emigrated. At last he reappeared at Namur with a squadron of the 12th Chasseur regiment (in which Murat served), which had brought him and the treasure of the army off through the rout. By the 9th March 1793 the former three armies, now three divisions, were formed up at Louvain, 'Ardennes' on the right, 'Belgique' in the centre, and the 'Nord' on the left. Happy for them was it that the slow Coburg had not followed up his success.[1]

Just as in 1792 he had for long refused to go south to stop Brunswick, so now Dumouriez clung to his expedition in Holland, urging, almost beseeching Miranda to hold firm and to give him time to finish his work in the north. At last the Government ordered him back and, leaving his motley forces in Holland under the command of de Flers, by the 11th March 1793 he had rejoined Miranda at Louvain. Already he was at open war with the Commissioners of the Assembly, who accused him of playing the Caesar. 'If', said Camus, 'you

---

[1] Chuquet, *Trahison*, 46–67; Jomini, *Rév.*, iii. 86–95; Lahure, 36–9; Belliard, i. 100–4; Bricard, 30–4; Langeron, 12–13, gives Coburg 28,000 men only.

were Caesar, I should be Brutus.' ' My dear Camus,' sneered Dumouriez, ' I am not Caesar, and you are not Brutus ; and the threat of dying by your hand is a warrant of immortality for me.' This was a very different spirit to that in which his successors were to meet such threats. Believing his troops too demoralized to stand a retreat and a long defensive attitude, he determined to advance and attack Coburg ; this too without waiting either for his army of Holland or for d'Harville's Corps at Namur. He had some 40,000 infantry and 4,500 horse. Coburg had 30,000 infantry and 9,000 cavalry. Valence took the right, M. de Chartres the centre, and Miranda the left. The *avant-garde* was led by Lamarche, the patron of Ney. On the 16th March Dumouriez was successful in retaking Tirlemont, which the enemy had captured from Lamarche. Coburg drew back and Dumouriez advanced. On the 18th March 1793 he found Coburg at Neerwinden. One victory would re-establish matters, and he attacked in eight columns. On the right and centre the struggle was indecisive, but Dumouriez believed himself the victor, until at night he discovered that his left had been repulsed and that Miranda, without waiting for orders, had withdrawn to Tirlemont.[1]

This battle caused some curious meetings of men who were to face one another on very different fields. Lt.-Colonel Moreau's volunteer battalion had headed the attack of the column of Champmorin, one of the best of Dumouriez's Generals, on the left, where the Archduke commanded the enemy. Twice this column was beaten back, and twice Moreau and Champmorin led it on again, when it was thrown into confusion by the fugitives of the column of Ruault, whose volunteers had behaved badly. Champmorin praised ' la conduite ferme et brave ' of Moreau.[2]

Lt.-Colonel Davout, full of Republican sentiments, presumably fought in the centre under the Orleanist Prince, M. de Chartres. Lieutenant Ney must have been with the right column, led by Lamarche, whose A.D.C. he was and who

---

[1] Chuquet, *Trahison*, 72-110 ; Jomini, *Rév.*, iii. 97-119 ; *Vict. et Conq.*, i. 109-20 ; Lahure, 36-40 ; Dumouriez, *Vie*, iv. 69-97 ; Bricard, 34-43 ; Langeron, 13 ; Plan in Jomini, *Rév.*, Atlas, vii ; *Vict. et Conq.*, i, iii ; Alison, Atlas, vii ; Rose and Broadley, *Dumouriez*, 170.

[2] Chuquet, *Trahison*, 107-8, and note 2, p. 108.

on the day before the battle had, with Valence, charged at the head of the 5th Hussars, to which he and Ney had belonged.[1] Ney, a cavalry officer, saw, and most probably was engaged in, the desperate attack on Overwinden, where the French cavalry was overthrown by the horse of the Austrians.[2] Lieutenant Murat also, if present, must have been in one of the columns on the right. Adjutant-General Brune is said to have been present, as is Captain Mortier, but I think he seems to have been with d'Harville, left at Namur, where also, I presume, Lt.-Colonel Jourdan was. One would have imagined that Lt.-Colonel Macdonald would have been by the side of the Commander-in-Chief, whose A.D.C. he was, but he was on his way from Paris to rejoin the army, which he did not reach till it got back to Brussels. Amongst the enemy one man won much praise. The victory was credited to Mack: any other chief, it was said, less skilful and less tenacious, would have lost the day.[3]

Dumouriez retired and desertion to an enormous extent began, especially amongst the volunteers, who covered the roads, shouting out patriotic songs, but going off for their homes. On the 21st March 1793, fighting now for his life, Dumouriez stood at Louvain, but was again defeated, partly by the failure of Ney's patron, General Lamarche. Again Dumouriez retired: sanguine as was his nature, he had lost heart, for his men, he said, if wolves, still ran like sheep. Lamarche was sent on to Douai, 'to look after his health', Ney no doubt accompanying him and so perhaps escaping the difficulty of choosing between Dumouriez and the Convention. On the 24th March 1793 the army passed through Brussels and here Macdonald, now full Colonel, rejoined from Paris and took the command of the 2nd regiment, the famous ' Picardie ',[4] much to the disgust of the officer who had been leading it in the campaign. Now at last, when too late, Dumouriez began calling in his detachments, and with d'Harville from Namur no doubt came Lt.-Colonel Jourdan and Captain Mortier. We may assume that, except perhaps Ney, all the future

---

[1] Bonnal, *Ney*, i. 15.
[2] Chuquet, *Trahison*, 100-1; Desbrière, *La Cav. pendant la Rév.: La crise*, 364.   [3] Langeron, 13.   [4] Susane, *Inf. franç.*, ii. 219, 223-7.

Marshals of the northern group, Brune, Davout, Jourdan, Mortier, and Murat, with Lt.-Colonels Moreau and Souham and Captain Hoche, A.D.C. to General Leveneur, were now with the massed armies. Negotiating with the enemy for an undisturbed retreat at the price of abandoning Belgium to them, Dumouriez withdrew his troops behind the fortresses; the Armée des Ardennes was at the Camp de Maulde, the 'Nord' at the Camp de Bruille,[1] and the Armée de la Belgique in Valenciennes, Condé, and other posts, whilst the troops of the Armée de la Hollande were called in to Lille, passing proudly through the enemy.[2]

As for Macdonald, it is difficult to understand his conduct. In January 1793, as we have seen, he had accompanied his General to Paris, and, when Dumouriez returned to his army for an active campaign in Holland, it would have seemed but natural, or rather inevitable, that his A.D.C. should accompany him, and the more so as Macdonald had been rewarded for his staff services by promotion. Yet he remained idle in the Capital whilst his General was fighting, detained, as he says, by the new Minister for War, General Beurnonville, who on the 1st March 1793 made him Colonel of the 2nd regiment, the famous 'Picardie'.[3] Some thirty-four years before, Roderick Random had been 'admitted into the regiment of Picardy, said to be the oldest corps in Europe',[4] but he was only a private. Macdonald says his promotion took some days, but why did he not start for his corps as soon as possible? He only joined the army at Brussels on the 24th March on its retreat after Neerwinden,[5] as we have seen. His 'some days' is not very frank. Why did he wait nearly two months after his General had gone and three weeks after his own promotion? He says that, on seeing him, Dumouriez reproached him for having abandoned him, and well might he do so, for his A.D.C., rewarded for his services by him, had, without reference to him, accepted a post removing him from his side. Was it only for this that Dumouriez reproached him? Can Dumouriez,

---

[1] Maulde is south, and Bruille still farther south, of Tournai.
[2] See Dellard, 8–10, for the withdrawal from Holland.
[3] See p. 156.
[4] Smollett, *Roderick Random*, Chap. XLIII.
[5] Macdonald, 17; Chuquet, *Trahison*, 123.

not a very cautious man, already revolving the idea of resistance to the Convention, have let his A.D.C. know what his thoughts were, and could Macdonald have been glad to break the tie between them ? This is a mere surmise, but there is something extraordinary in an officer remaining away, first from the General to whom he was A.D.C., and then from his regiment, during an important campaign.

The fact that his wife was *enceinte* had kept him from emigrating in 1792. I presume she was now in Paris, but there was a good interval between her two daughters,[1] and even the charms of a two years' wife could not tie an officer from a campaign. The incident is unpleasant. He answered the reproaches of Dumouriez by arguing that the General himself, 'under happier circumstances', would have obtained for him the same promotion ; but, as he writes, from Captain to Colonel in six months was more than he could have hoped for. Then he said that he was not leaving his General, as his regiment made part of the army, which again was not quite frank, for the relations between them must have been completely altered. Calming himself, Dumouriez told him of the bad situation of the army, and advised him to join his regiment at once and to try to keep it from the disorder which reigned around. Then the two parted, tears in their eyes, not to meet again, and going to very different destinies. Dumouriez must have been sorry, and Macdonald, let us hope, a little ashamed.[2]

Dumouriez, still confident in himself, now despaired of success under the Revolutionary régime. His troops had suffered very much under Maestricht throughout the winter. They had retaken heart on his arrival, but the two defeats had demoralized the volunteers, who went off for France in masses : Macdonald on his way to the army from Paris met them, still shouting patriotic songs. But it was not merely the forlorn state of his troops which told on the sanguine Dumouriez. He had wished for the preservation of the Monarchy ; and the King had been guillotined on the 21st January 1793. Full of plans, wanting to wield all the forces in the north and

---

[1] Anne-Charlotte, born on the 29th Feb. 1792 ; Adèle-Élisabeth, born on the 31st January 1794, both at Saint-Germain-en-Laye.
[2] Macdonald, *Souvenirs*, 16–18.

east of France, the General had found nothing but confusion in the Capital, and it was difficult to get any sane scheme considered, much less adopted. He had seen and known the leaders of the extreme and now all-powerful party, and he realized the incapacity, the suspicions, and the sanguinary nature of the men who were ruling the state. Also the growing inclination at Paris to interfere with the powers of the commanders of armies alarmed him. In his strife with the War Office officials he had made for himself a host of enemies, and their hour seemed coming. Even before Neerwinden he had had some thoughts of conflict with the Convention. Now, as after Valmy, he began negotiations with the enemy. At first, by abandoning his conquests, he wished to gain an unmolested retreat. Then he passed on to treason. Mack was sent by Coburg to negotiate with him, and Dumouriez now announced his plan. Still holding the fortresses, he would march on Paris, destroy the Jacobins, dissolve the Convention, and re-establish the Monarchical constitution of 1791. Who was to be King was left vague, but he believed the mass of the country would rally to this plan.[1]

Two things were fatal to Dumouriez. In the first place he attempted to act immediately after he had been defeated, whereas he required the utmost prestige possible. Monk could never have restored the Stuarts if he had come all draggle-tailed from defeat by the Scots. Secondly, he did not, perhaps could not, march at once on Paris before his troops had time to think and the Convention to act. He did not require all his army. One would have thought it possible to throw into the fortresses the troops and commanders on whom he could least count for his purpose. They would have been bound to preserve the 'patriotic' trust and to remain where posted. At the worst it would have been some days before they could determine on any joint action. Meantime he would have been on the march with his column for the Capital, only some 120 miles off. The cavalry, especially the heavy regiments, he could most trust, and they would have been the most useful. Indeed it would have been easy to push on an advanced guard under several reasonable pretexts.

[1] Dumouriez, *Vie*, iv. 121-2; Chuquet, *Trahison*, 140-6.

With any other man one might believe that the attempt was so desperate that he feared to commit himself to it until he were certain of his army. It is, however, impossible to put any limit to the daring of Dumouriez, and he and his staff were strangely confident in his hold on what he believed would be an army of Mamelukes: besides, the Convention was not yet the gloomy terror which it soon became when it had mastered France. The explanation of the delay probably is that, while too confident in his troops, he was not quite certain of the attitude of the enemy. An advance of Coburg would have ruined the plan. Whatever the explanation, he frittered away the precious days. On the 25th March 1793 he opened his plan to Mack. On the 30th he only proposed to march on Paris in a week. On the 1st April the Commissioners sent to arrest him found him still at his head-quarters at Saint-Amand. One fact shows how little he understood the management of such strokes. After any defeat of part of his forces, say in Spain, Napoleon in the height of his power was always careful to stop any officer from the beaten army reaching Paris. Indeed it is surprising how successful he was in concealing disasters. Now Dumouriez knew that his chief Lieutenant, Miranda, was opposed to his plan and openly avowed his intention, were it tried, of siding with the Republic. Yet he let Miranda, sore at having the responsibility for the defeat at Neerwinden thrown at him, go to Paris to work against him. This was not the way to prepare a *coup d'état*.

Whilst Dumouriez wasted time, the Convention acted with vigour and rapidity, for it was a question of their heads. Proclamations and emissaries were dispatched to the armies. Four Commissioners from the Convention, accompanied by the Minister for War, General Beurnonville, started for the north to order Dumouriez to appear before the Convention at Paris. Passing by Lille, they just missed taking with them Carnot, who was absent but who otherwise would have shared their fate. On the 1st April 1793 they arrived at the head-quarters at Saint-Amand. Part of the way they had been escorted by a party of Chasseurs, with whom were two Quadroons, distinguished cavalry officers—Colonel Saint-Georges, and Lt.-Colonel Alexandre Dumas, the father of the great

Dumas, both devoted to the Revolution.[1] The interview with the General was decisive. He refused to go to Paris, and, when the Commissioners declared him suspended, he in his turn arrested them and Beurnonville and handed them over to Coburg. They were imprisoned by the Austrians until December 1795, when they were exchanged for the Princess Marie-Thérèse, the unhappy daughter of Louis XVI.

The next days were passed by Dumouriez in doing what ought to have been done before, that is, in trying to get the main fortresses into the hands of Generals on whom he could depend, and in addressing his men, who all the time were being worked on by the emissaries and proclamations of the Convention. At first he could have counted on the cavalry and the regular infantry regiments. The volunteers were for the most part influenced by that strange respect for the so-called National Representation which for long enabled any faction which could seize power to rule France. Badly served, Dumouriez failed to hold the fortresses and the Convention ordered the troops to retire there from the camps. Meeting the volunteer battalion of Lt.-Colonel Davout, he was fired on by it and was almost taken prisoner. This led him into the fatal mistake of appearing before his men with an Austrian escort. The artillery, a body whose sympathies had from the first been with the Revolution, marched off, and their example,[2] with the hostility of the volunteers, told on the other troops. At last Dumouriez had to abandon his attempt and on the 5th April 1793 he passed over to the Austrians with a small body of cavalry and several Generals, including Valence, the commander of the Armée des Ardennes, and the Duc de Chartres, the future King Louis-Philippe.[3]

The declaration of Coburg received by Dumouriez shows

---

[1] They belonged to the 13th Chasseurs, formed 21st Feb. 1793 from the cavalry of the *Légion franche étrangère*, or *Légion américaine*, or *Légion noire* (from the number of blacks it contained). Susane, *Inf. franç.*, i. 349 ; ibid., *Cav. franç.*, i. 185 ; D'Hauterive, *Dumas*, 24–8. The corps had not yet been engaged.

[2] 'Le corps d'artillerie est la force de l'armée française.' Dumouriez, *Vie*, iv. 174.

[3] Ibid., 121–88 ; Chuquet, *Trahison*, 127–233 ; Jomini, *Rév.*, iii. 124–43; Thiers, *Rév.*, ii. 74–83 ; Vigier, *Davout*, i. 33–7 ; Foucart et Finot, *Déf. nat.*, i. 352–95 ; Fersen, ii. 66–71 ; Gaulot, *Un Ami de la Reine*, 333–40.

that the General did not betray France to her enemies. 'I engage myself on my honour not to come on French territory to make conquests. . . . If a strong place is remitted to my troops, I engage myself in the most express manner to give it up as soon as the government which shall be established in France, or the brave General Dumouriez, shall demand it. I will take the most rigorous measures that my troops shall not permit themselves the least exaction or the least violence. Whoever shall disobey my orders shall be punished with death.'[1] It is a question, however, whether the Austrians would have carried out this convention : certainly at first the Emperor, doubting the General's real intentions towards the Royal Family, ordered the armistice to be broken and, though he modified this order, which was not to be carried out unless the Duke of Orleans were declared King, still finally Coburg retracted his declaration, telling Dumouriez that, as his army had abandoned him, the Emperor had the right to retake the offensive.[2] Indeed, as Dumouriez could not carry out his share of the bargain, he could not expect the other side to adhere to it.

Dumouriez's life was far from ended, but it would be impossible to follow it here. He shuttle-cocked from land to land, even to England, distrusted by the Allies, until by the end of 1796 he was living near Hamburg, poor and supporting himself by his writings and Memoirs. In 1795 the young Duc d'Orléans came to him, and the General tried to get the Vendean leader, Charette, to adopt the Prince as King. Charette had a rude pen and replied, 'Tell the son of the citizen Égalité to go and get himself . . .' He believed in the elder branch, not anticipating that he would have to tell Louis XVIII that the cowardice of his brother had ruined everything.[3] Intriguing always, Dumouriez visited Paris in disguise in 1797, nearly falling into the hands of the Police at Fructidor. His *Tableau spéculatif de l'Europe* was issuing in edition after edition. In October 1799 he recognized Louis XVIII as his legitimate sovereign.[4] In 1799 he met Pichegru, each General remaining convinced that his own plan of opera-

---

[1] Pouget de Saint-André, *Dumouriez*, 153.   [2] Ibid., 164-8.
[3] Ibid., 199.   [4] Ibid., 215.

tions was the best.[1] He then visited the Comte de Provence, the future Louis XVIII, at Mittau. It may have been now, though it is generally placed at the Restoration, that Louis, with true Bourbon want of tact, refused to recognize him as holding any higher rank than that of *Maréchal de camp* ; shall we say General of Brigade ?

Then he visited the Czar, and, though he did not succeed in winning him to the enemies of France, Paul admired him, calling him the Monk of France. His position was now improved and he had overcome the suspicions of the Allies. London became his chief residence, but he wandered about, ever forming plans. He was in Paris several times, especially at or before the time of Georges Cadoudal's conspiracy. The unfortunate mistake of his name for that of Thumery led to Bonaparte's belief that he was with the Duc d'Enghien : a mistake so fatal to the Prince as causing him to seem to be involved with the inveterate plotter. In 1802 he might have rè-entered France under the amnesty, but he considered that would be to acknowledge himself culpable, and a life under the supervision of the Police would have been burdensome. He received a pension from England, but still wandered, even visiting Sweden.

The Restoration was a great disappointment to Dumouriez, who had expected to be made a Marshal, and, if thought too old for service, to be created a Peer-Marshal. Macdonald failed in his efforts to get him favoured and, if the Duc d'Orléans, as is said, did also advocate his claims, that must have come later and the support of the Prince could not have helped him. As Dumouriez himself said, the Royalists would never forgive two things, ' Champagne and Valmy '. Wise enough to anticipate a military revolt when the Allies should leave Paris, he threw himself on the side of the Orleanists and settled in England. At first he lived at Little Ealing, but when the Duke of Kent, who lived near him, died, he moved to Turville Park in the parish of Henley. Here he died on the 14th March 1823.

The Duke of Wellington, indeed, thought little of him, and

---

[1] Pouget de Saint-André, *Dumouriez*, 219-20 ; Sicotière, *Louis de Frotté*, ii. 209-10, 756-7.

to the remark that he had conquered Belgium replied, ' Yes, he conquered Belgium when there was no one to defend it. At the battle of Jemappes, which they talk so much about, there were only eleven thousand Austrians.'[1] It will be remembered that I make some 13,000, whilst Dumouriez had 40,000.[2]

The influence of Dumouriez on the career of the Republic was very great. Kellermann won the actual battle of Valmy, but that he fought there and that Brunswick was halted on his march to Paris was due to the daring of Dumouriez, which won admiration even from Napoleon. But his flight to the Allies was most disastrous to the armies of France. It gave foundation for all the marvellous suspicions of their commanders which so long reigned amongst the patriots, and which led General after General to the scaffold. He ruined military authority, for, without his act, the class of Saint-Just would never have tyrannized over the armies.

It is well that there should be no mistake about his position in France. Though a Commander-in-Chief, at no time was he Commander-in-Chief of the French armies. For instance, at the time of his flight he had no control over the armies in other theatres, the ' Moselle ', ' Rhin ', ' Alpes ', ' Pyrénées ', ' Côtes de la Manche ', or the ' Intérieur '.

As for the feelings and sympathies of the future Marshals present with the army during this trying time, we can be sure that Brune, Jourdan, and Murat would be on the side of the Convention. Ney probably took the same view. Lt.-Colonel Davout was strong in his opposition to Dumouriez, as was natural in a man with his record. Commissioned in 1788 at the age of eighteen, he had, while serving in the cavalry regiment, *Royal-Champagne*, thrown in his lot with the mass of the regiment and the National Guard against the officers, who in the heavy cavalry were generally opposed to the Revolution. Protesting against the discharge of some forty-nine men for a suspected plot, he was arrested and imprisoned for six weeks. He gave way and resigned his commission on the 15th September 1791, being released. He then joined the third battalion of the volunteers of his Depart-

---

[1] Stanhope, *Wellington*, 70.
[2] For his later life see Rose and Broadley, *Dumouriez*.

L'ARMÉE DU NORD, 1793

ment, Yonne (formed on the 23rd September),[1] and was elected second Lt.-Colonel by 400 votes out of 583.

Davout was short-sighted and wore glasses. A description of him in the year 1806 is given by Brandt,[2] 'A man of medium height, with a robust complexion and features which denote energy and intelligence. The general severity of his appearance is accentuated by premature baldness.'

As we have just seen, his battalion played the decisive card when they fired on their own commander, Dumouriez, and drove him to seek Austrian protection. Here Dumouriez's over-confidence in his men had led him astray. Meeting Davout's battalion marching in a different direction to his intention, he stopped and, directing it to go back, went into a house by the roadside to write his orders. This delay no doubt gave time for Davout and his men to prepare their resistance. Davout himself took pride in his action and regretted that that of others had prevented his taking Dumouriez prisoner.[3]

Macdonald's attitude is doubtful. He seems to have tried to keep clear of the whole affair. It is curious that neither of the two Generals concerned, Dumouriez and Beurnonville, both of whom had strong claims on him, confided their intentions to him. Dumouriez took leave of him at Brussels, when he went to take up the command of his regiment, without saying anything of the situation, and nothing further seems to have passed between them.

Beurnonville on his way to Dumouriez saw Macdonald, but made no communication as to the object of his journey. All this of course depends on whether Macdonald has given us a candid account.

The day after the arrest of the Commissioners, Macdonald was called into the quarters of his General, Miaczinski, at Orchies,[4] who in high spirits was reading to his officers a dispatch by which Macdonald learnt what had happened; he was then ordered to march his regiment on Lille, which he proceeded to do. His officers were uneasy, but he told them their duty was to obey orders without troubling themselves

---

[1] Susane, *Inf. franç.*, i. 345.
[2] Brandt, 5–6.
[3] Vigier, *Davout*, i. 34–7.
[4] South-east of Lille.

about what happened. Passing by Pont-à-Marcq, he had reached the suburbs of Lille, when he received orders from Miaczinski, now in that town, to stop where the message found him and to feed his men, but not to leave them. The gates of the town were closed and night was falling, when he was told from the walls to take his men to the Madeleine *faubourg*, where they would get food and tents. The men marched in disorder to the *faubourg*, but were refused admittance, while a voice from the place said that their Colonel was to come in to the assembled council. This the men said they would not allow, unless some of them accompanied him, and they showed their sentiments by declaring that these j—— f—— had killed their ' poor Capet ', and by crying ' Vive le Roi '. Macdonald quieted them, declaring that he recognized their voices and so intimidating them. He then entered the town, answering the assurance of the citizens inside that he need have no fear by the characteristic boast that the enemy had never frightened him, still less the French.

What had happened was this. Miaczinski had been ordered by Dumouriez to seize Lille, and it is evident from the obedience of Macdonald and the temper of that Colonel's men that he could have done this had he acted sensibly. Most foolishly he had told the two cavalry Colonels, the Quadroons Saint-Georges and Dumas, of his orders, inviting them to accompany him ; they refused and Saint-Georges told him he would warn General Duval in Lille and the administrators of the town. Instead of arresting them, he told them he would follow them and would be there as soon as they were. Then, setting off with his cavalry, he reached Lille before Macdonald. Here again most foolishly he entered the town, not with a mass of men, but with only one hundred troopers. Saint-Georges and Dumas had warned not only Duval, the commandant, but also the civil authorities, before whom Miaczinski was brought. He gave up the letter of Dumouriez, declared he would serve the Republic, and ordered the troops outside the town and those at Orchies to the Camp de la Madeleine under Lille, placing Macdonald in command of them.

Macdonald had succeeded in satisfying the authorities of his patriotism and he was sent out to take his troops to the camp.

The men now cried 'Vive la République', but when, on arrival at the camp, they found no food or supplies, they simply disbanded, leaving Macdonald to carry the regimental colour to his inn. Next morning, however, he succeeded in collecting the regiment again. A more severe test awaited him. Dumouriez, hearing of the failure to secure Lille, sent General Devaux on the 4th April to order the Dragoons in the Madeleine suburb to be ready to start during the night. Having given his message and being worn out, Devaux, a friend of Macdonald, went to that officer's quarters and, throwing himself on the bed, fell asleep. Macdonald had been called into the town again. The arrival of Devaux was known and Macdonald was ordered to arrest him. 'You speak of your patriotism,' said General Lavalette; 'I like to believe you, but this evening you will go and seize Devaux yourself.' The instructions of the *Conseil général* said of itself: 'Sure of the patriotic sentiments of Colonel Macdonald and of the troops under his orders, it is quite convinced that the Colonel will take all possible means of having Colonel[1] Devaux arrested, and that in any case he will not adhere to the proposals or the orders given by General Dumouriez.' It was a disagreeable task for a former A.D.C. of Dumouriez and for a friend of Devaux, but Macdonald had no choice. At eight that night he entered his own room and, as Devaux jumped up to throw himself into his arms, he said, ' My friend, I do not know what they want of you, but I have orders to arrest you '.[2] I give all this in detail as it is a good instance of the slackness of the Royalists and the energy of the patriots. Also this mission of Macdonald to Lille probably caused many of the doubts of his patriotism, under which doubts we shall find him suffering later. Miaczinski and Devaux went to the scaffold.[3]

Macdonald in his own account makes no mention of the disagreeable incident with Devaux. It is difficult to understand the action of the patriots towards him, as obviously he had been ready to act under the orders of Miaczinski and to seize Lille, had that General not placed himself in the hands

---

[1] Devaux had been promoted General by Dumouriez for this mission.
[2] Chuquet, *Trahison*, 184-90; Macdonald, *Souvenirs*, 21-5; Foucart et Finot, *Déf. nat.*, i. 370-3.   [3] Wallon, *Trib. rév.*, i. 102-4.

of the opponents of Dumouriez. He was lucky in saving his head ; but, though for long he was under suspicion, he was able to remain with the army and to rise in it.

Davout, on the other hand, for the moment was in favour, for, as I have said, he had played the final card in the matter. On the 1st May 1793 he was promoted Colonel, appointed Adjutant-General provisionally, and given command of a brigade formed of the 2nd battalion of the 104th regiment and of two volunteer battalions, his own 3rd Yonne and the 3rd Aube.[1] Still, his views were not advanced enough for the patriots and we shall find him transferred to La Vendée in July 1793.

Much that I have just written may at first sight seem but a part of the history of Dumouriez, having little relation to that of the future leaders who served under him. In reality the conduct and action of Dumouriez affected for long the whole course of the war. Hitherto, whatever interference there may have been from Paris, the commanders still ruled their armies. When Dumouriez ordered his troops to march, he could be certain that they would do so ; once he was in the Argonne, he called for more troops from the north under Beurnonville and they came. Unwise as the new Governments may have been, they had been obliged to give their commanders a free hand in most matters for active operations, All this was now changed. With Dumouriez fell the whole fabric of the old army. He had openly avowed his intention of overthrowing the Jacobins and of sowing salt on the site of their hall. He had defied the power of the Convention.

His open treason, followed by his defeat and flight, gave enormous ascendancy to the very party and Government he had abhorred. If the General that had foiled Brunswick and conquered Belgium could not stand against the Convention, which had wrung his troops from him, who after this could ever oppose that body ? By means of their Representatives with the armies the Convention now seized the management of all details of war. The commanders, retaining all their responsibility, became powerless to do anything not approved by the

---

[1] Dumouriez, *Vie*, iv. 167-71 ; Vigier, *Davout*, i. 37. Gavard, 14, makes him promoted Colonel provisionally in March 1793.

ignorant tyrants at their side. Had Dumouriez been victorious at Neerwinden, he and the other commanders would have retained the power necessary for the direction of operations. It was not for several years, after Robespierre had fallen, that the effects of this failure of Dumouriez ceased to be felt by the armies.

There is one point generally unnoticed. Not only did Dumouriez fall, but by sending General Beurnonville into captivity he also handed over the War Office to the Jacobins. *Poseur* and braggart as he was, Beurnonville understood his work and, like Dumouriez, had a healthy contempt for the mob. One of the meddlesome Sections of Paris sent a deputation to him to ask why he had employed a certain man : ' Give us a categorical answer ! ' ' Here is my answer,' replied the General ; ' I am off to bed. Good-night.' Beurnonville being a prisoner, the War Department passed into the hands of the Jacobins and free course was given for civilian incompetence and for the revenge of the civilians for their temporary submersion. Dumouriez, supported by the other commanders, had performed the miracle of overturning the incompetent Minister for War, Pache. Now the Generals were at the mercy of the War Office crew. Besides the Representatives with the armies, the Minister had his own special agents, distributing newspapers to the troops in which distrust of their officers was inculcated. These men hung about the camp-fires, sucking in every word that could be taken as a reason for declaring that any officer was ' suspect ', reporting any complaint made either by the men against their commanders, or, worse still, any grievance which any General might have against the Department. On their reports the Minister acted. No matter what an officer's rank or past might be, however useful or necessary his services, at a word from these spies he would find himself at best dismissed, if not sent to the guillotine. Of course personal feelings had much to do with these reports. Hitherto the armies had been ruled and directed by officers. Now begins the Revolutionary nightmare.

The new state of things was made worse by there being grounds for some suspicion of the officers, and it was not unnatural that there should have been a dull misgiving in the minds of the men. There is something pathetic about the manner in which, while the fate of Dumouriez's attempt to influence his army was yet undecided, the men, utterly puzzled as to what they ought to do, went off home in despair. 'The Lieutenant who commanded us,' says a volunteer, 'as well as the greater part of the company, was determined to leave. We went to our Lt.-Colonel to ask to leave in a body: he seemed very undecided, urging us to wait. We decided to start the same day.'[1] And off they went.

Obviously, however, the greater the liability of the men to distrust of their officers, the greater should have been the attempts to reassure both them and the officers, and the more so as many of the officers were influenced by fears as to their own fate if they remained in the Revolutionary armies. Indeed one wonders why so many remained. Davout, who had given such a great proof of his attachment to the cause, soon thought it wise to refuse a high command and to retire to his home.[2] Even then he was arrested and imprisoned for some time. Grouchy, now in La Vendée, another man who went with his whole heart with the Revolution, was struck by the law which prevented *ci-devant* Nobles from serving, and had to leave for a time. Even this law against Nobles did not save those who obeyed it. The French officers that had lost their 'de' used to laugh at their Scotch and Irish comrades, the Macdonalds and O'Morans, &c., whom they tried to assimilate to their own state by describing them as the '*ci-devant* Mac', and the '*ci-devant* O'', but there was an awkward truth in the jest, as Macdonald found in 1794.

---

[1] Bricard, 52.
[2] After his return to the 'Nord' from La Vendée.

OPERATIONS IN
FRANCE & BELGIUM
1792-4

X

L'ARMÉE DU NORD (*continued*), 1793

Dampierre the successor of Dumouriez. Reorganization of the group of armies. Positions of future Marshals. Davout's opinions. Murat promoted Captain; again at Paris; promoted Lt.-Colonel into 21st Chasseurs, under Landrieux, and posted at Pont-à-Marcq. Despair and death of Dampierre, who is succeeded by Lamarche, having Lieutenant Ney as A.D.C. Coburg drives Lamarche from the Camp de César. Accusations against Colonel Macdonald. English opinion of the Allies. Approximation of certain officers. Duke of York besieges Valenciennes. Use of balloons. The Duke's joke. Lamarche succeeded by Custine from the Rhine. Accusations against Custine, who attacks the Minister. The armament of Lille. Caution of Hoche. Davout answers for Custine. Custine is called to Paris and executed. Dies like a Christian. Bad effect of his execution on the army.

THE flight of Dumouriez and of Valence, who went with him, left the command of the Armée de la Belgique and of the 'Ardennes' vacant. General Dampierre, who was commanding at Le Quesnoy, had resisted Dumouriez's attempt to seize the place, although Dumouriez had counted on his support, and, as he was considered above suspicion, on the 4th April 1793 the *Conseil* appointed him to command the Armée de la Belgique,[1] that is, the army of which Dumouriez, commanding all the group of armies employed in Belgium and Holland, was officially the head. Lamarche, whose A.D.C. was Lieutenant Ney, was placed in command of the 'Ardennes' (with possibly an interregnum of Le Veneur), an appointment approved by the *Comité* on the 24th April 1793.[2] Miranda, as we have already seen, had gone to Paris, and his place as commander of the 'Nord' does not seem to have been filled at the moment. In fact, as the *Conseil* appears to have realized, it was not so much an army or armies of which Dampierre took command, but several groups of troops which had taken shelter in garrisons or camps. These settled down

---

[1] Aulard, *Recueil*, iii. 59, 87-9. Here and on subsequent pages *Conseil* is used for *Conseil exécutif provisoire*.
[2] Ibid., 421-2. Here and on subsequent pages *Comité* is used for *Comité de salut public*.

into two armies, the 'Nord' (which received the former components of the Nord, the Armée de la Belgique, the Armée de la Hollande, and the corps of d'Harville), and the 'Ardennes', the commander of which, Lamarche, was appointed to be under the command of Dampierre, who was described by the *Comité* on the 24th April 1793 as commanding the 'Nord',[1] although I do not find any formal appointment of him to that post, except when the Convention on the 4th April approved what they called his nomination by the *Conseil* to the command of the 'Nord' and 'Ardennes'.[2] Of course the title 'Armée de la Belgique' could no longer be used, and the Armée de la Hollande was broken up, its troops giving up the places they had seized and coming into Lille proudly enough through the Allies by virtue of their capitulations.[3]

The 'Ardennes', although nominally a distinct force, was, as I have said, almost always under the orders of the General commanding the 'Nord'. Usually it worked with the 'Nord', although every now and then it lent a hand to the 'Centre', which became the 'Armée de la Moselle'. The 'Ardennes' was the army of the Republic which had the least character and it was always a formless body. Just now it was very weak, a mere division: perhaps in the confusion some of its troops had joined the 'Nord'. In May 1793 Kilmaine, who then led it, after leaving the weakest possible garrisons in the many fortresses he had to hold, could only collect 7,000 infantry and from 800 to 900 cavalry as his active force.[4] Consequently the 'Nord' represented almost all the forces on this frontier. In name an army, it was really a long line of camps and fortresses, from some point or other of which a force every now and then advanced to make a more or less isolated attack, rather to allay dissatisfaction and to obey the Representatives, than with real hope of permanent success. Its main striking power lay to the south of its line, about the Camp de Famars. The troops really required rest, reorganization, and drill, but woe to any commander who tried to give them this!

The *ci-devant* Marquis de Dampierre, not realizing the com-

---

[1] Aulard, *Recueil*, iii. 422.   [2] Ibid., 64.   [3] Dellard, 7-10.
[4] Chuquet, *Valenciennes*, 82-3; id., *Hondschoote*, 59.

plete change of circumstances, received the perilous succession of Dumouriez with pleasure. From a youth he had sought every opportunity of distinguishing himself, whether at home, abroad, on the earth, in the water, or in the air. As an officer in the Swiss Guards, he had gone to Spain without permission, to take part in the siege of Gibraltar, and had been sent back under arrest. Then in 1788, having been too much absorbed in balloon ascents to remember the termination of his leave of absence, he had been again placed under arrest on his return to his regiment. Disgust with this sent him travelling in England.[1] Passing to Prussia, he became such an admirer of the system of the great Frederick as to make too pronounced a display of Prussian manners and dress. Louis XVI was noted for the raps over the knuckles which he administered to the courtiers, and his rough speeches won him many enemies. A remark of the King to Biron on Dampierre, 'Have you seen that lunatic with his Prussian manners?' hindered Dampierre's promotion and was as effectual in turning him into a good patriot as the 'parre' had been in the case of Luckner. Dumouriez, on his arrival amongst the Allies, had complained of Dampierre, who, he considered, had betrayed him. He had confided in him as a man of quality and ' fait pour bien penser '.[2] As I have said, it is just possible that he may have known that Dumouriez took a very different view of his conduct at Jemappes from what he himself did, and so may have been the less inclined to follow his commander's action against the Convention, but, boiling patriot that he was, his course seems natural enough. The Revolution had raised him rapidly; in ten months he had passed from Colonel of the 5th Dragoons to Commander-in-Chief of the main army of France.[3]

Putting aside technicalities, when the confusion caused by the flight of Dumouriez from his army, and by that of his army from him, had ceased, two armies, ' Nord ' and ' Ardennes ',

---

[1] There he met the William Augustus Miles, whose correspondence with Pierre Lebrun-Tondu, the Foreign Minister, is published, London, 1796, and London, Longmans, 1890, 2 vols.

[2] Fersen, ii. 70 ; Gaulot, 338 ; Chuquet, *Trahison*, 206.

[3] General Auguste-Henri-Marie Picot, Comte de Dampierre (1756–93). Michaud, *Biog. univ.*, x. 480–2 ; Chuquet, *Valenciennes*, 4–6; Foucart et Finot, *Déf. nat.*, i. 383, 384, 389, 390, 412.

occupied this theatre, in which served Adjutant-General Brune, sent with others by the *Conseil* to assist in reorganizing the army, Colonel Davout with his brigade, Lt.-Colonel Jourdan with his volunteer battalion, Colonel Macdonald at the head of his regiment of regulars, under General La Marlière (who commanded at the important Camp de la Madeleine under Lille), Captain Mortier in a volunteer battalion, Lieutenant Murat, soon to be Captain, in the 12th Chasseurs, and Lieutenant Ney, A.D.C. to General Lamarche. With these were Lt.-Colonel Moreau, commanding a volunteer battalion, and Captain Hoche of the regulars, A.D.C. to General Le Veneur in the ' Ardennes '. Sent to Paris by his General, to explain the situation to the *Comité* when Dumouriez fled,[1] Hoche made acquaintance with Marat and used the demagogue's paper to spread his own ideas. He had pleased the *Comité*, who promoted him to be Lt.-Colonel on the 15th May 1793 when he was starting to rejoin his General.[2] We shall mention him again in July 1793. General O'Moran, who was commanding in Flanders, had as A.D.C. the marvellous Jouy, some of whose adventures are told by Thiébault.[3]

Two at least of the future Marshals were known to Dampierre. Colonel Davout seems to have been on friendly terms with him, for towards the end of April two agents, really spies of the Minister, visited Dampierre and found Davout and an A.D.C. with him. In conversation Davout and the A.D.C. showed their dislike of Marat, Danton, and Robespierre, of whom they spoke with indignation, praising the Girondins, Pétion, Brissot, and Guadet, who were now being attacked by the extreme faction to which the Minister belonged. At dinner one of the agents, to draw the officers on, said Paris no doubt would not be quiet for long, as the Convention had sent Marat before the *Tribunal révolutionnaire*.[4] Falling into the snare, Davout and the staff officers replied that Marat well deserved the fate that they thought awaited him. The agent professed his surprise at the conduct of Davout. Was he not the man who had been driven from his regiment and

---

[1] Chuquet, *Trahison*, 196.   [2] Cuneo d'Ornano, *Hoche*, i. 42-55.
[3] Thiébault, i. 351, 352, 414-42.
[4] Thiers, *Rév.*, ii. 84-95 ; Marat triumphed.

imprisoned in the citadel of Arras ? It was he who in 1790 had taken the side of the patriot soldiers, who had given the example of a *pacte fédératif* between the citizens and the soldiers of the line. The agent went on to express his astonishment at seeing him so prejudiced against Marat, Robespierre, and the Jacobins. Was it not Robespierre and Marat who had defended him when he had been the victim of arbitrary power ? Davout replied, ' I am not prejudiced against those who were my defenders in 1790. Then I refused to serve the plans of a King who was my benefactor. Now, for the same reason, I refuse to serve the Jacobins and to support their plans, which seem disastrous to me.'[1] This is a good example of the spirit of many officers who were patriots, but not Jacobins : such an attitude did not suit the extreme party, and the agent denounced him. His action against Dumouriez, important as it had been, saved him for the moment, and his promotion to command a brigade may partly have been due to the good opinion of Dampierre, but, as I have said, we shall find him transferred to La Vendée in July.

As for Murat, on the 15th April 1793 we find him at Valenciennes, probably sent on some message and supping with Dampierre.[2] What he had been expecting had come to pass : his Colonel, d'Urre de Molans, had been promoted General of brigade [3] and had made such a report of his activity and courage that Dampierre had promoted him Captain on the 14th April 1793 and had approved his appointment as A.D.C. to General d'Urre, who now went to command at Hesdin [4] in the Pas-de-Calais, where Murat's regiment, the 12th Chasseurs, 'Champagne', was quartered, presumably in order to

---

[1] Chuquet, *Hondschoote*, note 3, pp. 49 and 50.
[2] The letter given in the correspondence of Murat, *Lettres*, i. 8–9. No. 7, and Lumbroso, *Murat*, 8–9, as of the 25th Feb. 1793, cannot be of that date, as Murat says he supped at Valenciennes with Dampierre on the 15th. ' On a repris le Camp de Famars.' Now on the 15th Feb. Dampierre and the armies were round Maestricht, but on the 15th April 1793 Dampierre, in command, marched on Valenciennes and retook the position of Famars (Chuquet, *Valenciennes*, 45). The letter shown as of the 15th Feb. 1793 seems to be of that date. Murat there called himself Lieutenant (Murat, *Lettres*, i. 7, No. 6).
[3] Susane, *Cav. franç.*, iii. 124, gives the 9th June 1793 as the date of appointment of d'Urre's successor in the regiment, but he probably had been promoted temporarily before.
[4] South-east of Montreuil.

rest and recover itself. Indeed, whatever Murat himself may have done, the action of the cavalry in the last campaign had been bad. It had suffered much in the disasters in Belgium, and the Generals described it now as ' nulle '.[1] Probably its losses in horses had been severe.

In April 1793 Murat had made one of his frequent trips to Paris, and on the 25th April we get a characteristic letter from him. To believe him, the army had always beaten the enemy. Once again he had been spoken of as deputy to the Convention, and, though he acknowledged not having much talent, he thought that, with his courage and his good intentions, he would have done more good there than some others. Struck by the horrors of war, he advised his brother not to come to him or to abandon their parents, but, if any others should come and ask for him, they would at least have a horse. He himself had two horses, which had cost him a hundred louis and twelve livres, and a third was to arrive. It is an amusing sign of the times that, when he found that the girl to whom he had paid some attention, Mion Bastit, was angry with him, he should have at once accused her and her family of being ' aristocrats '.[2]

Murat's run of luck continued. The regiment of *Hussards-Braconniers*, one of the newly raised bodies, came to Hesdin, where its commander, Landrieux, had been nominated Commandant, General d'Urre de Molans apparently going to command the 12th Division.[3] Jean Landrieux [4] was one of those adventurers thrown high by the Revolution. Dismissed from the seminary where he had been preparing for the priesthood, the protection of the Marquis de Montesquiou-Fézensac had got him the post of *Inspecteur des relais de Monsieur*, say inspector of the post-horses of the brother of the King, the Comte de Provence, the future Louis XVIII. A clever, daring man, using the Revolution to rise by, on the 9th September 1792 he obtained permission to form a free corps, of which

---

[1] Chuquet, *Hondschoote*, 62, 109.
[2] Murat, *Lettres*, i. 8–11, correcting date of letter No. 7 from February to April.   [3] Landrieux, *Méms.*, i. (56).
[4] Adjudant-Général Jean Landrieux (1756–c. 1825). See his *Méms.*, with a pestilent paging, the numbers of the pages of the introduction being put in brackets, those of the rest of the volume being numbered afresh.

he was provisionally nominated Colonel on the 19th January 1793. At Hesdin Landrieux had to superintend the raising of fortifications as well as to look after his regiment and, having only one Lt.-Colonel and admiring what he had seen of Murat, in May 1793 he offered him the post of 2nd Lt.-Colonel. Most officers in his position (Captain in a regular regiment and A.D.C. to a General) would have hesitated to accept such an offer and, as it turned out, Murat probably would have done better to have declined, but, dazzled by the rank and possibly doubtful about the future of his General, one of the suspected 'de's', he accepted. On the 8th May 1793 Landrieux wrote to Murat that he had got General d'Urre de Molans to apply for his being posted, by the order of the Minister and at the request of the Commander-in-Chief, Dampierre. So Murat was appointed, provisionally, to the post of 2nd Lt.-Colonel and was to join as soon as his General permitted.[1] On the 25th September the War Office informed Murat that he was given the place of *chef d'escadron*, Lt.-Colonel, in the 21st Chasseurs at Hesdin.[2] According to Gavard the date of appointment was 14th August 1793.[3] By some error this regiment of *Hussards-Braconniers* is sometimes styled the 16th Chasseurs for a moment, as there was a good deal of confusion about the numbers of the new cavalry regiments, but in reality the regiment became the 21st Chasseurs on the 14th August 1793. It then had 672 men.[4] Landrieux had been officially appointed Colonel to it, in its first state, on the 10th June 1793.

We shall meet Landrieux again in Italy in 1796 as Chief of the Staff to Kilmaine, but now he had a good deal to do with the fortunes of Murat. He must have been a strange character; the command of a newly formed regiment, and the superintendence of the works at Hesdin, did not content him and he roamed about the country on political work, arresting 'suspects' and even playing the part of a *mouton* to get a confession from a prisoner, the Duc de Châtelet. Whilst

---

[1] Landrieux, *Méms.*, i. (53–4).   [2] Murat, *Lettres*, i. 11–12.
[3] Gavard, No. 3.
[4] Desbrière, *La Cav. pendant la Rév.: La crise*, 147–9; Susane, *Cav. franç.*, i. 186; Murat, *Lettres*, i, note 1 and note 3, p. 11; Landrieux. *Méms.* i, note 4, p. (55).

their Colonel was thus absent, the two Lt.-Colonels had to equip and send to the front the squadrons as they could be organized. In July 1793 Taillefer, the 1st Lt.-Colonel, sent the first equipped squadron to the army, and in August and September Murat formed the second and third squadrons; then, still at Hesdin, he did the same with the fourth, whilst all the time Captains commanded the squadrons with the army. On the 24th September 1793 Landrieux resigned the command at Hesdin and on the 29th September, while escorting prisoners to Amiens, he wrote, ' Murat, I have left you at the regiment. You are there, and all should go well. Adieu, my lad, keep well. I am at the end of my last expedition : I am going to Abbeville with a brother of the Duke of Cumberland,[1] otherwise said to be a brother-in-law of the King of England, and forty-three fanatics or "prêtres non-assermentés".[2] Boulogne has been purged.' Then at last he rejoined the regiment, which seems to have been at Pont-à-Marcq [3] for some time. ' Situated in a marshy and wooded country, between the strategic positions of Cysoing and Orchies, at the junction of the roads from Douai and Lille, Pont-à-Marcq was the key of these two important towns.'[4] Consequently the regiment was constantly engaged with the enemy, and on the 31st October 1793 Landrieux was seriously wounded.[5] But this is anticipating matters and I must return to the Armée du Nord.

Taking command full of fire and energy, Dampierre soon found the task too heavy for him. Not only were the Austrians under Coburg in his front, but a Prussian Corps was coming up, to be joined by a British force under the Duke of York and another of Dutch troops. Neither side dared any wide strokes, both believing the line of fortresses must first be dealt with before the Allies could advance. Dampierre had to control not only his own active force and the Armée des Ardennes under Lamarche, but also the long line stretching to Dunkirk. He would have liked to give his men rest, while awaiting reinforcements, but the Allies were besieging Condé, and the Representatives urged him on.

---

[1] There is nothing to show to whom this refers.
[2] Priests refusing to swear to the civil constitution of the clergy, and who were treated as wild beasts.
[3] Landrieux, *Méms.*, i. (64–83). [4] Ibid., (83). [5] Ibid., (73).

On the 15th April 1793 he advanced on Valenciennes and the Camp de Famars, which he reoccupied. That night, as I have said, Captain Murat supped with him. On the 1st May 1793 he attacked Coburg on the left bank of the Escaut trying to throw him back on Quiévrain. Beside his own troops, with whom Davout and Murat and, I presume, Jourdan and Mortier served, he employed the Armée des Ardennes (where Ney was A.D.C. to Lamarche) and, on his left, the troops of La Marlière, amongst whom was Colonel Macdonald. The infantry fought well, but the cavalry failed to support the right, the army was repulsed, and Dampierre drew back. On the 8th May he again attacked. On the left La Marlière was successful. There Macdonald must have been near Colonel Blücher, a future opponent of his, who was very busy in this campaign and who was already distinguishing himself as a bold cavalry leader. La Marlière did not succeed in linking with the left of Dampierre and, to stop his progress, the Duke of York sent up the Coldstream and Grenadier Guards. These threw the French back, but in the end the Coldstream came on a position too strong for attack.[1]

Cramped and controlled by the Representatives in every operation, the iron entered into the soul of Dampierre and, feeling the toils closing round him, he despaired under his heavy task. The spies of the Minister were at head-quarters, tempting Davout and the staff of Dampierre to utterance against the Jacobins; indeed it may have been to Davout that one spy referred when he complained of the commander, 'Il est mal, très mal entouré'.[2] While the spies declared that Dampierre no longer mentioned the Republic, he himself was lamenting the way in which men only desirous to serve their country were treated, and one day, after a contest with a Representative, he exclaimed to Lahure, 'Ah, I wish I might have an arm or leg carried away, to be able to retire honourably'.[3] He was wrong; whatever wounds he might have received, they would not have saved him from disgrace and

---

[1] Calvert, 70-3; Chuquet, *Valenciennes*, 55-67; Jomini, *Rév.*, iii. 157-65; Desbrière, *La Cav. pendant la Rév.: La crise*, 366-7.

[2] Chuquet, *Valenciennes*, 60.

[3] Lahure, 47. To Colonel Tholosé he said he had no other hope than to die on the field of battle. Foucart et Finot, *Déf. nat.*, i. 440.

dishonour : even after his death on the field he was denounced as a traitor.[1] Fate, kind for once, gave him half his wish, adding the death which saved him from a bitterer end. In the battle of the 8th May his right thigh was shot off and he was carried from the field, to die next day. He was only thirty-seven. The pompous funeral given to his corpse, and the grave in one of the redoubts of the Camp de Famars, were far better than the scaffold and the bloody basket which awaited him had he lived.[2]

The Armée des Ardennes was fighting alongside of the 'Nord', and the old Lamarche, the leader of the former force, to whom Lieutenant Ney was A.D.C., was given the command of the 'Nord' by the Representatives at 5 p.m. on the 8th May, Kilmaine succeeding him with the 'Ardennes'. The men were exhausted, the fall of Dampierre had dispirited the troops, and all that could be done was to draw back to the Camp de Famars and Valenciennes. Next day passed in a cannonade, but on the 10th May the Allies retook what ground they had lost, and the French set to work to strengthen their position.[3]

At this moment the two armies were weakened by having to send fifty-four men from each battalion to La Vendée, to be replaced by recruits of the levy of 300,000 men, many of whom came only to leave almost immediately, unfit or deserters.[4] On the 14th May 1793 the volunteer battalion in which Captain Mortier served, 1st Nord, was ordered from Douai to Valenciennes to be *embrigadé* with the second battalion of the 83rd regiment of infantry.[5] Its formal *embrigadement* was, however, not carried out till the 4th January 1797, long after Mortier had quitted it.[6]

Lamarche [7] has a certain interest for us as the first patron

---

[1] By Couthon in the Convention. Chuquet, *Valenciennes*, 72.
[2] In 1836 his body was removed to the 'Quatre Chemins', at the forking of the roads of Paris and Condé. Foucart et Finot, *Déf. nat.*, i. 446-50 ; Chuquet, *Valenciennes*, note 1, p. 71.
[3] Chuquet, *Valenciennes*, 61-76 ; Jomini, *Rév.*, iii. 157-65 ; Calvert, 70-3 ; Langeron, 14-15 ; Foucart et Finot, *Déf. nat.*, i. 433-53 ; Lahure, 43-8. For plan see Jomini, *Rév.*, Atlas, ix.
[4] Chuquet, *Valenciennes*, 76-7 ; Aulard, *Recueil*, iii. 593-5.
[5] Foucart et Finot, *Déf. nat.*, i. 453.   [6] Susane, *Inf. franç.*, i. 453.
[7] Général François-Joseph Drouet, dit Lamarche (1733-c. 1800). Chuquet, *Valenciennes*, 73 ; Michaud, *Biog. univ.*, lxx. 14-15.

of Ney. Entering the service as a Dragoon, he had served mainly in the Hussars and on the 15th March 1791 had become Colonel of the regiment (*Colonel général* in that arm),[1] in which Ney was then *fourrier*, or Quartermaster-Sergeant. He probably had remarked Ney and, when after Valmy he became General of Brigade in October 1792,[2] with the 'Armée des Ardennes', he took the future Marshal, then *sous-lieutenant*, as his A.D.C.[3] On the 8th March 1793 Lamarche became General of Division.[4]

The Allies now intended to besiege Valenciennes and, as it was necessary first of all to drive the 'Nord' from the Camp de Famars, on the 23rd May 1793 Coburg advanced with his army to attack the French positions at Anzin and to the north of Valenciennes, whilst columns under the Duke of York and Ferraris swung round by the east to gain the rear of the Camp de Famars. Though York, crossing the Rhonelle to the south of the camp, soon halted, the English cavalry, turning the redoubts which covered the camp, entered them by their gorges, cutting down or capturing the defenders, an incident much taken to heart by the French.[5] The subject of open works is endless: here, it was said, the least obstacle would have stopped the horsemen. At Sebastopol, of the works assaulted by the French and English in September 1855, the closed redoubt of the Malakoff was the only one the assailants succeeded in retaining. Here the French cavalry tried to retake the works, but they were driven off. Although the French had held their ground to the north, Lamarche saw the danger to which he was exposed of being cut off by the further progress of the columns of the enemy south of him, and that night, leaving Ferrand to defend Valenciennes, he retired south-west to Bouchain, the Camp de César,[6] and Paillencourt.

---

[1] Susane, *Cav. franç.*, ii. 242.

[2] Chuquet, *Valenciennes*, 73, makes him appointed General of Brigade on the 3rd Feb. 1793, but he ceased to be Colonel of the 4th Hussars (*Colonel général*) in Oct. 1792, and Money shows him as then a General with the 'Ardennes'. Money, 134, 137, 140, &c. Michaud, lxx. 14, dates his promotion 10th Oct. 1792.

[3] Ney, *Méms.*, i. 34.

[4] Chuquet, *Valenciennes*, 73.

[5] Foucart et Finot, *Déf. nat.*, i. 460; Calvert, 76-7.

[6] North of Cambrai, on the heights of Saint-Olle and Paillencourt; see Gay de Vernon, 177-8.

The skilful Mack was wounded, but the French lost three colours, 300 prisoners, 3,000 killed and wounded, and seventeen guns. The messenger with such good news entered Vienna escorted by twenty-seven postilions, sounding their horns.[1] In this action Colonel and Adjutant-General Davout must have been engaged, and so must Lt.-Colonel Jourdan with his volunteer battalion. Captain Mortier had an opportunity of distinguishing himself and he held a post six hours after the army had retired.[2] Lt.-Colonel Murat must, I think, have been at Hesdin, just about to leave his post as A.D.C. and to join his new regiment, the 21st Chasseurs. Colonel Macdonald was with his regiment, forming part of the force round Lille under General La Marlière. That General on arrival had been warned against the Colonel of the 2nd regiment, but, on sending for him, found it was Macdonald whom he had remarked at Baisieux. Telling him to return to his post, he promised to be his defender. An opportunity soon came, for the Lt.-Colonel, disappointed of the post of Colonel when Macdonald had joined the regiment after Neerwinden,[3] now denounced him to the Representatives, and all his conduct at Lille and as A.D.C. to Beurnonville and Dumouriez, both now ' suspect ', was inquired into. La Marlière defended him and eventually it was decided to make him Adjutant-General, promoting his rival to command the regiment. Macdonald professed to see in this a censure and with some adroitness got his rival made Colonel and Adjutant-General, retaining his regiment himself.

Macdonald and his regiment consequently were with La Marlière when that General made a successful stroke which did something to comfort the French for the loss of Famars. On the 23rd May 1793 the Allies had made a general advance, not only on Valenciennes, as already described, but also on their right to the sea, and 500 Dutch had entered Tourcoing.[4] Next day La Marlière fell on this body with a far superior force, Macdonald's and another regiment, 400 gendarmes, volunteers, and a Dragoon regiment. He drove them through the place,

---

[1] Chuquet, *Valenciennes*, 86-94 ; Jomini, *Rév.*, iii. 166-73, and Atlas, ix ; Calvert, 75-7 ; Langeron, 15-16 ; Desbrière, *La Cav. pendant la Rév. : La crise*, 367-8. For the Camp de Famars see Dumouriez, *Vie*, ii. 336-8, Eng. ed. iii. 14-16.   [2] *Fastes*, i. 407.   [3] Macdonald, *Souvenirs*, 25-7.
[4] North-east of Lille, Jomini, *Rév.*, Atlas, viii.

taking almost all of them prisoners. One of Macdonald's grenadiers captured a colour, which was presented to the Convention next day amidst great applause. One Belgian in the French service distinguished himself this day, Dumonceau, who was to have the experience of being made Marshal by Louis Bonaparte, then King of Holland, and next being unmade promptly by Napoleon, who disapproved of what he considered a mere imitation of his own Marshalate.[1] On La Marlière's left part of his troops from Linselles drove the Dutch back on Menin.[2] The Dutch troops did not stand well with the Allies, ' from such friends and allies may the Lord deliver us ', wrote one of the Duke of York's staff. The Allies themselves, with some of the troops from Austria, were a most motley lot. ' The drawings which Captain Cook brought from the South Seas are nothing to some of our friends.'[3]

It is curious to think how near each other were certain officers at this period, some of whom were to be antagonists again in the future. With the Allies was the skilful Mack, really their Chief of the Staff, to whose plans the success of forcing the evacuation of the celebrated Camp de Famars was attributed. Colonel Blücher was already cursing the caution of his chiefs which so often prevented his pushing home his attacks on the French. The Duke of York, leading his men round Famars, had no idea that in 1799 he would have to retire before Brune, now in his front and a mere staff officer. With the Duke were Abercromby who was to die in Egypt, Lake who was to win so much glory in India, and Dundas, the master of drill.

Amongst the French, besides Brune, Davout (now Colonel Adjutant-General), was leading a brigade under Kilmaine in the ' Armée des Ardennes '. Jourdan, who must have won distinction in the last fights, had become General of Brigade on the 27th May 1793, that is, four days after the evacuation of Famars.

The Duke of York now began the siege of Valenciennes, and

---

[1] Général Comte Jean-Baptiste Dumonceau, alias Du Monceau (1780–1821). Michaud, *Biog. univ.*, lxiii. 128–32 ; *Biog. des Cont.*, ii. 1477–8. See *Corr. Nap.*, xviii, No. 14771, for Napoleon's objection to the Dutch Marshalate ; Hogendorp, 198, 252 ; *Méms. sur la Cour de Louis-Napoléon*, 68.'
[2] Chuquet, *Valenciennes*, 94-5 ; Jomini, *Rév.*, iii. 171-2.
[3] Calvert, 80.

one detail will show the extraordinary difficulties that the Allies manufactured for themselves. Two sieges had to be prepared for about the same time, those of Mainz and of Valenciennes. Instead of taking the nearest siege-train in each case, one toiled to Valenciennes from Vienna, whilst a Dutch train went to furnish the greater part of the siege batteries at Mainz. The truth was that the Austrians did not care very much to recover Mainz, which would fall again to its Elector, but Valenciennes would be a valuable addition to their own Netherlands, and therefore they helped that operation. The details of the important siege of Valenciennes can be read at length.[1] Here, as at Condé, the besieged made use of balloons, small ones apparently, in order to communicate with the outer world. At Condé a balloon fell into the hands of the enemy, giving them valuable information as to the straits in which the garrison was for food. From Valenciennes one balloon contained a pigeon bearing dispatches, but it was captured and the pigeon eaten. The Allies turned out to see the balloon, crying out that it was the Representatives flying from the place. The Duke of York got hold of a magniloquent French account of a sortie from Valenciennes. Thinking the garrison would laugh at this, he crammed it into a blind shell and fired it into the town. It fell unheeded amongst its murderous brethren, and till the surrender the garrison never knew of this well meant attempt to enliven it.[2]

Before the Allies besieged Le Quesnoy, General Gobert, who commanded the district, tried to arrange for communications between that fortress, if it were surrounded, and Cambrai ; he asked the *Conseil général* to supply pigeons. This the thrifty council agreed to do, stipulating that the birds should be paid for, but not by them.[3] In any case there was much solid sense in these bodies, witness the council of Cambrai, which resolved that, if the town were bombarded, they should assemble in the cellars of the Hôtel de Ville.[4] Could forethought for the public welfare go farther ?

---

[1] Foucart et Finot, *Déf. nat.*, i. 463–578 ; Jomini, *Rév.*, iii. 173–81 ; *Vict. et Conq.*, i. 212–24, with plan ; Chuquet, *Valenciennes*, 234–345 ; Calvert, 77–97 ; Musset-Pathay, *Sièges*, 239–53 and Plate III.
[2] Foucart et Finot, *Déf. nat.*, i. 511.
[3] Ibid., 625–6. [4] Ibid., 625.

Lamarche, a brave old trooper, had not liked taking the command, and even when given that of the 'Ardennes' had declared that, though he had goodwill and zeal, he had bad health and did not possess the necessary knowledge for a Commander-in-Chief. He had again objected when sent to command the 'Nord', only accepting because circumstances were so pressing. He had had, as we have seen, the good sense to do what required courage at the time, to retire from the Camp de Famars. Still, the agents of the Minister, men to be much distrusted, attacked him, saying he dined with the Representatives in the middle of the action and wasted his time in hunting the volunteers out of the cabarets, whilst his A.D.C., Ney, I presume, included, directed the defence of the outposts. The army was discouraged and in a state of demoralization, and now Lamarche insisted on being relieved from a post he had intended only to hold for three or four days. On the 9th May 1793 both the *Conseil exécutif* and the *Comité* nominated Kilmaine, who had succeeded Lamarche at the 'Armée des Ardennes', to replace him at the 'Nord', but this was subject to the opinion of the Representatives with the army and, when these proposed Custine, then commanding the 'Armée du Rhin', whom the army was said to demand, that General was appointed on the 13th May and arrived at Cambrai on the 27th May 1793.[1] He did Lamarche justice and, failing to get Stengel, asked for the former as Chief of his Staff, saying, 'This General has valour and intelligence when he is under guidance. He is an excellent citizen, but to command in chief is beyond his powers: he has proved this at Famars and acknowledges it himself.'[2] The appointment was refused and Lamarche, with Ney, went back to a division.

As in the case of his predecessor and in that of Dumouriez, Custine belonged to the class of Nobles that had thrown itself into the cause of the Revolution. Having won on the Rhine the first successes of the war, he had much prestige, though later checks had sent him on the downward path. Active and daring, in military matters he resembled Dumouriez rather than Dampierre who, indeed, had wished to hand over

---

[1] Chuquet, *Valenciennes*, 73-122; Wallon, *Rep.*, iv. 96-8; Aulard, *Recueil*, iv. 66-71, 129-37. [2] Wallon, *Rep.*, iv, note 2, p. 110.

the command to him. A strict disciplinarian, his selection for the command was good for an army which had become much disorganized and demoralized. Not having enough troops to relieve Condé and Valenciennes, both now besieged by the Allies, he proposed to reinforce his army with troops from the 'Moselle' (late 'Centre') and the 'Rhin'. Then, having raised the sieges, the 'Nord' could remain on the defensive, whilst all the other forces in the north and east could be thrown on the Rhine to raise the siege of Mainz. Naturally Houchard, commanding the 'Moselle', and Beauharnais, commanding the 'Rhin', protested against a plan which would prevent them doing anything at once to relieve Mainz, invested since the 31st March 1793. Unfortunately for Custine, when he had been on the Rhine he had proposed to use all the forces in the north for his own plans on the Rhine, thus bringing himself into opposition to Dumouriez, whilst his interference with Kellermann, when that General was commanding the 'Centre' or 'Moselle', had brought on an angry quarrel between them. It was therefore easy for the two Rhine commanders to represent him as always wanting to control the whole of the forces for his own plans and to direct them wherever he himself might be. The Minister for War objected that Mainz could not hold out long enough for Custine's plan, whilst the Government was more anxious to reinforce its troops in La Vendée than to operate elsewhere.

Condemned to the defensive, Custine set himself to work to re-establish order amongst the troops and in this task, for which he was well fitted, he was successful to a great degree. Getting rid of many useless men, by the 13th July 1793 he had 35,013 infantry and 4,385 horse. What was more, all these were armed and equipped, whilst before this many had had no muskets and others no bayonets. Thus engaged, the mass of his army remained in the Camp de César or de Paillencourt, whilst Kilmaine reorganized the Armée des Ardennes.

Farther north La Marlière from Lille carried on a series of small attacks, in which Colonel Macdonald, then placed at Lannoy and commanding the frontier from Armentières to Menin, took part. Meantime denunciations rained on Custine from the Jacobins. The very strictness with which he was getting his men into shape told against him with the foolish agitators at Paris. Were the defenders of Liberty to obey like machines, and that too under a General who still had his coat of arms engraved on his toilette articles ? Worse still, Custine came into open conflict with the Minister for War and denounced his incapacity. This brought on him the wrath of the men who were trying to drive all the former officers from command and who wished to keep the Generals under their control in the smallest details.

One charge against Custine is so curious, and shows so well the dangers to which the commanders were now exposed, that I give it in detail. Custine wanted to arm strongly the two Camps de César, under Cambrai and Bouchain, and that of the Madeleine under Lille. The fortresses had ample surplus ordnance, and guns were to be drawn from them, Lille furnishing seventy-six pieces. No commander of a fortress likes any diminution of his strength, and Lille was under Favart, an engineer, and therefore an officer the least likely to look with favour on this proceeding. He strongly remonstrated. Undoubtedly Custine was right ; Marescot, an engineer to be well known later, had determined with the staff officer Gay de Vernon what ordnance could be spared for the camps, and all that Favart really could plead was that, in case of a defeat of the force at the Madeleine camp, it would be impossible to get two hundred horses and drivers to bring the guns there back into Lille. Custine insisted and the operation was carried out, but it gave rise to discontent and absurdly exaggerated rumours were carried eagerly to Paris.[1]

At the moment, in the opinion of the Minister and of most Representatives, everything had to give way to the safety of the fortresses. In February 1793, when Custine was commanding on the Rhine, the Commissioners at Strasbourg had complained of his requiring guns from that fortress.[2] Now the Minister objected to the Commandant of Lille, Favart, being put under the orders of La Marlière, the General appointed by Custine to command on his left in West Flanders, and, when Custine refused to obey, he got first the *Conseil exécutif* and

---

[1] Gay de Vernon, *Custine et Houchard*, 179-82 ; Chuquet, *Valenciennes*, 181-5.   [2] Aulard, *Recueil*, ii. 137-9.

then the *Comité* to enforce his order.¹ So strong were the suspicions caused of Custine's good faith in this matter of the armament of Lille that even in 1805 the testimony of that honourable officer, Dejean, was needed to convince Napoleon, generally much misinformed about these campaigns in the north, that Gay de Vernon, on Custine's staff, had not been a party to a treacherous disarmament of Lille.² Such suspicions spread far. On the 8th January 1794 we find Hoche, then commanding the ' Moselle ', writing to the Minister that he had been asked, apparently by Pichegru, then commanding the ' Rhin ', to send twenty 24 Prs. from Strasbourg for the siege of Fort Vauban or Fort Louis : ' I cannot help believing this was intended as a snare for me. For, in drawing artillery and such a quantity of ammunition from Strasbourg, they would not have failed to say that I wanted to deliver up the place.' ³ Nor would they have failed to accuse him.

But while, with such charges, the enemies of Custine went for him open-mouthed, in the army his value was understood by the better class of officers. Davout, writing to his Department on the 2nd June 1793 in a manner prophetic of his attitude towards order in the ranks in later years, remarks on the ' discipline sévère et républicaine ' which was spreading in the whole army since the arrival of Custine. ' If one could answer for any one, I would guarantee the good faith of Custine ; I believe him to be Republican ; he has great military talents, which can be used to the advantage of the cause of Liberty.' ⁴ Another difficulty of the Convention, another cause of the animosity of Custine's enemies, was his popularity with the men. Some of his soldiers might grumble at his strictness, but the need for discipline was so acutely felt by the army that the men gradually turned against the attempts to discredit their General. They threw mud on the calumnious journals and hooted the Representatives. Now nothing was more dangerous to the Generals than any belief in their personal popularity with their men. Such a reputation always aroused the uneasy jealousy of the patriots.

---

[1] Chuquet, *Valenciennes*, 181-4. [2] Gay de Vernon, 182-4.
[3] Cuneo d'Ornano, *Hoche*, ii. 44-5 ; Rousselin, *Hoche*, ii. 47-8.
[4] Blocqueville, *Davout*, i. 307-8 ; Vigier, *Davout*, i. 36.

On the 12th July 1793 Condé fell: this was the first blow to Custine. It was thought too dangerous to arrest him while with his army, and he was simply called to Paris to consult with the *Comité de salut public* on the plans for the next campaign. The General did not think he had yet lost the game and on the 16th July 1793 he started for Paris, believing he could beat down his enemies. In the Capital he attacked the Minister for War most boldly, accusing him of a secret intention of ruining him and his army. The *Comité* believed it had the General at its mercy once he was away from his troops, but to their alarm, when he was seen in the streets, he was greeted by the people. On the 21st July the *Comité* ordered him not to appear in public without a gendarme. Next day he was arrested and imprisoned. Then came the news that first Mainz, then Valenciennes, had surrendered. Mainz had been taken by Custine, and he had failed to relieve it before he left the Rhine. Valenciennes had fallen while his Armée du Nord had not moved. His enemies had a free hand, and on the 27th August 1793 he was guillotined.

The mob of Paris had a curious delight in believing that the Generals fighting on the frontier for them were, if not traitors, certainly cowards, and it is constantly asserted that Custine showed ' faiblesse ' when going to his death. Rash, vindictive, brave as his sword, he regarded not man, but he feared God. Accepting the services of a ' prêtre assermenté ', he had made his confession and on arriving at the scaffold asked for and received the benediction of the priest, whilst the vile mob cried ' Ah, le lâche ! ' As the *Moniteur* announced, ' he knelt on the first steps of the ladder, then, getting up, he looked on the fatal blade and mounted the scaffold firmly,'[1] dying like an officer and a Christian amidst the jeers of the canaille.

His daughter-in-law, Delphine de Custine, at a time when every one shrank from a ' suspect ', had with rare courage sat on a stool at his feet during the trial, to assist in his defence. So beautiful was she, with her lovely face in its halo of the golden hair which was to enchant Chateaubriand,[2] that

---

[1] Wallon, *Rep.*, i. 226-52.
[2] Gribble, *Chateaubriand*, 97-8, with portrait.

Hébert appealed to the Judges not to be affected by the charm of her presence. He need not have troubled. As she left the court, the mob yelled, ' C'est la Custine, c'est la fille du traître ! ' but her brave countenance gained her passage. Her husband, the son of Custine, was executed on the 3rd January 1794, dying, as even the patriots allowed, ' avec fermeté et tranquillité '.[1]

There is something pathetic in the fate of Custine. He had served the Revolution in good faith on the frontiers. Indeed, in going to Paris and in believing he could oppose the Minister with a chance of success, he had given evidence of his sincerity. The wiser and more suspicious Dumouriez had avoided the snare set for him by the call to the Capital. How well advised the *Comité* had been in not attempting to arrest Custine when with the army, was shown by the attitude of the men, who had trusted him. Davout, for example, had seen the difference between him and Dumouriez, although Custine's opposition to the Jacobins can hardly have been unknown altogether. The absence of their commander had made the men uneasy. The news of his arrest confounded them. The Representatives, accompanied by his successor, had to go round the camps, assuring the troops that there were grave charges against him, but that, if found innocent, he would be sent back and his accusers would be punished. The troops received the harangue in gloomy silence. While some were dismayed at finding another commander suspected, others cried ' Vive Custine ! ' in the face of the Representatives. As a rule it was the volunteers who were more ready to believe in the wisdom of the Convention than the regulars, but there were exceptions. The volunteer battalion of Lt.-Colonel Moreau, when formed in square to hear the Representatives, along with a regular battalion which cried, ' Down with the Nobility ; no more Nobles to command us ! ' replied, ' We want Custine ; without Custine no army ! '[2] It took time and much persuasion to reconcile the troops, but the feeling of uneasy distrust of their commanders remained and grew.

---

[1] Wallon, *Trib. rév.*, ii. 316–24.
[2] Chuquet, *Hondschoote*, 51–2 ; Gay de Vernon, *Custine et Houchard*, 212.

XI

L'ARMÉE DU NORD (*continued*), 1793

Kilmaine succeeds Custine. His character. Strength of the ' Nord '. Position of future Marshals with the army. Tribulations of Lieutenant Ney. Davout transferred to La Vendée. The evil influence of Brune. Coburg advances, and Kilmaine withdraws the army from the Camp de César. Movements of the Duke of York, who is nearly taken prisoner. The skill of Kilmaine, whose ' Irish head ' is distrusted. Valenciennes surrenders to the Duke of York. Kilmaine is suspended. Houchard succeeds him, but finds his staff arrested. He wishes to be replaced, to escape from the atmosphere of suspicion. Desbrulys, the new Chief of the Staff. Carnot's strategy. Jourdan, entrusted with a column, comes on the red coats. The Allies divide their forces, and the Duke of York marches to besiege Dunkirk. Jourdan meets the father of Alexander Dumas. Macdonald surprises Blaton. The English under Lake rout the French from Linselles. Macdonald's triumph. Macdonald and Dupont praised and promoted Generals of Brigade, and Mortier made Lt.-Colonel. Jourdan meets Ernouf, his future Chief of the Staff.

CUSTINE was the last commander of the ' Nord ' to have any real power during the Jacobin supremacy. His temporary successor was Kilmaine, at the moment commanding the sister or dependent Armée des Ardennes. Kilmaine, who, as he put it, had ' the misfortune to have been born in Ireland ', although brought up in France,[1] belonged to the family of Jennings of Kilmaine, County Mayo, and, when eleven years old, had been brought to France by his father, a Roman Catholic, who practised as a doctor at Tonnay-Charente. Entering the cavalry, he soon distinguished himself, especially in the 6th Hussars, or *Régiment Lauzun*, which served in America under Rochambeau [2] and which became the 5th Hussars in 1792. When the Revolution came he rose rapidly, distinguishing himself by his patriotism and by his bravery in the field, as for instance at Jemappes under Dumouriez,

---

[1] General Charles-Édouard-Jennings de Kilmaine (1751–99). Michaud, *Biog. univ.*, lxviii. 517–21 ; *Biog. des Cont.*, ii. 2222–3 ; Chuquet, *Hondschoote*, 57–9 ; Chassin, *Pacifications de l'Ouest*, iii. 151–2.

[2] Susane, *Cav. franç.*, ii. 266–9.

who nominated him as Colonel. This promotion was not sanctioned by the Minister, who, however, made him General of Brigade on the 8th March 1793. One Representative, Dubois-Dubais, fixed his eyes on him as the General who could deal with the insurrection in La Vendée, for which he had ' a plan, wise and philanthropic '. He proposed him for the command of the Armée des Côtes de la Rochelle, but, fortunately for Kilmaine, his being a ' foreigner ' prevented this appointment being made.[1] Opposed to Dumouriez when that General turned against the Convention, he was made General of Division on the 15th May 1793 and commanded the *avantgarde* of the ' Nord ' under Dampierre in the severe combats in May 1793.[2] When Dampierre was killed, Kilmaine, rejected for the command of the ' Nord ', as we have seen, retained,[3] or was given, the command of the ' Ardennes ', replacing Lamarche. The so-called Armée des Ardennes was then but a mere division, disseminated in various garrisons, which he organized in some manner in the Camp de Villy, near Carignan.[4] Custine at one time hoped to use this force to occupy the head of the forest of Mormal, but that idea had to be abandoned, as the enemy was too strong.[5] Kilmaine himself had a plan for making a diversion on Namur and Liége in combination with the Armée de la Moselle, but Custine disapproved of this. Still Kilmaine's confidence, and some fortunate incursions made by him on the territory of the enemy, pleased the Representatives and won for him the temporary succession to Custine. The old General Diettmann, proposed for the permanent post by the Representatives with the Armée du Rhin, was wise enough to decline, and Houchard, then in command of the ' Moselle ', was the next choice ; he, however, could not arrive for some time. On the 15th July Kilmaine came to Cambrai to receive instructions from Custine, who left for Paris on the 16th July 1793.[6]

[1] Chassin, *Pac. de l'Ouest*, iii. 151 ; Chuquet, *Hondschoote*, 59.
[2] Chuquet, *Valenciennes*, 58-9, 68-70.
[3] He may have been given both ' Nord ' and ' Ardennes ' on the 9th May, Custine then taking the ' Nord '.
[4] Chuquet, *Hondschoote*, 59 ; Jomini, *Rév.*, iii. 166.
[5] Wallon, *Rep.*, iv. 104 ; Chuquet, *Valenciennes*, 132-3.
[6] Chuquet, *Hondschoote*, 48, 59 ; Gay de Vernon, *Custine et Houchard*, 206, 213 ; Aulard, *Recueil*, v. 380, 443 ; Wallon, *Rep.*, iv. 123.

A little time after Kilmaine took command, on the 30th July 1793, the strength of the ' Nord ', much of it wasted in garrisons, &c., and stretching over a long line, was 129,891, but with it were two divisions of the ' Ardennes ', the first, 8,682, and the so-called ' division de Maubeuge ', 11,787, making it up to 150,360, excluding the garrison of Valenciennes, 9,490, which soon surrendered to the Allies. Its sister army, the ' Ardennes ', left by Kilmaine under Champollon,[1] nominally was 47,756 strong, but as two of its divisions were detached with the ' Nord ', it only had its second division, 27,287 men, almost all in garrisons. Taking both armies as one force, commanded by Kilmaine, the total strength was 177,647. So large a part of this was left in the garrisons and camps that Kilmaine's active force in the Camp de César was but some 35,177 men. As the *amalgame* had not yet been carried out, the army was still a mass of incongruous units, regular battalions mixed with volunteers of all sorts.[2]

Almost all the future Marshals with this army were in the Camp de César. Jourdan, the ex-private, was made General of Division on the 30th July 1793. Kellermann had reached that rank before the Revolution, but Jourdan was the first of the future Marshals to attain it under the new conditions. Captain Mortier's volunteer battalion, 1st Nord, was in the *flanqueurs de gauche.* According to one authority he was promoted Lt.-Colonel Adjutant-General on the 3rd September 1793, a step otherwise stated only to have been won on the 16th October 1793.[3] In the *avant-garde* were the 4th Hussars, to which Lieutenant Ney belonged, and the volunteer battalion of Lt.-Colonel Moreau, which had only 344 men present in July.[4] Colonel Macdonald was with his regular regiment at Lille, under Béru, who had succeeded the unfortunate La Marlière.[5] On the 26th August 1793 Macdonald was promoted General of Brigade, remaining with the left wing of the army. Lt.-Colonel Hoche was in Dunkirk.[6] The newly formed cavalry.

---

[1] Chuquet, *Hondschoote*, 59.
[2] Dupuis, *Nord*, i. 7–30, 39–40, 114–15, 143–4.
[3] Gavard, 12, says 3rd Sept. *Fastes*, i. 407, says 16th Oct., really the date of Wattignies, but attributing it to his conduct at Hondschoote, which of course is wrong. [4] Chuquet, *Hondschoote*, 62.
[5] Macdonald, *Souvenirs*, 28. [6] Cuneo d'Ornano, *Hoche*, i. 56–7.

regiment, the 21st Chasseurs, in which Murat was Lt.-Colonel, is not shown in the return of the army for July 1793, except it be in one of its transmutations, the 16th Chasseurs, at Hesdin. Murat, writing on the 30th January 1794, describes his regiment as just having been relieved from Pont-à-Marcq, which it had held for seven months,[1] so perhaps it came up into line at Pont-à-Marcq in August 1793.[2]

Lieutenant Ney had his tribulations. Lamarche, his General, was now dismissed. The vile Ronsin, who was one of the friends of Brune and who had been sent by the Minister to this army, denounced him as a drunkard who had lost the confidence of the men. The retreat from Famars told against him and now the simple old trooper was reported to be 'the most astute of conspirators' and, if any proof of his treason were wanted, had he not been, since the arrest of his friend Custine, more taciturn and gloomy than ever?[3] He was suspended, but escaped death and, retiring to Épinal, lived there on a small pension. In 1800 his former A.D.C., then high in favour with the First Consul, got Lamarche the command of a brigade of veterans. It was a kindly act, but the old General died soon afterwards.[4]

Michel Ney, 'plain Michel Ney', as he was to say some forty-six years later, was born on the 10th January 1769 at Sarrelouis in Lorraine. His father had been a soldier, and, serving in the Seven Years' War, had, it is said, distinguished himself at Rossbach, hardly a battle, one would have thought, giving much opportunity for a private to do so. The old soldier had become a cooper, and did not wish his son to enter a service where a man of plebeian birth could get little but a share of the knocks and hardships of war, so, as his own trade was not a lucrative one, he intended his son for something better and placed him in a college taught by Augustinians. Unfortunately for his plans, the old soldier liked to fight his own battles over again by his fireside, and his tales excited the imagination of his son, who was ready to study,

[1] Murat, *Lettres*, i. 12.
[2] For the strength and stations of the army see Dupuis, *Nord*, i. 7-30, and Carte 2.
[3] Wallon, *Rep.*, iv. 131; Chuquet, *Hondschoote*, 64.
[4] Michaud, *Biog. univ.*, lxx. 15.

but who, once work was over, used to drill his comrades. Imperious then, as ever, he commanded the boys he had trained, to the amusement of an onlooker, M. Valette, a notary, who offered to take the lad into his office. This suited the father, and Michel Ney, then aged thirteen, was soon perched at a desk. Some of his writing done now was preserved with care in times when he had distinguished himself in other ways. Dissatisfied with this work, and probably wishing for a more active life, he became clerk to the *Procureur du Roi*, but found the criminal law repulsive. He was now fifteen and longed to enter the army, in which his elder brother Pierre [1] already served. Still, obedient to his father, he went to work at some iron mines at Appenweier. Again he wanted to enter the army, but again yielded to his family, and accepted a post of superintendent at the forges of Saleck. Two years passed in work which would have brought him in time to a comfortable position, but the old craving for the army returned, and the very neighbourhood told against his father's wishes for, wherever Ney turned, to Trier, Bergen, or Zweibrücken, he found garrisons and looked with longing eyes at their manœuvres. Fate called and, resigning his post, he set off for Metz to enlist. On the way he visited his home, where prayers and threats awaited him, but, tearing himself from his family, he set off on foot. 'Later, when Fortune had crowned his courage, he returned to Sarrelouis. The artillery thundered, the troops were under arms. The inhabitants flocked to see their countryman, of whom they were so proud. Remembering this road which, thirteen years before, he had travelled on foot, the Marshal, moved, recounted his early labours to the officers who surrounded him.'[2] Ney had a few happy days in his life.

Arrived at Metz, Ney enlisted in February 1787 or December 1788 [3] in the Hussar regiment, *Colonel général*, organized in 1783 by Kellermann, who now had left it. It seems to have been composed, at least mainly, from men of the frontier provinces. It was dressed in blue, with scarlet pelisse.[4] In

[1] Killed in Italy in 1796 when an infantry officer.
[2] Ney, *Méms.*, i. 5.
[3] 1st Feb. 1787, Ney, *Méms.*, i. 5 ; 12th Feb. 1787, *Fastes*, i. 425 ; 6th Dec. 1788, Gavard, No. 13, and Bonnal, *Ney*, 2.   [4] Susane, *Cav. franç.*, ii. 238.

1790 it became the 5th Hussars, but when the regiment of 'Saxe' emigrated in 1792 Ney's corps became the 4th Hussars.[1] This change causes confusion, for writers often represent Ney as entering the 4th Hussars.

Ney had been attracted to the regiment by the fact that a fellow countryman was a lieutenant in it, but there was something very suitable in his choice of corps. In France the Hussar was taken as the type of the dashing soldier, equally daring and equally fortunate, it was said and sung, in the service of Mars and of Cupid ; and very hard to hold. What Ney was now he remained all his life, bold, hardy, daring, and impetuous. He made good his place in the ranks by his fine horsemanship and dexterity with his sword, but neither these, nor any protection from his compatriot gave him the promotion which he owed to his right hand, it is true, but to its good handwriting. All armies are overwhelmed with paper work, a man who could write was valuable, and Ney was soon at a desk in the office of the Quartermaster, becoming in time Corporal.

The fencing-master of another cavalry regiment [2] in garrison with that of Ney, a bully who was the terror of the place, had fought and wounded the holder of the same post in the *Colonel général*, and had insulted the regiment. The *sous-officiers* of *Colonel général* chose Ney, as the most skilful, to avenge the insult, and he accepted the duty gladly. Alas, just as the two crossed sabres, Ney found himself seized by the pig-tail by his colonel, who ordered him to prison. Duelling was punishable by death, and only the energetic remonstrances of his comrades saved Ney from trial, after a long imprisonment. This did not check the unruly Ney, and the duel was again begun, but this time with more secrecy. The obnoxious fencing-master was disabled for life by a cut on his wrist, but in after years lived on a pension granted him by his antagonist.

Steady promotion now came to Ney, as was certain to a man good alike on parade and in the office. On the 1st January 1791 he was made *fourrier*, say Quartermaster-Sergeant, to

---

[1] Susane, *Cav. franç.*, ii. 244, 262.
[2] *Royal-Picardie*, late *Vintimille*. Susane, *Cav. franç.*, ii. 123-9.

a troop, on 1st February 1792 *maréchal des logis*, or Sergeant, and on 1st April *maréchal des logis chef*, Sergeant-Major. After certain changes of quarters the regiment, which had been detached, was collected at Phalsbourg in May 1792.[1] On the 14th June Ney was promoted *adjudant*, that is, to be a *sous-officier*, a little above our Regimental Sergeant-Major.

In handing over the command of the Armée des Ardennes, Lamarche had written a certificate for his A.D.C., describing his conduct from the 19th October 1792 to this day. Ney, he said, had 'fulfilled the duties of his post with all the intelligence, intrepidity, activity, *courrage*' (spelling was not a strong point with many Generals[2]) 'that a holder of that post could possibly show on all the occasions, however perilous, on which he has been employed. He has shown discernment and tactics of an uncommon kind.' Then Ney joined as Lieutenant the company of Captain Boyé of his regiment, now the 4th Hussars, where he remained until we shall find him A.D.C. to General Colaud on the 20th December 1793.

Davout had left the Armée du Nord. The fall of Custine was but a consequence of the failure of Dumouriez to overthrow the Jacobins, and that party was triumphant. In the Ministry of War all the men swept out by Beurnonville had been recalled, and the department, in accordance with a wish of Brune's, had been given a formation ' toute civique ',[3] so that the Minister was surrounded by none but true ' patriots ', just as in England the Secretary of State for War is, or was, never considered safe unless he has a band of civilians round him to prevent the military element prevailing in military matters. At the same time the regiments and the staffs of the armies were swept of officers in any way ' suspect ', and it probably was from doubts of his ' patriotism ' that Davout was removed from the ' Nord '. His friendship with Dampierre, his approval of Custine, his open dislike of the Jacobins, made him ' suspect ', but his volley on Dumouriez made it difficult to attack him directly. In July 1793 his rank as

---

[1] Susane, *Cav. franç.*, ii. 244.   [2] Bonnal, *Ney*, i. 21-2.
[3] Chuquet, *Hondschoote*, 45.

Colonel Adjutant-General being confirmed,[1] he was sent to join Berthier in La Vendée, in the Armée des Côtes de la Rochelle, the command of which another 'suspect', Biron, had reached on his way from the Armée du Rhin and that of 'Italie' to the scaffold. After seeing some fighting there alongside of Berthier, and becoming General of Brigade, Davout was retransferred to the 'Nord' in August 1793. On his way back he found at Paris that it was intended that he should command the Camp de la Madeleine, under Lille, as General of Division. Either suspecting some snare, or dreading the responsibility, he pleaded that the feeling against the *ci-devant* Nobles serving in the army stood in the way of his acceptance, and, resigning both his new and his actual rank, he retired to his home, where, as I have already said, he was arrested and imprisoned, not serving again until October 1794, when he went as General of Brigade to the Armée de la Moselle, late 'Centre'. Thus he drops out of the history of the 'Nord'.

It is not very easy to place Brune at this period. In fact this Marshal is rather an historical puzzle, as he took his place as General, later on, apparently with very little training, yet did well on the battle-field, winning the praise of Masséna and of Bonaparte in the army of Italy, no friendly censors of newcomers. Guillaume-Marie-Anne Brune was born on the 13th May 1763 at Brives, where his father was *Avocat du Roi* at the Tribunal. He was well educated by the Benedictines of his native town and, when twenty years old, went to Paris to study for the Law. Literature, however, had greater attractions for him, and, having taken a long holiday with some friends in Poitou and the Angoumois, he published a small work anonymously, *Un Voyage pittoresque et sentimental dans plusieurs provinces occidentales de la France*. This was partly in prose and partly in verse, for Brune much fancied himself as a poet.

Relinquishing all ideas of the Law, he became 'prote', say manager and corrector of the press, for a publisher, and then founded a newspaper, *Le Journal général de la cour et de la ville*, better known later as *Le Petit Gautier*, which appeared without interruption from September 1789 to

---

[1] Gavard, 14, makes him General of Brigade then.

August 1792. Under Brune this was a 'patriot' paper and favoured revolutionary views.[1]

On the formation of the National Guard in July 1791 he joined that body. Living near Danton and Camille Desmoulins, he became friends with both and took part in all the *émeutes* in the Capital, in which his tall stature and his ardour made him conspicuous and won from Danton the title of his 'Patagonian'.[2]

I have given these details of this part of Brune's life, for it is so extraordinary. With the other Marshals, when we know the circumstances of their early life, whether they were officers, soldiers, or civilians, we can guess many details: there is nothing surprising in Marmont's being in love, in Ney fighting duels; but for a future Marshal, when twenty-eight years old, to be one of the prominent men in the Revolutionary party at Paris, a friend of Danton, soon to be a follower of Robespierre, preparing to lead the mob one day, bolting the next at the first sign of danger, and then ending by becoming a good General, a capable commander of an army, a Marshal of the Empire, all this is too wonderful and would make us wish to believe there were two Brunes, one who led a consistent and vile life till 1796; and then another, a brave soldier. However, now, although released from prison, he may have believed it would be safer to get out of Paris. He became Adjutant-Major of a volunteer battalion, the 2nd Seine-et-Oise, formed on the 22nd October 1791, which went that month to Péronne, and joined the Armée du Rhin,[3] where we first find him in June 1792. His departure from the Capital when his party was not in the ascendant is much like that of his friend, Danton.

On the 7th April 1793, during the confusion caused by the stroke of Dumouriez, the *Comité* charged him, then Colonel Adjutant-General, among others to rally and reorganize the army and to take measures to stop desertion, which, as I have said, had set in largely, and to get the deserters to retake their places in the ranks.[4] He must have returned to Paris, for he

---

[1] *Revue des questions historiques*, 1st July 1912, pp. 223-4.
[2] Barras, iv. 36.
[3] Déprez, *Vol. nat.*, 492; Susane, *Inf. franç.*, i. 343.
[4] Aulard, *Recueil*, iii. 134.

was Chief of the Staff to the small force sent out by the Convention to stop the march of General Wimpffen on the Capital, which was done at the battle of Vernon on the 12th July 1793. For this, presumably, he was made General of Brigade on the 18th August 1793.[1] Two days later the *Comité* sent him with Colonel Calandini, one of the foes of La Marlière, to the ' Nord ' and ' Ardennes ', to take knowledge of everything concerning the state and the supply of the armies and the fortresses, and to report to them.[2] He can hardly have been long on this mission, for in September he is said to have been given command of a division of the Armée des Pyrénées-Occidentales,[3] but this probably applies to the force, rather a ragged one, brought against Bordeaux in October 1793. He returned to the Capital and after some adventures was attached to the *Comité militaire* on the 25th December 1793. We shall find him in Paris in 1794.

But wherever Brune was in 1793, present or absent, his thoughts were with the Armée du Nord, on which his evil influence was brought to bear. He was one of the band of men who were hunting the Generals to their death, and he himself was powerful from his connexion with the formidable Danton. Custine crushed, this band fell on La Marlière, the General we have seen protecting Macdonald. La Marlière made a good fight, accusing one of his assailants of having made his groom a Sergeant-Major, and the band got alarmed for themselves. It was to Brune they appealed : ' Dear Patagonian ' (the term used by Danton for the tall patriot), ' no laziness, the ground is giving under us ; see Danton.' There was indeed need for help, as the Representatives on the spot suspended General Lavalette (not the future Postmaster-General of the Empire), one of the men attacking La Marlière, whose post he wanted, but no less a personage than Robespierre intervened, and La Marlière, bitterly regretted by Macdonald,[4] went to the scaffold.[5] This murder, part of the responsibility for which doubtless rests with Brune,

---

[1] Aulard, *Recueil*, i, note 1, p. 281 ; *Fastes*, ii. 251.
[2] Aulard, *Recueil*, vi. 42.   [3] Ibid., i, note 1, p. 281.
[4] Macdonald, *Souvenirs*, 28.
[5] ' Le tapis brûle.' Chuquet, *Valenciennes*, 204-33 ; Wallon, *Trib. rév.*, ii. 102-20 ; Hamel, *Robespierre*, iii. 74-6.

shows that even when the Representatives on the spot saw the falseness of accusations they were powerless against the demagogues at Paris. The pack of calumniators hunted any game : we have seen La Marlière defend Macdonald, we shall soon find two of his successful assailants falling on Macdonald himself.

Even when in Normandy, breathing out slaughter against the Vendéans, we find Brune writing to Vincent, the assistant to the Minister Bouchotte, the enemy of Custine, on the 24th July 1793, ' It is a great stroke to have dismissed Custine. Does policy require the retention of La Marlière ? I do not understand this policy which perpetuates the evil and defers the good. Are O'Moran and Koting retained ? Shall we long be governed by Nobles and foreigners ? '[1] To show the regular system of hunting down the Generals, take this letter from one of the pack, Ronsin, writing to the same Vincent that Brune had addressed, ' You have overthrown Custine. I have contributed a little to the fall of Biron. Carry out, in the case of Beauharnais and of all the Nobles, the proscription which is so necessary to the maintenance of the Republic.'[2] Now of these Generals, Beauharnais (the husband of Josephine), Biron, whom we have seen with the ' Nord '[3] and who in turn commanded the ' Rhin ', ' Italie ', and the Armée des Côtes de la Rochelle in La Vendée, Custine, and La Marlière, all except Koting, went to the scaffold. The strangest of accusations were made against the Generals, whose very dress might imply treason. Defrenne, who had declared ' une guerre éternelle aux états-majors perfides ', announced with horror, ' Custine a eu l'audace de se présenter ici avec un chapeau à la Dumouriez '.[4]

It was not only in the hateful work against the commanders that Brune had influence : ignorant as he must have been of military matters, the opinion of such a patriot was valued. On the 29th August 1793, when preparations for some such stroke as was made at Hondschoote were contemplated, Berthelmy, the Chief of the Staff to Houchard, wrote to Brune, giving his ideas as to what had best be done, as if

---

[1] Wallon, *La Rév. du 31 Mai*, i. 538.　　[2] Chassin, *La Vendée patriote*, ii. 544.
[3] Wallon, *Rep.*, iv. 116-17.　　[4] Ibid.

Brune had a part in the decision. He wrote in patriot style, saying that by 'talking to the soldiers, thundering against the officers, they will be awakened and excited, and the thing must go well '.[1] It is of course true that Berthelmy, as we shall soon see, had only a short experience of the army, but that he was right about Brune's influence seems shown by the fact that on the 8th September 1793 the Minister, Bouchotte, telling Belair that he was promoted General of Division for a certain important command, wrote, ' Brune thinks that it would be of advantage to establish a camp at Mont-Saint-Quentin '.[2] How Brune got this influence is as mysterious as most of his early career, but civilians are apt to prefer one another's opinions to that of soldiers, as when Panmure considered the General in command in the Crimea must be wrong in thinking badly of the Army Works Corps, as Paxton, safe in England, differed. Brune's connexion with Danton does not explain all his power.

According to General Susane, from whom it is dangerous to differ, the first battalion of the 36th Regiment, ' Anjou ', to which Bernadotte belonged, had come to the ' Nord ' from the ' Rhin ' by May 1793,[3] but I think this must be wrong and I follow Dupuis in making it arrive much later, on the 31st August 1793,[4] when Bernadotte, a Captain, came to join General of Division Jourdan, General of Brigade Macdonald, Lt.-Colonel Murat, Captain or Lt.-Colonel Mortier, and Lieutenant Ney, as well as Lt.-Colonels Moreau and Hoche, although I take it he could actually have met Jourdan, Mortier, and Ney only, and perhaps Murat. There is another difficulty about Bernadotte's regiment, for Susane makes its second battalion go from the ' Rhin ' to the ' Moselle ' and remain there till it became part of the ' Sambre-et-Meuse ',[5] whilst Dupuis shows both first and second battalions as with the ' Nord ' in Balland's division in October 1793 at Wattignies.[6]

Born on the 26th January 1763 at Pau, Jean-Baptiste-Jules Bernadotte was intended for the Law, but, against the wishes

---

[1] Dupuis, *Nord*, i. 395–6 ; Chuquet, *Hondschoote*, 183–4.
[2] Dupuis, *Nord*, i. 295.   [3] Susane, *Inf. franç.*, iii. 409.
[4] Dupuis, *Nord*, i. 275, 278, 281, 402. The 36th is not shown as with the ' Nord ' in July 1793. Dupuis, *Nord*, i. 36–40.
[5] Susane, *Inf. franç.*, iii. 410.   [6] Dupuis, *Nord*, ii. 100–1.

of his family, determined to go into the army, and only the ranks were open to him. Brandt describes himself as lodged at Pau in 1812 ' near the house for post-horses and the house where Bernadotte first saw the light and had passed his early years. The Postmaster assured me he had known him well in his youth and had often seen him in times of pressure do the work of supplementary postilion.[1] It seems the future King of Sweden played the horn to perfection and did not at all disdain tips. I think I still see this cradle of one of the most astonishing fortunes, if not the most enviable, of our age, this pretty, tiny house of two stories, with their three windows in front and their great *jalousies*, all looking so quiet and so modest.'[2] When only seventeen years old he enlisted in the regiment *Royal-Marine*,[3] then in Corsica, but afterwards at Briançon and Grenoble. On the 16th June 1785 he became Corporal, in 1785 *fourrier*, and in 1788 Sergeant-Major, a good education no doubt helping him. In 1790 the regiment was at Marseilles, where the mob attacked the Colonel, the Marquis d'Ambert,[4] and was about to hang him when Bernadotte, now become *adjudant*, collected some men and rescued him, telling the crowd that, if the Colonel were to blame, the Law would deal with him, but they would have to march over his own body and that of his men to touch him.[5] In March the regiment, being entangled in the revolutionary movement, was moved to the north-west, and Bernadotte, whose conduct had been remarked, was on the 6th November 1791 appointed Lieutenant in the 36th Regiment, ' Anjou ', which had been abandoned by a great number of its officers. His new regiment in August 1792 joined the Armée du Rhin.

To return to Kilmaine, this General did one good thing during his temporary rule. His direct command and main force, some 35,000 strong, occupied the Camp de Paillencourt or de César, resting on the two fortresses, Bouchain and Cambrai :[6] its lines had been entrenched. The capture of

[1] ' Postillon auxiliaire.' [2] Brandt, *Souvenirs*, 213.
[3] For ' Royal-Marine ' see Susane, *Inf. franç.*, iv. 286–94.
[4] Colonel Agricole-Marie de Merle, Marquis d'Ambert.
[5] *Fastes*, i. 338.
[6] For description of the camp see Dupuis, *Nord*, i. 143–6, and Carte 2 ; Chuquet, *Hondschoote*, 79–80 ; Jomini, *Rév.*, iv, note 1, p. 29 ; Gay de Vernon, *Custine et Houchard*, 177–8.

Valenciennes made an attack by the Allies probable, and Kilmaine had thoughts of retiring southwards to Honnecourt and Le Catelet, covering Paris. At 7 a.m. on the morning of the 7th August 1793 he learnt that the enemy was advancing on his front and right. Coburg had formed a plan of crushing the French Army. Whilst demonstrations were to be made on the north of the camp, two columns from Hérin, together 16,000 strong, the most northerly under Clairfayt, and the other on its left under Colloredo, were to move against the camp north of Cambrai and to cross the Escaut (or Scheldt). To the left of these the Duke of York with some 25,000 English, Hanoverians, Hessians, and Austrians was to march from Villers-en-Cauchie and to make for Crèvecœur, the extreme southern point of the camp, circling past its front and aiming at the right and rear of the French. The first two columns reached the Escaut, but could not cross that day. The Duke of York got over the Escaut at Masnières and Crèvecœur, but he had been delayed by the intense heat and by the appearance of the French cavalry, who, however, did little,[1] so that, having done twelve miles only, he halted on the left bank of the Escaut and right in rear of the Camp de César.

Jomini praises this plan of Coburg's most highly, as honouring him or the officer who formed it, although the execution was not as good as the conception of it.[2] There, indeed, was the weak point, for York's column, parading round the position, was sure to give the French the earliest possible notice of what was in store for them. York's column should have had the twenty-four hours' start which Clairfayt recommended to Coburg,[3] and which might have been partly attained by a night march.[4] Langeron also is probably right in saying that the formation of the columns was wrong, and that more cavalry and less infantry would have been useful to York, the other columns having little need of horse.[5] As it was, Kilmaine at once saw his danger and assembled a council, where the Representative, Delbrel, advised such a stroke as we shall find Souham making successfully at the Duke of York

---

[1] Desbrière, *La Cav. pendant la Rév.: La crise*, 373-4.
[2] Jomini, *Rév.*, iv. 29.   [3] Langeron, 19.
[4] Jomini, *Rév.*, iv. 33; Dupuis, *Nord*, i. 165.   [5] Langeron, 19.

a little later, in September 1793. Leaving only posts to delay the other columns, the mass of the army was to be thrown on York and, when he was crushed, then the army might return northwards to deal with Clairfayt and Colloredo. York's column now, however, was too strong to be quickly crushed, and Kilmaine replied with truth that his army was not capable of such a manœuvre and that he had too little cavalry.[1] Kilmaine decided on retreat and adopted the advice of Gay de Vernon, not to draw back southwards, covering Paris directly, but to move westwards behind the Scarpe river, between Douai and Arras, placing the army on the flank of the Allies' advance and having Lille behind it.[2]

That night the army began to retire, the *flanqueurs de gauche* and the *avant-garde* (where Captain Mortier and Lt.-Colonel Moreau served, and Lieutenant Ney also, if he were with his regiment),[3] holding the connexion with Douai. Consequently when the Allies advanced on the 8th August 1793 their blow was dealt in the air; the French had gone and York, when he had worked round to the west, found even the strongly fortified heights of Bourlon abandoned. The other columns soon halted, but York pressed on in pursuit of the French to Marquion, on the road to Arras. The bridge over the Agache was broken and the village of Marquion had been set on fire by the French to prevent the Allies crossing. York himself galloped through the flames, accompanied only by an orderly and by Langeron. Coming on a French line of cavalry, and not knowing that his own squadrons had been stopped by the fire, he believed they were Hanoverians, whom they resembled in dress. Calling out, ' Here are my Hanoverians ', he went up to within a few paces of them, when Langeron, crying out that they were French, caught hold of his bridle and brought him back to Marquion.[4] If the French had captured him, would they have guillotined him, as Langeron assumes they would have done?

The Duke would have pressed the pursuit, but it was slow and difficult work to get his cavalry over the Agache through

---

[1] Chuquet, *Hondschoote*, 82–3.
[2] Ibid., 83; Gay de Vernon, *Custine et Houchard*, 221–2.
[3] Compare Dupuis, *Nord*, i. 7–8 and 158.   [4] Langeron, note 1, p. 20.

the burning Marquion and, though he sent part of his horse south to pass by Sains-les-Marquion, the passage there was narrow and the marshy ground prevented them coming up except by detachments. The French, therefore, would have got off without any fighting, had not two of their battalions, coming south by mistake, reached Marquion as York's cavalry got there. These troops could not cross, and York took the gun which they had with them, but Kilmaine brought up a mass of horse, when a cavalry affair ensued with more noise than loss and his superior force got the battalions off. Indeed the French only lost 3 guns and 150 prisoners. Unsupported by the other columns, except by eight squadrons which joined him, and having no artillery up to face that of the French,[1] the Duke went back to Bourlon, where he had a sharp dispute with Hohenlohe, 'whom he blamed rightly for the small success of the day'.[2] Indeed, Hohenlohe was to have supported either Clairfayt or York, according to circumstances,[3] and, as we have seen, Clairfayt had needed no help.

The affair at Marquion had been more important than it seemed. While Kilmaine had shown a bold front to York, there was confusion behind him. The 'Nord' for long was strangely liable to panic and now, when the army was marching safely to Arras, baggage in front, suddenly an alarm came from the front, the part farthest from the enemy, and 'sauve qui peut' was the cry; battalions disbanded and fled, a mere mob, to Arras, as if the foe had been at their heels; the artillery took refuge beyond Arras and was separated from the army for nearly twelve hours. If, says M. Chuquet, Coburg, Hohenlohe, and York had known what was behind the cavalry screen of Kilmaine![4] But York apparently did know, or at least suspect the state of affairs,[5] and hence probably his reproaches to Hohenlohe. Well might Kilmaine have refused to try with such troops the bold stroke suggested by Delbrel. He had done well, and now he placed his army

---

[1] Gay de Vernon, *Custine et Houchard*, 225. Kilmaine had 'artillerie légère', probably horse artillery, Lahure, 323; but Lahure, 324, gives the English an equal number of light guns.
[2] Langeron, 20. [3] Dupuis, *Nord*, 149-50.
[4] Chuquet, *Hondschoote*, 87; Dupuis, *Nord*, i. 163-4.
[5] Langeron, 20.

with its right at Arras and its left at Douai, head-quarters at Gavrelle, the position being often called the 'Camp de Gavrelle'.[1] The Camp de Biache, part of the position, was close to the Scarpe, south-east of Gavrelle. The *avant-garde* under Hédouville was on the right or east of the Scarpe, covering the army, Ney's regiment being at Monchy-le-Preux.

Kilmaine's choice of his new position may have been influenced by the fact that it could be occupied without fighting such a severe engagement as the position of York's column would have necessitated had the retirement been southwards; but the ease with which the transfer had been made was due to him. An excellent officer of cavalry, as Napoleon was to remark,[2] he had made good use of that arm, which at the time, bad as it might be, was unaltered in its organization and probably in better shape than the infantry, which had not yet been 'amalgamated'. Calvert, who is strangely brief in his record here, makes no mention of the delay in the march of the Duke of York's column on the 7th August, caused by the threatening attitude of the French cavalry,[3] but it seems that Kilmaine, forming a division of 3,000 horse (not, I think including Ney's regiment[4]) opposed them 'with much skill and success, to the enemy's columns, retarding their march, forcing their leading regiments to deploy, and feigning to attack when he only thought of defending himself and of gaining time',[5] that time being so valuable. Then, on the 8th August, he himself covered with his cavalry the retiring army, which probably would have become a screaming mob had the enemy got at it, alarmed as the infantry were by the cavalry of the Allies. Kilmaine's success with his own cavalry was the more creditable as that arm was not in a good state, indeed the new Chief of the Staff described it as 'nulle'.[6]

---

[1] Dupuis, *Nord*, i. 143–71, and Carte 2; Chuquet, *Hondschoote*, 79–91; Jomini, *Rév.*, iv. 28–35, and Atlas, ix; Gay de Vernon, *Custine et Houchard*, 220–6; Lahure, 52–5, 322–5; Langeron, 18–20; Calvert, 97–8.

[2] *Corr. Nap.*, xxix. 149.   [3] Calvert, 97–8.

[4] Ney's regiment, 4th Hussars, was with the cavalry of the *avant-garde*, sent on to Monchy-Boiry, to the west of Arras, apparently leading the army; I presume Kilmaine used Antoine's cavalry, for which see Desbrière, *La Cav. pendant la Rév.: La crise*, 371; Dupuis, i. 8, 156, and Carte 2.

[5] Gay de Vernon, *Custine et Houchard*, 222–3.

[6] Chuquet, *Hondschoote*, 62, 109–10; Desbrière, *La Cav. pendant la Rév.: La crise*, 364–5.

This deserves attention, as showing how the choice of commanders was made at this period. To Napoleon Kilmaine, after little if any further experience of war, was ' très propre à commander des corps d'observation détachés ', calm, taking in a situation at a glance, fit for ' toutes les commissions délicates qui exigent du discernement, de l'esprit, et une tête saine '.[1] To Marmont he was ' homme de tête, froid, calculateur, et brave ; cet officier était capable de combiner ses mouvements et d'agir par lui-même '.[2] Just the man, one would have imagined, for the command of the ' Nord ' at this moment. His ideas seemed patriotic enough ; he had approved the changes in the Generals made by the Minister, saying, ' Better to have no one than to have bad citizens. We want men who have no other alternative than the Republic or death ' ;[3] much the same formula as the famous, ' What have you done that you would be hung for if the Bourbons returned ? ' But he was Irish, and how could revolutionary ideas really enter an Irish head ? He himself, commanding temporarily, was anxious to go ; he offered to take again the command of the ' Ardennes ', from which he had come, or to serve under Barthel at Cassel. If sent against Ostend, that port would no longer exist ; wherever sent, he would do his duty. Yet the Representatives distrusted him, believing him to be a follower of Dumouriez, and, as in the case of Macdonald, his very calm seemed indifference.

M. Chuquet styles Kilmaine ' présomptueux, infatué de ses mérites ',[4] where a more lenient judge might see only the swagger natural to a very successful cavalry officer—and to an Irishman. Taking command with a light heart, approving the raid that the Minister had made on the Generals, he soon became depressed as his difficulties became more apparent to him. He demanded reinforcements, but the troops he had were slack. Disheartened by their defeats and by the changes in their commanders, disgusted at the loss of Custine, the men had little energy, and the white-coated line and the blue-coated volunteers still stood apart from one another. Kilmaine also found, as his successor, Houchard, was to find, the need for

---

[1] *Corr. Nap.*, xxix. 149.
[2] Marmont, i. 216–17.
[3] Chuquet, *Hondschoote*, 77.
[4] Ibid., 58.

good Generals. He foresaw the danger to the army if Valenciennes fell and he declared that the burden of command was too heavy for him.[1] On the 28th July 1793 Valenciennes surrendered to the Duke of York, the Allies, with the most culpable carelessness, only stipulating that its garrison, some 9,490 strong, should not serve against their armies during the war until exchanged, and not giving a thought to the insurrection in La Vendée and in the south, where these troops could be employed.[2]

The *Comité* had already suspended Kilmaine on the 4th August 1793, preferring the brave, stupid Houchard. The temporary command was to have been handed over to Barthel, then commanding a division at Cassel, but that General in all probability was not anxious to fill such a dangerous post, and an attack by the enemy delayed him, so that he did not reach head-quarters until after Houchard. He returned to Cassel without giving the letter of suspension to Kilmaine, who only knew of his removal on the 14th August and was much puzzled as to the successor to whom he was to hand over the army.[3] The *Comité* had based its decision on the allegation that he had family relations with the English and that, before Valenciennes had surrendered, he had given the Minister the greatest hopes of the success of the defence, whilst after its fall he had declared the garrison to have been too small. Still, his own wish not to command justified his removal and he went off to Passy, declaring that he remained inviolably attached to the Republic, disclaiming all ambition, but saying, ' You have need of a man like me to command your cavalry '. This was true enough, and Houchard wanted to use his knowledge of the country and to give him the command of the *avant-garde*,[4] but he had to leave and on the 29th December 1793 he was arrested. Robespierre denounced him for belonging to the English faction, his withdrawal from

---

[1] Chuquet, *Hondschoote*, 60–2 ; Gay de Vernon, *Custine et Houchard*, 213.

[2] Chuquet, *Valenciennes*, 256–345 ; Jomini, *Rév.*, iii. 175–81 ; Foucart et Finot, *Déf. nat.*, i. 460–577 ; Calvert, 81–95 ; Musset-Pathay, *Sièges*, 239–53, and Plate III. For strength of garrison see Dupuis, *Nord*, i. 20–1.

[3] Aulard, *Recueil*, v. 474 ; Chuquet, *Hondschoote*, 91–3. For Barthel see Dupuis, *Nord*, i, note 1, p. 63.

[4] Dupuis, *Nord*, i. 189–90 ; Wallon, *Rep.*, iv. 133.

the Camp de César without fighting was treated as a crime, and Saint-Just asked, ' Who can answer for an Englishman after Kilmaine, overwhelmed with favours amongst us ? '[1] He was fortunate to escape being tried, but, although released after Thermidor, it was not till 1795 that he was restored to the army. We shall find him in Italy, valued by Bonaparte. He was a possible Marshal, but he died in 1799.

Houchard, then commanding the Armée de la Moselle, succeeded Kilmaine with the ' Nord '. The Revolution had found him a Captain of Dragoons, his face all scarred and his body maimed by the wounds received on the many fields on which his stern face had looked. Tall, brave, a proved ' patriot ', the friend and A.D.C. of Custine on the Rhine, the ' Balafré ' had been rapidly raised to command, though Custine, a man of some insight, incurred his anger by prophesying that the command of an army would be an evil present to him. However, it was a time for surprises, as one incident will show. At Houchard's marriage in 1780 two of his friends, Landremont and Schauenbourg, were present. Little could they have thought that in 1793 all three would be Commanders-in-Chief of French armies and that all three would be removed from their commands almost on the same day.[2]

Already, however, Houchard knew what it meant to be given the command of an army of the Republic, and when, on his way from the Rhine, he stopped a few minutes at Sarrebourg to see his family, his efforts to hide his forecast of the future were betrayed by his melancholy, and to a friend he acknowledged that he despaired of escaping the fate he saw threatening him.[3]

On the 9th August 1793 Houchard arrived at Vitry. Coming fresh on the scene to take up his command in the presence of the enemy, he required all possible local information. Next morning he woke up without any staff. They had all been arrested, while the whole of the order and letter-books of his head-quarters' office had been sealed up by the Representa-

---

[1] Chuquet, *Hondschoote*, 90–4 ; Aulard, *Recueil*, v. 474.
[2] Houchard (' Nord '), removed 24th Sept. 1793 ; Schauenbourg (' Moselle ') and Landremont (' Rhin '), both removed 29th Sept. 1793. Chuquet, *Hondschoote*, note 1, p. 99.
[3] Gay de Vernon, *Custine et Houchard*, note 2, p. 249.

tives. Naturally he sent at once to the Representative, Billaud-Varennes, to request that he might at least have the books, but Billaud refused. He had found the books in a kitchen and intended to send them to Paris, to show how carelessly the work of the army was managed.[1] The explanation was easy. The staff had just arrived at Vitry and, finding that the only room in the house allotted to them that was large enough for their work was a kitchen, they had established themselves there. Two sentries guarded the doors and two officers slept inside. This had shocked the Representative, who had seized the books and had arrested General Desbrulys, Chief of the Staff, and twenty-two of his assistants. At the same time he sent the *gendarmerie* to arrest General O'Moran, who commanded at Mont-Cassel, on a charge of treachery. O'Moran was guillotined for refusing to drink the health of Marat, it was said, but more probably for writing to Custine that the presence of two Representatives, Carnot and Duquesnoy, prevented the severity necessary to re-establish discipline.[2] What became of the staff is not clear. Desbrulys [3] saved his life, to blow out his own brains in 1809 rather than surrender the island of Réunion to the English. The office books reached Paris and, though the *Comité de salut public* had the good sense to return them at once, well might Houchard ask if there were any more cruel position than his?

Even before his arrival Houchard recognized the deadly atmosphere into which he was coming, where every General, every officer, was suspected. 'My life is poisoned,' wrote the honest old soldier to the Minister, 'and since I have been accused, calumniated with impunity, whilst all my being, all my efforts, are employed for the good of the Republic, I cannot any longer be fit to lead an army: everywhere calumny has preceded me, everywhere I have suffered the last agony, since I have found nothing but distrust in all the persons who do not know me.' Colaud, one of the future commanders of Ney in 1796, wrote in the same strain when he found there

[1] Gay de Vernon, *Custine et Houchard*, 229–31 ; Chuquet, *Hondschoote*, 107–8.
[2] For O'Moran see Alger, *Englishmen in the French Rev.*, 177–8 ; Chuquet, *Hondschoote*, 73–4 ; Wallon, *Trib. rév.*, ii. 462–3 ; Thiébault, i. 351–2.
[3] General Baron Desbrulys (Nicolas-Ernault de Rignac) (1757–1809) *Fastes*, iv. 260–1 ; Chuquet, *Hondschoote*, note 3, p. 66.

were four denunciations against him, asking why he was left in command of troops (he had that of the *flanqueurs de gauche*) if he were ' suspect ' ? He wanted to be sent back to his regiment, there he could serve without fear: the very privates were saying they would not be Generals: ' Ils ont, ma foi, bien raison . . .' Well might Houchard wish to be replaced in command as soon as possible ; it would be unjust to require him to serve as General.[1] Such a request the patriots were always loath to comply with, storing it up for use as a charge in the future : the Republic played with its Generals as a cat with mice, and Houchard was to find that something worse was in store for him than what he thought was his ' dernier supplice ', one charge that the brave old man, all scarred with wounds, never dreamt could be made against him.

For his Chief of the Staff, to replace Desbrulys, Houchard insisted on having his late A.D.C., Berthelmy. Although the Minister suspected that officer, Houchard got him. Berthelmy was one of the better specimens of the men thrown up by the Revolution. A sub-engineer of the ' *Ponts et chaussées* ' at Tulle, he had risen through the volunteers and had won the favour of Custine, against whom, however, he had turned before that General left the Rhine. Now he was made General of Brigade and *chef d'état-major* to the ' Nord '. Scenting the danger like Houchard, he declared that he was too young and had not the necessary knowledge, and said he could not be forced to become a General. ' Humainement parlant,' replied the Minister, ' on ne peut pas vous forcer à être général, mais il faudra bien que vous acceptiez.'[2] Disgraced with Houchard and imprisoned till Thermidor, he escaped death through the influence of Brune and his group[3] and, after serving again, returned to his old profession and even became a member of the *Cinq-Cents*, dying in his bed in 1841.[4] Although Houchard liked and trusted him, one quite understands the indignation

---

[1] Dupuis, *Nord*, i. 59–65.
[2] Chuquet, *Hondschoote*, 106. Berthelmy took up his duties on the 14th Aug., Thuring having acted after the arrest of Desbrulys. Dupuis, *Nord*, note 1, p. 190.
[3] Chuquet, *Hondschoote*, 336–8.
[4] General Étienne-Ambroise Berthelmy or Berthelemy (1764–1841). Ibid., 104–7, 336–8 : Dupuis, *Nord*, note 1, p. 189.

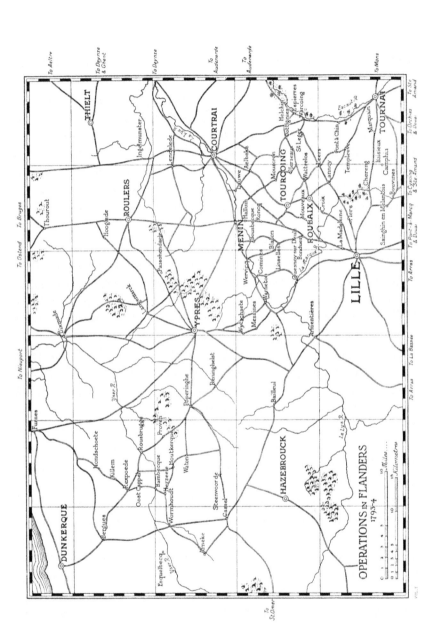

of the old trooper when Berthelmy became, as we shall find him, too insistent as to what should be done after Hondschoote : ' You are too young to teach me war.' [1]

Carnot, who was now on the *Comité de salut public*, influencing the movements of armies, and whose strategy was always to operate on the flank of the enemy, had set his heart on an advance by the coast on Ostend. Houchard agreed, and it was determined that General Barthel, who was commanding at Cassel, should move by the coast on Ostend with 12,000 men. To cover this movement Jourdan, who with a flying column of 7,000 men was watching the frontier from Douai to Lille, was to march to Lille with his own men and 3,000 under Romanet. At Lille he was to join Béru, under whom Macdonald served, and he was to throw the Dutch back from Menin. The whole operation was intended to be a mere raid, for, Ostend burnt, both columns were to draw back. Still, the choice of Jourdan was a compliment to him ; Houchard said his intelligence and bravery were known and he would certainly serve the Republic with the same zeal as he had shown during the course of the war.[2] Much to the astonishment of the Generals, as Jourdan marched from the camp of Gavrelle [3] he found that two columns of red coats were moving alongside of him. This was the army of the Duke of York, which came almost in sight of the French camps.

How Jourdan stumbled on the English is explained as follows. France really was at the mercy of the Allies, who had some 118,000 men [4] ready to be thrown into the gap made in the line of fortresses by the capture of Condé and Valenciennes. Carnot, as we have seen, was thinking of his flank, not of his centre. The troops were dispirited, and Houchard was only a brave Dragoon leader. The salvation of France came from the Allies, who chose this moment to split their forces. Dumouriez had warned them that they would be like hungry robbers who, having plundered a coach, then quarrelled about the spoils. The English wished to hold Dunkirk as a useful base for their operations, and the Duke

---

[1] Chuquet, *Hondschoote*, 224. [2] Ibid., 135-6 ; Dupuis, *Nord*, i. 193-203.
[3] Between Arras and Douai.
[4] Dupuis, *Nord*, i. 30-5 ; Jomini, *Rév.*, iv. 36.

of York determined to march to besiege that town with a mixed force of some 37,000 English, Hanoverians, Hessians, and Austrians. Then the Prussians of Knobelsdorf, 8,000 strong, with whom Colonel Blücher served, left Coburg for Luxembourg and Trier to join their King, who with the Austrians under Wurmser was opposed to the armies of the ' Moselle ' and ' Rhin '. Beaulieu with 3,000 Dutch and 5,000 Austrians joined Coburg, but, though this nominally compensated for the departure of the Prussians, the increased proportion of the Dutch became a danger, as that nation was getting discontented with the share, or no share, of the spoils likely to fall to it and was very lukewarm in the war. The main body of the Dutch, under the Prince of Orange, was placed at Menin, to mask Lille and the Camp de la Madeleine and to link the Duke of York with Coburg, who remained to besiege Le Quesnoy (which surrendered on the 10th September 1793). Had the Allies but remained united, the march of Jourdan northwards would have enabled them to make short work of Houchard.

At Pont-à-Marcq Jourdan probably passed the regiment in which Lt.-Colonel Murat served, but already at Mons-en-Pévèle [1] he had picked up the brigade of no less a man than General Alexandre Dumas,[2] the father of the great Alexander of glorious memory. We have already met that officer before Dumouriez went over, and we shall come across him several times, but I mention him here, for there is something pleasant in imagining him, fit as he was to be one of the heroes of his son's romances, marching alongside of the sober, matter-of-fact Jourdan. Many years afterwards the son of Dumas came to Jourdan to claim his protection, when the worthy old Marshal failed to anticipate any future greatness in the lad,[3] but who could have foreseen the great, the glorious, the omniscient Dumas ? With Jourdan also were the 4th Hussars, to which Lieutenant Ney belonged.[4]

On the 17th August 1793 Jourdan and Béru had planned a strong reconnaissance from Lille on Roubaix, to the northeast, but on the 18th Jourdan heard that the posts to the

---

[1] South-west of Orchies. [2] Gay de Vernon, *Custine et Houchard*, 238.
[3] Maurel, *Les Trois Dumas*, 77. [4] Dupuis, *Nord*, i. 201.

north had been attacked by the enemy. The Prince of Orange, with some 10,000 men, was holding Menin and the line of posts to the south of that place, Wervicq, Halluin, Roncq, Mouscron, Wattrelos, and Lannoy. Partly to cover the march of the Duke, partly to take advantage of the presence of the Duke's troops to give himself room, the Prince had ordered an advance, he himself moving from Menin on Linselles, and another column on Blaton, to the north-west of Linselles ; and both these places were taken from the French, whilst the Duke of York continued his march in rear of this movement by Roncq on Menin. Hearing of this, Jourdan and Béru determined to recapture the two posts they had lost. This was done, and one column retook Linselles, whilst the brigade of Macdonald from Quesnoy[1] surprised the garrison of Blaton and captured seven guns. 'The interior of the redoubts,' says Dellard, who came up after the action, 'which had just been taken, afforded a spectacle of fearful carnage.'[2]

When the Dutch fell back from Linselles the Prince of Orange asked for reinforcements from the Duke of York, and the Duke sent up three battalions of the Guards[3] under Lake, who was to do so much and so well in India in later years. Lake tried to rally the Dutch under cover of the Guards, but they had had enough and Lake, a gallant leader, always ready for the offensive, determined to attack the French with his own men alone, some 1,122. The French held a large and strong redoubt and the road was defended by other works, while woods and ditches covered the flanks of the position. The intrepidity of the troops, says Calvert, made up for the paucity of their numbers, and part of the French had dispersed to plunder.

Advancing under a heavy fire of case the Guards, after several volleys, threw themselves on the works and, taking the redoubt, chased the French through the village and, when they tried to stand, again broke them. Béru's men fled south to Bondues ; ' It was not a retreat but a rout ', wrote Jourdan, who covered the fugitives with a battalion and even attempted

---

[1] Quesnoy-sur-Deule.   [2] Dellard, 17–18 ; Jomini, *Rév.*, Atlas, viii.
[3] One battalion of the 1st and another of the 3rd Guards, and a battalion of the Coldstream Guards.

later a fresh attack, but the Guards had been supported and held the place, taking seven guns.

Macdonald, to the left at Blaton, hearing of this, evacuated that post and fell back for Quesnoy. Béru was in despair, but next day the Duke, in order to continue his march on Dunkirk, drew off his men with bands playing and, though the French retired on Lille, their patrols still held Linselles and Wervicq. Macdonald, by telling General Béru that his own successes at Blaton made up for the defeat at Linselles and that the disappearance of the enemy made the operations seem successful, cheered up his commander, and the columns re-entered Lille in triumph. Macdonald got a large part of the credit, which drew down jealousy on him, although he professes to have enjoyed his favour discreetly.[1]

Then followed two promotions which I have already mentioned. Jourdan, relieved on the 26th August 1793 in command of his division by Leclaire, was sent to replace Barthel, thought to be inefficient, in charge of Cassel and Dunkirk.[2] Houchard also nominated Macdonald and Dupont for Generals of Brigade on the 26th August 1793 and, the Representatives agreeing, wrote to the *Comité* to get these promotions confirmed. Of Macdonald they said, ' He has military talents and has given proofs of the self-possession and courage which characterize good Generals in the affair of the 18th at Blaton, where we had a complete success '. Of Dupont they praised not only the talents but also the ' patriotisme raisonné ' which did not seem equivocal, a praise not given to Macdonald. Houchard thought most highly of this Dupont[3] and later proposed him for the important command of Maubeuge. ' He is the only one capable of making dispositions on a large scale and of giving vigour to the corps of Maubeuge. He will leave a great gap in the Camp de la Madeleine, and I shall be in the same embarrassment to

---

[1] Dupuis, *Nord*, 203–19; Chuquet, *Hondschoote*, 137–8; Jomini, *Rév.*, iv. 42–3; Macdonald, *Souvenirs*, 29; Calvert, 106–7. For plan see Carte 3 in Dupuis, *Nord*, i, and Jomini, *Rév.*, Atlas, viii.

[2] Dupuis, *Nord*, i. 312–13, 368–9.

[3] General Comte Pierre Dupont de l'Étang. His brother, General Pierre-Antoine Dupont-Chaumont, had been promoted on the 15th May 1793. See *Fastes*, iii. 195–200.

replace him.'[1] In fact every one thought most highly of Dupont till Baylen.

On the 13th September the Representatives were complaining that the Minister had not 'deigned' to confirm the appointments of Macdonald and Dupont; a protégé of the Minister, an assistant staff officer, a clerk, would already have had his commission, they declared.[2] On the 3rd September 1793, that is, just before Hondschoote, Captain Mortier, promoted Lt.-Colonel Adjutant-General, went on the staff, but to what division is not stated.[3]

It was now that Jourdan first met a man who was to have some influence on his fortunes, Ernouf, who, entering the volunteers as a Lieutenant in 1791, had become Lt.-Colonel Adjutant-General in this army on the 30th July 1793. In giving Jourdan his instructions on the 26th August, Houchard told him he would have under his orders Ernouf, 'whose talents and patriotism are valuable'.[4] Indeed, so well did Jourdan think of him that he took him as Chief of his Staff when he himself succeeded Houchard, leaving with him in disgrace in January 1794, after Wattignies. We shall find Ernouf again as Chief of the Staff to Jourdan when that General commanded the Armée de la Moselle and that of the Sambre-et-Meuse in 1794-6, and going with his commander to the Armée de Mayence and the Armée du Danube in 1798-9. His career under the Empire was crushed by his surrender of Guadeloupe, of which he was governor, to the English in 1810.[5] His action in 1799 when left in command for a moment by Jourdan did that commander much harm. However, he must have some of the credit for Wattignies and Fleurus and for the organization of the 'Sambre-et-Meuse' in 1794-6.[6] Napoleon described him as a 'fameux jacobin'.[7]

---

[1] Dupuis, *Nord*, i. 312-13, 410; ii. 287. [2] Ibid., ii. 233.
[3] I follow Gavard, but other authorities make the promotion after Wattignies.
[4] Dupuis, *Nord*, i. 369. [5] *Corr. Nap.*, xxiii, No. 18510.
[6] General Baron Jean-Augustin Ernouf (1753-1827). Foucart et Finot, *Déf. nat.*, ii. 267-8; Dupuis, *Nord*, i, note 1, p. 232; *Fastes*, v. 282-3.
[7] *Corr. Nap.*, xxxi. 86.

XII

L'ARMÉE DU NORD (*continued*), 1793

The Duke of York besieges Dunkirk. Houchard complains of his officers. The difficulties of General Leclaire, one of Jourdan's brigadiers. Jourdan communicates with Dunkirk, but is brought back to Cassel. Houchard throws Macdonald, Dupont, and Alexander Dumas on the Dutch, but they are beaten off. Houchard proposes to attack the Duke of York. His strategy. Interference of the Representatives and of the Minister. Houchard's grimace. The regiment of Captain Bernadotte surprised. Houchard's plans. Hedging directions of the *Comité*. The position of the Duke of York's force in front of Dunkirk. Hoche in Dunkirk. The six columns with which Houchard attacks the Duke of York. The first day's fighting. Jourdan takes Rexpoede. Freytag, with the covering army, attacks him, but is beaten and captured. Escape of Prince Adolphus of Cambridge. Walmoden falls on Jourdan and routs the division, which retires and releases Freytag. Extraordinary position of the French columns. Houchard again advances. Walmoden fights at Hondschoote to cover retreat of the Duke of York, but is beaten. The *sans-culottes* capture a store of trousers. Houchard will not pursue. The missing column of Dumesny. Hostile attitude of the Representatives towards Houchard. Hoche in Dunkirk is praised, promoted Colonel, arrested, and then made General of Brigade. The Dutch defeated at Menin and Wervicq. Victory turned to disaster. Menin retaken by Beaulieu. Failure of the right of the 'Nord' to relieve Le Quesnoy. Route of Declaye's column. Arrest of Houchard, who is guillotined. His character cleared by Bonaparte.

THESE flank affairs had no effect on the main operations, for the Duke of York marched on to besiege Dunkirk. His left or flanking column had driven the French from Oost Cappel on the 21st August and by the 22nd he had cleared the French from the left bank of the Yser, the fighting being remarkable only from the bad behaviour of the French troops, who had fled in confusion, losing eleven guns.[1] Houchard took all this to heart and wrote to the Minister, throwing the blame on the officers : ' The soldiers are good, but the cowardice

---

[1] Dupuis, *Nord*, i. 227-34, and Carte 4 ; Chuquet, *Hondschoote*, 140-4 ; Marmottan, 75-6.

and crass ignorance of the officers make them learn cowardice, and to fly before the enemy is nothing to them ', the Representatives adding that, whilst the officers were always in the town instead of on the alert, those nominated by the Ministers often did not join for more than two months. The Minister, Bouchotte, held firm, however, to his principles, that what was wanted was true *sans-culottes*, not ' ces prétendus hommes à talents '.[1] He would not give Houchard the Adjutant-General Jarry, who, like Berthier, had been thought so well of in the times when Rochambeau commanded the ' Nord ', and who was reserved to train the English Staff College.

Meantime Jourdan with his division, in which Lieutenant Ney served, was moving slowly westwards for Cassel. On the 18th August he was at Lille, his troops having taken but a small part in the affairs of the 17th, and it was only on the 23rd that he reached Cassel, pushing north towards Wormhoudt an advanced guard, of which Ney's regiment formed part.[2] This place Jourdan took on the 24th, when we have an amusing account from one of his Brigadiers, Leclaire, forced by the Representatives to attack Esquelbecq, on the west of Jourdan's point. The poor Brigadier, who was very ill, marched with three Representatives and seven battalions, knowing nothing of the enemy and still less of any other movement by the French. He took the village at night, when Jourdan arrived, asking him what the devil he was doing there and telling him his fire had nearly routed his, Jourdan's, troops : there was no sense in what he was doing, and he would lose his artillery, for 12,000 men would fall on him at once. Whilst Jourdan ordered him back and the Representatives listened amazed, on came the enemy and, losing a gun, Leclaire fell back on Cassel. He found that he was one battalion short, but that had been sent by Jourdan to Wormhoudt. ' Drenched with sweat as if I had been taken out of the water, I fell off my horse from weakness and pain.' His gunners hoisted him up again, and he got to bed in Cassel. Next morning in came the Representatives to congratulate him on his victory ! He thought they were joking, ' but I never could persuade Duquesnoy that I had lost a 4 pdr.' Indeed, the

---

[1] Dupuis, *Nord*, i. 310–12, 378. [2] Ibid., 233–4.

Representatives praised him to the Convention highly, saying not a word of the gun. To make the matter complete, next day, the 25th August, the enemy retook both places, the French losing several guns ; the enemy said nineteen.[1]

Ordered, though not by Houchard, to draw near Dunkirk, and circling round by Waton, Jourdan's division reached Loon on the 26th August 1793, when Jourdan himself went into Dunkirk. Finding that it feared an attack, he reinforced the garrison. The town, be it remarked, was never surrounded by the enemy and could always receive supplies and reinforcements from the west.

Then came fresh orders, this time from Houchard. Arriving at Lille on the 24th August, he found that the Representative at Cassel, Duquesnoy, at the request of the municipality of Dunkirk, had ordered the division of Jourdan on that town. This was one of the checks to which the commanders of armies of the Republic were exposed, and Houchard felt it strongly, for he had intended to recall Jourdan to Lille, to assist in an operation against Menin which should call back York from Dunkirk, and he deplored the dispersion of this ' belle division '. However, he resolved to get Jourdan himself back, and on the 26th August he ordered him to hand over his division to Leclaire and, coming back to Cassel, to relieve Barthel and to take command from Dunkirk to Bailleul. He was to drive the enemy from this part of the frontier, ' employing all the means which his talents and his complete devotion to the cause of Liberty shall suggest to him '. Jourdan was to communicate on his right with Béru, the General under whom Macdonald served, who commanded the troops eastward to Armentières, that is, to the Lys river, Macdonald taking the section from Menin to Armentières.[2] Jourdan accordingly set off for Cassel. In the distribution which Leclaire made of his division, part in Dunkirk, we find 50 Chasseurs only of the 4th Hussars, Ney's regiment, placed at Waton, that is, east of Cassel.[3] Next, after certain hesitations and changes of plan which do not concern us, Houchard, bringing up to Lille

[1] Dupuis, *Nord*, i. 339–43, and Carte 4 ; Chuquet, *Hondschoote*, 146–7.
[2] Macdonald, *Souvenirs*, 28 ; Dupuis, *Nord*, i. 367–8, and Carte 1 ; Chuquet, *Hondschoote*, 149–51 ; Foucart et Finot, *Déf. nat.*, ii. 98.
[3] Dupuis, *Nord*, i. 370.

six battalions from Landrin in Cassel, launched some 15,000 men northwards on the posts of the Dutch on the 27th August 1793.

The plan was that of the staff officer, Gay de Vernon, whose knowledge and activity the Representative Duquesnoy admitted, but ' il a des yeux qui ne me plaisent pas ', so hard was it to satisfy a patriot.[1] Three young Generals of Brigade were to lead three columns : Macdonald on the right was to move on Lannoy, in the centre Pierre Dupont went through Mouveaux on Tourcoing, Houchard himself with General Béru and two Representatives accompanying this body, while on the left Alexandre Dumas, promoted Brigadier on the 30th July,[2] moved on Linselles. Certain demonstrations on the flanks can be neglected. Macdonald and Dumas were both beaten back by the Dutch, the first losing a gun. As for the centre column, it took Tourcoing, then only a large village surrounded by thick woods, after a long struggle in which Houchard described the troops as ' cruellement maltraités '. Then, as so often happened at this period, the men dispersed to plunder and, when the Generals attempted to stop them, they levelled their muskets at them, crying that the inhabitants of Tourcoing were aristocrats who must be despoiled. However, the mere sight of two small bodies of the enemy's cavalry sent them flying. Houchard had hoped to have advanced on Menin, but, in dread of what might happen, he drew back his mob on Mouveaux, the civilian drivers of the artillery cutting their traces, so that altogether this day the French lost seven guns and took a howitzer.[3]

Alexandre Dumas, whom I have just mentioned, we have already met ; he was Lt.-Colonel of the 13th Chasseurs at the time of the treason of Dumouriez. It is he, I presume, then Adjutant-General, whom we find the Minister on the 20th August 1793 ordering to Soissons to direct the march of the reinforcements from the other armies for the ' Nord '.[4] Promoted General of Brigade on the 30th July 1793,[5] he seems to have been placed in command at the important cross station, Pont-à-Marcq. Here probably he had Lt.-Colonel

---

[1] Dupuis, *Nord*, i, note 1, p. 379.   [2] D'Hauterive, *Dumas*, 36.
[3] Gay de Vernon, 244–5 ; Chuquet, *Hondschoote*, 164–8 ; Dupuis, *Nord*, i. 377–89 ; Jomini, *Rév.*, iv. 54–5, and Atlas, viii.
[4] Dupuis, *Nord*, i. 276–80.   [5] D'Hauterive, *Dumas*, 36.

Murat of the 21st Chasseurs, now brought up into line, under his orders.[1] On the 3rd September he was promoted General of Division by the Minister against the wish of the Representatives, and on the 8th of that month he was nominated to command the Armée des Pyrénées-Occidentales. In the advance, which I have just described, Murat, if he were not with Dumas, most probably was with the diversion attempted by the troops at Pont-à-Marcq on the right of Macdonald against Cysoing, to their north-east; they were beaten off with the loss of four guns.[2]

Houchard had at first suspected that the flank march of the Duke of York, extraordinary as it was, concealed some snare to induce him to divide his own troops, but when he realized that the Duke intended seriously to besiege Dunkirk, he and the Representatives determined to throw the weight of his army on the Duke. Chuquet, whom I usually follow with gratitude, speaks of this resolution as if it proved a complete change in the situation and deserved high praise as marking 'a revolution in the history of strategy'.[3] Surely strategy had not fallen so low even in the first armies of the Republic that when a General saw the enemy divide their forces and form them into two masses, one at the extremity of either wing, we should praise him for determining to throw his weight first on one body and then on the other? Neither the execution of the plan, nor the subsequent history of the war in this district give reason to think highly of the conception. Indeed, it is obvious that the highest strategy would have been to let York amuse himself before Dunkirk, and to strike at Coburg. Nor again is there any reason for special praise of the proposal 'to attack, and to attack *en masse*'. The claim by the leaders of the 'Nord' to be reinforced from the other armies was but common for all commanders of armies at that and at any other time. Dumouriez and Custine had each wished to collect all the forces available, wherever they themselves were, and Napoleon was to fulminate against the belief of all his generals that the decisive point was where each of them stood.

---

[1] D'Hauterive, *Dumas*, 36; Chuquet, *Hondschoote*, 41, 43.
[2] Dupuis, *Nord*, i. 380, 385–6.   [3] Chuquet, *Hondschoote*, 154, 157.

L'ARMÉE DU NORD, 1793

As for concentrating forces, let me quote a French writer on cavalry during this campaign : ' Besides the 4,000 men at Lille, the 20,000 at the Camp de la Madeleine, the 10,000 with Jourdan at the Faubourg des Malades, there are, also, 20,000 at the Camp de Biache, 5,000 at Mons-en-Pévèle, 10,000 at the Camp de Sin and at Douai, 10,000 under Cassel, the whole within a radius of less than 25 miles from Linselles. They have allowed the 35,000 men of the Duke of York to defile under their eyes and to take a post from them, then . . . to lay siege to Dunkirk.'[1] So much for ideas of concentration at this period. Still, although all armies wanted reinforcements, the ' Nord ' really had claims to pre-eminence and it received 2,750 men from the ' Ardennes ', the extraordinary Jouy conducting the operation,[2] and some 28,250 men from the twin armies, ' Moselle ' and ' Rhin ', or 31,000 in all, only 1,000 of these being cavalry, an arm in which it was very deficient.[3]

Houchard certainly had no idea of massing his troops to strike one decisive blow at York. A considerable part of the ' Nord ' had been brought over to the left, drawn as if by a magnet by York, as it would have been had the Duke moved in any other direction, and Houchard's first plan was to make what was a mere demonstration with this part of the army, to the east of the Duke, in hopes that it would attract him away from Dunkirk. The ' Nord ' was to be reorganized in three groups ; that of the Right or of Maubeuge consisted of the garrisons of Maubeuge and of Le Quesnoy, &c., 18,000 : the *Corps principal*, or the Centre, had the division of Jourdan, the three divisions in the Camp de la Madeleine, under Lille, a division of the troops at Mons-en-Pévèle and at Pont-à-Marcq, another division at the Camp de Biache,[4] &c., some 58,900 strong. Here, I take it, Jourdan, Mortier, and Ney all served. It is doubtful whether Macdonald should be added to the list ; if so, he would most probably have been with the *Groupe du nord*, 23,300 strong, on the left, which was commanded by Barthel and held Cassel and Dunkirk. In the

---

[1] Desbrière, *La Cav. pendant la Rév.: La crise*, 385.   [2] Thiébault, i. 417
[3] Dupuis, *Nord*, i. 71, 267-85.
[4] Ibid., 305-8; Desbrière, *La Cav. pendant la Rév.: La crise*, 387-9.

various numbers here given are included only those troops who were to take the field, and they depended on the arrival of the large reinforcements ordered from the ' Ardennes ', ' Moselle ', and ' Rhin '.

The reinforcement from the Rhine frontier, including the first battalion of the infantry regiment, the 36th, in which Captain Bernadotte served,[1] arrived on the 5th September 1793, and Houchard collected some 45,000 men at Cassel. The news of the execution of his predecessor and former commander, Custine, had reached him a few days before. Here we have a good instance of the real effect of this system of slaughtering Generals, which is sometimes believed to have stirred on the commanders of the armies of the Revolution to greater efforts. Little knowledge of human nature is required to anticipate the results. With a disgraceful death staring him in the face, sure to be condemned if he opposed the Representatives, sure also to die if those blunderers were as unsuccessful as they deserved to be, Houchard fell into a state of dejection and let the Representatives have even a freer hand than before. ' Then there is a regular determination to guillotine the Generals ? ' he cried. ' And you too,' snapped Levasseur, 'if you betray us. Not one traitor shall escape us.'[2] The Pro-Consuls were to be the judges of what was treachery : one sure sign was defeat, but Houchard was to find that even victory could not clear him.

It was not only from the Representatives with his army that Houchard suffered. These local despots often took on themselves to nullify the orders from Paris and now those on the Eastern frontier kept back 10,000 of the troops he should have received and on which he had counted.[3] At the Capital Bouchotte, the Minister for War, played his part in disorganizing the army ; a process defended by Chuquet with the amazing apology that, if he removed Generals and staff officers, on the other hand he appointed others.[4] Now Abraham Lincoln had a sound axiom that it was bad to swop horses when crossing a stream. I take the head-lines of two contiguous

---

[1] Dupuis, *Nord*, i. 275, 281, 283, 402.
[2] Levasseur tried, later, to soften the brutality of his answer. Dupuis, *Nord*, i. 411 ; Chuquet, *Hondschoote*, 185 ; Wallon, *Rep.*, iv. 140–1.
[3] Dupuis, *Nord*, i. 273–85. [4] Chuquet, *Hondschoote*, 41.

paragraphs of Chuquet's valuable work: 'From Paris Bouchotte stimulated the Generals. . . . But at the same moment Bouchotte cashiered the *commissaire-ordonnateur en chef*, Petitjean,' one of the most skilful and indefatigable officers of his class. Fancy the effect on an army just about to march of the removal of the official on whom all the supplies depended, and then, only on second thoughts, the replacement of him by a man who had worked on the northern frontier. Small wonder that the Representatives resentfully reported that Houchard was ' affecté de ces contrariétés '.[1] Also he wanted cavalry, and when he heard that he was only to get a few, and especially that he was not to get his pet regiment, the fine Carabiniers,[2] the news, said the Representatives, ' lui a-t-elle fait faire la plus terrible grimace du monde '.[3]

The collection of forces round Cassel made Freytag, commanding York's covering army, uneasy, and on the 5th September 1793 he sent a small body in two columns from Wormhoudt and Esquelbec to attack Arneke,[4] ' to observe the rear of the Camp of Cassel '. The village was taken, the French losing 200 killed and wounded and 4 officers and 57 men prisoners, but consoling themselves by the capture of an English Colonel,[5] ' whose rich spoils ', wrote Houchard, ' passed to our *tirailleurs* '. This affair made Freytag believe he was about to be attacked and he asked for reinforcements, but I mention it because the loss of the village was attributed to the fact that the 36th Regiment, that of Captain Bernadotte, had been surprised, not having got up, wrote Houchard, as early as ordered. ' This regiment has suffered some losses, which nevertheless are not very heavy. I am now making its chief feel that he ought to have been more vigilant.'[6]

There were two means of relieving Dunkirk; a movement by Menin and Ypres on the rear of the besiegers, forcing them to raise the siege and to cut their way back, or else a direct attack, quicker but less effective.

---

[1] Chuquet, *Hondschoote*, 177–81 ; Foucart et Finot, *Déf. nat.*, ii. 91.
[2] Susane, *Cav. franç.*, ii. 187–207.
[3] Dupuis, *Nord*, i. 408 ; Chuquet, *Hondschoote*, 182.
[4] North-west of Cassel.
[5] Probably a Hanoverian, the French taking all red coats for English.
[6] Dupuis, *Nord*, i. 344–6, and Carte 7 ; Chuquet, *Hondschoote*, 182.

Houchard probably would have adopted the bolder, wider plan, but the *Comité* did not approve[1] and, besides many reasons connected with the state of the army, thrown into confusion by the Minister and the Representatives, he had also to consider how the state of Dunkirk would affect his own operations. The garrison was weak for the long lines it had to hold, and not only might the town fall during his march north, but on any sudden appeal from Souham, the Commandant, the Representatives would not have hesitated to halt him. We have to take much of the criticism on Houchard and other commanders at this time as it stands, as if they had full liberty of action, and as if we knew all their difficulties and motives. Doubtless no General of the time was foolish enough to let even his pillow know what his real thoughts were of his masters, the Representatives, whilst those gorgeously dressed personages[2] strutted out their hour. Most probably Houchard was wise in determining on a direct attack, especially as the tendency of his men to break, if only for the sake of plunder,[3] made it dangerous to throw them in rear of such troops as the English and Hanoverians. Indeed, the stroke at York's rear, while raising the siege, might well have led to a defeat if the Duke could have brought his whole force against this part of the 'Nord'. Hedging, as it often did, the *Comité* told Houchard to 'deal the enemy a terrible blow, without, however, risking any decisive action if it be at all doubtful'.[4] Now, if the troops were thrown on the rear of the enemy, the battle must be fought to the end, defeat meaning ruin for either side, whilst in the direct attack retreat was always open to the French. Small wonder Houchard chose the direct course, knowing well that his head was at stake.

The operations which ensued, and the battle of Hondschoote, can be studied in detail in the work of Captain Dupuis,[5] which I take as my chief authority, but I give a sketch of them

---

[1] Gay de Vernon, *Custine et Houchard*, 248-9; Dupuis, *Nord*, i. 397-8. Dupuis considers the *Comité* left Houchard free (*Nord*, 407-17), as does Chuquet (*Hondschoote*, 172-5).

[2] See Saint-Sauveur, *Costumes, etc.*

[3] Dupuis, *Nord*, i. 388.

[4] 'porter à l'ennemi un coup terrible, sans cependant risquer aucune action décisive pour peur qu'elle ne soit douteuse.' Dupuis, *Nord*, i. 413.

[5] Dupuis, *Nord*. See list of authorities.

because several future Marshals, Bernadotte, Jourdan, Mortier, and Ney, not to speak of the future Generals, Moreau and Hoche, were engaged, and also because they show some of the difficulties which the commanders of the armies of the Republic had to deal with at this period. The arrangements of the siege of Dunkirk offered every possible facility for the relief of the town. The English Navy gave no support to the Duke of York until too late, so that the besiegers were exposed to a cannonade on their sea flank when the French vessels chose to come out of the port. Then the besieged had been able to inundate the country from Dunkirk to Bergues, so that the front of the Duke had to be extended over a long distance. Also a great swamp of morass, the Moerkercke Ruine, Grande-Moer, lay parallel to the coast-line for some considerable part of the distance from Dunkirk to Furnes, obliging the besiegers to divide their forces. Dunkirk itself was not in a good state of defence. Souham, who on the 26th August was sent to command there instead of O'Moran, reported that it could not hold out for more than five days and that the garrison of 5,000 ought to be 15,000. The *Comité* was indignant, and removed him from the command. Souham was replaced by Jacques Ferrand on the 5th September,[1] but both Houchard and the Municipality so praised him that on the 11th September he resumed the command.

The garrison of Dunkirk was increased by 2,500 men, and although the troops at first were nervous and alarmed, Souham, and then Ferrand, acted vigorously and well. Most writers are apt to give the credit of the defence to the Chief of the Staff to these Generals, the young Lt.-Colonel Hoche, who, by one of the usual incidents of the time, had just been released from arrest for showing his indignation at the arrest of General Le Veneur, to whom he had been A.D.C.[2] The tribunal of Douai had acquitted him and he had been sent to Dunkirk, highly recommended by Berthelmy, Chief of the Staff to Houchard.[3] Hoche had the knack of catching the tone of the patriots at the moment, and he put himself forward, writing,

[1] Foucart et Finot, *Déf. nat.*, ii. 89–90, 122–3 ; Dupuis, *Nord*, 358–66.
[2] Chuquet, *Hondschoote*, 64–5 ; Lahure, 55–7 ; Cuneo d'Ornano, *Hoche*, 56–7.
[3] Dupuis, *Nord*, i. 358.

for instance, direct to the *Comité*,[1] which brought him high promotion, as we shall see, and makes him seem to have occupied a higher position at Dunkirk than he really did.

One of Hoche's correspondents was Robespierre. These letters have disappeared; probably they were full of the denunciations of which Hoche was always so profuse and which at that time often meant death to the person attacked. The Commandant of Dunkirk, not, I presume, Souham, but his predecessor, O'Moran, was denounced by Hoche.

Houchard, intending to strike at the covering army under Freytag, broke up the 45,800 men he meant to use into six columns, the title of some, *flanqueurs de gauche*, &c., having no real relation to their employment. On the right, or east, Dumesny had 9,000 men at Bailleul. Next, and to the north-west, came Lt.-Colonel Vandamme with 4,400 troops, amongst whom was the volunteer battalion of Lt.-Colonel Moreau. We shall soon find Moreau as General of Division, commanding General of Brigade Vandamme. To the west was Hédouville[2] at Steenvoorde with 7,400 men, including an infantry brigade under Colaud to which the 4th Hussars, Ney's regiment, was attached. The conjunction of Colaud and Ney should be noted; in 1796 we shall find Ney as General of Brigade leading the advanced guard of Colaud, who, as I believe, had some influence in forming his character. West again, at Cassel, was the *corps de bataille* under Jourdan, 13,000 men, including the infantry regiment of Captain Bernadotte, who was to rise to divisional rank under Jourdan in 1794. A little north, on the hill of Cassel, was Landrin with 6,000 men. Here served the volunteer battalion of Mortier, but that officer had just before been promoted Lt.-Colonel Adjutant-General, on the 3rd September 1793. Still, he may have been with this division. A good deal north, at Bergues, was Leclaire, with 6,000 men. Besides these troops Houchard intended to use all the garrison of Dunkirk, except 2,000 men, say roughly 6,000 men, for a sortie. Altogether some 51,000 men were to act against York's 35,000; the main blow to be delivered at the

---

[1] Cuneo d'Ornano, *Hoche*, i. 65–6, ii. 6–12; Hamel, *Robespierre*, iii. 164–5, and note; Dupuis, *Nord*, i. 346, 357–8.

[2] Joseph, Vicomte de Hédouville (1774–1818), Dupuis, *Nord*, i, note 1, p. 401; not Gabriel Hédouville, the General of the Empire.

covering army, some 16,000. The French front extended over eighteen miles.[1]

On the 6th September 1793 Vandamme, taking rather a circuitous course, advanced with but little fighting past Poperinghe to Proven, south-east of Rousbrugge. On Vandamme's left Hédouville, less Colaud's brigade, drove the enemy from Poperinghe and, advancing through Proven, took Rousbrugge, crossed the Yser, and halted at Oost-Cappel.

On the left Landrin, moving north, was stopped by the enemy, who held Wormhoudt. On the extreme left Leclaire tried an advance from Bergues, but had to draw back there in the evening, whilst the garrison of Dunkirk, coming out 6,000 strong, was beaten back by York.

Now for the centre. Colaud's brigade, leaving Hédouville, had moved north and had driven the enemy from Houtkerque, whence the Hussars of Ney pursued them. Now Houchard came up with Jourdan's division and unfortunately, at the instance of the staff officer, Ernouf, gave up his first idea of joining Hédouville by Rousbrugge and of then moving with both columns on Hondschoote. Instead he sent Colaud to Proven to rejoin Hédouville, and himself turned west for Herzeele. The village was soon taken by Jourdan's troops, that General heading them, sword in hand. Inspirited by this success, Houchard determined to force the passage of the Yser and to take Bambecque. The bridge was protected by a *tête de pont*, the troops were beaten off, and, when a violent storm broke on the column and the ammunition began to fail, for the men were very wasteful, Jourdan sent back to ask Houchard if the advance had not better be stopped. The indignant Chief of the Staff, Berthelmy, cried, 'We must conquer at any price; failing cartridges, are there not bayonets?' Bernadotte's regiment was sent to ford the river, the passage was won, and Bambecque was taken. By this time it was 6 p.m. of a September day, the troops were tired and the roads bad, so that Houchard intended to halt for the night abreast of Hédouville, whom he knew to be also over the river on his right at Oost-Cappel. Houchard, however, was not the master, and the Representative Hentz announced that, 'Free

[1] Dupuis, *Nord*, i. 420-8, and Carte 7.

men were never too tired to fight the slaves of tyrants; therefore the army should continue its movement'. Accordingly Houchard ordered the troops on, and Rexpoede was taken and occupied by three regiments of Jourdan and by a regiment of cavalry. Ernouf, who knew the country, undertook to place the posts, and the men, exposed as they were to heavy rain, disbanded to get food and shelter in the houses, notwithstanding the exertions of Jourdan.[1]

Houchard, his staff, with, I presume, Jourdan and the Representative Delbrel, got into a house where they came on a treasure, some loaves of bread and some pots of beer, most grateful to men who had been on horseback all day without time to eat anything. While they were enjoying these and talking of the success they hoped to win next day, a storm of fire fell on the village and the enemy was on them before they could mount their horses. Freytag, commanding the covering army, mostly Hanoverians, had been alarmed by the progress made that day by the French, who had got nearer to Hondschoote than most of his own troops, and who next day might take that village and so cut his connexion with York and the besieging army. At 8 p.m., therefore, he had begun his retreat on Rexpoede, which he believed still to be held by his own men. He moved in two columns, himself riding at the head of the right one (that nearest the French, consisting mostly of artillery and cavalry), and having with him Prince Adolphus of Cambridge and Scharnhorst, the future organizer of the Prussian army of 1813, which did so much when the bones of most of the Grand Army lay in Spain and Russia. He was at this time a Captain in the Hanoverian army. Ernouf must have placed his posts fairly well, for, when Freytag's column reached the village, they were charged by a body of French cavalry. The head of the column broke, the guns obstructed the road, so that the Hanoverian horse could do nothing, and the whole body, falling into confusion, threw itself on the left and wandered in the country. Prince Adolphus, whom the French claim to have taken for a moment, escaped by the devotion of his A.D.C., but Freytag, wounded in the head and

---

[1] Dupuis, *Nord*, i. 430-43, and Carte 7; Gay de Vernon, *Custine et Houchard*, 255-9; Foucart et Finot, *Déf. nat.*, ii. 92-4; Chuquet, *Hondschoote*, 193-9.

weak from loss of blood, fell from his horse into a ditch and was taken prisoner.

The tired French settled down again to rest, when suddenly out of the darkness the guns of the enemy opened on them and the Hanoverians were in the village, almost catching Houchard, as we have seen. Walmoden, marching with the second or left column, mainly infantry, had nearly got abreast of Rexpoede when he heard of Freytag's disaster. At once he rose to the occasion and, though his men were worn and had only eight cartridges apiece, he called on them to rescue their comrades and, making his way to the village, fell on the three battalions which Jourdan had left there. The surprise was complete; the French, not realizing how small a force was attacking them, fell into the most complete confusion and their state was the worse as all the ground was new to them, whilst the Hanoverians had occupied it for some days. Jourdan found that his men only thought of getting cover and, being without staff or orderlies, he most foolishly went back to Houchard and was ordered to withdraw on Bambecque. He need not have troubled himself, for when he regained Rexpoede he was met by a volley of musketry and went back to Bambecque, where news of his death had been spread. His men had fled, some to Bambecque, others to Oost-Cappel, and others right back to Cassel, Bernadotte's battalion being, apparently, specially blamed.[1] Bad as matters were, it was, says an eye-witness (Gay de Vernon), only owing to the vigour of Jourdan that this night affray had not been a complete rout. Rescuing Freytag, who was taken to Furnes, Walmoden brought both columns to Hondschoote by 6 a.m. on the 7th September.[2]

So thoroughly demoralized were the troops of Jourdan that Houchard in dismay drew back southwards over the Yser to Herzeele, where he remained all the 7th September, restoring order and supplying the men with food and ammunition, whilst in front of him a curious state of affairs existed. On the left (or west) Leclaire, advancing again from near Bergues, found himself at last in presence of a column, which turned

---

[1] Dupuis, *Nord*, ii. 230-1, but I am not sure that he was with this battalion.
[2] Gay de Vernon, 259-62; Chuquet, *Hondschoote*, 199-205; Dupuis, *Nord*, i. 443-51, and Carte 7.

out to be that of Hédouville, coming up from Oost-Cappel, so that these two bodies, having had only to deal with small posts of the enemy, actually met to the front of their discomfited commander. The situation promised to be most interesting, for the two Generals meant to attack the enemy at Hondschoote, but the night fell, and Hédouville halted at Rexpoede and Leclaire at the Maison Blanche. In the rear (or south) of these columns, Landrin occupied Wormhoudt and Esquelbecq on the right bank of the Yser, so that he was about abreast and to the west of Houchard at Herzeele. To the north again Vandamme, starting from Proven, went through Rousbrugge and Oost-Cappel for Hondschoote. Here with his 4,400 men he came on Walmoden's army of 13,000 and, losing three guns, drew back south-west to Killem. Could there be an odder situation ? 13,000 enemy were at Hondschoote with three of Houchard's columns to their south-west at Killem, Oost-Cappel, and the Maison Blanche, one of these having been checked, but the others, 13,400 strong, not having met any real resistance. Behind these three columns, altogether 17,800 strong, was Houchard with Jourdan's 13,000, thoroughly beaten, having alongside Landrin's 6,000 untouched. Yet another column of 9,000 under Dumesny, with which I shall deal later, was remaining quietly at Bailleul.[1]

Houchard, it will be seen, had disseminated his force, and it would have been better had he formed one really strong column in the centre. It is true that it was owing to the action of the Representative Hentz that Jourdan had not halted at Bambecque,[2] where he would have linked with Hédouville on his right at Oost-Cappel. Still, if Hédouville's column had been united to that of Jourdan the mass could not have been crushed and the Hanoverians could not have cut their way through.[3] Also Houchard had not acted as commander of the army: he had simply directed Jourdan's division, and no superintendence seems to have existed over the other columns, that of Dumesny's for example. No doubt his staff was bad, the country difficult for communications,

[1] Dupuis, *Nord*, i. 450-8, and Carte 7 ; Chuquet, *Hondschoote*, 205-6 ; Gay de Vernon, *Custine et Houchard*, 260-3 ; Du Casse, *Vandamme*, i. 44-7.
[2] Gay de Vernon, *Custine et Houchard*, 261.
[3] Jomini, *Rév.*, iv. 56, 57.

and the presence of the Representative complicated matters, for had Houchard not been with Jourdan, he could not have told where the division might be sent (an argument for making it stronger), and his absence might well have been made a crime against him.

There might have been some excuse for the manner in which Houchard had spread his columns on the first advance, but there was none now for the repetition of the fault when the blow should have been dealt with full force on the left of the enemy at Hondschoote. On the 8th September 1793 Jourdan's division was to move by Rexpoede on Hondschoote, flanked on its left (or preceded) by Vandamme from Killem, and having on its right the brigade of Colaud (where Lieutenant Ney was in the 4th Hussars), detached from Hédouville. Hédouville, instead of flanking on the left, was, without Colaud's brigade, to move north-west to Bergues and was then to turn eastwards for the battle expected at Hondschoote, if he met no enemy. By a strange plan, whilst Hédouville was thus detached on Bergues, Leclaire was to march from the Maison Blanche, close to Bergues, on Hondschoote, and Landrin was sent in to Dunkirk to strengthen the garrison, by whose sorties York was to be prevented from supporting Walmoden. Thus of his total force of 43,000,[1] Houchard used only some 22,000 directly for the all-important battle at Hondschoote, some 12,000 being sent on Bergues and Dunkirk, that is, on the least important wing of the enemy. Dumesny's force of 9,000 was to be far away east, threatening Ypres.

Nevertheless, Houchard with his 22,000 men was far superior to Walmoden, who with his covering army, reinforced to about 14,600,[2] stood at Hondschoote in a strong position, but one in which the thick hedges gave the French skirmishers the cover they were so quick to use and also neutralized his cavalry, 4,000 strong, the arm which the Allies generally employed with advantage. Indeed, we may take Walmoden's fighting force as practically some 9,000, almost all Hanoverians. As these troops then wore red coats, in all the contemporary

---

[1] I follow here Dupuis, *Nord*, i. 461, although in pp. 420-1 he makes the strength 45,800, but I suppose here he allows for previous losses.
[2] Dupuis, *Nord*, i. 458.

French accounts, as well as in many modern histories, they are described as English.[1] I make the correction as a mere technical one, for the gallant Hanoverian army had no need to fear any comparison with other troops. Walmoden would have drawn back farther eastwards, but the Duke of York, having learnt of the retirement of the covering army, was raising the siege of Dunkirk and called on him to hold his ground to cover the withdrawal of the siege train, an operation the Duke then hoped to perform.[2]

On the 8th September 1793, as the French drew near Hondschoote, they came on no outposts of the enemy, for Walmoden, certain he would be attacked, had drawn in all his troops to his position. This puzzled the French at first, but then enabled them to reconnoitre more closely than usual the line they had to attack.[3] As the enemy's right was covered by a creek and by the inundation, and their left by hedges and ditches, Houchard determined to attack their centre from the Killem road. Vandamme had already engaged on the west of this road, and Jourdan's men threw themselves as skirmishers on each side of it, on the right of Vandamme. A long struggle ensued with a heavy fire of musketry and artillery, the opposed ranks coming to such close quarters that the men were described as stabbing one another. By 10 a.m., although Colaud had come up on the French right and Leclaire was getting near the enemy's right, the French centre was being forced back, at any moment the guns might have to be withdrawn to the rear, when the troops probably would break, so that Houchard believed the battle was lost. But, encouraged by Jourdan and the Representatives, he determined that, whilst Jourdan brought up three fresh battalions, he himself should go to Colaud's brigade on the right, and that, when his drums there sounded the charge and he attacked, Jourdan should advance, as also should Vandamme and Leclaire on the left.

While Houchard went off to the right, the struggle con-

---

[1] Alison, ii, Chapter XIII, calls them Dutch and Austrians. The real composition was 15 battalions, 16 squadrons Hanoverians ; 3 battalions, 2 squadrons Austrians ; 5 squadrons Hessians ; 10 squadrons, English ; one battalion Émigrés. Dupuis, Nord, i. 224.
[2] Dupuis, Nord, 458–60 ; Chuquet, Hondschoote, 206–7.
[3] Gay de Vernon, Custine et Houchard, 264–5.

L'ARMÉE DU NORD, 1793

tinued in the centre, and the enemy, who had already delivered two counter-attacks, now came on so vehemently that the French line fell back. In this emergency, although no signal came from Houchard, Jourdan, in order to prevent a rout, proposed a fresh assault. There still remained one battalion in rear, guarding the colours. This he would take to form the head of a column, to be launched at the charge on the enemy, whilst the available cavalry hunted back the fugitives, so that, as he put it, the column would grow like a snowball as it advanced and the left wing would join when they heard the drums. But, said Jourdan, he was tied by the orders of Houchard until the signal should come from the right. We shall find Jourdan very skilful in using those formidable people, the Representatives, and here one of them, Delbrel, at once assisted him by ordering him to do what he proposed, and then offered to act as A.D.C. to him. At this moment Jourdan was wounded by a bullet which scraped his chest, but which put him *hors de combat* for the moment. Then at last, about noon, came the sound of the drums beating the charge on the right. Houchard had had a purpose in leaving the centre, where Jourdan could lead the troops. Arrived at Colaud's brigade, the old cavalry leader put himself at the head of the 17th Regiment of cavalry and deployed the squadrons. It is permissible to believe, or at least to imagine, that Ney's Hussars joined in this movement. At all events Houchard, now in his own element, sword in hand and followed by his staff, led the charge, which was supported by the infantry and taken up both by the centre and by the left of the line, where Leclaire was throwing back the enemy's right.

Walmoden had only held to give York time to retreat, and when Hondschoote was now taken, he drew off eastwards, his troops falling into disorder, but being shielded by his cavalry. On the 9th September he reached Furnes unpursued, where by noon he was joined by the army of the Duke of York, which had beaten off the sorties from Dunkirk, unsupported as they were by the division of Landrin,[1] and had drawn off along the coast, untouched by the French, but leaving all its siege train before Dunkirk.

[1] Chuquet, *Hondschoote*, 255–6.

In the four days' fighting, 5th–8th September, Walmoden's 9,000 infantry had lost 2,331 officers and men. A Hessian General, Cochenhausen, who was taken prisoner, died from his wounds and was buried with military honours by Vandamme.[1] The French loss is not stated : Jomini is probably correct in putting it as about equal to that of the enemy, but Gay de Vernon, who was there, makes it 1,800.[2] General Jourdan was slightly, and Colaud seriously wounded. One part of the spoil, some clothing, and especially a number of trousers, was most welcome to the ragged *Sans-culottes*.[3]

There was no pursuit by the French. The heads of the different columns, penetrating into the village after the long fight, had got entangled, and the whole fell into confusion. Leclaire, explaining how the men asked him where their battalions were, and how he formed them into squads, goes on, ' It was indeed at this moment that I felt the necessity for diversity in uniforms '.[4] Houchard had been cowed by the check at Rexpoede and by the tendency of his young troops to fall into confusion. Still he had fresh troops, for, when the battle was over, Hédouville appeared, having spent his time in reconnoitring about Bergues, whence of course the enemy had disappeared. Houchard reproached him for his conduct,[5] but Hédouville ought never to have been given any choice of direction. What happened at Bergues mattered nothing, every man was required at Hondschoote. Houchard did send Hédouville in pursuit, but that General, finding a bridge broken, halted at once. Then Houchard was advised to push Vandamme, who knew the country, across the great marsh with 4,000 cavalry, to fall on the Duke of York.

The enemy believed the marsh to be passable ; Houchard did not and, fearing to compromise his cavalry, he only gave Vandamme three cavalry regiments,[6] who got across and,

---

[1] Chuquet, *Hondschoote*, 221 ; Dupuis, *Nord*, i. 483 ; Du Casse, *Vandamme*, i. 53.
[2] Jomini, *Rév.*, iv. 60 ; Gay de Vernon, *Custine et Houchard*, 273.
[3] Lahure, 60.   [4] Dupuis, *Nord*, i. 482.
[5] Gay de Vernon, *Custine et Houchard*, 270–1.
[6] Dupuis, *Nord*, i. 485, says only sixty cuirassiers, but I follow Du Casse, *Vandamme*, i. 48. For Hondschoote see Dupuis, *Nord*, i. 417–95 ; Chuquet, *Hondschoote*, 188–261 ; Jomini, *Rév.*, iv. 55–72 ; Gay de Vernon, *Custine et Houchard*, 264–75 ; *Vict. et Conq.*, ii. 14–20 ; Foucart et Finot, *Déf. nat.*,

taking some baggage, were seen in the distance by York's column. By 5 p.m., abandoning all further operations, Houchard quartered himself at Hondschoote.

Houchard's difficulties were increased by the ineffectiveness of his cavalry, which ought to have bound the columns together, instead of letting them wander about at haphazard.

One could not see, says Desbrière, more formal proof of the radical incompetence of the cavalry for service in the field, for one cannot attribute the failure of their role to the activity of the opposed horse, kept in rear of its infantry.[1]

Of the six columns which Houchard had intended to use, I have left one, that of Dumesny, unaccounted for, but its proceedings show the extraordinary difficulties the commanders at this period had to contend with On the commencement of the operations on the 6th September, Vandamme was at first to form the advanced guard, or to clear the way for Dumesny [2] and then, when Vandamme had passed Reninghelst and while he turned to the north-west for Poperinghe, Dumesny was to move with his 9,000 men and ten siege-pieces from Bailleul on Ypres, to try to take the citadel there, and in any case to prevent the Dutch at Menin from reinforcing the covering army of the enemy. The staff officer concerned, Gay de Vernon, knowing apparently that Dumesny had a good deal of the limpet in him, thought it wisest not to trust to a written order to him, but to get Vandamme to ride on ahead of his own men, and himself to tell Dumesny that he was to move. This Vandamme did, and he was not the man to whisper his message, but Dumesny remained quiet, not only that day, but also on the 7th September, leaving Houchard's right flank uncovered.[3] Then came fresh orders, and on the 8th September, the day of the battle of Hondschoote, he at last advanced and his batteries fired on Ypres, without much effect, all the

---

ii. 92–120; Calvert, 108–21; Langeron, 21–2; Lahure, 58–60; Du Casse, *Vandamme*, i. 45–8. For plan see Dupuis, *Nord*, Cartes 7 and 8; *Vict. et Conq.*, ii. 9; Chuquet, *Hondschoote*, end.

[1] Desbrière, *La Cav. pendant la Rév.: La crise*, 391.

[2] General Pierre-Joseph-Michel-Salomon Dumesny or Dumesnil, really Salomon (1739– ?), dismissed 18th Sept. 1793; re-employed, but retired 25th Nov. 1797. Chuquet, *Hondschoote*, note 1, pp. 191–2; Dupuis, *Nord*, i, note 2, pp. 308–9.

[3] Gay de Vernon, *Custine et Houchard*, 255, 262–4.

9th September. He had covered his right by a detachment of 2,700 men from Armentières and other posts under Joslet, and he only had to deal with a garrison of some 2,000, but at night on the 10th, alarmed by a demonstration of the garrison and believing that the enemy was advancing from Menin on him, he and Joslet retired, leaving some sixty prisoners to the enemy. Thus, whilst Houchard fought Hondschoote with, say 22,000 men, some 11,700 of his troops were making this timid demonstration far on his right. The perfect satisfaction of Dumesny and of Joslet, and indeed of the worthy Dellard, who was with the column, is remarkable. Joslet said he commanded not men, but devils, a phrase he meant to be complimentary, but which might be read with the acknowledgement that they ' se sont un peu livrés au pillage ', the ' un peu ' not agreeing with a report by the Commissary, Chivaille. It was not to Houchard that the lagging Dumesny reported, but to the Representatives.[1]

The victory was not a great one; indeed, considering the extraordinary way in which Freytag's force, or even the whole army of York, had been exposed to the attacks of the ' Nord ', it was rather wonderful that Houchard had not done more. Still it was undoubtedly a victory when one was sorely needed to restore the courage of the army and of the nation. The enemy, checked at Valmy and beaten at Jemappes, had again been forced from a position, and men did not look too closely at the comparative strength of the opponents. The victory did, however, little good to Houchard. The Representatives had been unsympathizing witnesses of his hesitations and uncertainties, partly caused by their presence with him. His difficulties they could not understand. It is true that, with troops in the uncertain state of the ' Nord ', the sight of the Representatives in the field had done good. When Levasseur and Delbrel appeared at the head of the columns of Jourdan and Colaud, ' the brilliant courage of these Deputies, the sight of the plumes and tri-coloured scarves which floated from their hats, produced, as always, an electrical effect '.[2] But if they

---

[1] Dupuis, *Nord*, i. 423, 430-1, 456, 462-5, and Carte 7 ; Foucart et Finot, *Déf. nat.*, ii. 93, 112-16 ; Dellard, 18-21 ; Chuquet, *Hondschoote*, 208-9 ; Jomini, *Rév.*, iv. 61-2.

[2] Gay de Vernon, *Custine et Houchard*, 268.

appeared on the field, they considered they had a right to advise, and practically to order. We have seen Delbrel ordering Jourdan on before the signal had been given for which Houchard had told him to wait, and this, had it not happened to concur with the signal, might well have led to a disastrous repulse.

Submissive as Houchard usually was to them, he did stand at last. When urged to throw his confused forces on the rear of the English, retiring sullenly but untouched, Houchard, who may have heard of Minden, refused. It was natural enough for the old trooper to rebuke his Chief of the Staff: 'You are too young to teach me how to make war;' but, when he told a Representative, 'Vous n'êtes pas militaire',[1] he was on dangerous ground. The Representatives, affirming that the roads were as bad for the Allies as for the French, forgot that roads wear by the passage of an army and the first-comers get the easier ways; but for a General to claim superiority in knowledge over a Representative was criminal. Also men fighting well on the field mistook the duties of a commander, and it was to the presence of the Representatives with the troops that was due the extraordinary accusation which came later that the brave old Houchard was a coward. At the moment, however, the Convention was pleased, and on the 17th September it decreed that the Armée du Nord had 'bien mérité de la patrie', and charged its President to write a letter expressing its satisfaction to the army and to Generals Jourdan and Colaud, 'seriously wounded after having contributed to the victory'.[2]

The defence of Dunkirk began the real career of Hoche, who as Lt.-Colonel Adjutant-General had been the Chief of the Staff to the commanders Souham and Ferrand and whose 'flamboyant' style suited the patriots. Now he wrote, 'At last they have departed, these vile slaves of tyrants', and, although he soon fell ill, showing signs of the disease from

---

[1] Chuquet, *Hondschoote*, 223-4. I do not understand how M. Chuquet considers Gay de Vernon as believing that the English could have been crushed, he only seems to have thought the cavalry could have been turned on them; the crushing he thought an absurd idea. Gay de Vernon, *Custine et Houchard*, 272-5, especially note, p. 274: 'It is seen how absurd is the opinion ... that General Houchard could turn the English Army and make them lay down their arms.'

[2] Chuquet, *Hondschoote*, note 2, p. 227.

which he was to die, he was clamouring for employment and proposed to the *Comité* an invasion of England, which was not to be a matter of skill or manœuvring, but one of steel, fire, and patriotism. In 1796 he was to have his chance at such an invasion. On the 10th September 1793 the Representatives promoted him Colonel Adjutant-General, when, according to revolutionary routine, he was at once denounced as a royalist, an accusation which he met successfully with a scream of anger. On the 13th September 1793 he became General of Brigade.[1]

One other victory could be claimed by Houchard. Having remained at Hondschoote to give time to the garrison of Dunkirk to bring into the town the enemy's siege train, he went to Cassel and planned a stroke at the Dutch at Menin. These beaten, and the communication between York and Coburg thus cut, he intended to leave 20,000 men to contain York, and to march himself with 30,000 to raise the siege of Le Quesnoy.[2] For Menin, he used some 26,000 to 27,000 men against 10,000 Dutch, who were scattered ; but to the south Beaulieu with 6,000 Austrians was coming up northwards from Cysoing[3] to support them. On the 11th September Hédouville with his division and the *Chasseurs à pied* of Colaud, 6,500 men, marched south to Bailleul, where he joined Dumesny with 10,000, and where Béru met them to plan the stroke on Menin. On the 12th September 1793 the French columns advanced northwards. On their right or eastern flank Béru came from the camps under Lille with 10,000 to 11,000 men in three columns, Dupont on the right, Béru himself in the centre, with Macdonald on his left, whilst to the west Hédouville and Dumesny moved down the left bank of the Lys for Wervicq. That day the French were repulsed, but on the 13th September they carried everything before them. Béru took Menin and came on the fugitives from the left, driven back by Hédouville.

The enemy was thrown into confusion, and at Wervicq his cavalry, perhaps three squadrons, sent up by Beaulieu,

---

[1] Cuneo d'Ornano, *Hoche*, i. 57-81, ii. 6-15 ; Rousselin, *Hoche*, i. 58-89, ii. 1-11.

[2] Dupuis, *Nord*, ii. 6.   [3] South-east of Lille.

had to gallop through the French, each man laid on his horse's neck, whilst the French, sheltered along the houses, could only deliver a few shots and some bayonet thrusts.[1] Beaulieu on the previous evening had reached Lauwe, not three miles east of Menin. On the 13th he had crossed the Lys below Menin, but, afraid of being involved in the flying mob, he did little to cover the retreat of the Dutch, great numbers of whom reached Bruges, whilst their commander, the Prince of Orange, drew back through Courtrai to Deynze, having lost 88 officers and 3,000 men, of whom 1,200 were prisoners, and 40 guns. Béru, who was weak in cavalry, said that with more squadrons he would have taken half the Dutch. Then the French gave themselves up to pillage, not thinking of Beaulieu, who had withdrawn to the north-east to Lendelede. The Representative Levasseur wrote of the attack made by 'les braves divisions que commandent les braves Béru, Macdonald et Dupont'.[2] Ney's regiment, the 4th Hussars, had been ordered to join Hédouville on the morning of the 13th September, so he must have been in this affair.[3]

Following victory, came disaster after disaster. Not knowing that Le Quesnoy had surrendered on the 11th September, Houchard continued his movement east for its relief, and Hédouville and Dumesny were ordered from Menin south for Lille. They came, but in full flight. On hearing of the defeat of the Dutch, the Duke of York had marched eastwards to cover them, but they had been avenged by Beaulieu. Hédouville, leaving Menin on the 15th September 1793, had thrown Demars's brigade, some 3,000, down the Lys to threaten Courtrai, and when Demars showed some natural reluctance for his mission Hédouville urged him on by threats of denouncing him to Houchard. He must take Courtrai or burn it with his shells.

Beaulieu had occupied Courtrai and, as Demars approached, he came out in fine temper, fell on Demars, and drove him back.

[1] Dellard, 23.
[2] Dupuis, Nord, ii. 3-15, 213, 219-22, and Carte 1; Foucart et Finot, Déf. nat., ii. 136-8; Chuquet, Hondschoote, 262-9; Jomini, Rév., iv. 62-5, and Atlas, viii; Dellard, 21-4; Desbrière, La Cav. pendant la Rév.: La crise, 392; Vict. et Conq., ii. 24-6; Calvert, 131-6.
[3] Dupuis, Nord, ii, note 4, p. 6.

Hédouville brought up reinforcements, but Demars was driven back to Menin. The mass of the division was on its way to Lille, and Demars was left outside Menin to hold till night. On came the Austrians, and when Demars's men saw their cavalry they set off in full flight through Menin for Lille. The Dutchman, Daendels, commanding in Menin, checked the rout for a time, but it began again and the French were pursued into and through the town, many being drowned in the river. Béru, the commander of Macdonald, at last came up with some light guns and, with the aid of the Representatives, drove back the Austrians and brought the column off, for which he was made General of Division next day, whilst Hédouville and Dumesny were of course arrested and sent to Paris. Hédouville, praised by Houchard, was acquitted and, not being employed again, died in 1818.[1] Dumesny, also acquitted, served again in La Vendée.[2] We hear nothing of Macdonald.

The French lost 500 killed and wounded, 200 prisoners, and two guns.[3] Béru, as I have said, was promoted, but it is amusing to read the attack made on him for a number of imaginary crimes committed in this affair, his denouncer kindly giving the *Comité* the defence he assumed Béru to make to each charge, 'Because I am a Noble', &c.[4] Ney's regiment was probably in the rout of Hédouville's division.[5]

In these operations we have been concerned with the left of the 'Nord', where Jourdan, Mortier, Murat, and Ney had been serving with Hoche and Moreau. I now return to the right of the army and to the events which occurred after Houchard had been drawn westwards by the march of the Duke of York. Coburg, when York had left him, had first cleared the French from the forest of Mormal on the 17th–18th August 1793, driving their force into Landrecies and

---

[1] Wallon, *Trib. rév.*, ii. 367.
[2] Dupuis, *Nord*, i, note 2, pp. 308–9.
[3] Ibid., ii. 15–22, 232–3 ; Chuquet, *Hondschoote*, 306–14 ; Gay de Vernon, *Custine et Houchard*, 284–5 ; Jomini, *Rév.*, 65–6, Atlas, viii ; Foucart et Finot, *Déf. nat.*, ii. 139–40 ; Aulard, *Recueil*, vi. 511, 577, vii. 101.
[4] Dupuis, *Nord*, ii. 244–5.
[5] It is, I think, by mistake that Dupuis (ii. 18) puts the 4th Hussars at Gavrelle on the 15th Sept. This must have been the 7th Hussars ; see his pp. 221–6..

Bouchain; he then besieged Le Quesnoy, which surrendered on the 11th September 1793.[1] Houchard had ordered that an attempt should be made to relieve the town, and on the night of the 11th September 1793 two columns advanced; Ihler from Maubeuge, with 14,000 men, moved through Landrecies and Avesnes, picking up troops from both places, but was beaten back, retiring in the greatest disorder. Then Declaye advanced from Cambrai with some 4,663 men, taken from his own garrison and that of Bouchain. The bells of Cambrai rang gaily for some hours in honour of Houchard's success, but late in the day they gave way to the 'general assembly' to man the ramparts. Declaye had been crushed. His troops were new levies and dragged with them two guillotines, but these heroes soon found the difference between beheading defenceless fellow countrymen and meeting in the field the men they loved to describe as 'the slaves of tyrants'.

Moving north-east for Saulzoir, on the east of Villers-en-Cauchie, appeared the enemy's cavalry. Declaye tried to draw back on Avesnes-le-Sec, but the Austrian squadrons with the *émigré* regiment, *Royal-Allemand*, broke his cavalry, which galloped for Bouchain, followed by Declaye himself. The French infantry then formed square, but the Austrian horse went over them and but few escaped; 2,000 were killed, and 2,000 were taken prisoners when the troopers were sick of slaying. Eighteen guns were left on the field by their drivers. Even this was not the worst, for Cambrai and Bouchain had been stripped of troops to make up Declaye's force and, had Coburg but followed up his stroke, Bouchain, left with a garrison of only 500 men, must have surrendered at a summons. The Allies, however, did not make war in that style, and Coburg, thinking the matter over, settled down to besiege Maubeuge, whilst the French hurried men and food into Bouchain and Cambrai. One thing was really marvellous: Declaye, when arrested, did not lose his head, but went to work for which he was better fitted, the suppressing of the revolt of Lyons against the Convention.[2]

---

[1] Dupuis, *Nord*, ii. 225, 234, 235. In Foucart et Finot, *Déf. nat.*, ii. 157–9, the date is given differently. The garrison marched out on the 13th Sept. 1793.
[2] Dupuis, *Nord*, ii. 24–32, 210–11, 215–18, 222, 229–31, 250–60; Chuquet,

These defeats were fatal to Houchard, who was denounced at once in Paris as incapable, for which much might be said, and as a traitor, which was absurd ; his arrest and death were inevitable. The Convention and the Representatives were too strong now to make it necessary to adopt such precautions as in the earlier case of Custine, but still some care was taken to prevent either resistance or flight on the part of the victim, although he was asking to be relieved of his command.[1] First several of the staff were arrested, and the consent of General Duquesnoy to accept the interim command was obtained. Then, when Houchard, all bewildered, came to the Representatives on the 23rd September 1793 to know what was happening, he was told he was in arrest. Always anxious to degrade commanders, the Representatives had him taken to the common prison and sneered at his complaints of being treated like a private. Then much was made of finding amongst his papers letters from foreign officers, containing commonplaces of war on exchange of prisoners, &c.[2] Meantime, pathetically enough, the old soldier was explaining to the Representatives his fears lest the enemy should be marching on Maubeuge. Later, in Paris, when very near the scaffold, he was writing on the proper system of drilling men in the riding school.[3] Even in the Convention complaints were made of his removal, but these were crushed by Robespierre.[4]

Houchard soon found himself a prisoner, first in the Abbaye and then in the Conciergerie at Paris. There he must have been confirmed in his belief as to the determination to guillotine the Generals by finding twenty-four officers of that rank prisoners with him. In his defence against the charge of treason, he said, ' I only wished for the rank of Captain of Dragoons, and I had obtained that. A stranger to all ambition, to all intrigue, I did not ask for any of the posts I have filled. I did not want to be Colonel, nor General of Brigade, nor

---

Hondschoote, 270–306 ; Foucart et Finot, *Déf. nat.*, i. 632–60, ii. 156–63 ; Gay de Vernon, *Custine et Houchard*, 280–5 ; Jomini, *Rév.*, iv. 37–41 ; Thiébault, i. 447–51 ; Langeron, 23–5 ; Calvert, 132–6 ; *Vict. et Conq.*, ii. 20–4. See plan for L'Échec du Cateau, Coutanceau, *Nord*, IIe Partie, i.

[1] Dupuis, *Nord*, ii. 49. [2] Ibid., 248–9 ; Aulard, *Recueil*, vii. 70–2.
[3] Desbrière, *La Cav. pendant la Rév.: La crise*, note 3, p. 291.
[4] Hamel, *Robespierre*, iii. 141–8.

General of Division, nor General of an army, and I was forced to take the commands which to-day bring me insults and a prison. What ? I have thirty-eight years' service, I have always fought bravely and no one has doubted my courage. I have six wounds, which are so many certificates of my bravery. A musket shot has gone through my face, a second through my thigh, a third in the leg, and three sabre-cuts.' So spake the simple-hearted trooper to his butchers in Paris. But why continue ? One word felled him. ' They called me coward.' After that, death was sweet. Condemned as traitor and coward, he died on the 16th November 1793.[1]

If the Revolutionary Tribunal could condemn Houchard to infamy, the army, which knew his faults, knew also his gallantry and his patriotism, and neither it nor the country accepted the sentence of the Tribunal. It was given to the wise generosity of the two Napoleons to wipe out many such bloody stains in the military history of France. It is pleasant to read the quaint but serviceable legal fiction by which on the 10th September 1800 the First Consul gave a pension to the widow of the General who had died as a traitor. ' General Houchard, having been in employment at the moment he was brought before the Revolutionary Tribunal, is considered as having died on active service.'[2] The money may have been needed by the widow, but far sweeter must have been the implied reparation to her husband's name. So felt the widow of Ney in later years when, before the massed troops and dignitaries of France, under the Prince President, she saw the Marshal rise again in his statue, defying his foes.

---

[1] Wallon, *Rep.*, iv. 150-1 ; ibid., *Trib. rév.*, ii. 82-90 ; Chuquet, *Hondschoote*, 314-36 ; Beugnot, i. 226-9 ; Aulard, *Recueil*, vii. 83-4.

[2] *Corr. Nap.*, vi, No. 5096. In June 1890 a monument to Houchard was raised on the field of Hondschoote.

XIII

L' ARMÉE DU NORD (*continued*), 1793-4

Jourdan succeeds Houchard. He finds the army in confusion, but the troops becoming inured to war. His personal advantages. Position of future Marshals with the army. Difference in their ranks. One division armed with pikes. Jourdan advances with Carnot to relieve Maubeuge. Clairfayt announces that, if the French take the position held by the army covering the siege, he will become a *sans-culotte*. French beaten in the first day of the battle of Wattignies; 15th October 1793. Second day Clairfayt retires, but Jourdan remains, half checked. How his right column ran. Absurd attitude of the garrison of Maubeuge. The inconsistencies of the Carnot legend of Wattignies. The opinion of Soult and of Napoleon. Evidence that Jourdan was hampered in his operations. The French artillery win the day. Want of skill and tenacity of the Allies. Position of the future Marshals with the army. The left of the ' Nord ' also advances, but has to retreat. Hoche goes to command the Armée de la Moselle. Moreau made General of Brigade, but leads a division. The difficulties of Macdonald. Souham protects him. Jourdan threatens to resign and is permitted to take up winter quarters. He is called to Paris. The Representative Duquesnoy protects him against Carnot, who is splashed with ink. Jourdan dismissed by Carnot. He retires to his home and places his uniform of General in his shop.

THE bloody inheritance of Houchard fell to Jourdan, who, put *hors de combat* for a week by his wound,[1] had just gone to Maubeuge to take command of the Armée des Ardennes, to which he had been nominated on the 9th September 1793, the day after Hondschoote.[2] The appointment of Kellermann, an old officer and a General before the Revolution, to the command of an army had been natural enough and might have occurred under the *ancien régime*; and, after all, he had only 16,000 men of his own at Valmy. Now Jourdan, whom the Revolution had found a discharged private, leapt into command of more than 104,000 men.[3] At first on the 22nd September he was chosen to act as Commander-in-

[1] Dupuis, *Nord*, ii. 215. [2] Foucart et Finot, *Déf. nat.*, ii. 164.
[3] Dupuis, *Nord*, ii. 54.

Chief of the ' Nord ' ' provisoirement ',[1] the ' Ardennes ' being put under him on the 2nd October.[2] On the 23rd September he received the first order, and reached Guise on the 24th, and the camp at Gavrelle, between Douai and Arras, on the 25th. He came most unwillingly, telling the Representatives that he had neither the talents nor the experience necessary for such an important command, so that it was his duty to refuse it, but the Representatives reminded him of a decree ordering the arrest of any citizen who did not accept the employment assigned to him, and he had to obey.[3] Carnot, who had been on the field, recommended his appointment,[4] and Robespierre, who doubtless knew nothing of his absence from the final charge, represented him as taking Hondschoote and used his virtues to attack Houchard.[5]

Born in 1762 Jourdan had enlisted in 1778 and served six years in the army. On discharge he became a linen-draper and, marrying a dressmaker, the two joined trades. As he is described as travelling for orders with a pack on his back, his business does not seem to have been a large one ; possibly indeed the word ' pedlar ' might describe him with some accuracy. The first movements of the Revolution recalled him to the ranks, and he became Captain of the *Chasseurs à pied* of the National Guard of Limoges in 1790. When battalions of volunteers were formed from the National Guard in June 1791 to serve with the regular troops, he was elected commander of the second battalion of the Department of Haute-Vienne. We have followed him in his subsequent career.

Jourdan had great personal advantages for command at this moment. As a former private soldier, he was not open to the charge of a love for the *ancien régime*, which had given him no career, and he was too plebeian to suffer from the suspicions which had done such harm to Dumouriez, Custine, Dampierre, and even to Houchard. In theory at least he was a thorough ' patriot ', and for long had an almost touching belief in the Revolutionary watchwords. While possessing a certain sense of his own worth, he was very modest and was not likely to

---

[1] Dupuis, *Nord*, ii. 49, 242-3. [2] Ibid., 95, 264.
[3] Ibid., 49-50. [4] Carnot, i. 408.
[5] Hamel, *Robespierre*, iii. 142, 147-8.

awaken the uneasy jealousy of the Representatives : indeed, until the end of the system under which that body existed, he was singularly successful in conciliating those with his commands, and, what was better, in using their influence for his own aims. He was not a great General : he cannot be placed higher than in, say, the third rank of commanders, men capable of command, but liable to serious errors. He rose early in his career to be Commander-in-Chief, too early indeed for his permanent fame. The reader who has followed my account of what may seem mere skirmishes or unimportant fights will realize how bad a school were these campaigns for a future Commander-in-Chief. Half-organized troops, acting in a desultory and indolent fashion along the frontier, making ill-arranged dashes at the enemy, seldom achieving combined action, taking little thought beforehand for their flanks and then easily frightened by flank attacks, all this was bad training. Still he was just the man for the odd sort of war now being carried on in this district ; to concentrate at one point or another of a long line, and then to attack enemies who spread themselves largely. The daring warfare of Bonaparte, which required so much long marching and hard fighting from the men, such skill and tenacity from the Generals, would have brought ruin on the troops at this period. Such a patient pause as Masséna made before Zurich in 1799 would have led him to the scaffold in 1793 : indeed, we shall find similar caution on the part of Jourdan nearly bringing him to that end. Above all, Jourdan possessed that dogged obstinacy which to the end of his career in the field made him undaunted by defeat. Throw his army back over a river, rout it from a field of battle, and he was ready to begin again next day. Honesty and tenacity of purpose go far in war, as in other matters.

The future Marshals and other distinguished men serving in the 'Nord' under Jourdan, besides that General himself, were Captain Bernadotte in the 36th Regiment, General of Brigade Macdonald, Lt.-Colonel and Adjutant-General Mortier, Lt.-Colonel Murat of the 21st Chasseurs, and Lieutenant Ney of the 4th Hussars, besides Lt.-Colonel Moreau at the head of the 1st volunteers of Ille-et-Vilaine, and General of Brigade

Hoche. Of these Bernadotte, Mortier, and Ney alone went to the right of the army and were engaged at Wattignies, the others remaining on the left. Mortier served as staff officer, say Chief of the Staff, in the division of Balland, who had been a drummer in the battalion of the National Guard of Paris to which Thiébault belonged ; Balland had cleaned the boots of that vivacious writer, who was furious when this man, ' sans forme et sans fond ', made Colonel at Jemappes, was given a division.[1] We shall find that Mortier probably suffered from having such a chief. One incident will show the great difference in the rank of the future Marshals at this time. At the first council held to determine the next movements, Jourdan was present as the Commander-in-Chief of the main army of the Republic, on which everything depended. Carnot's order to introduce a miller, from whom information was wanted, was carried out by one of the junior staff officers, Lt.-Colonel Mortier.[2] Had the whole army been there, Lieutenant Ney might well have been outside in charge of an escort, and Captain Bernadotte in command of a guard.

Jourdan found everything in wild confusion from the arrests among the staff, and he reported that he knew neither the strength of his troops nor what Generals led them. Carnot, coming down from Paris to inquire, found he had not exaggerated the state of affairs. But the situation really was not so gloomy as it seemed, for in the constant fighting the troops were getting inured to war and most of the incompetent officers had been weeded out. Also there were signs that the French were beginning to understand that to cover a frontier by a long line of posts was not the best way to defend it. It is significant that whilst one cause of Custine's ruin was the lamentation of the commander of Lille at the way in which he tried to draw men and ordnance from that fortress, now a similar wail about the weakness of the garrison was met by the Representatives with the reply that they would cover the place, that is to say, by an advance. However, they and Jourdan felt the danger of this. ' Jourdan is worthy of the command entrusted to him ', wrote Carnot after Wattignies. ' But victory was

---

[1] Thiébault, i. 263, 444 ; Dupuis, *Nord*, ii, note 1, p. 92.
[2] Foucart et Finot, *Déf. nat.*, ii. 244.

necessary to him. He was lost if he had failed; already he was denounced as a traitor, and I also, for having drawn the garrisons from the towns to join the army.'[1] The Allies were 106,000 to 128,000 strong,[2] but, with less excuse than the French, they wasted their force by stretching their line unnecessarily. They were incapable of the boldness which would have led to a concentration for a march on Paris, or for a vigorous and prolonged onslaught on the main body of the French until it were shattered. Also their armies were of three nations with different aims, and the absurd excursion of the English to Dunkirk and the crushing of the Dutch at Menin had weakened the union, the Dutch giving much trouble.[3]

Jourdan submitted his plans for the campaign,[4] but his hand was forced by Coburg, who began the siege of Maubeuge with a corps of 26,000 men, mostly Dutch, covered by a *corps d'observation* of 37,000, posted two leagues off at Wattignies and along a line of villages in front of it,[5] stretching far to their flanks. The Duke of York was coming up from Menin, but he was very weak, as the 19th, 27th, 42nd, and 57th English Regiments had left him for Ostend and the West Indies, the 14th was at Courtrai, and the 53rd at Nieuport, so that he had only the Guards, reduced by sickness to 1,400 men, four weak Hanoverian battalions, and seven English cavalry regiments, some 5,000 men.[6] Just as Houchard had concentrated on his left to relieve Dunkirk, so now Jourdan concentrated on his right to save Maubeuge, and he began collecting some 44,276 men of the 'Nord' and the 'Ardennes' at Guise. This force consisted of the division of Fromentin (in which was Lieutenant Ney's regiment, the 4th Hussars [7]), the division of Balland (where was the 36th Regiment in which Bernadotte was Captain), and those of Duquesnoy, of Cordellier, and of Beauregard,[8] the last belonging to the 'Ardennes'. The

[1] Dupuis, *Nord*, ii. 134-5.
[2] Ibid., i, note 1, p. 260, ii. 74-5; Jomini (*Rév.*, iv. 36) makes them 163,000, probably the nominal strength.
[3] Dupuis, *Nord*, ii. 105-6; Langeron, 26. [4] Dupuis, *Nord*, ii. 55-8.
[5] Ibid., 59-75, 109, 113, 155, 176-7, 198-9.
[6] Ibid., 107, 193; Calvert, 142-54.
[7] See Dupuis, *Nord*, ii. 282-3, for the transfer of the 4th Hussars from Balland to Fromentin.
[8] See ibid., 100-3, 280.

volunteer battalion of Lt.-Colonel Mortier was in Cordellier's division, but he seems to have been appointed Adjutant-General on the 3rd September and to have been in Balland's division.[1]

A mass of men was left unused, for instance 10,000 between Arras and Douai, but Arras was the country of Robespierre, and woe to the General who 'uncovered' that sacred spot. Still it is difficult to know the value of the men left in rear, for example, a division of troops of the new levy held the camp at Guise. These men were armed with pikes only, and some older battalions had to stay to guard them, this being, says Jomini, the only instance of a large corps requiring a detachment to protect it.[2] The Republic was very short of muskets, and not only were pikes being manufactured, but there were thoughts of 're-establishing the use of bows and arrows'.[3] On the 14th October 1793 Carnot came again from Paris and acted as adviser and companion to Jourdan. Of course he is often given the credit of the success won, which I believe really was due to Jourdan himself.

After a delay caused by want of ammunition, Jourdan advanced to strike the force covering the siege of Maubeuge, and on the 15th and 16th October 1793 was fought the battle of Wattignies. The Austrian *corps d'observation* under Clairfayt lay to the south of Maubeuge, with its right on the Sambre, by Berlaimont, whence its line stretched eastwards to and beyond Wattignies.[4] Nominally Clairfayt had 37,000 men, but his line extended so far that he only had 21,000,[5] Langeron says 18,000,[6] to meet Jourdan, who had 45,000.[7] In his rear Maubeuge was blockaded by a mixed force of 26,000 under the Prince of Orange, 16,000 Dutch on the left bank of the Sambre, and 10,000 Austrians on the right bank of that river. Little help could be drawn from this force, as the Prince of Orange refused to send any troops over to the right bank of

---

[1] Gavard, 12.
[2] Jomini, *Rév.*, iv. 123. See Ernouf's *Souvenirs d'un jeune abbé*, 1-7, for an account by a private.
[3] Dupuis, *Nord*, ii, note 1, p. 137.
[4] See Carte 2 in Dupuis, *Nord*, ii.
[5] Dupuis, *Nord*, ii. 113, 154-5, note 3, p. 198. [6] Langeron, 27.
[7] Dupuis, *Nord*, ii. 113; Thiers, *Rév.*, ii. 295; Carnot, i. 40; Jomini, *Rév.*, iv. 123-4, makes him 50,000 to 60,000.

the Sambre. Maubeuge itself was held by 20,000 French troops, who were expected by both sides to make a sortie to help Jourdan. The French also had the advantage of approach by a country much wooded and broken, so that they could avoid much of the power of the Austrian squadrons; still, the Austrian position was entrenched, and Coburg was so confident in the superiority of his troops that it was announced that, if the French succeeded, he would become a *sans-culotte*. This delighted the army of Jourdan, which, getting wind of the tale, set to work to make a pair of trousers for presentation next day.[1] Although Clairfayt commanded the covering force with which Jourdan had to deal, Coburg, the Generalissimo of the Allies, was on the ground and seems to have controlled the operations.[2]

Jourdan was a 'patriot', and before the battle he wrote from Avesnes in the style of his party to the Minister. The enemy, he said, had 64,000 infantry and 25,000 cavalry, but he counted on the courage and energy of the Republicans whom he commanded. 'One ought to be worth two', and he would fall 'with the most decided audacity on this horde which is only encouraged by the little resistance opposed hitherto to their efforts and to the perfidy of the leaders. . . . I have only time to tell you that my country will be triumphant, or I shall perish in defending it.'[3] It was lucky for him that his Republicans had not to meet not double, but even equal forces. He had to learn a good deal, and it is probable that his views on the perfidy of the chiefs may have altered after the treatment he himself soon received.

The details of the battle do not concern us much and can be followed in Lt.-Colonel Dupuis's excellent work.[4] The plan for the first day, the 15th October 1793, smacks of Carnot, for both wings attacked those of the enemy, whilst Balland's division in the centre, where Bernadotte and Mortier were, was to be thrown on the enemy's centre when their wings had been driven back. Some assistance was expected from a body, 3,500 strong, of new levies under Élie, marching far on the right

---

[1] *Vict. et Conq.*, ii. 86–7 ; Foucart et Finot, *Déf. nat.*, ii. 247 ; Fricasse, 18–19.
[2] Langeron, 27–9 ; Calvert, 154–6.   [3] Marmottan, *Fromentin*, 88.
[4] Dupuis, *Nord*, ii. 153–70, and Cartes 2 and 4.

from Philippeville on Beaumont; but these men were to be kept from actual contact with the enemy and were only to be seen at a distance, not to fight. At first Fromentin on the left, and Duquesnoy on the right, made good progress, and Carnot at once proposed to throw Balland in the centre on Dourlers. It was too soon, and Jourdan urged that it should not be done until the left had made more progress. Carnot, however, persisted in his opinion and, when he said that such prudence would allow victory to escape them, Jourdan gave way to what he described as pride and the vivacity of his age:[1] we may rather believe that he saw his danger if he disregarded Carnot and if he were then defeated. Anyhow, he put himself at the head of Balland's division and advanced on Dourlers. Here he met a stern resistance, his heavy batteries could not get up in time, and his light infantry was crushed by the enemy's guns. Meantime Duquesnoy was checked at Wattignies, and on the left Fromentin, venturing his division into the plain by the Sambre, contrary to the intention of Jourdan, if not to the letter of his instructions,[2] was caught by the Austrians and was thrown back. The French were beaten off with the loss of 12 guns, Balland alone losing about 1,500 men.[3]

Lieutenant Ney, it is to be presumed, was with his regiment, the 4th Hussars, in the division of Fromentin. It was used on the day before the battle to reconnoitre the Avesnes wood[4] and probably was overwhelmed by the Austrian cavalry on the 15th. Of course we have no mention of him, a simple Lieutenant. A squadron of his regiment, under Captain Boyé, distinguished itself by slashing its way through the enemy's infantry when cut off by their cavalry.[5] Fromentin attributed part of his defeat that day to the Colonel of the 25th Cavalry, who refused to obey the order to charge and made his way off the field instead.[6] The Austrian squadrons, on the other hand, on both days of the battle were used with great effect in attacks on the French infantry in the open, or when debouching from villages which they had taken.[7]

---

[1] Dupuis, *Nord*, ii. 164.
[2] Ibid., 161-2.
[3] Ibid., 170. See other authorities farther on, for the whole battle.
[4] Ibid., 293.
[5] Ibid., note 2, p. 160.
[6] Marmottan, *Fromentin*, 91, 102-3.
[7] Desbrière, *La Cav. pendant la Rév.: La crise*, 398.

There is a difficulty about Mortier, who in some accounts was wounded on the 16th October, the second day of the battle, at Dourlers and was made Lt.-Colonel Adjutant-General in consequence. In reality he was given that rank on the 3rd September, according to Gavard,[1] or by other accounts for his behaviour at Hondschoote.[2] Certainly he was on the staff when Jourdan held his first council on coming to command this army and we may take him as serving in Balland's division, which attacked Dourlers. Here he was wounded on the 15th, the first day, and was carried into the château to have his wound dressed.[3] There, it is said, he was visited by Carnot, who appointed him Adjutant-General, but more likely confirmed his appointment to that post. The accounts which place his wound on the second day, the 16th, probably are wrong, for there was little or no struggle at Dourlers then.[4] Bernadotte, in the same division, is said to have distinguished himself the first day [5] Marmottan places Marceau here in command of a battalion of volunteers, but in reality he then was Adjutant-General in La Vendée.

That night Jourdan adopted a more sensible plan; the decisive attack was to be made by the right, whilst the centre and left only held the enemy in their front. Some 6,000 men were taken from Balland and were formed into a body to act on the left of Duquesnoy, under Jourdan himself. This brought the right wing, the divisions of Duquesnoy and Beauregard and Jourdan's body, up to 22,000 men. On the other hand Coburg had strengthened his left with some four battalions from the left bank of the Sambre, making the *corps d'observation* 22,400 men (16,400 infantry and 6,000 cavalry [6]). Reports told him that Jourdan had been reinforced by new levies from Paris, so that the French had 100,000 men, but, still confident in his troops, he determined to stand. It will be seen, however, that the great increase to the French right gave them every

---

[1] Gavard, 12.
[2] Michaud, *Biog. univ.*, lxxiv, 435; *Fastes*, i. 407, with the date of Wattignies.
[3] Piérart, *Wattignies*, 56; Marmottan (92) puts the wound as received at Saint-Aubin, a little south of Dourlers.
[4] Dupuis, *Nord*, ii. 178.
[5] Marmottan, *Fromentin*, 92.   [6] Dupuis, *Nord*, ii. 176–7.

chance of beating back the Austrian left, for their force there was equal to the whole *corps d'observation*. In Jourdan's arrangements there was some attempt at making the army more manageable by forming Wing-Commands. On the left Cordellier was put under Fromentin, and Duquesnoy was given power to issue orders to Beauregard on his right.[1]

On the second day of the battle, 16th October 1793, Jourdan and Carnot went to the right, where the decisive battle was fought, the centre and left doing little. A thick fog covered the advance till 9 a.m. Twice the French advanced, as the enemy said, ' avec un acharnement indicible ', but were twice swept back. At last Lecourbe, who commanded four battalions on Duquesnoy's left, rallied the men of several regiments. He dismounted, took a musket, and with his Adjutant, Gauthier, beating the charge on a drum, led the men on again. Duquesnoy's column advanced whilst Jourdan on his left was rallying his men and trying to prevent them from retreating. All the columns now joined in the attack on Wattignies ; it was taken and after another struggle the slopes beyond were cleared of the enemy.[2]

' Lecourbe will go far ', said Moreau,[3] then with the part of the army left in the north, a well-founded prophecy, but a curious one when the different ends of the two men are considered, Moreau himself getting further than he can ever have dreamt of in these years, and becoming adviser of the Allied Monarchs.

Jourdan had won Wattignies, but there were many deductions to be made from his success. The day had been doubtful once or twice : Gratien, bringing up a brigade of young soldiers on the left of Duquesnoy to support the attack on Wattignies, was caught by the Austrian cavalry in the open, when his men ran in on the main attack and threw it into confusion. For

---

[1] Dupuis, *Nord*, ii. 289-90.
[2] For Wattignies see Jourdan's dispatch in Bonnal, *Carnot*, 153-4, and in Marmottan's *Fromentin*, 95-6. Dupuis, *Nord*, ii. 153-88 ; Jomini, *Rév.*, iv. 123-35 ; *Vict. et Conq.*, ii. 85-93 ; Foucart et Finot, *Déf. nat.*, ii. 237-58 ; Piérart, *Wattignies* ; Thiers, *Rév.*, ii. 295-8 ; Philebert, *Lecourbe*, 47-51 ; Marmottan, *Fromentin*, 87-99 ; Calvert, 148-57 ; Langeron, 26-31. For plan see those with Dupuis, *Nord*, ii ; *Vict. et Conq.*, ii. 74 ; and Thiers, *Rév.*, Atlas, xi.
[3] Philebert, *Lecourbe*, 50.

this he was sent to the rear to be 'shortened', although he escaped that fate.[1]

On the right matters had been very bad. Beauregard's division, belonging to the 'Ardennes', bad troops under a bad General, reached Obrechies on the Austrian left, but retired on the mere sight of the Austrian cavalry and was pursued right back to Solre-le-Château, losing five guns and leaving Duquesnoy's right flank exposed. This check was far more severe than the French allow. They make Beauregard halt at Solrinnes, about half-way between Obrechies and Solre-le-Château.[2] Perhaps he may have occupied that post eventually, but Calvert, who was on the field, corroborates the statement that Beauregard was pursued to Solre-le-Château,[3] well in rear of Jourdan's right and not to be confused with Solre on the Sambre, near Merbes-le-Château. Langeron asserts that the Austrians not only reached Solrinnes, but penetrated to Solre-le-Château, whereupon the French abandoned Wattignies and Dourlers, leaving thirty guns on the field.[4] Certainly, as we shall see, the French seem to have received a blow which deadened their advance.

A recital of the fortunes of the extreme right column, that of Élie moving from Philippeville on Beaumont, will show with what materials Jourdan had to work and what were part of the forces which kept Coburg from Paris. Élie had some 3,500 men, two-thirds of whom were *réquisitionnaires*, forced into the ranks and utterly unfit for the field. Élie, however, one of the conquerors of the Bastille, hoped that love of their country, the character of Republican soldiers, and the desire to vanquish tyrants, would be at least an equivalent to experience on their part. Naturally he harangued them, and the patriotic and Republican voices which cried 'Vive la République' and 'Vive la Montagne' presaged victory to his heart. Full of confidence, and proud to lead soldiers of Liberty against those of despots, he started on the 15th October and threw out advanced and flanking parties in proper style. Unfortunately his main body, becoming alarmed, fired on these men, wounding

---

[1] Général Baron Pierre-Guillaume Gratien (1764–1814), *Fastes*, iii. 252–3 Dupuis, *Nord*, ii, note 1, p. 186.
[2] Dupuis, *Nord*, ii. 187–8, and Carte 4.
[3] Calvert, 156.
[4] Langeron, 29.

some. Next, about half-past one in the morning, a bad time for courage according to Napoleon, nearly the hour when Joubert was to be ordered to attack at Rivoli, an outpost was surprised and then the enemy attacked. The moment the balls sang overhead the patriotic voices shouted, ' Nous sommes perdus '. The fire of their own guns (for here as elsewhere the gunners stuck manfully to their pieces), horrified the men still more, and they broke and ran, overwhelming the corps in rear. Élie succeeded in rallying them and drew them up in two lines by the village of Bossu, whence he prepared to advance again at daybreak. The soldiers of despots, however, again came on, this time ' doucement ' through a thick fog, when the second line of the soldiers of Freedom fired on the first line in front of them, and the whole, throwing away arms and packs, made off to the rear. Loison, then Adjutant-General (known later in Portugal, after he had lost an arm, as ' Maneta '), at the head of the cavalry, by his brilliant valour saved the column from being massacred. ' If I had had soldiers ', wailed Élie, but unfortunately he led men more careful of their lives than of the patriotic sentiment: *vivre libre ou mourir*. He had lost 12 guns and 400 men. As some compensation he announced that the enemy had lost 1,100 men, a marvellous statement, only to be explained by their fatigue in pursuing his flying mob, but they only acknowledged a loss of 138 men. The most astonishing thing about this affair was that Élie was not guillotined. At all events he had employed an Austrian force which had better have been at Wattignies ![1]

In the French account of Wattignies before the publication of the work of Lt.-Colonel Dupuis, Jourdan was represented as triumphant and the retreat of the enemy as certain. It was, however, evident that this was not true. Even on the 17th October he was still at Avesnes. He had lost 3,000 men and, far from considering that he had won a decisive victory, on the evening of the 16th he was preparing to receive a counterstroke from the enemy. Duquesnoy was to be reinforced and was to intrench himself on the plateau of Wattignies. Coburg, however, had lost 365 killed, 1,753 wounded,

[1] See Élie's report in Rousset's *Volontaires*, 258-63; Dupuis, *Nord*, ii. 188-93, 203, 302-3.

and 369 prisoners or missing. The Duke of York had come up to Englefontaine on the afternoon of the 16th with his 3,500 men, the *corps d'observation* was still 20,000 strong, and there was still the Austrian part of the besieging army, 10,000 men, to reckon with. Although Jourdan still had 40,000 men, and there were 20,000 French in Maubeuge, Coburg meant to stand, but the Prince of Orange refused to bring any of the Dutch troops over to the right bank of the Sambre. Covered by a fog, the Allies withdrew, and the French had lost contact so completely that it was only at two on the afternoon of the 17th October that Jourdan and Carnot entered Maubeuge, finding no vestiges of the enemy except some wounded, some gabions, and many entrenching tools.[1]

Part of the hesitation of the French came from the inaction of the 25,000 men in Maubeuge, from whom much had been expected, as they could have taken Coburg in rear. On the first day of the battle the garrison had made a badly organized sortie, but on the second day it had hardly moved and remained listening with interest to the guns of the army engaged in its relief. So it would have remained, a sort of military sleeping Princess, had not a peasant girl strolled into the town on the morning of the 17th with much the same news as brought by the lepers into Samaria. The enemy had gone, and the delighted garrison, declaring ' Nous sommes débloqués ', and anxious to do something, turned out and presented arms to the world in general. Then they sent out a column, not in pursuit of the enemy but to meet Jourdan, who, much disgusted, ordered it back in the right direction. There was generally blood in the farces of the Revolution, and the Second-in-Command in the town, Chancel, with doubtful justice was guillotined for the inaction of the garrison.[2]

In describing Wattignies I have discarded altogether the Carnot legend. In most accounts it is Carnot who rides the whirlwind and directs the storm throughout the two days, minor but important parts being played by his younger brother, Carnot-Feulins, and the other Representative,

---

[1] Dupuis, *Nord*, ii. 193–5; Marmottan, *Fromentin*, 95–6; Bonnal, *Carnot*, 153–4.
[2] Dupuis, *Nord*, ii. 195–8, 301–2; Thiébault, i. 460–5; Fricasse, 12–20.

Duquesnoy.¹ Jourdan is assigned the part of a respectable figure-head, issuing orders only to be corrected by the Representatives. The General is indeed given part of the responsibility for the premature advance of Balland, but at the end of the first day it is to Carnot that all look. Amongst the assembled Generals Jourdan proposes a feigned attack on Dourlers, while the left wing is to perform the curious manœuvre of crushing both wings of the enemy. Meantime Carnot, having read a dispatch telling of the loss of the lines of Wissembourg by the Armée du Rhin, plunged in thought, considers the situation. At last he lifts his head and declares that, if Wattignies be won, victory is assured. Jourdan combats this striking opinion, but Carnot is not only ready with the conception of the necessary plan, but will undertake its execution.

Finally, after long discussion, Jourdan agrees. Then during the last day's battle it is the Representatives, with the younger Carnot, who lead the columns, rally broken troops, and find time to dismount and discharge the muskets of raw soldiers, till at the end Carnot and Duquesnoy meet on the plateau at Wattignies, embracing with a cry which announces victory to one army and defeat to the other; little being left for Jourdan and the odd 40,000 men to do. Yet, with curious inconsistency, when pursuit was to be expected, we are treated to a view of Carnot at nightfall, alone, without a horse, and harassed by the thought how necessary he may be at headquarters in rear at Avesnes, which he contrives to reach at last by the help of a party of cavalry, who give him a horse and take him to the town.²

None of this rhodomontade will stand examination. The mistakes and achievements of the battle were those characteristic of Jourdan and of the armies of the period. The attacks on both wings of the enemy on the first day may pass as the favourite plan of Carnot in strategy and tactics, but the interposition of a central attack points to a compromise between him and Jourdan. Certainly his interference has not always been admired. Long years afterwards Soult, with his

---

¹ There were two Duquesnoys, brothers, with the army, one a General of Division, and the other a Representative.

² Carnot, i. 410–20; Martin, *Hist. de France*, ii. 84–6; Dreyfous, *Les Trois Carnot*, 64–7; Tissot, *Méms. sur Carnot*, 54–9; Rioust, *Carnot*, 32–6.

great experience, criticized Jourdan's proceedings and, though he had not been with this army, he had much knowledge of the period. Blaming him for spreading his forces everywhere on the first day, while Wattignies might have been seized and Maubeuge reached, he says, ' There is also ground for believing that the arrangements of Jourdan were often dictated to him, that his authority had to yield to that of the Representatives, whose will was all powerful, and, finally, that he had to struggle against rivalry in the command and did not always succeed in obtaining obedience '.[1] I know that in later years Napoleon attributed the success of Wattignies to Carnot, but in the first place the Emperor was badly informed about these campaigns in the north, and in the next place he disliked the man he had to make a Marshal, but to whom he would not give a Duchy : I venture to think he was more anxious to take credit from Jourdan than to give it to Carnot. The great mistake, almost a fatal one, of the first day, the premature advance of Balland, Jourdan distinctly states to have been due to his yielding, against his own opinions, to the persistence, and to what practically was the veiled threat, of Carnot, who urged on the movement.[2] On such a point Jourdan was modest enough to be trusted.

The opinion of Soult, that Jourdan would have done better without Carnot, is curiously supported by contemporary evidence. Celliez and Berton, two agents sent to the army by the Minister for War, reported, ' We know that Jourdan is so hampered in his operations that he would have already sent in his resignation had it not been for some patriots who dissuaded him ; but that has not hindered him from being often annoyed to see men covered with the National inviolability be everything with the army, except what they ought to be '. They went on to complain of the deference towards the Representatives which Jourdan, according to them, carried to weakness in letting them act as Generals, although the real motive is clear. ' He feared to displease the Representation of the Nation, he perhaps feared being denounced by the Representatives. . . . However this may be, Jourdan is pure.'[3] Now these very men had been hard at work denouncing the

---

[1] Soult, *Méms.*, i. 55. [2] Dupuis, *Nord*, ii. 165.
[3] Wallon, *Rep.*, iv. 148-9 ; Dupuis, *Nord*, ii. 117.

Generals and officers of the army and, allowing for any jealousy of the Representatives on their part, it is startling to find them taking this line and unwittingly showing how the raids on the Generals had demoralized the commanders. Consequently, when the *Comité de salut public* at Paris, though urged to leave Carnot with the army, declared they could not spare him from Paris, they may have had good though unavowed reasons for their action.

To me, Jourdan at Wattignies seems much what he always was on the field of battle : his failure to grasp the whole situation being compensated for by a certain amount of obstinacy, which enabled him to grope his way to victory whenever he had not an active commander opposed to him. However well his troops may have fought, it was, says Calvert, a spectator, ' their immense artillery ' which really won the day.[1] It would, however, be unfair not to acknowledge how much Jourdan owed to the faults of his enemy. The Dutch would not allow Coburg to draw men from the army of investment in order to reinforce the body which Jourdan fought, and it is obvious that the Duke of York could have been brought up on the field : indeed, one of his staff, Calvert, whom I have just quoted, was there. The Allies totally failed to see that the best way to defend the length of the frontier was to concentrate and to crush Jourdan, and although they were well informed about his collecting his troops at Guise,[2] they allowed him to bring up slowly superior forces against one link of their long chain, as if their posts were so many players, each bound to defend his own wicket. Also Coburg gave way too easily. The defeat of the French at Neerwinden had been attributed by Langeron not only to the skill, but to the tenacity of Mack, and, had that General been here, the Austrians would have fought the battle to a finish, probably with results disastrous to Jourdan.

Jourdan has criticized himself, saying that he was wrong in not sending more troops to his right ; 10,000 men dispersed in the wood of the Haies d'Avesnes would have held the centre and left of the Austrians in check, whilst in attacking Wattignies with the rest of his army he would have gained a more

[1] Calvert, 154-6. [2] Ibid., 155.

complete victory. As far as the French were concerned, there is nothing to add to this, but, in something of the spirit of Saint-Cyr, he goes on to point out the faults of his adversary, to which, modestly enough, he says he partly owed his victory. Coburg, according to him, placed his army too near Maubeuge and could have found a better position farther off, taking Avesnes and forcing Jourdan to move to his right and to expose his communications with Guise. Jourdan would thus have been delayed until the garrison of Maubeuge, weakly commanded, had surrendered. Certainly he is right in blaming Coburg for not bringing his reserve up to Wattignies, when on the morning of the 16th it was evident that the principal forces of the French were attacking that point. He also blames the detachment of a force under Benjovski at Beaumont,[1] the body which crushed Élie, as, if placed at Obrechies, it might (I presume after the repulse of Beauregard), have fallen on the right of the French at Wattignies.[2] This is all concerned with the second day. As for the first day, he thought that Coburg, if he had followed up Balland's division when it was repulsed, might have crushed it and then, turning on the right flank of Fromentin, have dispersed that division and have gained a complete victory.[3] In this, however, he is not criticizing himself, for, as I have said before, he treats Balland's advance as due to Carnot and made against his own advice.

If we except Carnot, there was no other claimant to Jourdan's laurels, for certainly he owed little to his Generals of Division, all of whom, except Beauregard, had served like him in the ranks before the Revolution, and none of whom did any service under Napoleon.

Carnot, describing Jourdan as 'un brave et honnête sans-culotte', went on, 'General Duquesnoy[4] also is very good: the others, such as Balland,[5] Fromentin,[6] Lemaire,[7] also have much good will, but are weak in talents. Cordellier[8] has not appeared. I believe the Commander-in-Chief does not yet

---

[1] Dupuis, *Nord*, ii. 109. [2] Ibid., 202-3. [3] Ibid., 165.
[4] General Antoine Duquesnoy (1761-96). Ibid., note 5, p. 93.
[5] General Antoine Balland (1751-1821). Ibid., note 1, p. 92.
[6] General Jacques-Pierre Fromentin (1754-1830). Marmottan, *Fromentin*.
[7] General André-Joseph Lemaire (1788- ?). Dupuis, *Nord*, i, note 1, p. 439.
[8] General Étienne-Jean-François Cordellier (1767-1845). Ibid., ii, note 1, p. 103.

know where he is.¹ It seems to me he is of little account.'²
Beauregard had been an officer, a Lt.-Colonel, under the
ancien régime. Kilmaine had denounced him as ' vrai procureur de l'ancien régime, un vil intrigant qui met toute la
division en désordre '.³ It will be remembered how little his
division had done. Jourdan had had to exert himself. ' If it
be considered that Jourdan, after having passed the day on the
field of battle, was present on the evening of the same day
at a council of war and issued two series of orders ; if besides
it be remarked that he was at the bifurcation of the Longe⁴ on
the 16th about 4 a.m. and was present at a battle which lasted
until night fell, it will easily be admitted that Jourdan had
made proof of great physical vigour. It is true that this
Commander-in-Chief was in the prime of life, he was then
thirty-two.'⁵ As for that, however, Luckner at seventy was
vigour itself.

As for the distribution of the future Marshals and of the
men with whom we are concerned, who belonged to the ' Nord '
at the time Wattignies was fought, Jourdan, a Commander-
in-Chief, was on the field, as were Lt.-Colonel Mortier, Captain
Bernadotte, and apparently Lieutenant Ney. General of
Brigade Macdonald, and Lt.-Colonel Murat,⁶ with General of
Brigade Hoche and Lt.-Colonel Moreau, were all away with
the left of the ' Nord ' ; Macdonald being with the Lille force,
under Souham, Murat probably at Pont-à-Marcq, Moreau by
Lille,⁷ and Hoche on the extreme left, at Dunkirk.

There was much resemblance between the battles of Wattignies and Hondschoote, for in each case the French had
broken up a siege by beating the covering army, weaker than
themselves because, for reasons not the same in both cases, it
could not be properly reinforced from the besieging army.

¹ His division had been under Fromentin. Dupuis, *Nord*, ii. 289.
² Ibid., 201.
³ General Pierre-Raphael Paillot de Beauregard (1734- ?). Ibid., note 2, p. 96.
⁴ The road-junction about 2½ miles N.E. of Avesnes.
⁵ Ibid., 175.
⁶ The 21st Chasseurs mentioned by Jourdan as at Gavrelle on the 5th Oct.
1793 in Balland's division were *Chasseurs à pied*, not the 21st *Chasseurs à cheval* to which Murat belonged. See ibid., 269, 272.
⁷ I do not know why Philebert, *Lecourbe*, 50, writes as if Moreau had watched Lecourbe at Wattignies.

No attempt was made to follow up the victory, and Jourdan certainly had good reasons for not doing so. Coburg now had some 65,000 men concentrated on the west of the Sambre, from Solesmes to Thuin, with the forest of Mormal behind him and, as Jourdan put it, 'retranché de la manière la plus respectable'.[1] Jourdan considered he could not attack without exposing himself to be beaten. He ought to have been, for now, supposing he could draw 18,000 from Maubeuge, rather a large number, he would have 60,000 men. Of these we have seen what the division of Beauregard was worth and the troops from Maubeuge probably were of much the same stamp.

Nominally there were other new battalions, but some of these were not even armed, one such corps marching up with its arms on carts, which started some days after it.[2] When they were armed they were rather dangerous. At Landrecies the Commandant, believing the place might be besieged, got a battalion of these men turned out, when 200 of the enemy's cavalry dispersed them.[3] Jourdan therefore halted, nominally for ammunition

Coburg might well have tried a stroke, but he went into winter quarters. It was all, says Langeron, from Mack's being away. 'The expedition to Dunkirk which broke up the army, the retreat from Maubeuge, the slowness of all the movements, finally this disastrous system of forming a cordon, which causes one to be weak everywhere, have hindered the Allies this year from terminating at Paris, or at least on the Oise, a campaign whose commencement had been so brilliant.'[4]

Besides this movement of the right of his large army to relieve Maubeuge, Jourdan had been ordered to make an advance in Flanders with his left, and this he carried out, but the 'Nord', always sprawling on a long line, suffered much from want of command, and now the left failed, just as the right had done whilst Houchard had been with his left at Hondschoote. Davaine, who had the chief command on the left, wasted time in correspondence with Jourdan and, when the left did advance on the 21st October 1793, all its strength was wasted in different columns with different aims: in fact the

[1] Dupuis, *Nord*, ii. 200.
[2] Ibid., 247, 260, 281, 299.
[3] Ibid., 260-1.
[4] Langeron, 30-1.

operation would not be worth our consideration if Macdonald and Moreau, and perhaps Murat, had not been engaged in it. Béru, Macdonald's commander, who had done well in the field, had been suspended on the 9th October as an ex-Noble, just as he was offering to resign the command he had accepted unwillingly. On the 14th October Souham from Dunkirk succeeded him in command of the Camp de la Madeleine, under Lille, an appointment disliked by Souham, who complained that he would have preferred to remain at Dunkirk. He asked to have as assistant General of Brigade Hoche, who had served under him there. ' Ma confiance en ses lumières et en sa capacité vous répond de la sûreté et du salut de ce poste ',[1] but, as we shall see, he did not get Hoche.

Souham moved northwards with his three brigades, Macdonald, Michel, and Dumonceau. On the left Macdonald fell on a body of *émigrés* in Wervicq, and in the centre Dumonceau took Menin with many stores. Farther to the right Michel threatened the camp of Cysoing, against which Osten moved from Pont-à-Marcq with a force probably containing Lt.-Colonel Murat's Chasseur regiment. Still farther south-east Ransonnet took Marchiennes. Matters soon changed, for the Duke of York, who had been at Englefontaine,[2] marched to strike Souham's right, and on the 28th October Abercromby attacked Lannoy, taking four guns. Souham's advanced position was now dangerous: already on the 27th October he had ordered Macdonald, then at Menin, to evacuate the town silently at night, when his brigades fell back safely on Lille, but Ransonnet's division was crushed by the Austrians.[3]

Farther on the left Davaine was to have advanced on Ypres, but, clamouring for reinforcements, he remained at Cassel, only throwing forward on Poperinghe Bertin's brigade and Lt.-Colonel Moreau. This was the first command of Moreau; hitherto he had lead a volunteer battalion, but on the 8th October Vandamme, called away for a higher post, had handed over to him a small column.[4] This attack was

[1] Dupuis, *Nord*, ii, note 2, p. 118. [2] A little south of Le Quesnoy.
[3] Foucart et Finot, *Déf. nat.*, ii. 266–72 ; Jomini, *Rév.*, iv. 137–40 ; *Vict. et Conq.*, ii. 117–20 ; Langeron, 30 ; Calvert, 160–5. For map see Jomini, *Rév.*, Atlas, viii ; Dupuis, *Nord*, i, Carte 3.
[4] Du Casse, *Vandamme*, i. 62.

successful. So also was that on the extreme left, where Vandamme, with the brigades of Hoche and Gougelot, marched from Dunkirk for Furnes and Nieuport.

Furnes was taken by Vandamme with Gougelot's brigade and Hoche attacked Nieuport, the siege of which, if siege be the right name, was directed by him, Vandamme having remained in rear at Furnes till next day, the 22nd October 1793. Then Vandamme came up, and the place was summoned, but it was too strong for the French field artillery and, as the enemy began flooding the country, even the ardent Hoche protested against the order to attack again and advised a retreat on Furnes, which Vandamme eventually ordered and which was effected in some disorder. Furnes was held, but otherwise all the left retook its former positions, Vandamme, who had done all that was possible, being placed in arrest and being kept there till the 11th November 1793.[1]

Several changes amongst the Generals occurred after these operations of the left. Hoche, already General of Brigade, had been nominated as Chief of the Staff to the Armée de la Moselle, late 'Centre', on the 22nd September 1793, whilst he was engaged in Flanders; but on the 22nd October, by an extraordinary promotion, when only 25, he was sent to command the 'Moselle', not, however, as a Commander-in-Chief, as was the rule in such cases, but only as a General of Division, a point which might have proved to be of some importance. His ardour, his declamation, and his correspondence with the patriots, Robespierre, &c., had brought him this promotion, and accordingly he now left for ever the 'Nord' on the 25th October 1793.[2]

Davaine went to the scaffold,[3] and Souham in his place gave Macdonald the command from Bailleul to Dunkirk.[4] As for

---

[1] Foucart et Finot, *Déf. nat.*, ii. 273–80; Wallon, *Rep.*, iv, note 2, p. 163; Cuneo d'Ornano, *Hoche*, 81–2; Rousselin, *Hoche*, i. 89–92; Du Casse, *Vandamme*, i. 65–92; Jomini, *Rév.*, iv. 137–41; Calvert, 165; Langeron, 30; map in Jomini, *Rév.*, Atlas, viii; Coutanceau, *Nord*, IIe Partie, ii, Carte des opérations des divisions de Souham et Moreau, Feuille Nord.

[2] Cuneo d'Ornano, *Hoche*, i. 82–3; Rousselin, *Hoche*, i. 92–3; Chuquet, *Hoche*, 57–8, 171–2; Aulard, *Recueil*, vii. 564–5; Du Casse, *Vandamme*, i. 74, 81.

[3] Wallon, *Trib. Rév.*, ii. 462–3. He was sentenced with O'Moran and Chancel.

[4] Foucart et Finot, *Déf. nat.*, ii. 280.

L'ARMÉE DU NORD, 1793-4   267

Moreau, I suppose that it was for his service to which I have just alluded that on the 20th December 1793 the Representatives nominated him General of Brigade. This was confirmed on the 6th February 1794.¹ It is difficult to understand his position at this time. Later on he said that he was General of Division when the new Commander-in-Chief, Pichegru, arrived,² that is, in February 1794. This is not in accordance with the records, but Moreau probably was right when he went on to say that he then had 25,000 men under his command. Certainly he seems soon to have been entrusted with a force equal to a division, even before he had received his commission as General of Brigade.³ As for Souham, whether or not he were the General directing these last operations, he now certainly became the leading General in this part of the theatre of the Armée du Nord.

His subordinate, Macdonald, was meanwhile serving under the sort of recurring difficulties which show how hard was the fate of the Generals of the Republic. Like a true Scot, he had done his best to get a protector and, finding that one Representative wished to be present at some affair, he arranged an attack in which the Representative heard the balls whistle round him and, delighted at his own prowess, not only graciously permitted Macdonald to cite his deeds in his report, but drew up a report of his own, in which his modesty did not prevent his doing justice to his own gallantry as well as to that of the General, to whom he gave the kiss of brotherhood, and whom he assured that he could reckon on him for life and death. Then, also, when Souham came to take over the command from Béru on the 14th October 1793, that General found he could rely on Macdonald for the security of that portion of the line entrusted to him, and the two began a friendship which was to last permanently.⁴ When the amalgamation of the regulars and the volunteers was to be made, Souham gave that work over to Macdonald, reporting that he had done it with activity, although some of the instructions as to accounts had not been understood.⁵ One observer

¹ *Fastes*, iii. 426.   ² Dontenville, *Moreau*, 10–11.
³ Coutanceau, *Nord*, IIᵉ Partie, ii, Docts. Annexes, 14.
⁴ Macdonald, *Souvenirs*, 30–1.   ⁵ Coutanceau, *Nord*, Iᵉ Partie, 356.

describes Macdonald at this time as a young man, looking not older than 30 or 32 (really he was only 28), full of military talent and even of tactical knowledge.[1]

One would have thought that a General with such a reputation, successful in the field, trusted by his General of Division, praised by a Representative, would have been safe; but Macdonald was a master of jeers and it was a dangerous time to give offence to any patriot. Lavalette,[2] ' Général Républicain et Révolutionnaire au superlatif ', as Macdonald puts it, and a friend of Brune's, had shown cowardice at the recent attack on Menin, and Macdonald had joined in ridiculing him. Another enemy was a ' General ' Dufresse,[3] formerly an actor, but now commanding one of the vile local revolutionary armies, used for the slaughter of citizens : a man who had a guillotine engraved on his seal. Also one of Macdonald's own Lt.-Colonels, Wattel, whom he had placed in arrest for foolish conduct in the field, took his revenge by denouncing his General for sending a *parlementaire* to the enemy.[4] When fresh Representatives, Saint-Just and Le Bas, came to the army, these men denounced Macdonald to them and Saint-Just intended to dismiss him and to send him before the Revolutionary Tribunal of Arras, whence no one returned.[5] Indeed, it was said that court had guillotined one man as ' soupçonné d'être suspect '.[6] The crime Saint-Just alleged against Macdonald was that he had not ' une figure à la Comité Révolutionnaire ', and that, having a Scotch name, he must be an aristocrat.[7]

Souham did his best for his subordinate at a time when it was dangerous to defend any one ' suspect ', telling Saint-Just, ' I do not know if at the bottom of his heart he is Republican, I cannot read his soul, but I know he is an excellent officer, who on every occasion has served the Republic well, and I answer on my head that, instead of betraying, he will serve it as a good and brave soldier '. Saint-Just replied that

---

[1] David, 246.
[2] General Louis-Jean-Baptiste-Thomas Lavalette, guillotined with Robespierre 28th July 1794. Chuquet, *Valenciennes*, 208–11 ; Wallon, *Trib. Rév.*, v. 252.
[3] General Dufresse (1763–1833). Chuquet, *Valenciennes*, 211–15 ; Wallon, *Rep.*, iv. 167–9.
[4] Coutanceau, I^e Partie, i. 36–7.   [5] Wallon, *Rep.*, v. 84–121.
[6] David, 246–7.   [7] Ibid., 245–6 ; Macdonald, *Souvenirs*, 31–2.

they only wanted well-pronounced Republicans and that Macdonald had not the face nor the name of a Republican, his objection to the name coming oddly from a 'Saint'. However, Souham obtained that Macdonald should only be brought in to Lille, to be imprisoned there. Then, sending for the General, he warned him of what was about to be done and hinted that he could emigrate, but Macdonald knew how cold a reception from the *émigrés* awaited such tardy and unwilling recruits, and he determined to try for the help of the friendly Representative, although warned by Souham that he had already done so in vain.

Souham was right, the Representative, perhaps scenting danger for himself, told Macdonald he was not a Republican, and he himself would not meddle in the matter, replying to reminders of his former promises that 'les temps sont bien changés'. Souham again pressed Macdonald to decide, but the General determined to remain, and fortunately for him Saint-Just was recalled.[1] Then Souham, getting a free hand, placed him at Cassel, with the command from Bailleul to Dunkirk, as I have said, having eleven other Generals of Brigade and 40,000 men under him.[2]

The *Comité* or its mouthpiece, Carnot, now ordered Jourdan to advance down the Sambre on Charleroi with his right, but the preparations took time and, when the General was ready to cross the river, he found the passage opposed; rain flooded the country, the roads became impassable, and all movement was stopped. Carnot, snug and dry in Paris, kept on urging an advance, but Jourdan, making a stand which, for the period, was very bold, wrote on the 4th November 1793 that, if the *Comité* insisted on the advance, he must resign, 'I cannot bear the heart-breaking sight of an army destroyed without fighting. I render justice to the brave soldiers who compose it: not the least murmur has escaped from them, although they are half-naked and shoeless, exposed to all the effects of the weather, as it has been impossible to move the wagons.'[3]

Many a General has offered his resignation to escape from a difficult position, or, like Bonaparte in 1796, when anxious to force the hand of a Government, but this letter required

---
[1] David, 246-7; Macdonald, *Souvenirs*, 32-4.   [2] Ibid., 33-4.
[3] Wallon, *Rep.*, iv. 165-6; Foucart et Finot, *Déf. nat.*, ii. 283.

more courage than many a feat in the field. Jourdan staked his head for the good of his men, and from this act we may begin to recognize the honourable qualities of the man. Carnot replied, requesting him to come to Paris to consult with the *Comité*, a measure which usually was an invitation to the scaffold, and Jourdan must have had many misgivings as, handing over the temporary command to General Duquesnoy, he went to Paris. However, it was rather too soon after Wattignies to deal with him in the usual style of the *Comité* and, when matters were discussed, the *Comité* could talk but could not supply boots, and Jourdan, sent back to his army, was permitted to place his troops in winter quarters.[1] Before leaving Paris he had appeared at the Jacobins, on the 11th November 1793. I fancy to the end of his life he believed in the patriotism of this body and now ' the frankness of his explanations, his promise never to employ his sword except to combat kings and to defend the rights of the people, raised the acclamations of the assembly '. Hébert, who had been attacking him, retracted and apologized, but Jourdan escaped the accolade of this wretch, which fell to Duquesnoy.[2] He did not dream he would ever be helping a king to crush the Spaniards.

Indeed, the situation had been too trying even for the temper of the much-enduring Jourdan, and we have curious proof of this in a letter which he, in conjunction with his Chief of the Staff, Ernouf, and the Representative Duquesnoy, wrote about this time to the violent ' patriot ' Hébert. We only have some fragments: ' Behold the labyrinth in which we are lost from false plans, you may well believe they come from false patriots; we have spoken to you of the man; inform yourself, brother, we open our hearts to you; you are the man who can remedy the evils of the Republic.' Then, in a postscript of his own, Jourdan burst out, ' I am in a rage, I too! F—— The army wants everything and, thousand bombs, b—— who have their feet warm want to make the infantry march without shoes, the cavalry without forage, and the artillery without horses. Adieu, F—— Jourdan.' Three years later Carnot brought this letter before the Directory,

---

[1] Jomini, *Rév.*, iv. 141-6; Foucart et Finot, *Déf. nat.*, ii. 282-4; Wallon, *Rep.*, iv. 169-73.   [2] Hamel, *Robespierre*, iii. 208.

alleging that he himself was ' the man ' referred to. The other Directors affected to regret the style of the letter, for 1796 was very different from 1793, but thought it had nothing to do with the circumstances of the day. Exasperated, Carnot gave them each a copy, hoping that on reflection they would not keep in the command of the ' Sambre-et-Meuse ' this ' soudard de 1793 '.[1] This sounds as if the joint action of Duquesnoy and Jourdan had not been pleasing to the Representative, who tried as Director to avenge himself. As for Jourdan, he always had a strange belief in the patriots, but he might well say, ' Did I not well to be angry ? '

The needs of La Vendée soon weakened the ' Nord ' ; 10,000 men were sent there, under General Duquesnoy, and another 10,000 went to the Armée de la Moselle, now under Hoche. The comparative quiet enabled the local patriots to give trouble, as when for instance the *Société populaire* of Maubeuge, meddling with military matters, denounced General Meyer. A number of certificates of character were presented in the General's favour, but it was sagaciously observed that most of the signatories were officers, and what could they know of the character of a General ? Their conduct was ordered to be inquired into, while the soldiers were requested to give their opinion. Poor Jourdan was requested to put in orders an invitation to his army to express its wishes about General Meyer, and a little later he was asked to invite his whole army to make accusations against General Gudin, the uncle of the well-known General of the Empire. Next, a Colonel came to the *Société* to request permission to go to Paris to denounce General Duquesnoy, then on his way to La Vendée, as we have just seen. This was probably a clever manœuvre to strike that General, really a hot patriot, for some private grievance, while away from his brother, the Representative, and he was arrested.[2] In Paris, however, the Representative, supported by Robespierre, defended him before the Convention and brought the General off from the accusation of Hébert. Otherwise he would have gone to the scaffold.[3]

From this wasps' nest Jourdan was soon to escape. Of course

---

[1] Barras, ii. 278–80.   [2] Foucart et Finot, *Déf. nat.*, ii. 292–7.
[3] Hamel, *Robespierre*, iii. 205–8.

it was impossible to prevent the enemy from making incursions on the frontier, and each *commune* visited by the enemy made its shriek of treason heard in Paris. On the 6th January 1794 the Minister complained that, with 150,000 men, Jourdan did not stop the incursions between Landrecies and Cambrai. On the 10th Jourdan replied that he had only 15,000, not 150,000 men there, but the patriots did not wait for troublesome explanations and that day the Minister requested him to come to Paris with his Chief of Staff, Ernouf; the *Comité* ordered that both should be dismissed and arrested, this reward for Wattignies being in the handwriting of one of the signatories, Carnot. Jourdan remained in Paris for some time after his arrival, until he was called before the *Comité*, living meantime with Ernouf near the Tuileries and watching the procession of carts to the guillotine, which any day he might join. Fortunately for him he had usually been on good terms with the Representatives accompanying his army, and now Duquesnoy, who had been some time with him, defended him warmly against the attacks of Carnot for not pursuing the enemy. Duquesnoy simply overwhelmed Carnot, who burst into tears under his reproaches, whilst Duquesnoy in his wrath struck a large ink-pot, which was on the table, so furiously that his unlucky colleagues were covered with splashes of ink. At last Robespierre, who was not on good terms with Carnot, demanded whether Duquesnoy would answer with his head for the patriotism of Jourdan and of Ernouf, and, on a satisfactory reply, the *Comité* decided only to remove Jourdan from his command. In the Carnot legend this figures as Carnot saving the life of Jourdan. Ernouf's real sin, it is alleged, was that he had roughly ejected from a quarter, marked for Jourdan, a nephew of Carnot's, who was in the Commissariat.[1]

In the memoirs of Carnot by his son, Carnot is made to shield Jourdan, and it is given as a proof of this that only he and Prieur signed the decree of the 7th January 1794 altering the order to arrest Jourdan into a simple call to Paris to excuse his conduct.[2] One wonders if there can be any confusion here,

---

[1] Foucart et Finot, *Déf. nat.*, ii. 314; Wallon, *Rep.*, iv. 206-7; Ernouf, 269-71; Dreyfous, *Les Trois Carnot*, 67-8.

[2] Carnot, *Méms.*, 448-9.

for M. Wallon states that the order of the 10th January 1794, that Jourdan and Ernouf were to be 'destitués et mis en état d'arrestation', was in the handwriting of Carnot and was signed by Collot d'Herbois, Billaud-Varennes, Carnot, Barère, and Robespierre. 'Les mots "destitués", etc., sont en surcharge. Le vainqueur de Wattignies destitué par une surcharge de la main de Carnot!'[1] It is usual to defend part of Carnot's conduct by declaring him not to be responsible for what he merely signed. But when he writes a document?

One is almost tempted to believe that the *Comité*, or at least the Minister, was a little ashamed of the compromise that was made, from the tone of the letter written by Bouchotte on the 19th January 1794: 'The intention of the *Conseil exécutif provisoire*, citizen, is that you should proceed without delay to the place of your domicile; they do not think that your stay at Paris at this moment is necessary. If eventually circumstances permit it, you will be again employed in the service of the Republic. It is with regret that they find themselves reduced, by the effect of the stagnation in which the Armée du Nord remains, to the necessity for not employing you at this moment.[2] The *Conseil* knows that you have no fortune. It will remind the *Comité de salut public* of this. It is not the intention of the Nation and of the Convention that he who led our brothers in arms of the Armée du Nord to the deliverance of Maubeuge should suffer poverty.' The *Comité*, indeed, had saved many Generals from all anxiety as to their pecuniary future, and Jourdan must have blessed Duquesnoy and Wattignies each time he felt his head on his shoulders. On the 27th January 1794 he arrived at Limoges and restarted his little haberdashery shop. The *Comité* gave him a pension of 3,000 livres, say £120, so that doubtless he did not experience want. Still, even the mildest and most modest of men may show a little resentment for ingratitude, and the haberdasher who had won Wattignies and who had relieved Maubeuge quietly placed his uniform as General at the back of his shop.[3]

---

[1] Wallon, *Rep.*, iv. 207 and note 2.
[2] Pichegru had been nominated to succeed him, 6th Jan. 1794.
[3] Wallon, *Rep.*, iv. 207-8; Foucart et Finot, *Déf. nat.*, ii. 314-15.

Lieutenant Ney, disgusted with the disgrace of his patron, General Lamarche, had been with his regiment, the 4th Hussars, from the 1st August 1793. Now, on the 20th December 1793,[1] he again left the regiment to become A.D.C. to General Colaud,[2] one of the senior officers of the army ; indeed, we shall soon find Pichegru leaving Colaud for a time in command of the ' Nord '. On his nomination Ney received a certificate of bravery, dated the 21st December 1793, from the officers, *sous-officiers*, and men of his regiment. His association with Colaud probably had not a good effect on his character, rough and unruly as he was, for Colaud seems not to have been easy to rule and we shall find him giving trouble to Jourdan in the ' Sambre-et-Meuse '. At present it suffices to describe him as ' homme à humeur, frondeur impitoyable du gouvernement et peut-être même de la Révolution ', having the reputation of a man of probity and delicacy, timid and fumbling before the enemy, passing for a good General.[3] Like Ney's first patron, Lamarche, Colaud had been a Hussar officer and had much disliked commanding infantry. Early in January 1794 he was sent to instruct light troops, presumably light cavalry, in the garrisons of Rheims and Châlons, Ney of course going with him.

[1] Bonnal, *Ney*, i. 22.
[2] General Baron Jean-Jacques-Bernardin Colaud de la Salcette (1759–1834). *Fastes*, ii. 273–4 ; Michaud, *Biog. univ.*, lxi. 188–9 ; Chuquet, *Hondschoote*, 195–6.
[3] Chuquet, *Hondschoote*, note 1, pp. 195–6.

XIV

L'ARMÉE DU NORD (*continued*), 1794

Pichegru in command of the 'Nord'. Asks for advice. Remarks Macdonald. Positions of future Marshals with the army. History of Moreau. His relations with the future Marshals. Vandamme. Position of Macdonald, ordered to leave the army and to be arrested if he did so. Colaud, one of the patrons of Ney. Curious credit of Pichegru for battles not won by him. His large command. Promotion of Bernadotte and Ney. The Allies besiege Landrecies. The right of the 'Nord' attempts its relief but is beaten. Bernadotte's General shot by his own men. Bernadotte declines promotion to General of Division until more discipline is established. The right of the 'Nord' is again advanced. The column under Chapuis cut up by English cavalry. General Mansell seeks death. Gallantry of French *gendarmes*. English recruits to be fitted from the kits of the dead. National spirit of the Hungarians and Austrians. The stolid English. The slow strategy of the Allies and of Mack. Kléber joins from La Vendée. Murat suspected to be an aristocrat. Ridiculous phrases of Macdonald. The left of the 'Nord' advances on Menin. Garrison breaks out. The Duke of York beats off Bonnaud.

PICHEGRU, the new commander of the 'Nord', had been at the head of the Armée du Rhin, which in conjunction with the Armée de la Moselle had just succeeded in relieving Landau on the Rhine. Hoche, the commander of the 'Moselle', had been in chief command of the two bodies, the appointment being fought for by the Representatives with each army, each of whom wanted it for his own General, so that the Government thought it best to withdraw Pichegru from that theatre.

He had visited Paris on his way[1] and it was not till the 8th February that he arrived at 'Réunion-sur-Oise' (or Guise), relieving Ferrand, who had held the post temporarily from the 13th January 1794 after Jourdan had left.[2] Pichegru came in a curious mood for a commander who had just won, or at least claimed, a brilliant success, for in his first circular

---

[1] Coutanceau, *Nord*, IIe Partie, i. 124 ; ibid., Docts. Annexes, 510.
[2] Ibid., note 2, pp. 122, 125–6.

to his Generals he began by stating the 'insuffisance de mes moyens', and requesting information and advice. 'Finally I ask for your good will, until I can merit your friendship.'[1] Then, instead of carrying out the plan of campaign prepared for him, he placed Colaud in command on the 27th February and set off for a tour of inspection of his army, beginning with the left wing and, though he returned to Guise for a time on the 10th March, it was only on the 17th of that month that he finally settled down in his post.[2] During this tour, on the 2nd March at Lille, he was a spectator of a foray on Cysoing, where several cart-loads of corn were brought in. 'This operation was commanded by a young General of Brigade, named Macdonald, who is said to be a good officer, but whose Republican opinions are not very pronounced.'[3]

The future Marshals and other men of interest with the 'Nord' when Pichegru arrived at that army were General of Brigade Macdonald, Lt.-Colonel and Adjutant-General Mortier, Lt.-Colonel Murat, Bernadotte, made Lt.-Colonel on the 8th February 1794, the very day Pichegru arrived at Guise,[4] and Lieutenant Ney; besides Moreau, promoted General of Brigade on the 6th February 1794. Of these Macdonald and Murat, with Moreau, remained with the left of the army. Murat probably saw little if anything of Pichegru. Writing from Lille on the 30th January 1794 to his family, he said his regiment, after fighting like devils three days before at Pont-à-Marcq, which they had defended for seven months, had been called in to Lille to refit, all naked as they were. By the 18th February 1794 he was on the extreme left at Dunkirk, in the division of Michaud. He wanted his baptismal certificate, as the War Office believed he was Noble. He thought the matter grave enough to talk of what would happen if he lost his place. He was young and would go home and help his parents. However, 'Je suis à ma patrie avant d'être à vous.' He was refusing to be Adjutant-General, a thing I shall refer to later. At Dunkirk he was expecting either to enter Holland or to form part of a descent on England. 'May there be one cry from one end of the universe to the other: " Vive la Liberté,

---

[1] Coutanceau, *Nord*, IIe Partie, i. 127. [2] Ibid., 134-43.
[3] Ibid., 140-1. [4] Ibid., Docts. Annexes, 510.

vive l'Égalité!"' 'For the future all the nations no longer compose more than a single family of brothers, friends, and Republicans', wrote the future King. At Lille he described himself as commanding the field squadrons of the regiment, 21st Chasseurs,[1] so that the new Colonel, Duprès, appointed on the 18th November 1793 to replace Landrieux, may not yet have joined.[2] All the others, Bernadotte, Mortier, and Ney, now appear on the right, a change which in June 1794 took them away from this army to join a new force, the 'Sambre-et-Meuse'. By that time we shall find Bernadotte, a full Colonel on the 4th April 1794, getting his brigade on the 26th June, just as he was leaving this army. Ney got his Captaincy on the 25th April 1794. Macdonald and Murat were to serve on under Pichegru till April 1795, Macdonald getting his division on the 28th November 1794. Murat then went to Paris and Macdonald remained with the 'Nord', first under Moreau and then under Beurnonville; indeed, he remained until the Armée du Nord ceased to exist in 1797. Jourdan and Macdonald then are the only Marshals who won their divisional commands in the 'Nord'. Besides them, the principal personages this army produced are Pichegru and Moreau. Pichegru will be better known by his conduct on the Rhine, when he commanded the Armée du Rhin in 1793 and the Rhin-et-Moselle in 1795-6. Some description of Moreau had better come here.

Moreau was born at Morlaix in Brittany in 1763.[3] He was the son of an *avocat* of high character, who intended him to adopt his own profession, but the young lad chose to enlist in a regiment. His father bought him out, and Moreau, studying at Rennes, became *Prévot* at the *École de Droit* there and had a great hold over the other students. In 1787, in consequence of the quarrel between the Court and the provincial *Parlement*, an attempt was made to disperse the *Parlement* by the garrison, but the Bretons opposed force to force, when the young Moreau used his influence to calm the

[1] Murat, *Lettres*, i. 12-14; Lumbroso, *Corr. Murat*, 10-12; Coutanceau, *Nord*, IIe Partie, ii. 68.
[2] Landrieux, (115).
[3] *Biog. Cont.*, iii. 680, gives his date of birth as 11th Aug. 1745, which must be too early.

people and was styled 'Le Général du Parlement'. At the election for the States-General at Rennes in January 1789, the Nobles, meeting in the monastery of the Jacobins, were blockaded by a mob stated to have been led by Moreau. Amongst these Nobles was the young Chateaubriand, another Breton, who was to have so different a career from Moreau's. Finally the Nobles cut their way through the mob, sword in hand.[1] When the National Guard was formed, Moreau raised a volunteer company of gunners, in which he was Captain. Tiring of this, he tried to enter the *Gendarmerie*, being ready to accept a low rank, but this application was refused.[2] On the formation of the volunteer battalions, Moreau, popular as he was, became Lt.-Colonel of the first battalion formed in his Department, the 1st Ille-et-Vilaine, which was organized on the 10th September 1791.[3]

We have followed his career in the ' Nord ' up to the time when he became General of Division on the 14th April 1794, but he appears to have been really in command of a division when Pichegru joined the ' Nord '. The career of Moreau for the next few months, at all events till the triumphant advance of the ' Nord ' began, should be followed with some attention, as the ordinary biographies tend to represent him as holding at this period a position higher than that of leader of a division. It will be seen that Souham occupied a higher position in the left wing than did Moreau, Souham being the fighting General and, indeed, having Moreau under his command for a most important time, the battle of Tourcoing. In fact both now and later the work of Moreau was mainly that of sieges, and it is not easy to account even for his promotion to the head of a brigade and of a division.[4] ' Pichegru ', says one authority, having got him made General of Division, ' at once entrusted him with a corps destined to act in maritime Flanders ; Moreau first got possession of Menin.'[5] This gives the idea of the command of a separate corps, but the following pages will show that Menin was taken under the immediate direction of Pichegru, whilst Souham covered the operation. The similar

---

[1] Gribble, 21-2.   [2] Michaud, *Biog. univ.*, xxx. 86 ; Dontenville, 9-10.
[3] Susane, *Inf. franç.*, i. 330 ; Déprez, *Vol. Nat.*, 436.
[4] Compare *Fastes*, iii. 426, lines 32-3.   [5] Michaud, *Biog. univ.*, xxx. 86.

passage in the *Fastes* refers to a later period, the final advance of the ' Nord '.

As afterwards there were suspicions that Moreau was inclined to royalism, I notice here a fact which occurred in July 1794, when the ' Nord ' was in full tide of success, advancing rapidly through Belgium, and when Moreau himself had just taken the island of Kadzand. The father of Moreau, Gabriel-Louis Moreau, formerly Judge of the tribunal of Morlaix, had acted as agent for several *émigrés*, receiving and transmitting their revenues. In July 1794 he was accused of sending money to an *émigré*, Barbier de Lescoët, and, after trial at Brest, was guillotined on the 31st July 1794. This execution was remarkable, for the fall of Robespierre was then known, but locally the Terror continued. Also four sons of the prisoner were serving in the armies, and the fact that one of them, General Moreau, was taking such a prominent position amongst the defenders of the Republic, must have been common information. General Moreau, hearing of the peril of his father, wrote in his defence to the *Accusateur Public*, but the letter arrived after the execution and that official only wrote on it ' Condamné à mort '.[1] Naturally one would assume that this would indispose Moreau towards the Republic, and some suspicion clung to him. It is perhaps due to the knowledge of this that we find Fabre de l'Aude describing him later, when on a visit to Paris, probably after the army had halted on the Rhine, as ' trop peu indigné du supplice de son père et trop parfait républicain ; le républicanisme lui sortait par tous les pores ; ses discours respiraient un enthousiasme qui ne se peignait pas dans ses yeux '.[2]

At this time, 1794, a contemporary described Moreau as thinking properly, say well disposed to the Government, but as at bottom a Royalist. ' He is a man full of talent, but lazy. He is 28 years old. He is very brave, calculates well, but lets himself be led by General Vandamme ', for whom he had a strong friendship throughout this campaign.[3] Another writer paints Moreau as stout, about ' six pieds, deux pouces ' high, and of more agreeable manner than the gloomy Pichegru.

---

[1] Wallon, *Rep.*, ii. 66.   [2] Fabre de l'Aude, ii. 370-1 ; *Fastes*, iii. 426.
[3] Coutanceau, *Nord*, Ie Partie, i, note 1, p. xli.

'Il ne lui manque que de vivre ailleurs qu'aux armées pour être un homme tout-à-fait aimable.' Here also we learn that neither Moreau nor the volunteer battalion he had commanded liked the Constitution of 1793, that which was proposed after the destruction of Royalty but was found unworkable.[1] It was only with difficulty that the battalion could be got to accept it: 'Je l'ai entendu quelquefois raisonner très-juste sur ce Code anarchique, et il pénétrait très-bien ce qui est arrivé.' Still less was he the partisan of what was styled the Revolutionary Government.[2] Here again we get a hint of the tendency of Moreau to Royalism, which his end as the professed adviser of the Allied Sovereigns may seem to justify. I have already mentioned the dissatisfaction at the removal of Custine from command which his battalion so openly expressed.

One of the many mistakes often made about Moreau is to confuse him, Jean-Victor Moreau, with General René Moreaux, whose name is frequently spelt as 'Moreau', an officer of distinction who had served as a private in America and won the rank of General of Brigade at the head of his volunteer battalion at Thionville. Serving with the Armée de la Moselle, he died in command of it on the 10th February 1795.[3]

Although Moreau had become one of the leading Generals before the arrival of Pichegru, it was due to the friendship which soon existed between them that Moreau owed his rise to command. Indeed, it is hard to understand why Moreau took such a prominent position except by the favour of Pichegru: during the advance into Holland his chief work was done away from the main army, in sieges, and it was by such work alone that he was known in other forces.[4] We shall find him leaving his own division and accompanying Pichegru, as he was to do with Schérer in Italy in 1799, as a sort of adviser. Souham was senior to him, and only the disgrace or eclipse of that General could have enabled Pichegru to give Moreau the temporary command of the army when he himself fell ill at the end of 1794. Souham indeed seems to have been a friend of Pichegru, at least he suffered at Fructidor in 1797

---

[1] Thiers, *Rév.*, ii. 175-6, 228, 273-4.   [2] David, 245.
[3] General René Moreaux (1758-95). See Léon Moreaux, *Le Général René Moreaux*.   [4] Saint-Cyr, *Rhin*, iii. 1-2.

from suspicion of complicity with him.[1] It was on the recommendation of Pichegru that Moreau followed him in command, first of the ' Nord ', and then of the ' Rhin-et-Moselle '. The friendship between the two was ruinous to Moreau : in 1797 it was to involve him in the fall of Pichegru owing to what was at best his concealment of the treachery of his predecessor, and in 1804 it entangled him in the conspiracy against Bonaparte. It is important to bear this in mind, for the conduct of Moreau in 1804 is too often judged without reference to his former connexion with Pichegru. Both ended in strange fashion for French Generals, Pichegru committing suicide in preference to facing an open trial with the exposure of all his treachery, and Moreau killed amongst the enemies of France by a French shot.

One word, it might well be a volume, of the rough, violent, plundering, hard-fighting Vandamme, who was a native of the district in which he was now fighting.[2] Having been a pupil in the *École militaire de Paris*, patronized by the Maréchal de Biron, he enlisted as a private in 1788 and served in America, leaving his regiment and returning to France in 1790. In July 1790 he became Captain of the grenadiers of the sedentary guard of Cassel ; but on the 7th June 1791 he enlisted as a private in the Régiment de Brie, the 25th, then the 24th Regiment.[3] Leaving this on the 25th August 1792, having ' très bien et fidèlement servi ',[4] he raised a *compagnie de Chasseurs francs* called *Chasseurs du Mont-de-Cassel*, with which he served in the campaign of Dumouriez in Holland. When his company was amalgamated with others to form a light battalion of the ' Mont-de-Cassel ', Vandamme became Lt.-Colonel of the new body on the 1st August 1793 and, distinguishing himself at Hondschoote, became General of Brigade on the 27th September 1793. At one time he had Moreau under him, and then he passed under the command of that General. In time he passed to the Rhine, becoming General of Division on the 5th February 1799. His life was full of fine fighting, the

---

[1] *Fastes*, iii. 561.
[2] General Comte Dominique-Joseph-René Vandamme (1770-1830), Comte d'Unsenbourg. Du Casse, *Le Général Vandamme* ; *Fastes*, iv. 17-19 ; Michaud, *Biog. univ.*, lxxxiv. 436-51 ; *Biog. des Cont.*, v. 839-40 ; De Fezensac, 396-7.
[3] Susane, *Inf. franç.*, iii. 258-61. [4] Du Casse, *Vandamme*, i. 11.

rewards for which fell to others, much to his outspoken disgust, for what his bravery and daring should have won on the field was lost by his evil reputation for violence and plundering. Napoleon understood how to treat him and, when the General's *fourgons*, laden with linen and other goods, came to the French frontier, they were stopped and their contents seized, whilst Vandamme, with ' le cœur ulcéré ', wailed over such an unjust proceeding, for all were but presents from the grateful country he had occupied. ' If there were two General Vandammes,' said Napoleon, ' I should shoot one.' Frequently disgraced, still Vandamme was too valuable a man in the field not to be forgiven, and on the 1st April 1809 he was made Comte d'Unsenbourg.[1] In 1813 in all probability he would have become Marshal, had it not been for Kulm, where he was little to blame. Taken prisoner, he only returned to France to fight at Ligny, and under Grouchy at Wavre, dying in 1830, a man to be condemned and to be much admired. The combination at this time of the fiery Vandamme with the cool, precise Moreau may have been a very happy thing. Poor Vandamme is described as the most reckless General of the army, making no combinations, yielding to, and acting on, his first impulse. Capable of making great mistakes, he was, says the critic, only good for pursuing a column in flight, for he loved blood. He now was 22, a fine man, without education, as indeed his letters show,[2] ' emporté et dévoué à la République '.[3] His disaster at Kulm in 1813, when pursuing a retreating, not a flying column, gives weight to this rather ill-natured criticism. The reference to his devotion to the Republic makes it the more strange that some wisehead amongst the English tried to get him to desert with as many men and guns as he could, when he would receive a large sum, 240,000 livres. With some skill, it was suggested that he had become ' suspect ' to the Convention, and he was told to write to ' Lord Twedel ', No. 1,659 rue de Bœur, ' Ceci n'est pas une plaisanterie ', and a treaty, signed by York and Coburg, was offered to him. One would suspect this to be an attempt to discredit the

---

[1] A title often confused with that of Hunebourg, borne by Clarke.
[2] See later, on the ' Nord ' reaching Brussels.
[3] Coutanceau, *Nord*, Ie Partie, i, note 4, pp. xxxix–xl.

General, were not wholesale endeavours being made to get the men to desert, either singly or in bodies. With much good sense Vandamme got his commander, Moreau, to come to him (had he been arrested with the letters on him, he would have been ' suspect ' indeed), and laid them before him. It was characteristic of the times that Moreau forwarded the letters to the *Comité de salut public,* only sending copies to Pichegru. Finally the *Comité* expressed their satisfaction with the courage and incorruptibility of the General. It would have been pleasant to have heard Vandamme on the subject.[1]

Towards the end of April 1794 Macdonald again occupied a very awkward position. A decree ordered that all Nobles should retire to thirty leagues from the frontier and from the Capital. One does not see why Macdonald should have been considered a Noble except perhaps as a *ci-devant* ' Mac ', but so it was ; however, he had given the staff of the army much information on the frontier and Pichegru, who, to do him justice, did not balk at such things, recommended that he should be retained. The Representatives agreed and told Macdonald that in virtue of their powers they would employ him. Naturally, whilst expressing his readiness to act, he asked for a written order, otherwise in case of reverse he would be accused of remaining in order to get the army beaten, a most certain conclusion. The Representatives declined, when Macdonald announced that he would retire. ' If you leave the army, we will have you arrested and tried.'[2] It was under these cheerful circumstances that Macdonald fought, and his danger can be understood by the fact that it was the powerful and sanguinary Representatives Saint-Just and Le Bas who had announced their intention of dismissing him ; whilst, for remaining with the army, he could only rely on Florent Guiot and Choudieu.[3]

Ney, who had been A.D.C. to Colaud since the 20th December 1793, rejoined his own regiment, the 4th Hussars, when promoted Captain on the 25th April 1794. Colaud gave him a certificate that he had filled his post with zeal and activity

---

[1] Coutanceau, *Nord,* I^e Partie, i. 49–60 ; Foucart et Finot, *Déf. nat.,* ii. 345–6, with portrait of Vandamme, p. 357. The ' Lord ' is omitted before ' Twedel ' in one letter. Du Casse, *Vandamme,* i. 117–21.

[2] Macdonald, *Souvenirs,* 34–5.   [3] Coutanceau, *Nord,* I^e Partie, i. 35–40.

and that in his service he had shown all the intelligence and the patriotism of a pronounced Republican.¹ As I have said, Ney was again to serve under Colaud in the 'Sambre-et-Meuse' in 1796. In the *Mémoires* of Ney his promotion to Captain is put as after the affair of Famars, 'si fâcheuse pour le respectable Lamarche'. But that was on the 23rd April 1793.²

As for Pichegru, he came with a dubious fame from the Armée du Rhin and, if in the 'Nord' he gained distinction, it was not from actions of his own; indeed, nothing is more remarkable than the manner in which he managed to be absent when his army fought, whether successfully or not. In fact, it would be interesting to get those who consider him a commander of whom Napoleon was jealous to give the name of any battle won by him in person, or at which he was even present in this theatre. If Wellington had been at Brussels when Quatre-Bras was fought, had come up at Waterloo on the 19th June, and had still got full credit for those battles, we should have a similar case. Here Pichegru was successful in a strange fashion, his divisions winning battles for him in his absence, and even the feat of capturing the Dutch fleet by cavalry we shall find taken from him. Just as on the Rhine he had but followed up the success of the sister army, the 'Moselle', with his own force, the 'Rhin', so here he got the credit really due to Jourdan and his new army, the 'Sambre-et-Meuse'. However, he was overweighted in command, for the 'Nord' was too big for any commander of the time. In March 1794 it was 126,035 strong, or, if the garrisons be included, 194,930. Nor was this all, for he was also responsible for the Armée des Ardennes, 6,757 strong or, with garrisons, 32,773, which gave him a grand total of 227,703, or perhaps more.³ Now in 1796, when the *amalgame* had stiffened the armies and made them more manageable, and the staffs were much improved, Saint-Cyr, looking back with great experience, considered that the 110,000 men that the combined armies on the Rhine would have totalled, was too large a force for any

---

[1] Bonnal, *Ney*, i. 22, giving 13th April 1794 as the date of promotion of Ney.
[2] Ney, *Méms.*, i. 45.
[3] Coutanceau, *Nord*, IIe Partie, i. 103-5. The strength varied very much.

one then to be fit to command.¹ The long line on which the troops of the 'Nord' were stretched made the difficulty all the greater.

On the 29th March 1794, for some reason hard to understand, instead of carrying out the plan of campaign, Pichegru ordered an attack on Cateau-Cambrésis² by the division of Fromentin, in which served the 4th Hussars, to which Lieutenant Ney belonged. Fromentin moved from Avesnes, and two other divisions came from Guise, that of Balland (whose Chief of the Staff was Lt.-Colonel Mortier) and that of Goguet, where Lt.-Colonel Bernadotte served in the 36th Regiment. The attack was beaten off, the French losing 1,200 men and 4 guns against an Austrian loss of 293 men. Ney's regiment had behaved well, better than the Dragoons with them, and on the next day, the 30th March, being sent out from Catillon, it checked the cavalry of the enemy. One of its Captains, Boyé, whose company Lieutenant Ney had joined when he left Lamarche in July 1793, so distinguished himself the first day that he was made General of Brigade, so that the regiment was a good school for Ney. Lt.-Colonel Bernadotte also must have distinguished himself, for he was promoted full Colonel on the 4th April 1794.³

The plans of the Allies were as bad as those of the French, and the Emperor, who had arrived in person, had upset much that Mack had tried to arrange.⁴ It had been determined to begin with the siege of Landrecies, one of the places which the Archduke Charles thought should have been neglected,⁵ and on the 17th and 18th April 1794 Coburg advanced and threw back the divisions of Balland and Goguet on Guise with some loss, whilst to the east Fromentin was forced over to the right bank of the Helpe river. Pichegru, as usual in moments of difficulty, was away, this time at Lille, the French line was surprised, and the Allies began the siege of Landrecies, a petty place. Balland, the senior General of this group of divisions, took on himself to strike back in order to recover communica-

---

¹ Saint-Cyr, *Rhin-et-Moselle*, iii. 201.
² South-west of Landrecies, now famous as Le Cateau.
³ Coutanceau, *Nord*, IIᵉ Partie, i. 172-81, Docts. Annexes, 533-51, with map; Jomini, *Rév.*, v. 44-7; Marmottan, *Fromentin*, 111-15.
⁴ Coutanceau, *Nord*, IIᵉ Partie, i. 32-69. ⁵ Ibid., 109.

tion with the town, and on the 21st April the divisions advanced. That part of the enemy which was commanded by Alvinzi, one of the future antagonists of Bonaparte in Italy, was forced over the Sambre at Barzy, but the attack failed and next day the French retired, Balland and Goguet alone losing 500 killed and 4 guns.[1]

In the attack on the 21st April Bernadotte, just promoted Colonel, is said to have led a brigade of one infantry and one cavalry regiment in Goguet's division. Whilst Balland was not seriously engaged, Goguet was met by the Austrians and his division was routed, flying in disorder back to Guise. Bernadotte, sent to the left, brought up his brigade just in time to find his General shot down by the fugitives of one regiment, as Théobald Dillon had been in 1792. Whilst the murderers were boasting of their crime, Bernadotte vowed vengeance, but Goguet, disregarding his own wounds, advised him to keep calm and to prepare to resist the enemy, as he would be attacked next day; his men had been deceived about himself. Bernadotte, however, delivered a harangue to the men who sympathized with the criminals. A fervid speaker, he succeeded in turning the indignation of his men against the murderers, so that now he had to prevent them taking justice into their own hands. In 1792 this would have been impossible, for fresh cries of treachery would have been raised and he would have been another victim.[2] It was no doubt this incident that made him soon afterwards decline to be made General of a Division before being promoted General of Brigade, saying significantly, 'It is, besides, enough trouble and danger for me to command a brigade, until more discipline and subordination be established in the army'.[3] Indeed, as a Captain of a regular regiment was sentenced to death for inciting the men to fire on Goguet, matters must have been bad enough.[4]

Pichegru now took a measure which, considering the long line on which the 'Nord' sprawled, it is wonderful that he had

---

[1] Coutanceau, *Nord*, IIe Partie, i, 210–350, Docts. Annexes, 570–651; Jomini, *Rév.*, v. 47–52; Marmottan, *Fromentin*, 118, 125; Foucart et Finot, *Déf. nat.*, vi. 347–54; Langeron, 58–9; Calvert, 188–93.
[2] Jomini, *Rév.*, v. 50–2; *Fastes*, i. 338–9; Coutanceau, *Nord*, IIe Partie, i. 325–6, Docts. Annexes, 630–2. [3] *Fastes*, i. 334.
[4] Coutanceau, *Nord*, IIe Partie, i, Docts. Annexes, 632.

not taken before. Remaining with his left wing, where his Chief of the Staff, Liébert, was in bed with fever,[1] he nominated General Ferrand on the 19th April 1794 to command the divisions of his right from Maubeuge to Cambrai. On the 24th April Ferrand advanced in order to what he called ' réattaquer ',[2] to save Landrecies. In this operation Ney's Hussar regiment was in Soland's brigade from Avesnes, Lt.-Colonel Mortier was with Balland, and Colonel Bernadotte, I presume, was with the division lately Goguet's. The divisions round Maubeuge (Favereau, Despeaux-Muller, and Desjardins) had been placed under Favereau from the 19th April 1794,[3] Favereau now working under Ferrand and a little system being thus put into the hitherto spineless right. The attack, which took place on the 26th April, was a total failure ; the divisions fought separately and were beaten back.[4] Goguet's late division was not much engaged, but Balland's division, where Mortier served, was regularly routed.[5]

The worst fate befell Chapuis from Cambrai, on whose flank at Troisvilles the Duke of York sent a column of heavy cavalry, the Zeschwitz Cuirassiers and the Blues, Royals, 1st, 3rd, and 5th Dragoon Guards, with the 16th Light Dragoons. The heavy cavalry took twenty-six guns, and another column, the 7th and 11th Light Dragoons and some Austrian Hussars, took nine more pieces, the Allies altogether capturing ninety guns. Chapuis and some thousands of his men were taken prisoners, the General himself being the first to surrender,[6] and with him the Allies got the plan of campaign that Pichegru was following, and thus learnt that their right under Clairfayt in Flanders was to be attacked. The English General Mansell had fallen in the battle under peculiar circumstances. On the 24th April the 15th Light Dragoons and two squadrons of Austrian Hussars had a brilliant affair at Villers-en-Cauchie, where Mansell was to have supported them with

[1] Coutanceau, *Nord*, IIe Partie, i, Docts. Annexes, 708–9.
[2] Ibid., 351.   [3] Marmottan, *Fromentin*, 119.
[4] Coutanceau, IIe Partie, i. 351–453, Docts. Annexes, 665–710 ; Jomini, *Rév.*, v. 52–7 ; *Vict. et Conq.*, ii. 233–5 ; Langeron, 59–61 ; Calvert, 194–7.
[5] Coutanceau, IIe Partie, i. 438–42, Docts. Annexes, 705.
[6] See Dellard, 27–32 ; Jones, 19 ; Wilson, *Life*, i. 65–73 ; Coutanceau, *Nord*, IIe Partie, i. 416–29, Docts. Annexes, 690–712 ; Desbrière, *La Cav. pendant la Rév.: La crise* 403–5 ; Langeron, 59–60 ; Calvert, i. 196–7.

some English and Austrian cavalry. By an error in the orders Mansell did not come up, and the 15th Light Dragoons and the Leopold Hussars had a desperate but successful struggle with superior numbers to prevent the Emperor being intercepted. Mansell had at first been deprived of his command, but on the very day, the 26th April 1794, when Chapuis was defeated, on the circumstances being understood, he had been reinstated. Still he had resolved not to survive what he considered his disgrace and, having sent 'his son and Brigade-Major to different points of the line, and commanded his orderly Dragoon not to follow him, he darted on the enemy and met an inevitable death. His body was found after the action, and the Duke of York and others attended the interment. As far as I could judge from the countenances of these personages, they seemed to feel that a brave man had been untowardly sacrificed.'[1]

In the case of Chapuis's division,[2] as in some others I have mentioned, the infantry had been composed of raw troops whom all the self-sacrifice of their artillery and cavalry could not save. It was far otherwise where good French troops had to be met, and some of these affairs, unimportant as they may seem in contrast to the decisive battles of later campaigns, were fought out with a determination and bitterness hard to exceed, and with a great display of spirit and gallantry on either side. Thus Wilson describes how five French *gendarmes*, separated from their comrades, ' determined to cut their way through or die in the attempt, and at all events made their attempt memorable '. Piercing the Blues, they kept on, few caring to close with them ; one fell and three at last sank, ' quite colandered with balls, and the fifth, being dismounted, by his horse receiving a leg wound, stood like Mars, bidding defiance to the crowds that assailed him and refusing to yield his sword. At length a trumpeter took deliberate aim, and the hero sank to earth with a wave of his sword hand, as if he were exulting in his doom.'[3] It was not a mere phrase

---

[1] Wilson, *Life*, i. 73 ; Jones, 16–17 ; Coutanceau, *Nord*, IIe Partie, i. 421–2, Docts. Annexes, 661 –711.

[2] 'The eight battalions that composed it all included a large number of raw soldiers, without experience and not yet having any steadiness under fire.' Dellard, 28.   [3] Wilson, *Life*, i. 77–8.

to describe the French as engaging to the shout of ' Vive la
République ' : even as the sword fell on them, they gave it
as their last cry. Mahan says with great truth, ' If ever, for
good or ill, men had the single eye, it was to be found in the
French soldiers of 1793, as they starved and bled and died that
the country might live. Given time—and the Allies gave it—
units animated by such a spirit, and driven forward by such
an impetus as the Committee knew how to impart, were soon
knit in an overpowering organism, as superior in temper as
they were in numbers to the trained machines before them.'[1]
With the latter part of this passage I, however, disagree. No
impetus was given by the denunciations that the *Comité* poured
on the Generals and officers who were doing so much for the
Nation, and it is a great mistake to believe that there was no
national spirit amongst the troops who fought the first Revolutionary levies, or that the Allies brought none but old troops
into the field. England certainly sent out troopers not even
clothed, ' presuming that they might be fitted out from the
dead men's kits, as if the effects of the slain were regularly
collected and stored '.[2] Yet such men and drafts from the
jails are soon described as having ' afforded the most exemplary
proof of national courage ',[3] when, with drums beating and
colours flying, they bore down the troops of Macdonald on the
22nd May 1794. This, too, after a memorable and undeserved
defeat. Machines do not work in that fashion. It was the
same with the gallant Austrians, who took up the national
quarrel, their men calling the French ' King-eaters ' and
' assassins ', whilst the Republicans replied by abuse of them
as satellites of slaves. The wounded Hungarian grenadiers
who sang their national songs as they were borne off the
field of Templeuve [4] had as much national spirit as the men
who marched to the *Marseillaise*. National characteristics
must be allowed for, and the English soldier, going into the

---

[1] Mahan, *Sea Power*, i. 94–5.   [2] Wilson, *Life*, i. 97–8.
[3] Ibid., i. 97. Lord Panmure to Lord Raglan, 1st June 1855 : ' It has been suggested to send out ticket-of-leave men to the army, but I have set my face against that, though I daresay they would fight as well as honester men.' Lord Raglan to Lord Panmure, 23rd June 1855 : ' Pray save us from ticket-of-leave men.' *Panmure Papers*, i. 221–31, 252.
[4] Wilson, *Life*, i. 95.

zone of fire, will, after the manner of his race, say nothing of the country for which he is ready to die.

General Duhesme, who wrote the account of what his brigade had done, asked in later years the indulgence of the reader for a period when he and all the leaders were but infants in the art of war,[1] and it is but fair to remember how short a time it was since Pichegru, who had to wield 227,000 men, had been in the ranks of the artillery.[2] The Allies, however, could not plead such excuse, and it seems wonderful that they did not use their success to crush at once the French line of divisions in their front, on which they had just dealt such a heavy blow. That was not their way, and the very fact they had learnt that Pichegru was about to throw himself on their right, and would therefore be out of the way for some time, was only a reason for halting and weakening themselves to reinforce their right. Mack planned many campaigns, including that of Austerlitz, but in his own way he was leading the Allies skilfully enough, step by step, with a pause for consideration between each operation. One really feels sympathy for him when in 1805, bent over his game of chess, prepared, as he thought, for the appearance of Napoleon on his board, he suddenly found himself struck as if by a thunderbolt from a clear sky. Even here, although Landrecies surrendered on the 30th April,[3] his success was ended and the initiative was to pass to the French.

The changes amongst commanders of division are worth noting for the convenience of students. At Cambrai the division which had lost its General, Chapuis, in the rout of Troisvilles on the 26th April, had at first been led by Proteau, but Bonnaud, much protesting, was posted to it on the 30th April.[4] At Guise Dubois from the Armée du Rhin took the place of Goguet[5] in the division where Bernadotte served. As for Balland, whose Chief of the Staff was Lt.-Colonel Mortier, there had been much dissatisfaction with him. This,

[1] Coutanceau, *Nord*, IIe Partie, i, Docts. Annexes, note 1, p. 644.
[2] Not two years.
[3] For siege of Landrecies see Coutanceau, *Nord*, IIe Partie, i. 182-491, Docts. Annexes, 605-813; Foucart et Finot, *Déf. nat.*, ii. 360-75; *Vict. et Conq.*, ii. 238, 239; Langeron, 58-9.
[4] Coutanceau, *Nord*, IIe Partie, i. 472, Docts. Annexes, 751.
[5] Ibid., 460, 468, Docts. Annexes, 749.

I think, must be the man whom Thiébault describes as in 1790 a drummer in the Feuillants' companies of the National Guard of Paris, and who had cleaned the boots and run the messages of those who chose to employ him.[1] Now it was complained that his division had not fought well and had not seconded the others, and Fromentin wrote of his 'stagnante conduite' on the 29th April, declaring that 'tout le monde récrimine contre lui'.[2] Consequently on the 11th May he was replaced by General Kléber,[3] who was to have replaced Goguet and who joined from La Vendée about the 11th May 1794.[4] All this must have been bad for Mortier.

Pichegru had attempted to save Landrecies, not only by throwing forward his right, in conjunction with the Armée des Ardennes, the movement we have just seen, but also by advancing into west or maritime Flanders with his left wing, the divisions of Souham, Moreau, and Michaud. Here Macdonald led a brigade in Souham's division and Vandamme in that of Moreau. Lt.-Colonel Murat's Chasseur regiment belonged to the division of Michaud,[5] although we shall find it detached to that of Moreau.

Macdonald, like Murat, was under the dangerous suspicion of disliking the Republic, besides being a Noble and a foreigner. 'Watch Macdonald', wrote the Minister, Bouchotte, to Pichegru, 'who is very cold towards the Republic.' Macdonald took matters with a very high hand, especially considering that Robespierre still lived. Hitherto he had been guarding the line down the Lys from Armentières to Wervicq and then eastwards to Linselles, but on the 26th February 1794 Souham ordered him to command the troops at Five. This really was a larger body, but Macdonald remonstrated in the most outspoken fashion. An attempt, he told Souham, was being made not only to disgust him, but to force him to leave a post where

---

[1] General Antoine Balland (1751-1821). A former private and Sergeant-Major, not employed after June 1795, and so not the General in Italy in 1797, notwithstanding the editor of Thiébault, i. 262-3 and note 1, p. 444.
[2] Coutançeau, *Nord*, IIe Partie, i. 467-8, 486-7, Docts. Annexes, 803-4, 806.
[3] Ibid., 460, 468, Docts. Annexes, 749.
[4] Foucart et Finot, *Déf. nat.*, ii. 390.
[5] I cannot trace this Michaud, who was not the General Claude-Ignace-François Michaud who served in, and at one time commanded, the Armée du Rhin. *Fastes*, iii. 399-401.

he thought himself useful. Not only did he know the troops he was with, and was known by them, but also he was well acquainted with the country. Now a General knowing nothing either of the troops or of the country was to relieve him in what he considered a much more important post than that to which it was proposed to send him. Souham met him in the same style, refusing to reply to 'all the ridiculous phrases which your letter contains', and told him that the armed force must essentially be obedient. ' Thus, you have received an order : obey.' Macdonald one would have thought to be Republican enough : he had just proposed for the parole, ' Republicans, to arms, let us revenge ourselves ! '[1] He was soon to do something to make up for Flodden.

Slipping away from his right, which was about to undertake the direct relief of Landrecies, Pichegru arrived at Lille on the 13th April 1794, intending to use some 50,000 men from the divisions of Souham (31,856) under Lille ; of Moreau at Cassel on Souham's left (15,968) ; and of Michaud (13,943) under Dunkirk ; besides Osten's brigade (7,822) on the right at Mons-en-Pévèle and Pont-à-Marcq, Murat's old station. To strengthen Souham's division he transferred one of the brigades (Desenfans) of Moreau to it, making up the strength of Moreau with one brigade (say half the force) of the division of Michaud ; this caused the regiment of Lt.-Colonel Murat to serve under Moreau in this campaign. The advance was made easily enough, Michaud on the left, ordered on Furnes, inclined to his right on Rousbrugge, but he had only a small part in these operations. Souham's division moved down the Lys, Macdonald with 15,000 men turning Mouscron, and the division occupying Courtrai, whilst Moreau went down the left bank of the Lys for Menin, which he began to bombard on the 28th April.[2] This advance of the left of the ' Nord ' had met with but little opposition, as the English, who had repaired Menin, had long been called in eastwards to the main army for the siege of Landrecies, and, just before the advance, Clairfayt, who had 28,000 Austrians and Hanoverians, had, much to his

---

[1] Coutanceau, *Nord*, IIe Partie, ii. 6–9.
[2] Ibid., Docts. Annexes, 264 (page not numbered) : ibid., pp. 56–106 ; Du Casse, *Vandamme*, i. 124–5.

annoyance, been also brought in by Mack to Denain.[1] The danger of Menin had been foreseen[2] and, when the plan of Pichegru had been found on the captured General, Chapuis, Clairfayt had marched back westwards and reinforcements had been sent after him. Coming up from Tournai to the south-east on the 28th April, Clairfayt attacked the right of Pichegru at Mouscron and drove Bertin's brigade back in confusion on Tourcoing, Jardon's troops retiring northwards to Aelbeke.[3] Clairfayt wanted to save Menin, but he had better have waited for reinforcements, for, though Pichegru, as usual when stirring events were about to happen, was away from the important point, Souham, whose division was menaced, acted with praiseworthy decision.

Determining to strike back at once, he sent Macdonald with his brigade eastwards to Aelbeke, whence he was to attack Clairfayt with his own troops, those of Jardon, and Bertin's brigade from Tourcoing, some 16,000 strong, all of whom Macdonald was to command, reinforced by Daendel's brigade, altogether 24,000 men. Clairfayt believed the French were about to retreat and he had taken no measures of defence. Yet when their attack came Bertin's brigade was once more broken and both Macdonald and Daendels were twice beaten back. The impatient Souham at 2 p.m. ordered Macdonald once more to attack, and the two Generals charged at the head of the troops, whilst their artillery crushed that of the enemy and forced Clairfayt to retreat, although for a moment the young troops became panic-stricken. The park of the enemy fell into the hands of the French, who took 33 guns, 4 colours, and 3,000 men. Clairfayt himself was wounded. Early next morning most of the garrison of Menin broke out, led by the battalion of *Loyal-Émigrans*[4] to whom capture meant death, and, though hampered by trying to take guns with them, the bulk cut through the division of Moreau, partly, it is suggested, from the usual carelessness of Vandamme, and got clear to the north, bearing off three French guns together with most of their own field pieces, a feat the French acknowledged to be

---

[1] South-west of Valenciennes. For Clairfayt's objection see Langeron, 62.
[2] Calvert, 181-2, 183, 198.
[3] Coutanceau, *Nord*, IIe Partie, ii. 107-13.   [4] Ibid., 171-2.

most creditable to Von Hammerstein, the Hanoverian commander. A small force left in Menin then surrendered.[1] Clairfayt's force was really but the head of the column of the whole army of the Allies, which, having taken Landrecies, was now moving against the left of the 'Nord', and one would have thought that the whole mass would have been kept together to strike one heavy blow in the rear of the two divisions of the French at Courtrai and Menin, but the Allies scattered their troops. Clairfayt was sent north of Courtrai, whilst the Duke of York arrived at Marquain, west of Tournai, and other troops of the Allies threatened Courtrai from the east. This led to some fighting which might be passed over had not Macdonald been engaged. On the 10th May 1794, whilst Moreau held the Lys, Souham with part of his division, including Macdonald, struck southwards from Courtrai at General von dem Bussche, who was to the west of Mouscron, and who soon drew off. Meantime Clairfayt had attacked Courtrai and, reaching the *faubourg*, might have got in had he pressed on. Souham now, by Pichegru's orders, brought his troops back westwards and, while Vandamme and Daendels, coming out of Courtrai, attacked Clairfayt, Macdonald and Malbrancq (who had superseded Bertin), with their brigades were sent over the Lys through Menin for the same purpose, but they came up too late. At night Clairfayt drew off to the north. With him was a small body of English, two battalions and three squadrons, which had been landed at Ostend [2] and which were placed under General White.[3] Farther south an attack was made on the 10th May 1794 on the Duke of York at Marquain, before Tournai, by the division of Bonnaud, late Chapuis, which Pichegru had ordered up from Cambrai to Sainghin [4] and which, taking up Osten's brigade, was now 23,000 strong.[5] The chief part of the fight took place at Baisieux and Camphin, on the road from Tournai to Lille.

---

[1] Coutanceau, *Nord*, IIe Partie, ii. 116–79 ; Jomini, *Rév.*, v. 59–62 ; *Vict. et Conq.*, ii. 235–8 ; Foucart et Finot, *Déf. nat.*, ii. 359–60 ; Du Casse, *Vandamme*, i. 125–6 ; Langeron, 62–3 ; Calvert, 198–200. For plan see Jomini, *Rév.*, Atlas, viii, and in Coutanceau, *Nord* ; Desbrière, *La Cav. pendant la Rév.: La crise*, 406–8.

[2] Coutanceau, *Nord*, IIe Partie, ii. 180–221, 225–41.

[3] Ibid., 213. [4] Between Tournai and Lille.

[5] Coutanceau, *Nord*, IIe Partie, ii. 191–222.

L'ARMÉE DU NORD, 1794

The Duke turned the French right with his heavy cavalry under Dundas, Laurie, and Vyse, when part of the French cavalry became demoralized and fled. Their infantry then retreated in what seemed to the English good style, but at the end Dundas's brigade cut into them, and when this attack was supported by some guns the French went off in disorder, leaving, says Calvert, 14 guns. The French acknowledge a loss of 5 guns and 500 men.[1]

[1] Coutanceau, *Nord*, IIe Partie, ii. 221-5; Jomini, *Rév.*, v. 66-7; Calvert, 203-5; Jones, 28-34.

XV

L'ARMÉE DU NORD (*continued*), 1794

Battle of Tourcoing, 18th May 1794. Mack's plan to surround the left of the ' Nord '. His six columns. The Duke of York's column exposed in spite of his remonstrances. The Archduke Charles's column lags in rear. The Archduke's illness. Council of Souham, Moreau, Reynier, Liébert, and Macdonald. Self-sacrifice of Moreau, who is left to contain Clairfayt in the north, whilst Souham and Bonnaud attack the Duke of York, whose column is crushed. The Emperor takes the responsibility for the Duke's position. The guns block the retreat of the cavalry. Horrible scene. The soldier's wife. Narrow escape of the Duke of York. Amount of loss. Ludicrous scenes. French gunner's death. Praise of Macdonald. Position of Murat. Souham's history. Battle of Pont-à-Chin, 22nd May 1794. Pichegru attacks Allies, but is beaten off. Gallant sight at attack of Macdonald by the English, who capture Pichegru's dinner. Loss at this ' butchery without plan, success, or result '. The work of Colonel Coutanceau. Pichegru advances with the left of the ' Nord '. Moreau besieges Ypres, whilst the rest of the force beats off Clairfayt from Rousselaere on the 13th June 1794. Praise of Macdonald.

Now in the battle of Tourcoing came a defeat to the Allies, and a great but undeserved disaster to the English under the Duke of York. The Duke may have had the first idea of a combined stroke by himself from the south and Clairfayt from the north at the two French divisions at Courtrai and Menin,[1] but it was the scientific Mack who prepared a plan which was said to have been his masterpiece. Some 73,350 men, formed in six columns in a circle round the French, were to make a concentric attack and to catch the two divisions, Souham and Moreau, as if in a net. By the 17th May 1794 the columns were to be placed ready to attack on the 18th. To the north-west Clairfayt from Thielt, with some 19,600 men, was to cross the Lys above Menin at Wervicq, and was to push on south-east for Tourcoing to meet the other bodies. To the east the first column, under Bussche, 4,000 Hanoverians, was to move from Warcoing on the Escaut northwards to Dottignies, and

[1] Coutanceau, *Nord*, IIe Partie, ii. 257-8.

then westwards for Mouscron. On Bussche's left the second column, 10,000 strong, under Otto, was to move north-westwards by Leers and Wattrelos for Tourcoing. On Otto's left the third column, under the Duke of York, 10,750 strong, was to move on a parallel line from Templeuve by Lannoy and Roubaix for Mouveaux. On York's left Kinsky with the fourth column, 11,000, was to move from Marquain, linking on his right and left with the third and fifth columns, and to force the passage of the Marque at Bouvines. The Archduke Charles with the fifth column, 18,000, was to march from Marquain for Pont-à-Marcq; his column and that of Kinsky would have to deal with Bonnaud's division from Lille.[1]

If the French only stood to receive the attack, the task of the columns would be as simple as those at Leipzig, but should the French attempt a counterstroke, then to prevent any single column being overwhelmed it was plain that each commander should press forward as fast as he could, and that, if checked, he ought to keep contact with, and to hold as many of the enemy on his front as possible. Also it was important that all the columns should be at their appointed stations on the day before the final attack, 17th May 1794. Most of the Generals of the Allies were not on a level with the situation: only two really did their duty, York and Otto, who consequently received the brunt of the French attack. Also Mack's plan, like most of those of the Austrians, attempted too much. The fifth column, the Archduke Charles, was sent on too wide an arc, as if to sweep Bonnaud from Lille into the net, and had better have been kept farther north.[2] This plan may be compared with others of the Austrians in Italy, for instance with those of the campaigns of Castiglione and Rivoli, for, different though the ground there was, the slackness of the Austrians and the energy of the French determined the result in both battles. On the 17th May 1794 the columns advanced, but all did not reach their proper posts. To the north Clairfayt reached Wervicq on the Lys, but could not cross till 1 a.m.

[1] I estimate the strength of Clairfayt from Coutanceau, *Nord*, IIe Partie, ii. 261 He may have been stronger. The strength of the other columns is given in that work, p. 263. For the plan of the Allies see that work, 256-64, and Docts. Annexes, 249-52.
[2] Compare Coutanceau, *Nord*, IIe Partie, ii. 327.

on the 18th, thus giving the French time to oppose him by Vandamme's brigade. The first column, Bussche, got to Mouscron, but was repulsed by Compère to Dottignies and Herseaux, south of Mouscron, instead of holding Mouscron. Otto and York got to their posts, Otto to Tourcoing, and York (first taking Lannoy) to Roubaix. Here, between 5 and 6 p.m., the Duke, knowing that the attack on Mouscron had failed and also that the fourth and fifth columns were not covering his left, as they should have done, determined to halt for the night. Unfortunately the Emperor sent him a positive order to attack Mouveaux, still farther on. 'Nothing can equal the madness that dictated this order, except the blind obstinacy with which it was persisted in, in spite of every representation.'[1] Abercromby took Mouveaux gallantly enough with four battalions of the Guards, Lt.-Colonel Churchill leading the 7th and 15th Light Dragoons over the ditch of the works protecting the village.[2] On the left of the Duke, Kinsky threw back Bonnaud westwards on Flers, but halted on the right of the Marque by Bouvines. The Archduke Charles, after a long march from Saint-Amand, also threw back the troops of Bonnaud on his front from Pont-à-Marcq, but halted with his advanced guard at Grand Ennetières, south of Lille, instead of at Lannoy to the east of that town.

Feeling his position dangerous, as Kinsky and the Archduke were not covering his left, the Duke of York at 9 p.m. on the 17th, and again at 6 and at 9 a.m. on the 18th, sent to the Emperor to get permission to abandon Mouveaux and Roubaix and to fall back to Lannoy. Mack, however, having sent orders to the Archduke to start early on the 18th to make up for his delay, and thinking Kinsky would press on, assured the Duke that he would be supported, and directed him to remain where he was. At 1 a.m. on the 18th Mack had sent Captain Koller to the Archduke to beg him to march at once on Lannoy. By 4 a.m. Koller reached the quarters of the Archduke, but the staff of the Prince refused to awaken him. In reality the Prince had had an attack, during the night, of the epilepsy to which he was subject, and this probably influenced his staff,

---

[1] Calvert, 215.
[2] Coutanceau, *Nord*, IIe Partie, ii. 285-6; Calvert, 210, 211; Jones, 36-8.

who, however, did not take the obvious course of acquainting the next senior General with the message.[1] At 3 a.m. on the 18th Mack had given fresh orders for this column to leave ten battalions and twenty squadrons before Lille, and then to move on Lannoy with Kinsky.

All through the 17th May the most disastrous news came pouring into Courtrai where the leading French Generals were assembled. On almost every side the enemy was advancing and a great circle of fire was forming round the two advanced divisions. Fortunately for the French, Pichegru had gone off to his right, and on the 13th May Souham had taken command of all troops from Sainghin to Courtrai, say the divisions of Souham and Moreau by Courtrai and Menin, and the division of Bonnaud by Lille, but apparently not that of Michaud to the west by Furnes.[2] With Souham this day were Moreau, Reynier (the staff officer of Souham), Macdonald with his staff officer, Pamphile Lacroix, and General Liébert (the Chief of the Staff to Pichegru), who, according to the odd custom of this army, often did not accompany his General.[3] Souham's resolution, whoever originated the plan, was a fine one. Whilst Moreau was to hold the line of the Lys from Courtrai up to Comines, that is, to act against Clairfayt, Souham, marching south-west from Courtrai, and Bonnaud, marching north-east from the neighbourhood of Lille, were to strike the centre of the enemy with all their force, say 40,000 men. The garrison of Lille was to make a demonstration to its south-east, and the division of Drut at Douai, south of Lille, was to demonstrate to its north-east. We, who know the position of the Allies, see that, while Moreau was to hold against the right column (Clairfayt) and the garrisons of Lille and Douai were to delay the Archduke Charles with the left column of the Allies, Souham and Bonnaud with some 40,000 men were to dash at the two advanced columns, Otto and York, some 20,000 men, attacking early in the morning.[4]

[1] Langeron, note 1, p. 66; Coutanceau, *Nord*, IIe Partie, ii. 296, 315-17. See Wellington on the Archduke: ' He is admirable for five or six hours ... but after that he falls into a kind of epileptic stupor.' Croker, i. 338.
[2] Coutanceau, *Nord*, IIe Partie, ii. 268. [3] Ibid., Ie Partie, i. 159.
[4] Ibid., IIe Partie, ii. 271-8, 297, 305, Docts. Annexes, 213-18; Jomini, *Rév.*, v. 88-9.

The mass of troops that Souham and Bonnaud were about to use seemed in no special danger, for at the worst it would have been hard if, in the event of a repulse, they had not been able to cut their way to Lille or to the west of that town. Moreau, however, was in a very different position, for, if Clairfayt made his way to Tourcoing, Moreau would be cut off, and also that General practically could only rely on one of his brigades, that of Vandamme. The other, Desenfans, from Michaud's division, was watching Ypres and was not in close contact with him.[1] Even if Souham were successful, Moreau and Vandamme might be cut off by Clairfayt and the next column of the Allies: indeed, we shall find Vandamme losing heavily, although not pressed by Clairfayt to the last point. Still, though seeing his danger, Moreau undertook the tasks, saying: 'It would require a piece of good fortune, on which we cannot count, to prevent half of my division and myself being sacrificed according to this plan, but still it is the best which can be proposed, and consequently it should be adopted.'[2]

At 1 a.m. on the 18th May 1794 Clairfayt passed the Lys at Wervicq and marched south-east for Linselles and Blaton, throwing Vandamme back northwards to Bousbecque on the Lys. Much of this success was due to the 8th Dragoons of the English army, who, according to Vandamme himself, 'charged the infantry with the greatest impetuosity and pierced the battalions';[3] indeed, they charged down the Lys as far as Halluin, close to Menin, making the artillery fly in disorder. Here, however, Clairfayt halted. The French say that, reinforced by two battalions, the tired, discouraged, and alarmed men of Vandamme took fresh heart and threw the enemy back on Linselles and Bousbecque, capturing a standard from the Dragoons.[4] Clairfayt himself says that, believing the French to have been reinforced by 5,000 men, he thought it necessary to draw back on his bridges and therefore took post on the fortified heights of Blaton, ready to take the offensive next day. It was Vandamme alone who had checked this column;

---

[1] Moreau did not even know exactly where Desenfans was. Coutanceau, *Nord*, IIe Partie, ii. 312, 313, and Docts. Annexes, 220.
[2] Thiébault, i. 492. [3] Coutanceau, *Nord*, IIe Partie, ii. 305-9.
[4] Ibid., Docts. Annexes, 232-4.

the brigade of Desenfans, in which the regiment of Lt.-Colonel Murat served, was watching Ypres, instead of acting against the right of Clairfayt, and had retired far to the south-west on Bailleul.[1] That evening Souham, having crushed York and thrown back Otto, sent back the brigades of Malbrancq, Macdonald, and Daendels to reinforce Vandamme and to attack Clairfayt next morning, 19th May. In the night of the 18th, however, Clairfayt received news of the disaster to the rest of the Allies and the order to retire north on Rousselaere (Roulers), so he drew back across the Lys and made good his retreat almost unmolested. Macdonald and Malbrancq were sent through Menin to try to cut off the enemy, but a sortie made by the garrison of that town against the Hanoverians, who were watching it, was repulsed and was so sharply attacked by the cavalry that two-thirds of the troops of Vandamme composing the party were captured; this probably delayed Macdonald and Daendels. Clairfayt carried off 7 guns and 300 prisoners.[2] The right of the Allies, Clairfayt, thus had done but little to draw off the French from the rest of the force, and, beyond retaining one brigade of the French, this column had only called back part of the French force from following up its victory. The two left columns of the Allies had done less. Kinsky, when pressed by the A.D.C. of the Emperor, the Duke of York, and the Archduke, to advance against Sainghin, announced that 'Kinsky knows what he has to do', but he and his 10,000 men did nothing, whilst on their right the Duke of York was being crushed

At 2 p.m., hearing of the defeat, Kinsky drew back with the Archduke eastwards on Marquain, in front of Tournai. As for the Archduke Charles, ordered to leave 10 battalions and 20 squadrons before Lille, he chose also to leave another 10 battalions and 20 squadrons at Pont-à-Marcq to guard against the garrison of Douai. By 6 a.m. he knew of the orders to start early for Lannoy with Kinsky,[3] and the urgency of the situation should have been manifest. This scientific Prince only moved off late, explaining that his troops were tired.

[1] Coutanceau, *Nord*, IIe Partie, ii, Docts. Annexes, 220–1, 229–30, 234.
[2] Ibid., 305–13, 329–34; ibid., Docts. Annexes, 232–4, 243, 244, 259–62 Jomini, *Rév.*, v. 97–8; Du Casse, *Vandamme*, i. 140–2, 144–5.
[3] Langeron, 66.

How fresh were the regiments who marched from Verona to fight at Rivoli, and then that night marched to Mantua to fight there again ? [1] By noon he had only got as far north as the road from Lille to Tournai. Here he received orders to return to camp and, joining Kinsky at Chereng, he fell back on Marquain to meet the rest of the army before Tournai. As far as the battle was concerned, the 29,000 men of these two columns might have been a hundred miles away.

Now for the second and third columns under Otto and the Duke of York. At 3 a.m. on the 18th May the left of Souham, the brigades of Thierry and Compière, with Daendels, moving by Herseaux on their outer flank, attacked that part of Otto's column at Wattrelos, while his right, Macdonald and Malbrancq, attacked the troops holding Tourcoing. Otto held firm on the east of Tourcoing and prevented Macdonald from debouching. He received support from two Austrian battalions, sent by the Duke of York to link with him, but which joined him altogether. Then Souham, who was directing the operation in person, sent Malbrancq from the right of Macdonald on Mouveaux, held by the English, whilst Bonnaud, coming up from the south-west, sent his left to join Malbrancq in an attack on the head of the Duke of York's column at Mouveaux, while the rest of his division struck at the rear of the Duke, the troops holding Roubaix and Lannoy. This body even pressed on right behind the Duke to threaten the rear of Otto, who in consequence had to retreat eastwards from Tourcoing to Wattrelos. There Otto was threatened from the north by Compère, Thierry, and Daendels, and he fell back again eastwards on Leers, where he stood for the rest of that day. It must be remembered that this attack of Bonnaud, so telling in the way it fell on the rear of the Duke and of Otto, should have been averted by the columns of Kinsky and of the Archduke, which were on the contrary lagging far south. The Duke of York, himself at Roubaix, had placed Lieut.-General Abercromby, with the 1st Infantry or Guards Brigade (the 1st, the Coldstream, and the 3rd Grenadier Guards), to hold Mouveaux. Roubaix was covered by four or five Austrian

[1] Coutanceau, *Nord*, II⁰ Partie, ii. 314–17 ; ibid., Docts. Annexes, 253, 254 ; Jomini, *Rév.*, v. 96.

battalions, part of Otto's column being in rear of that place. Major-General Fox, with the 2nd Infantry or 'Little Brigade', the 14th, 37th, and 53rd Regiments, was on the left, on the main road from Roubaix to Lille, watching Croix to the south-west; Lannoy in rear was held by two Hessian battalions. The nature of the country prevented the cavalry being used except for patrolling, so that arm, the 7th, 11th, 15th, and 16th Light Dragoons, was divided between the different corps, as was the artillery. The Rocket Troop was at Mouveaux.[1]

At daybreak on the 18th May 1794, when Otto was attacked, Colonel Devay, commanding the left of that column, asked the Duke of York for help to cover his flank, and the Duke sent two Austrian battalions, the regiment of the Grand Duke of Tuscany, with orders to fall back on him if pressed, but this body never returned. Into the gap thus made poured the French skirmishers, 'sharp-sighted as ferrets, and active as squirrels'.[2] Roubaix was taken by Bonnaud from the Austrians and Lannoy from the Hessians, the troops there retiring in disorder. Abercromby at Mouveaux was cut off, but he made his way south-east on Roubaix, when, finding the French in possession and the left of Malbrancq's brigade trying to cut him off from Leers, he went on for Lannoy. Here again he found the French in possession, but they had not yet penetrated beyond that place, so he marched rapidly for Templeuve. His safety was due to the fine behaviour of his men and also to the 'extreme vigour' of a diversion made by Otto.[3] The account of Wilson, who commanded the rear-guard, should be read.[4]

The Duke of York himself had a narrow escape of being captured. He at first had been in Roubaix and, when he saw the Austrians there giving way, tried to reach the Guards at Mouveaux, but that was impossible. Then he attempted to form a body of troops to relieve the Guards, and so he made for

---

[1] Jones, 37-8; Calvert, 211-12, 215-16; Wilson, *Life*, i. 85-6; Coutanceau, *Nord*, IIe Partie, ii. 320.

[2] Wilson, *Life*, i. 86.

[3] Coutanceau, IIe Partie, ii. 325, seems to doubt Otto's statement on this point, but I follow Wilson, *Life*, i. 93.

[4] Wilson, *Life*, i. 86-94; Jones, 39-41; Coutanceau, *Nord*, IIe Partie, ii. 324-5; ibid., Docts. Annexes, 257-8.

Fox's brigade to the west of Roubaix, but the enemy held the suburbs of that place. Then, turning eastwards, he tried to get to Wattrelos, hoping to find Otto's troops there and to arrange for succour for the Guards at Mouveaux : Wattrelos was unoccupied, and he and the few officers and troopers with him had almost passed through the village when he came under fire from the enemy, which wounded an officer's horse by his side. Taking to the fields and clearing a wide ditch, the Duke ' after many difficulties and perplexities ' was ' fortunate enough to reach Leers, where General Otto was ', but no relief could be sent to his men, as Lannoy was lost. Thence he went to Templeuve, where he was well received by Abercromby's brigade of Guards, which, as we have seen, had reached that place. ' No mobbed fox ', wrote Calvert, who had been in this ride, ' was ever more put to it to make his escape than we were, being at times nearly surrounded.' Next morning Fox's ' Little Brigade ' joined from Leers.[1] ' Son méprisable Altesse ', wrote Souham, ' required better horses for himself than for his artillery, for he was within an ace of accompanying his guns to Lille.'[2]

As for Fox and his gallant ' Little Brigade ',[3] they had held until surrounded and then, finding the rest of the column had retreated, cut their way through the different bodies of the enemy, each of whom expected such a handful of men to surrender. They made good their road towards Leers, where next morning they joined the Duke and Otto. They had had 1,120 men under arms and only brought off 530. ' The ability and coolness with which Lieut.-General Abercromby and Major-General Fox conducted their corps, under such trying circumstances, has done them immortal honour.'[4] One thing remained to remove any possible blame from the Duke for any alleged rashness. ' The Emperor has done us a bit of justice in publicly acknowledging that the Duke's column was the only one of the five that completed the service expected

---

[1] Calvert, 216-20 ; Wilson, *Life*, i. 87, 93 ; Jones, 38-9 ; Coutanceau, *Nord*, IIe Partie, ii, 324, Docts. Annexes, 228, 257-8.
[2] Coutanceau, *Nord*, IIe Partie, ii, Docts. Annexes, 236.
[3] ' Though his body be little, his honour is great.' Irish song for the Wren on St. Stephen's Day.
[4] Jones, 40-1 ; Coutanceau, *Nord*, IIe Partie, ii, Docts. Annexes, 259.

from them ',[1] and on the 27th May Coburg wrote by order of the Emperor to the Duke, assuring him of the Emperor's perfect satisfaction, and that nothing had been done by him except under orders.[2]

No real pursuit was made of either York or Otto, as the attention of Souham was drawn off to the north by the advance of Clairfayt, easily as that commander had been checked. Even as it was, another three-quarters of an hour, wrote Souham, would have linked him with the forces of the Allies advancing from the east.[3] Leaving Compère, Thierry, and Bonnaud to hold Wattrelos and Lannoy, and to watch the Duke of York, Souham called off Macdonald, Daendels, and Malbrancq, and sent them back westwards against Clairfayt, but the way was long and only Malbrancq got engaged, and that but slightly. Moreau took command of these brigades and prepared to attack Clairfayt next morning with them and with Vandamme, but that night, as we know, Clairfayt retired on Thielt, whilst the other columns fell back on Tournai, the French resuming pretty nearly their former positions.

The artillery lost heavily; fifty-six guns with their wagons stood on the road from Roubaix, 'the drivers having cut the traces and escaped with the horses when they found the enemy's fire surrounding them. Such was the consequence of sending out as drivers the refuse of our jails—for that was the practice at that day.'[4] Such incidents taught a lesson, and who now bear fire so well as those hardest-worked of men, the drivers of the artillery? The cavalry was even worse treated. Its whole mass was jammed soon after emerging from Roubaix, apparently by coming on the abandoned guns. As the head of their column fell back a little, the shock threw down some three-fourths of the horses and, whilst the horses and riders battled to gain their feet again, the French poured volleys into the struggling mass, until the scene became too horrible even for them, and a few moments' pause in the fire gave breathing time to the survivors. The camp-followers suffered too.

[1] Calvert, 217. [2] Ibid., 224-7.
[3] Coutanceau, *Nord*, IIe Partie, ii, Docts. Annexes, 236.
[4] Wilson, *Life*, i. 91. The English artillery lost 31 horses killed and 70 wounded or missing. Jones, 43.

'I saw a soldier's wife take a baby from her breast and, giving it a kiss, fling it into the stream or ditch, when she frantically rushed forwards and, before she had got ten yards, was rent in pieces by a discharge of grape that entered her back, sounding like a sack of coals being emptied.'[1]

The latest French authority makes the loss of the Duke's column to have been 53 officers and 1,830 men, besides 32 guns.[2] This seems exaggerated, and Jones gives as the English loss 65 killed and 875 wounded and missing, whilst the Duke, expressing his perfect satisfaction with his troops, wrote that the loss appeared to be less than might have been expected from the nature of the action.[3] The total loss of the Allies, according to the French, was 1,000 officers, 4,000 men, and 1,500 prisoners.[4] Jomini is more moderate, putting the loss of the Allies at 3,000 men.[5] The French loss is not given, but as Clairfayt had drawn off after inflicting damage, and only the Duke of York's column had been crushed, there seems no reason for supposing there was a great inequality in that matter, as far as the infantry was concerned. Here, as at Vittoria, it was the block caused by the guns which made the day so disastrous, at least to the cavalry.

There are ludicrous scenes even on a battle-field. Souham, seeing a volunteer limping along, asked him what was the matter and, when the man replied that he was wounded, told him to go quickly to the hospital. Off went the man, straight and rapid as a flash of lightning. Macdonald's staff officer, Pamphile Lacroix, who tells the story, says that, though busy rallying his men, he laughed till he cried at the sudden rapidity of the disappearance of what had been a slow limper.[6] A better instance of the spirit of the men is given by Lahure, whose horse was killed in the engagement of the 13th June by a round-shot, which struck a gunner behind him. 'Are you wounded, Commandant', said the man; then, finding Lahure had escaped with a scratch, 'Ah, so much the better. I shall not get off so cheaply: my thigh has been carried away—my wife, who has just done a hundred miles to see me, is there in rear; she

---

[1] Wilson, *Life*, 88–91. [2] Coutanceau, *Nord*, IIe Partie, ii. 325.
[3] Jones, 42–6, 51. [4] Coutanceau, *Nord*, IIe Partie, ii. 325–6.
[5] Jomini, *Rév.*, v. 98.
[6] Coutanceau, *Nord*, IIe Partie, ii, Docts. Annexes, 109–10.

will be nicely taken in. Vive la Liberté!' and so saying he fell back in his blood, to rise no more.[1]

Macdonald was the only future Marshal present at this battle. He himself includes it as one of those in which he had the greatest part [2] and, although one does not quite see this, yet he seems to have been the right arm of Souham notwithstanding the late argument between them. Already, in the affair at Mouscron, Pichegru, although not present, had very justly reported that the success had been due to the audacity of Souham and the ' bravoure réfléchie ' of Macdonald. ' They were seen everywhere, always marching at the head of our battalions in their different charges, rallying them calmly each time the enemy repulsed them : at the end it was they who bore down the enemy'; praise repeated by Pamphile Lacroix, who must have been by the side of Macdonald.[3] Much the same report would be true here, where Macdonald had had great difficulty in getting through Tourcoing, and at one time the rout of a battalion, and confusion amongst some cavalry, had augured badly for the day.[4]

Lt.-Colonel Murat had been far away with Desenfans' brigade, really belonging to Michaud, but attached to Moreau. Only two weak squadrons of his regiment, the 21st Chasseurs, were actually present with the brigade ; indeed Desenfans does not even mention it in giving the posts of his brigade which, on Clairfayt's reaching Wervicq, had retired from near Ypres to Bailleul, as I have said. On the 21st May Desenfans, visiting Comines, on the Lys near Menin, left Lt.-Colonel Murat there with fifty Chasseurs to reconnoitre in front and to link up with the brigade then at Wytschaete, south of Ypres, watching that town.[5]

This had distinctly been Souham's battle, planned and carried out by him. I say ' planned ', for, though the idea is attributed by Thiébault to an unnamed Colonel, perhaps Reynier, in a council of war much advice may be given, but the responsibility

---

[1] Lahure, 74–5.
[2] Macdonald, *Souvenirs*, 35. Pichegru wrote, ' Macdonald, who had most to suffer from the enemy's fire '. Coutanceau, *Nord*, IIe Partie, ii, Docts. Annexes, 243.
[3] Coutanceau, *Nord*, IIe Partie, ii. 135 ; ibid., Docts. Annexes, 109.
[4] Ibid., 322–3.   [5] Ibid., 312–13, 342 ; ibid., Docts. Annexes, 221, 264.

for the course adopted must lie with the commander. Jomini calls Souham ' un homme médiocre ', but sensible enough to refer to those who knew more than he did.[1] Surely this is, unintentionally, to praise Souham highly ! Most commanders get good advice, and some counsellors of Rehoboam were excellent : happy is the army whose commanders know what *is* good advice. But all through this part of the campaign Souham showed knowledge and decision and, when Pichegru went wrong, pointed out the error at once.[2] At Mouscron on the 29th April he had struck hard and rapidly on his own initiative. Here at Tourcoing he had done what Saint-Cyr considered much harder than making a plan—he had carried it out—giving a new direction, for instance, to the attack of Malbrancq's brigade. At a time when the troops required personal example, he himself led his men on to the attack. All this is not what one would have expected from ' un homme médiocre '.

Souham,[3] the tall, stuttering General of the Republic, was born at Lubersac in the Department of the Corrèze on the 30th May 1767 and had enlisted as a private in the 8th regiment of cavalry, Cuirassiers,[4] but at the beginning of the Revolution he returned home and, when the volunteers were organized, he, like many such old soldiers, became Lt.-Colonel of a battalion, the 2nd Corrèze, which joined the ' Nord '. He became General of Brigade on the 30th July 1793, and got the command of a division on the 13th September the same year. He seems always to have distinguished himself, making a useful diversion in Flanders over the same ground as we have been dealing with, when Jourdan was advancing for Wattignies. He did a great deal of fighting throughout the time of the Republic and the Empire, being twice disgraced for suspected complicity with Moreau, first in 1797 and then in 1804. This last affair no doubt was the reason why it was not till the 4th June 1810 that he received any mark of favour

---

[1] Jomini, *Rév.*, v, note 1, p. 89.
[2] Coutanceau, *Nord*, IIe Partie, ii. 113–15.
[3] General Comte Joseph Souham (1767–1837). Fage, *Le Général Souham*; *Fastes*, iii. 560–2 ; *Biog. des Cont.*, iv. 1362–3 ; Michaud, *Biog. univ.*, lxxxii. 391–2.
[4] I suppose the Cuirassiers du Roi. Susane, *Cav. franç.*, ii. 65–75.

L'ARMÉE DU NORD, 1794

from Napoleon, becoming Comte on that date,[1] a reward which Thiébault, the young General of the Empire, who was rather inclined to sneer at the old General of the Republic, by mistake attributes to the slightest of operations of Souham, under Marmont, against Wellington in 1811.[2] In 1814 Souham was concerned with Marmont in carrying the 6th Corps over to the enemy, a matter which endeared him to the Bourbons. Placed in retirement by Louis-Philippe, he died in 1837. Love of gambling, and his irregular life, it is said, stood in the way of his advancement.

Pichegru, who at the time received all the credit for the battle, arrived next day only from the right of the army. He now ordered an attack on the Allies, who lay before Tournai, resting on the Escaut both above and below the town, but with their right pushed needlessly forward northwards, down the river to the Espierre stream. Moreau was left to guard Courtrai and the Lys against Clairfayt with the brigades of Vandamme and Malbrancq, that of Desenfans, where Murat served, still watching Ypres. Dewinter's brigade, placed at Helchin,[3] was to link him with the attacking force. On the left Daendels' brigade was to move by the main road from Courtrai for Warcoing, and then up the Escaut, flanked on his right by Macdonald, who had his own brigade and that of Jardon, probably about 16,000 men, and who marched by Aelbeke and Tombrouck for Saint-Léger, joining Daendels on the Espierre. On Macdonald's right came the brigades of Thierry and Compère, all these four bodies, really so many divisions,[4] being under Souham. Farther south the division of Bonnaud was to attack the centre of the enemy, only demonstrating against their extreme left. Altogether some 62,000 men were probably employed.[5] The battle of Pont-à-Chin, or of Tournai, began early, about 5 a.m., on the 22nd May 1794, and was continued all day, becoming a series of attacks, made and opposed on either side with the greatest obstinacy, for the French troops were inspirited by their late success and were rapidly taking shape. We meet with no trace of any direction

---

[1] Révérend, *Armorial*, iv. 260.   [2] Thiébault, iv. 526-62.
[3] Near the Escaut; below Espierres.   [4] Jomini, *Rév.*, v. 99.
[5] Coutanceau, IIe Partie, ii, Docts. Annexes, 264-73.

on the part of Pichegru, save when, in the afternoon, his mistaken view of the position, or an error in the delivery of his order, caused Souham to make a fresh attempt to gain the village of Pont-à-Chin.[1] In the end, late in the day all the attacks of the French were beaten off, the weak demonstration against the left of the Allies being made so faintly as to enable them to reinforce their line elsewhere. For us the interest lies on the left, where Macdonald fought and where indeed was the main stress of the struggle.

Macdonald and Daendels, meeting, forced the Allies back up the left bank of the Escaut till they reached Pecq, where Daendels proposed to pass the river and march on Tournai by the right bank, when they might have found the town unprotected.[2] This, however, would have been so dangerous, as, in case of defeat, their retreat would have been cut off easily on the left bank, that the plan was abandoned and, while Daendels held Pecq and watched the river, Macdonald, putting himself at the head of five cavalry regiments,[3] made a dash up the left bank for Pont-à-Chin, but, checked by the artillery of the enemy, he had to wait for his infantry to take the village. Then began a long and desperate struggle for this post, which Souham ordered Macdonald to take. 'From 10 a.m. till nine at night the fire of both artillery and musketry was heavier than the oldest soldier in the field had ever before witnessed.'[4] Four times was Pont-à-Chin taken and recaptured, Macdonald holding it at the end.

At last the Duke of York, set free on the left, sent up seven Austrian battalions and his second brigade, and at 7 p.m. Fox's men, the 'Little Brigade', the 14th, 37th, and 53rd Regiments, which had lost so heavily on the 18th May, advanced to throw off Macdonald. 'Nothing', says Wilson, 'could exceed the pride of that moment for an Englishman.' The Austrians were, by order, most properly and naturally lying down after their long struggle in which Macdonald's men had been repulsed five times from Pont-à-Chin. 'It was never-

[1] Coutanceau, *Nord*, IIe Partie, ii. 357 ; ibid., Docts. Annexes, 283.
[2] Ibid., 355 ; Langeron, 68.
[3] Jomini, *Rév.*, v. 100, makes Macdonald charge at the head of the fifth cavalry regiment, but I follow Coutanceau, 355. Desbrière, *La Cav. pendant la Rév.: La crise*, 417, says four regiments.
[4] Calvert, 222.

theless a gallant sight—and the Austrians themselves by their cheers acknowledged it—to view this handful of brave men step through them into the rain of fire that poured as they appeared and with inflexible intrepidity press to the charge.'[1] Macdonald's men, panic-stricken, broke and fled; the English artillery came up fresh into action, and their well-directed fire prevented the French ever rallying. They retired, and at ten at night the last gun was fired.

This battle, 'butchery without plan, success, or result', as Thiébault describes it,[2] was very murderous for both sides, as the troops had fought desperately. The Allies lost 4,000 men, of whom 196 (all except three were from Fox's brigade) were English.[3] The French lost seven guns and some 6,000 men or more. In one place 280 of them lay headless from the fire of an Austrian battery, which had caught them wedged in an orchard. 'Such a beheading carnage was perhaps never paralleled. The Emperor was so pleased with the intrepid gallantry of the British " Little Brigade ", which had returned to the charge with colours flying and music playing, that he gave an order for the Austrian battalions always to move to the attack in the same formation, but this order was not one of long duration.'[4] It was Pichegru's battle, and a very different one from that of Souham at Tourcoing.[5] One incident was especially pleasing to the Allies, who believed their late defeat at Tourcoing had been due to Pichegru. That General had been dining behind Pont-à-Chin when the last action there took place, believing that the Allies were finally repulsed. Suddenly there was a cry, 'Les Anglais, les habits rouges!' The scramble was universal, and some of the officers got out of the window in order to gain their horses sooner. The dinner was found by 'les Anglais' and was a good prize; the plate also left was a more valuable one.[6] To eat your adversary's dinner always gives a zest to victory.

---

[1] Wilson, *Life*, i. 95-6.   [2] Thiébault, i. 492.
[3] Jones, 57.   [4] Wilson, *Life*, i. 97.
[5] For this battle see Coutanceau, *Nord*, IIe Partie, ii. 342-61, and ibid., Docts. Annexes, 274-91; Jomini, *Rév.*, v. 98-104; Dellard, 38-44; Langeron, 67-8; Jones, 52-7; Calvert, 221-2; Wilson, *Life*, i. 94-8. For plan see Coutanceau, *Nord*, IIe Partie, i, Docts. et Cartes; Alison, Atlas, ix; Jomini, *Rév.*, Atlas, viii.   [6] Wilson, *Life*, i. 96.

On the 30th May 1794 the Emperor left the head-quarters of the Allies to visit Clairfayt on the left and then to join his army which was defending Charleroi from the attacks of the right of the 'Nord' and the Armée des Ardennes, whence he returned to Vienna, his departure dispiriting his troops. With him went Mack, who had resigned his post as Quartermaster-General, in which he was succeeded by the Prince of Waldeck. The Prince of Coburg commanded the whole of the Allies. Alarmed by the operations against Charleroi, of which I shall soon speak, the Allies weakened their force at Tournai, where the Duke of York remained, and Pichegru took advantage of this to attack Ypres, which was besieged by the division of Moreau, in which I suppose Lt.-Colonel Murat still served in the brigade of Desenfans. The siege was covered by the division of Souham (in which Macdonald led a brigade), with that of Despeaux, brought up from Courtrai, on his right and that of Michaud on his left. The operations of the Allies, curious enough in a study of their strategy, need not detain us. Puzzled by the attacks on their left at Charleroi and on their right at Ypres, they let the initiative pass to the French and wasted their strength in trying alternately to reinforce one or other of their wings, each march having to be cancelled by some fresh advance or threat of the French. The Duke of York, meanwhile, much against his will, was left to guard Tournai on the Escaut, a town which the Austrians had neglected to fortify properly, and which now became a burden to their cause.[1]

On the 1st June 1794 the division of Moreau, covered by that of Michaud, began the siege of Ypres, and on the 10th June Pichegru advanced with his other three divisions to attack Clairfayt at Rousselaere,[2] where he hoped to outflank him, but the Austrians drew back on Thielt. On the 13th June Clairfayt, anxious to save Ypres and reinforced by six battalions from Coburg, suddenly attacked the French at 7 a.m., his blow falling first on Despeaux, one of whose brigades (Malbrancq) was broken, and the other (Salm) thrown back towards Menin.

---

[1] Jomini, *Rév.*, v. 104, 119-25; Langeron, 68-76; Calvert, 222-59. See Jones, 64, for plan of position of the Duke of York before Tournai.
[2] Roulers.

L'ARMÉE DU NORD, 1794   313

The storm then fell on Macdonald, whose brigade, reinforced by a regiment from the left, held the plateau of Hooglede, north of Rousselaere. Macdonald says he commanded alone. This is not correct, but he certainly bore the brunt of the fight. His brigade was nearly surrounded, but thanks, it is said, to the bravery, firmness, and intrepidity, joined to the talents and rare coolness of its commander, it held for six hours, although Clairfayt poured his cavalry on it. Then Dewinter's brigade came up on its left, Salm advanced, and the enemy, exhausted, retired as suddenly as he had come. 'This combat', says Jomini, 'did as much honour to General Macdonald as to his brigade.' It settled matters in this district, for, while the Allies were moving from the east to relieve it, Ypres surrendered on the 18th June [1] and Clairfayt retired, pursued by Souham, who struck him at Deynze and who followed him to the gates of Ghent.[2]

[1] Musset-Pathay, 335–60, and Plan VIII.
[2] Jomini, *Rév.*, v. 119–24, 153; Foucart et Finot, *Déf. nat.*, ii. 381–2; *Vict. et Conq.*, iii. 32–8, with plan of siege of Ypres; Macdonald, *Souvenirs*, 35; Lahure, 74–8; Calvert, 230–59; Langeron, 74–5; Du Casse, *Vandamme*, i. 149–60.

XVI

L'ARMÉE DU NORD (*continued*), 1794-5

Change in the composition of the 'Nord'. Its right, with the Armée des Ardennes, joins a force brought by Jourdan from the Armée de la Moselle, and becomes a new army, the 'Sambre-et-Meuse'. Redistribution of the future Marshals. Attack on Charleroi. The 'Nord' directed away northwards from the 'Sambre-et-Meuse'. Jourdan wins the battle of Fleurus. Extraordinary campaign. Advance of the 'Nord'. Pichegru enters Brussels. Bad spelling of Pichegru and Vandamme. Allies bewildered. An Englishman's prayer. English again capture Pichegru's dinner. The 'Nord' occupies Antwerp, and the two armies, 'Nord' and 'Sambre-et-Meuse', halt whilst the fortresses are besieged. The fall of Robespierre. Sieges carried on by Moreau on the coast. The treatment of the *émigrés* captured in the places. Decree that no quarter be given to English and Hanoverians. Soldiers suggest that the Convention might eat the prisoners, but refuse to kill them. The fortresses taken, the two armies again advance. Capture of Bois-le-Duc and Nijmegen. Wellington engaged at Boxtel. The Comte d'Artois joins the English. The 'Nord' passes the Meuse. Disaster to the English 37th Regiment. Moreau takes the place of Pichegru, who falls ill, Macdonald, now General of Division, taking the place of Moreau with the division. The Duke of York leaves the English army. Pichegru resumes command. Macdonald leads across the Waal. Pichegru only receives the capitulation of provinces. Capture of Dutch fleet by French. Hardships of the English retreat. Bad hospitals. Wellington learns what not to do. Moreau and Macdonald on the right bank of the Rhine. Macdonald's commands. Pichegru leaves for the 'Rhin-et-Moselle'.

A GREAT change in the composition of the 'Nord' now took place. That army had always been too large for its commander to handle, weighted also as he was with the superior command of the Armée des Ardennes, so that his front extended from Dunkirk to Longwy.[1] We have just seen that, whilst his left had been extricating itself from a most dangerous position at Tourcoing, Pichegru had been away, visiting the Armée des Ardennes. Now the *Comité* formed an entirely new army of the right wing of the 'Nord', the effective divisions of the

[1] Coutanceau, *Nord*, IIe Partie, i, Docts. Annexes, 602-3.

L'ARMÉE DU NORD, 1794-5

'Ardennes', and of a force brought from the Armée de la Moselle by its commander, Jourdan; the whole taking the title of the Armée de Sambre-et-Meuse. By this change the 'Nord' lost three future Marshals; Bernadotte, made Colonel on the 4th April, who had been serving in Goguet's late division, which had passed under Dubois; Lt.-Colonel and Adjutant-General Mortier, employed in Balland's late division, now under Kléber (although I do not know if he continued under that General); and Ney, made Captain on the 25th April, who served in Fromentin's division. Besides these the 'Nord' lost Kléber, who had joined from La Vendée, and Schérer, who had come from the Armée du Rhin.[1] All these, with Marceau, who, coming as a General of Division from La Vendée, had joined the Armée des Ardennes on the 14th April 1794,[2] now definitely separated from General of Brigade Macdonald and Lt.-Colonel Murat, who remained with the 'Nord', whilst the others went to join Jourdan, Lefebvre, and Soult, who came from the 'Moselle' to the 'Sambre-et-Meuse'. These made up what I may call the Jourdan group of Marshals. Lt.-Colonel Lecourbe, denounced after Wattignies, where he had fought in the 'Nord', had long been a prisoner on some of the usual charges of want of patriotism, launched by officers who had been punished for improper conduct. He had been sent, still a prisoner, to La Vendée: now at the end of May 1794 he joined the Armée des Ardennes, where on the 12th June he was made General of Brigade in Meyer's division, with which he passed to the new force, the 'Sambre-et-Meuse'.[3]

It was, however, not till the 29th June 1794 that the Armée de Sambre-et-Meuse actually received its name by decree of the Convention. Meanwhile, before its formation was contemplated, Pichegru, with the Representatives Saint-Just and Le Bas, had on the 6th May 1794 formed a plan for the operations of the 'Nord'. A garrison of 2,000 was to be left at Avesnes, 7,000 to 8,000 in Maubeuge, and 6,000 in Cambrai and Bouchain. The rest of the army was formed in three masses. On the right 60,000, part from the 'Ardennes' under Charbonnier and part from the right of the 'Nord' under

---

[1] Coutanceau, *Nord*, IIe Partie, i. 460, 468, Docts. Annexes, 749.
[2] Maze, *Marceau*, 41.   [3] Philebert, *Lecourbe*, 53-88.

Desjardins, were to concentrate at Jeumont[1] and then, crossing the Sambre at Thuin, to march on Mons. In the centre Ferrand with 24,000 men was to hold the enemy in his front and maintain the communications of Maubeuge and Avesnes with Guise. On the left by the coast Pichegru himself with 70,000 men was to take Ypres and Tournai and, seizing the navigation of the Escaut, make the enemy's work of provisioning himself most difficult. Pichegru did not count on the co-operation of the ' Moselle ', looking on the check it had received at Arlon as final. His plan was to attack by both wings, thus giving the Allies the opportunity of falling on one or other of his two great bodies. His centre was to be ready to advance if the wings were successful, and to enable it to do this, or to reinforce them if they were beaten, he wished to have it strengthened by 25,000 men, either from the ' Moselle ' or from the coast and La Vendée. Thus he would have called in the force under Jourdan from the ' Moselle ', not to the nearest point, his own right, but to his centre and, wherever he was to get his 25,000 men, some time must be taken before they were available.[2]

Pichegru had already been trying to use the ' Ardennes ' to support his right, but for the sake of clearness I have omitted its operations, which had little effect. How [3] the advance of the right became an attack on Charleroi, in which in time Jourdan with his force from the ' Moselle ' joined, leading to the formation of the ' Sambre-et-Meuse ' and the battle of Fleurus, will be told in the history of that army. Although the divisions of the ' Nord ', thus detached under Desjardins, technically belonged to the ' Nord ' till the 13th or 24th June, it will be more convenient to treat them in all their operations, with those of the ' Ardennes ', as part of the force to which they were soon to belong, the ' Sambre-et-Meuse ', while we return to the former left wing of the ' Nord ', which now began to act ; remembering that of the men with whom we are concerned, we have here only General of Brigade Macdonald, Lt.-Colonel Murat, and General of Division Moreau.

[1] On the Sambre, below Maubeuge.
[2] Coutanceau, *Nord*, IIe Partie, i. 505 ; Dupuis, *Fleurus*, 82–7.
[3] Ibid., 506 ; ibid., 33–82.

L'ARMÉE DU NORD, 1794-5

It had been intended that the 'Nord' should advance, wheel to its right, and cross the Escaut at Audenarde, whilst it was hoped that Jourdan with his army would be able to advance by Mons and meet it. Clairfayt would then have been cut off from Coburg on the right, and a formidable mass would have been concentrated against the centre and left of the Allies. The old hankering for a stroke along the coast, which had attracted Dumouriez in 1793, now prevailed, and on the 26th June 1794, when the army had its leading troops engaged with the English [1] before Audenarde, it received orders to move north, apparently, says Jomini,[2] to assist a maritime expedition against Holland. That very day Jourdan won the battle of Fleurus before Charleroi, which fortress had just surrendered to him, and the main force of the Allies had thus been beaten off by one French army. The whole of this campaign is extraordinary, for the Allies, possessing the central position and able to throw their weight with ease on either flank, allowed two French armies, neither of them led by great Generals, to threaten and beat off their wings and eventually to besiege and capture the two fortresses on which those wings had rested. Nor had these sieges been successful from sheer rapidity of execution, as in the case of some of Wellington's captures in Spain, for Ypres had been threatened ever since Houchard had relieved Dunkirk. Its fortifications had been destroyed by Joseph II, and the Austrians, although partially restoring them, had never been awake to the importance of the work.

The case of Charleroi was even more wonderful, for, when Jourdan crossed the Sambre for his final attack on it, it was the fifth time the French had crossed for that purpose in May and June of this year. Jomini remarks on the isolation in which Clairfayt had fought, whilst 30,000 Austrians remained inactive at Tournai, and 7,000 English under Lord Moira rested at Ostend after their passage from England.[3] This is not quite correct, for Lord Moira reached Ostend on the 26th June and marched from it two days later, eventually, on

---

[1] Calvert, 266.
[2] Jomini, *Rév.*, v. 153-4 ; *Carnot, par son Fils*, i. 483-4.
[3] Jomini, *Rév.*, v. 124.

account of the general retreat of the Allies, meeting the Duke on the 9th July at Malines. In this operation Lord Moira acted much on his own responsibility.[1] To the French belongs the credit of some daring and certainly of considerable perseverance, but the folly and sloth of the Generals of the Allies were so great that part of the merits of the winners is discounted. It will be seen that the French armies were fast gaining consistency and confidence, for the *amalgame* was doing its work, whilst the names of Generals who belong to history now emerge from the crowd.

What happened was more like a dream than the story of a campaign. Moving forwards, Pichegru was at Bruges on the 1st July 1794, Moreau, under whom I suppose Lt.-Colonel Murat still to have been, having entered that town two days before. Scattering his divisions, Pichegru waited, watching the Duke of York at Audenarde, while Jourdan, having, as I said, beaten off Coburg at Fleurus in front of Charleroi, swung round his left wing in an enormous semicircle northwards. The Allies had lost all heart and, instead of falling in strength on either French army, thought of nothing but retreating. On the 10th July Pichegru, always eager to snatch credit from others, entered Brussels, already reached by the left wing of the ' Sambre-et-Meuse '.[2] By this event the worthy Vandamme won a watch most honestly. ' Je promoit une montre à repetition en argent au général Vandamme à l'arrivée de l'armée à Brussel, Le général en chef de l'armé du Nord, Pichegru.'[3] Time apparently did not permit of better spelling, but the ' Nord ' was not strong in orthography. Some four years later Vandamme wrote a delicious letter to Lecourbe in acknowledgement of a loan—' Ce tegmoniage non équivoc du dézir d'obliger votre camarade . . . Mais que puige y faire obéire est mon devoir et je le fait . . . Mille chosses je vous prie de ma part à votre chère damme '.[4] Vandamme would surely

[1] Calvert, 266· Jones, 81–9. Lord Moira had 7,000 men, including the 19th, 27th, 28th, 40th, 42nd, 54th, 57th, 59th, 87th, and 89th Regiments, and apparently the 8th, 15th, and 16th Light Dragoons.

[2] Jomini, *Rév.*, v. 153–6, 162–3 ; Foucart et Finot, *Déf. nat.*, ii. 409–13 ; Calvert, 259–75 ; Jones, 73–90.

[3] Vandamme's brigade reached Brussels on the 15th September 1794. Du Casse, *Vandamme*, i. 182, and note 1, p. 183.

[4] Philebert, *Lecourbe*, 134.

have been rejected by any of our modern boards of examination, but, if he jumbled up his letters, he knew the right place for his men in the field, and after all that was something.

The march northwards of the Armée du Nord was a marvellous one, and it seemed to cry out to Coburg to disregard such a false step and to throw the bulk of his forces on Jourdan and the 'Sambre-et-Meuse'. Nothing which had occurred gave the least reason for believing that Jourdan could have stood such a blow, for at Fleurus the Duke of York had been absent, and his force would have undoubtedly turned the scale there. Yet, 'so strange a thing is war' that this very false movement seems to have bewildered Coburg and the Allies more than a really formidable operation would have done. All this campaign reminds me of an action in the American Civil War between some Federal gun-boats and a large Southern ram; the smaller craft, by constant ramming and audacity, simply bullied the more formidable vessel into surrender. It is true that the Southerner had had her steering gear shot away, but that put her much in the position of the Allies, whose directing power seems to have vanished. Altogether this is a very curious campaign to study, and so difficult is it to understand the actions of Coburg, that Calvert, one of the Duke of York's staff, like a sensible man, was amazed and found it hard not to suspect there was some treachery at work. Thanking God daily that he was an Englishman, he prayed 'the time may arrive when it may be no longer necessary for us to have connexion with the fools and villains who are playing the principal parts on the Continent of Europe'.[1]

By the 11th July 1794 the two armies, the 'Nord' under Pichegru, with whom Macdonald, Murat, and Moreau served, and the 'Sambre-et-Meuse' under Jourdan, with whom Bernadotte, Lefebvre, Mortier, Ney, and Soult served, with Kléber and Marceau, were united on a long line stretching from Namur on the east, through Brussels, with the left on the Vilvorde canal towards Malines. Thus the state of affairs in the time of Dumouriez had nearly been restored, but on a sounder basis, and this time without any decisive battle. All behind the French was now clear, except the fortresses captured by the

[1] Calvert, 303-4.

Allies, Landrecies, Le Quesnoy, Valenciennes, and Condé. Coburg with Clairfayt, that is to say the Austrians, had retired to Louvain and Tirlemont; the Dutch and English were on the Dyle, the Duke of York being at Contich,[1] covering Antwerp. The retreat, as so often happens with a combined army, had sown distrust between the different nationalities and had brought out the differences between their objects. The English and Dutch covered Holland, whilst Coburg thought of Maestricht and of his communications with Germany by Köln and Koblenz.

This junction of the two armies, the ' Nord ' and the ' Sambre-et-Meuse ', seemed to invite a combined movement, but several reasons stopped the advance of the immense force and broke it up almost as soon as it was formed. The *Comité* suddenly became nervous and insisted on the recapture of the fortresses taken by the Allies before any further advance were made. The consequent sieges fell to the ' Sambre-et-Meuse '. Other causes kept the armies apart. Neither of the two commanders wished to lose his independence, and this feeling was shared, as often, by the Representatives with each army. It is, indeed, said that Pichegru was destined by the Representatives for the chief command of the whole mass, but that General, as on the Rhine in 1793 at the relief of Landau, showed his indecision too plainly. Thus the armies separated, and while Jourdan, with greater vigour, moved against Coburg at Louvain, Pichegru on the 13th July 1794 only made a slow advance on Antwerp against the English and Dutch. Souham commanded three divisions, besides the so-styled brigades of Macdonald and Dewinter. Coburg, falling back before Jourdan, crossed the Meuse at Maestricht, whilst the Dutch, followed by the English, retreated behind Breda, Antwerp being occupied by the ' Nord ' without resistance on the 27th July. There was much desultory fighting, and on the 22nd July at Boxtel on the Dommel the English once more captured the dinner of Pichegru, who must have been unlucky about his food.[2] Again the two French armies halted on a long line, Jourdan to the east, with his right at Liége, whilst Pichegru had his left at

---

[1] Between Malines, held by the Hessians, and Antwerp.
[2] Wilson, *Life*, i. 100–1.

Antwerp, a post at Diest connecting the two forces.[1] On the 9th Thermidor, 27th July 1794, the bloody dictatorship of Robespierre had ended, and a great sigh of relief went up from France.

Before the advance of the ' Nord ', Moreau, in whose division the regiment of Lt.-Colonel Murat served, had been sent along the coast on the extreme left, first occupying Ostend and then marching against Nieuport, in front of which he arrived on the 4th July, and which he besieged with the brigade of Vandamme, obtaining its surrender on the 18th July.[2] Moreau then marched on, still along the coast, to besiege Fort l'Écluse, or Sluys. First the island of Kadzand had to be taken, and on the 28th July his men, some in boats, others swimming, forced the passage under the fire of the enemy's guns, a deed described as one of the boldest in the campaign.[3] Seeing one of the boats carried away by the current and almost sinking, Moreau dashed into the water and, swimming out, brought a grenadier to shore.[4] The Convention decreed an honourable mention of the passage. It was now that Moreau heard of the danger of his father, who was guillotined. The siege of Fort l'Écluse was carried on under the greatest difficulties, the men often having mud and water up to their waists and suffering much from fever ; indeed, whilst only 120 men were killed and wounded by fire, more than seven thousand were sent to hospital from the brigades of Vandamme, Daendels, and Laurent, notwithstanding all the precautions of Moreau. At last, on the 25th August 1794, the place surrendered and, after resting his men in good quarters till the 13th September, Moreau rejoined the army.[5] All this brought credit to Moreau : indeed his captures were considered by the Allies as most disastrous to them, endangering their right.[6] In both sieges Moreau had done all he could to save his men from fever, feeding them well and providing all the remedies then known for the curse of the

---

[1] Jomini, *Rév.*, v. 163-74 ; Lahure, 78-80 ; *Vict. et Conq.*, iii. 101-3 ; Langeron, 81-7 ; Calvert, 273-95 ; Jones, 89-119.
[2] *Vict. et Conq.*, ii. 91-8 ; Musset-Pathay, 433-52, and Plan XIII ; Du Casse, *Vandamme*, 160-2, 168-76.
[3] *Vict. et Conq.*, iii. 109-16.   [4] Musset-Pathay, 410.
[5] Ibid., 405-32, and Plan XII ; *Vict. et Conq.*, iii. 137-44 ; Foucart et Finot, *Déf. nat.*, ii. 413-14 ; Du Casse, *Vandamme*, i. 163-4, 178-82.
[6] Calvert, 275-6, 288-90, 309, 312, 320.

swamps, issuing much vinegar and 'une grande quantité de petite bière'.[1]

One unpleasant incident of these two sieges was the treatment of the *émigrés* in the garrisons, who, by the decree of the Convention, were to be killed. At Nieuport some *émigrés* escaped in a small vessel under the fire of the besiegers and reached the English fleet in the offing.[2] On the capitulation the article proposed by the besieged, that three such vessels should be permitted to sail out, obviously for the safety of the *émigrés*, was refused and the *émigrés* were specially excepted from the terms. These unfortunate men tried to escape, hiding themselves in the farms in the inundation round the place, but they were almost all discovered and shot.[3] Some 300 were thus slaughtered.[4] In the capitulation of Fort l'Écluse Moreau again excepted the *émigrés*,[5] but we are not told of their fate, which no doubt was the same as of those at Nieuport. It would be unfair to blame Moreau, who according even to the survivors wished to save them,[6] but he had to deal with the Representatives and with the decree of the Convention; Vandamme seems to have had no scruples in the matter.[7]

A more important question, that of the slaughter of all the garrisons, had been rather avoided than solved. The Convention had decreed that no English or Hanoverians were to be made prisoners. The Duke of York on the 7th June 1794 announced this to the troops of those two nations under him, expressing his confidence that they would not adopt such a principle of war until it were proved that the French army submitted to such an atrocious order.[8] He was right, and Lahure, then with the 'Nord', writes, 'I ought to say, for the honour of the army, that the soldiers never consented to put this infamous measure into execution'.[9] In some cases the men, sending their prisoners to the interior, suggested that the Convention might eat them if it liked: they would not sully their hands with such blood.[10] The decree, indeed, was unwork-

[1] *Vict. et Conq.*, iii. 144.   [2] Musset-Pathay, 438–9.   [3] Ibid., 444, 449.
[4] Calvert, 288.   [5] Musset-Pathay, 428.   [6] Calvert, 288.
[7] Du Casse, *Vandamme*, i. 68–9, 161–2, 171–5.
[8] Calvert, 234–8; Jones, 64–8.
[9] Lahure, 80.   [10] *Vict. et Conq.*, iii. 39.

able, and the day before Nieuport fell Carnot wrote, practically annulling it as far as this garrison was concerned. The decree, he said, did not refer to the Hessians, who were to be kept prisoners : the others were to be sent back in exchange for an equal number of soldiers or sailors. ' As for the *émigrés*, there can be no manner of mercy for them.'[1] As a matter of fact, the troops of the garrison of Nieuport, some 2,000 strong, almost all Hanoverians, were made prisoners of war.[2] We have seen the fate of the *émigrés*.

The Hanoverians in Nieuport had been fortunate. Moreau, realizing that the garrison, if driven to desperation, would hold out to the last, asked what he was to do if it wished to capitulate, and the Representatives on the spot, wanting his force for the attack on the island of Walcheren, supported the request for indulgence, but the *Comité* was inflexible. Pichegru saw the folly of this and, writing to Moreau, said, ' I see beforehand all the *pleasure* this will give you ! This will lengthen an operation which, I think, would have been ended in a few days, and which will perhaps cost us four times what it would have cost us under the other supposition.' However, the Representatives on the spot took on themselves to allow a capitulation before the answer of the *Comité* had arrived, but they assured the *Comité* that they would not have done this had they known of the decision in time. It is to be remarked that, while the Generals wanted to save time, the civilians dreamt of giving ' a terrible example of the inflexibility of an outraged nation and of the measure of its vengeance '.[3] I presume the milder decision given by Carnot came later.[4]

According to Moreau's own account, given later, he went very far, answering the order for slaughter sent by Pichegru that with 6,000 men he could never take a place defended by 8,000, if these were driven to despair ; besides, he would not undertake such work and asked to be relieved from it. Pichegru, who was sensible enough in such matters, told Moreau that he had thrown this letter into the fire, ' de peur qu'elle ne le perdit ', as assuredly it would have done, and the order

---

[1] ' Quant aux émigrés, il ne peut y avoir de grâce pour eux d'aucune manière.' Wallon, *Rep.*, iv. 241.
[2] Musset-Pathay, 444.
[3] Wallon, *Rep.*, iv. 269-70.
[4] Compare ibid., 241 and 269-70, which hardly agree.

was maintained. Moreau then went to the Representatives present and, not telling them of the confirmation of the order, induced them to authorize him to receive a capitulation of the garrison, alleging the resistance he would otherwise meet. Robespierre in the Convention did not forget this. ' Perish ', he said, ' 10,000 men rather than a principle ', but he fell too soon to be able to punish Moreau.

It may be interesting to give a state of the ' Nord ' on the 1st September 1794, as until lately it has been difficult to know any details of it.[1] It is to be remembered that Macdonald led a brigade under Souham, Vandamme another under Moreau, whilst Lt.-Colonel Murat's Chasseur regiment was also, I think, with Moreau.[2]

Divisions.	Infantry.	Cavalry.	Artillery.	Guns.	Howitzers.	Mortars.
1st Souham	14,813	3,436	1,311	60	9	—
2nd Moreau	11,053	1,026	577	39	2	—
3rd Lemaire	11,255	1,118	595	35	3	—
4th Despeaux	5,432	647	283	16	2	—
5th Bonnaud	9,103	1,558	658	34	5	—
6th Delmas	4,481	380	241	16	2	—
Artillery Park	—	—	901	51	22	10
	56,137	8,165	4,566	251	45	10

Infantry	56,137
Cavalry	8,165
Artillery	4,566
	68,868

By the middle of September 1794 the ' Sambre-et-Meuse ' had finished the recapture of the fortresses in rear, and the advance of both armies recommenced. On the right Jourdan, with the ' Sambre-et-Meuse ', forced the Austrians over the Rhine, but the progress of the ' Nord ' was much slower, indeed the apparent slackness of Pichegru in the pursuit of the English caused murmurs amongst his troops.[3] Much desultory fighting took place between the advancing and retiring forces, and on the 14th September 1794 the French made a night attack on

[1] Desbrière, *La Fin de la Convention*, 131-2.
[2] See the table state of the army, 3rd July, in Jomini, *Rév.*, v. 134 ; probably founded on the nominal strength of regiments, where the 21st Chasseurs are shown with Moreau.
[3] François, *Journal*, 58 ; *Vict. et Conq.*, iii. 161-2.

the post at Boxtel on the Dommel river, where Lt.-Colonel Wellesley, then commanding the 33rd Regiment, saw his first engagement, his men covering the retreat of the English Guards down a lane. His regiment had left Cork in May and, landing at Ostend, had joined the English force. Macdonald was engaged in this affair, where the Duke of York lost nearly 1,500 men, mostly Hessians.[1] Two days later the Comte d'Artois, the future Charles X, joined the Duke; ' he appears a polite, gentleman-like man ', says Calvert.[2]

The Prince, joining an army in full retreat, remained long with it, going through all the painful experiences of an exile whose cause was taken up at most half-heartedly by the Allies. Remaining after the English army had left, it was only on the 7th August 1795 that he landed in England, too late for the disastrous expedition to Quiberon.[3] I mention the Prince because it is pleasant to think of his surprise had he been told he would be one of the patrons for a statue of Pichegru, before whom he now was retiring.

The Duke of York now drew back to the right bank of the Meuse, below Grave, and Pichegru besieged Bois-le-Duc or Hertogenbosch. Macdonald's brigade was part of the force under Delmas covering the siege and, when the place surrendered rather hastily on the 9th October 1794, the Dutch, knowing that he had been in garrison there when in the service of Holland, attributed this to him, but in reality the Commandant, an old officer, is said to have lost his head and to have capitulated prematurely.[4] But Lahure, who was with Macdonald, calls the defence honourable.[5] Amongst the garrison were eleven hundred *émigrés*, who almost all passed out with it. Pichegru sent them word that he did not wish their death and that, if they marched out mixed with the garrison, no notice would be taken of them.[6] This was very honourable to Pichegru: indeed there is a striking difference between the

---

[1] Calvert, 324-8; Jones, 120-5; *Vict. et Conq.*, iii. 159-61; Jomini, *Rév.*, vi. 24-5; Macdonald, *Souvenirs*, 35.
[2] Calvert, 328-37.
[3] Ernest Daudet, *Hist. de l'Émigration*, i. 272-81, 293-6, 324.
[4] Musset-Pathay, 485-94, and Plate XV; *Vict. et Conq.*, iii. 173-9, with plan; Macdonald, *Souvenirs*, 35; Lahure, 81; François, *Journal*, 59-60; Jomini, *Rév.*, vi. 48. [5] Lahure, 81.
[6] Calvert, 360 (the mention of Jourdan is a mistake); François, *Journal*, 60.

action of the demagogues at Paris and that of the Generals on the frontier. Thus, at the siege of Nijmegen by Souham, when the place was treating for a capitulation on the 8th November 1794,[1] the French troops penetrated into the town, but Souham yet allowed the garrison to become prisoners of war.[2] Here let me say that, if it be true, as the French allege, that the English troops that had been in the place and had evacuated it before the surrender fired on the Dutch who were trying to pass the river also, the explanation would seem to be that some of the Dutch were firing on English and French alike, and were therefore believed to be enemies.

On the 6th October 1794 Moreau, who had come up to Venlo and was now on the right of the army, learnt that the 'Sambre-et-Meuse', on his right, had passed through Roermond or Ruremonde, and by the 14th October his division was over the Meuse. He himself went, as we shall see, to replace Pichegru temporarily, and the division under Laurent besieged Venlo, which capitulated on the 26th October.[3] Pichegru had determined to pass the Meuse by Grave, in the centre of the enemy's line, and on the 18th October Souham and Bonnaud crossed over, the Duke of York with most of his force having retired to Nijmegen. Next day Souham, no doubt having Macdonald under him, attacked the advanced posts of the enemy in front of Nijmegen between the Meuse and the Waal, and one of his columns fell on the English 37th Regiment, under the future General Hope, which was marching along a dyke and which was almost destroyed. They had been acting with part of the Austrian 'Hussars of Rohan', a body of *émigrés*, and the 9th Hussars of Souham's division rode up, calling out that they were the Rohan regiment, whose uniform theirs resembled: getting thus amongst the 37th on the top of the dyke, they drove them off it, taking the greater part of them, with one colour and their regimental guns.[4] The English

---

[1] Musset-Pathay, 515–28, and Plate XVIII; François, *Journal*, 63–6.
[2] *Vict. et Conq.*, iii. 219–20; François, *Journal*, 66; David, 127. Compare Musset-Pathay, 526, and *Vict. et Conq.*, iii. 219, with François, *Journal*, 65, and Jones, 141–2.
[3] Musset-Pathay, 495–514, and Plate XVII; Jomini, *Rév.*, vi. 56; *Vict. et Conq.*, iii. 195–9; François, *Journal*, 61–2; Du Casse, *Vandamme*, i. 165–6.
[4] Jomini, *Rév.*, vi. 49–56; *Vict. et Conq.*, iii. 190–3; David, 111–17; Jones, 132–4; Calvert, 361–2, 365–6.

believed the French copied the uniform of the *émigrés* exactly. 'There is not a man on earth who might not have been deceived under similar circumstances ',[1] but we may assume that the *émigrés* adopted their former uniforms.

The French in Italy seem to have thought the proper way to meet such an attack was for the infantry to slip off the dyke, so that the cavalry could not reach them, and then to fire on their foes, but here we may suppose the French infantry followed up the charge.

Pichegru now fell ill and remained in Brussels, while Moreau on the 15th October [2] took temporary command of the army, a post which one would have thought would have fallen to Souham, the senior of the two, but that General seems not to have been employed after the capture of Nijmegen.[3] I think Souham was succeeded in the command of the division by Macdonald, who was promoted General of Division on the 28th November 1794, and who now commanded the right of the army, the two former divisions of Souham and Moreau (now under Laurent, soon succeeded by Vandamme),[4] his line stretching from Nijmegen up the Rhine to Urdingen [5] where it linked with the left of the 'Sambre-et-Meuse', which also had reached the river. The Allies now were on the right bank of the Rhine, the Dutch on the lower river; the Duke of York had his head-quarters at Arnhem, on the right bank of the Neder Rijn, hoping to hold the country between the Rhine and the Yssel. On the left of the Duke, the Austrians had their head-quarters at Emmerich on the Rhine.[6] Then, expecting nothing to happen during the winter, the Duke went to England on the 2nd December 1794. 'Here the British army lost a father and a friend who had endeared himself to them by his humanity, justice, and benevolence.' [7] He did not return, but was succeeded by General Walmoden in the command of the mixed corps he had led, the English troops being under Dundas and Abercromby. Dundas was the only General from

---
[1] Jones, 133.
[2] Musset Pathay, 499, 18th October; Desbrière, *La Fin de la Convention*, 136.
[3] *Fastes*, iii. 561.
[4] François, *Journal*, 61; Du Casse, *Vandamme*, i. 166, 185.
[5] Below Düsseldorf. For these posts see Vogel, Atlas, xii.
[6] North-east of Cleves. [7] Jones, 144.

head-quarters whom Wellington saw between October and January.[1]

Pichegru resumed command in the middle of December 1794, Moreau remaining with him; grown confident, he told the Dutch, who wished to negotiate, that he would treat in Amsterdam, and he only waited for the first frosts to pass the Waal. Macdonald at Nijmegen, living on ration bread and cheese, at least when that was procurable, was watching the ice and on the 8th January 1795 he observed that the enemy on the other bank was preparing to retire, and even saw a gun taken away. The ice had not formed in front of the town, but he threw his men across above and below, where it did bear, and, although the English, after abandoning the position on the frost setting in, returned when a thaw began, eventually the French made good their hold on the right bank. The English retired northwards, up the Yssel to Zutphen, where they placed their left, their line running to the sea. The Austrians also had retired. The whole 'Nord' advanced joyfully, the march becoming a triumphal procession.[2]

While the English and Austrians went off, the Dutch troops withdrew into their fortresses and the road to Amsterdam lay open. The severe weather and the state of the frozen country told on the French, but Victory cheered the way, and on the 20th January 1795 Pichegru entered Amsterdam. The Stadtholder left for England, and the Commissioners of the Convention, taking possession of his palace, inscribed on it their wish to 'transform this magnificent palace into crystal so that the people could be witnesses of all their actions'. No change of material, however, was required to show the harsh measures adopted towards all who did not welcome the new Government. Macdonald had joined in the race to be first at Amsterdam, but he had to bully and cajole the fortress of Naarden into surrender,[3] so that, when he did get to the capital, he found Pichegru already there and in such a state of triumph that he professed to consider anything beneath the capitulation of a

[1] Stanhope, *Wellington*, 182.
[2] Macdonald, *Souvenirs*, 36–40 ; *Vict. et Conq.*, iv. 8–13, 18–21 ; Jomini, *Rév.*, vi. 193–8 ; David, 152–4 ; Lahure, 83–4 ; François, *Journal*, 74–5 ; Jones, 155–76 ; Vogel, Atlas, xii.
[3] Macdonald, *Souvenirs*, 40–1.

L'ARMÉE DU NORD, 1794-5

province unworthy of his acknowledgement. In reality the success of Jourdan on his right, won by hard fighting, had prevented the 'Nord' being resisted. The forts, with their ditches frozen, lost half their strength, and the Dutch were utterly demoralized. Lahure, sent with a small force on Haarlem, arrived by accident in his carriage at the gate of the town before his men. Finding the garrison under arms repressing the population, which was anxious for the entry of the French, he boldly announced to the Commandant that he was master of the town and that resistance would be useless, for he was at the head of a large body of troops. Then, unbending, he offered a capitulation, which was accepted. The French were not to have so easy a prey until they swept over Prussia after Jena.[1]

The capture of the Dutch fleet, caught in the ice by the French troops, is often attributed to Macdonald or to Pichegru. This curious feat was really due to Lt.-Colonel Lahure, then commanding a sort of flying column. He was sent from Amsterdam with three battalions, two light guns, and a squadron of Hussars, to march on Haarlem and to penetrate into North Holland. Passing Haarlem, he marched for the Helder, or the Hook of Holland. Arriving at Alkmaar at eight in the evening of the 22nd January 1795, after making two Dutch cavalry regiments and some infantry battalions surrender, he found that a Dutch squadron, fourteen ships he says, was stuck in the ice between the Helder and the island of Texel; he determined to try and capture it by a *coup de main*. Six or seven leagues of country had to be crossed in intense cold, but, collecting all the carts of the district, he got enough to carry one company of infantry, and he set off with these and his squadron of Hussars, the rest of his men following as best they could. He closed the gate of the town and started at 1 a.m.; the barrel of spirits of a *cantinière* enabled the cavalry to withstand the cold, and about 6 a.m. on the 23rd January he reached the shore alongside the squadron. As soon as it was light enough, he mounted his infantry behind his horsemen and set off silently across the ice. In the gloom of the winter morning the ships could not

[1] Lahure, 86-7.

ascertain his strength and he was requested to go on board the flag-ship, when he declared to the Admiral that he was but the advanced guard of a *corps d'armée* and that the ships could not resist the French, who now held all Holland. The Admiral listened and surrendered, when the French took not only the squadron, but also several merchantmen and an English ship which was cutting her way through the ice. Large stores were also seized at the Helder, and some French prisoners at the Texel were released : a quaint performance, although the Dutch must have been very half-hearted in the matter.

'Sic vos, non vobis', and in the general scamper over Holland, though the deed was remembered, the planner of it was forgotten. When Louis-Philippe in later years was forming the historical gallery at Versailles, a picture of this incident by Mozin was exhibited with the inscription, 'Prise de la Flotte Hollandaise par l'Armée de Pichegru'. Lahure found that Macdonald and Bonnaud were credited with the capture, while in the picture General Officers were shown, with some guns and a large body of troops,[1] instead of the handful of shivering men really employed. On the 7th March 1836 he wrote to Fain, then *Intendant* of the Civil List, pointing out that neither Macdonald nor Bonnaud had commanded in North Holland at that moment and that he himself, commanding the *avant-garde* of Salm's brigade, had imagined and carried out the capture. At the same time he wrote to Macdonald, 'Suum cuique. You are too rich in your own deeds to object to my claiming one which belongs exclusively to me. I request you will read the enclosed copy of a letter which I have written to Baron Fain. . . . I would have held my tongue if the picture in question had only been the fruit of the imagination of a painter ; but, as it is ordered by the Civil List and is destined for the Museum at Versailles, it ought to show the truth, and truth does not admit there either the brilliant uniforms of General Officers or the guns, which destroy the originality of this deed of arms.' Macdonald, always an honourable man, submitted this letter to the King, guaranteeing its truth, and Lahure's name was placed alone in the notice of the picture, guns and Generals, however, remaining. Indeed, there might

[1] See for example the plate in Dreyfous, *Les Trois Carnot*, 80.

be much altering of pictures if Generals and Princes were only to be put in their real positions.[1]

To do Pichegru justice, he did not refuse the gifts Fortune was thrusting into his hands, and he pushed on Macdonald with his two divisions, Moreau remaining with him at headquarters and leaving his division to be led, under Macdonald, by the hard-hitting Vandamme. The march northward on Groningen, where the English still lingered, was troublesome, for the thaw had begun, and instead of, as before, sliding to victory, the troops were now wading through the inundations. Macdonald was given the task of clearing the north-eastern provinces, Drente, Friesland, and Groningen, and finally he took post on the river Ems.[2] The English had crossed that river on the 12th February 1795 at Rheine and had gone on to Bremen. On the 14th April 1795 they embarked for England at Lehe,[3] leaving their cavalry for the moment.[4] One of the last acts of their commander at Bremen was to thank Vandamme for his care of their wounded left at Zwoll.[5]

The retreat had been a melancholy one for the English. 'The sufferings of the army', wrote an officer with it, 'are beyond the power of words to describe, numbers dying every hour through cold and fatigue : they marched through a dreary desert, where the snow drifted so strongly that it was almost impossible to get forward until, nature being at last overcome and the spirits quite exhausted, without a possibility of relief, men, women, and children, who by the darkness of night or through fatigue were unable to keep up with their respective columns and sat down to rest their weary limbs, sunk immediately to sleep, never to wake again. . . . It frequently happened from the deepness of the ruts that the wagons with the sick got into such situations that it was impossible to extricate them, and the consequence was generally fatal to the unfortunate persons who were in them. The whole of the retreat as far as

---

[1] Lahure, 86-96. Compare Jomini, *Rév.*, vi. 208 ; *Vict. et Conq.*, iv. 29-30 ; Thiers, *Rév.*, iii. 158 ; Alison, iii, chapter xvi, para. 100 ; Desbrière, *La Fin de la Convention*, 138-9.

[2] See Vogel, Atlas, vi.

[3] Below Bremerhaven, on the right bank of the mouth of the Weser, ibid.

[4] Calvert, 422-3 ; Jones, 175-83.   [5] Du Casse, *Vandamme*, i. 243.

Deventer was marked with scenes of the most affecting nature ; it would be unpleasant to the reader to dwell on this subject.'¹ Captain Jones considered, I presume, that a campaign, as the Duke of Wellington said of a battle, was like a ball-room where it might not ' be quite decorous to tell all he saw '.²

The French no doubt suffered also. ' For three months ', says Lahure, ' we had marched, fought, in cold of from 15° to 20°, hardly clothed, and the troops shoeless. Our soldiers wore sabots, or covered their feet with trusses of hay. The officers partook the food of their men ; it was often reduced to frozen ammunition bread with a morsel of cheese.'³ After a similar experience one can fancy Wellington's feelings towards the officer who warned him that often he would literally have no dinner, and not be ' merely roughing it on a beefsteak or a bottle of port wine '.⁴ But it is easier for an advancing army to find shelter for its sick, stragglers, and wounded than for one retreating. Here the sympathy of the inhabitants was all for the invaders, and the behaviour of the men whose battles the English thought they had been fighting was in painful contrast with that of their open enemy. ' It was a march of fearful suffering, and not alleviated by any friendly sympathy or aid from those whose country we had sought to defend. The Dutch peasantry inhabiting those dreary and inhospitable provinces were enemies more cruel to our exhausted soldiers than the victorious French who harassed and pursued them.'⁵ Jones, saying that the inhabitants welcomed the French, goes on (and he was an eyewitness), ' But their conduct to the British was cruel and vindictive to a degree scarcely to be credited ; in many instances they were so barbarous as to let them die at their doors rather than afford them shelter ; they were greater enemies than the French, as the latter always took care of such sick or wounded as came within their power, but the inhabitants frequently murdered them and in every instance distressed them as much as they could.'⁶ This behaviour of the French troops was the more honourable to them as the orders of the Convention prohibited

---

¹ Jones, 171–2.   ² Jennings, *Croker Papers*, i. 352.
³ Lahure, 97. ' Tout soldat blessé mourait gelé.' François, *Journal*, 72.
⁴ Stanhope, *Wellington*, iii.
⁵ Calvert, 423. Compare François, *Journal*, 77.   ⁶ Jones, 175–6.

the giving of quarter to the English. This order was disobeyed, and sometimes even the *émigrés* captured were not merely spared but were also fed.[1]

One misery added to the ordinary burden of the English soldier was the fearful state of the hospitals. That at Reenen [2] was well supplied, but the staff was complained of, and it got such a bad name that men ordered there became dejected, believing their death-warrants were signed. Some regiments, finding no one returned from the hospital, adopted a rule not to send any one there on any account. The army must have been exceptionally fortunate in its staff, for this plan was not interfered with, and nine-tenths of the sick, kept with their regiments in untainted air, recovered in a few days.[3]

Such a state of things was not unexampled. Dellard, taken prisoner by the Austrians whilst Macdonald was being swept back at Pont-à-Chin in May 1794, and sent down the Danube with a convoy of other prisoners, says that every one put into the boat that served as an infirmary was at once attacked by a sort of pest and soon died. This boat had a deck, and the air below was so contaminated that the Doctors did not venture to enter, but administered their medicines through port-holes made for that purpose. No one dared to acknowledge they were sick from fear of being sent to this death-trap.[4]

Thus ended without glory, but without shame, an English expedition whose history might be written in detail with great advantage. If the strategy had been bad, the fighting had been most severe, and the first campaign of Wellington deserves to be fully recorded. He had come in only for the disastrous end, and it is significant how much the differences between the Allies, and not the faults of the army, had to do with the result, that he, whose first lesson in war had been this long retreat, should have commenced his struggle with the fine troops of the Empire by declaring that he at least would not be afraid of them. In later years, when told that this experience must have been very useful to him, he replied, ' Why, I learnt what one ought not to do, and that is always something '.[5]

---

[1] Lahure, 80, 92–3. Compare Calvert, 233–8, 254. [2] West of Arnhem.
[3] Jones, 170–1. [4] Dellard, 48–50. [5] Stanhope, *Wellington*, 182.

Macdonald's movement on the right bank of the Rhine had been covered, as I have said, by the division of Moreau, who now again took command of his own troops. First one, and then another division (Lefebvre and Morlot), from Jourdan's Armée de Sambre-et-Meuse, was also brought over the river in support, so that in the first week of February 1795 Macdonald was on the left, on the Yssel from Deventer northwards, Moreau on his right at Zutphen, and the divisions of the ' Sambre-et-Meuse ' on the right again at Doesburg.[1]

Holland having been cleared, the army swung round almost facing south, to front the Austrians in the Duchy of Berg. On the 4th March 1795 Moreau even occupied Bentheim, but soon fell back on the same line as the army.[2] Then in April a body of Prussians replaced the Austrians, alarming Macdonald, who believed this was an accession of strength to the enemy, but, as the peace of Bâle between France and Prussia had been signed on the 5th April 1795,[3] the Prussians only came to occupy their own country, and the troops on either side were soon on friendly terms, drinking the health of the Republic, but not of the King of Prussia.[4] The work of the ' Nord ' was now finished and the interest of the war passed to the armies farther up the Rhine, the ' Rhin-et-Moselle ' at Strasbourg, linking about Mainz with the ' Sambre-et-Meuse ', under Jourdan, which again linked with the ' Nord ' below Düsseldorf, the two divisions belonging to that army, Lefebvre and Morlot, having repassed to the left bank of the Rhine to rejoin their proper army.

The French armies, as I have said, seldom had much love for one another, and this detachment of two divisions of the ' Sambre-et-Meuse ' into the theatre of action of the ' Nord ' had led to a quarrel between Pichegru and Lefebvre, which had better be narrated in dealing with the ' Sambre-et-Meuse '. As for the ' Nord ', now left to itself, it was formed into territorial divisions, Macdonald commanding the first, the provinces of Drente, Friesland, and Groningen, and placing his head-quarters at Groningen. Three months later he com-

---

[1] Jomini, *Rév.*, vi. 209–12 ; *Vict. et Conq.*, 61–3.
[2] Between Osnabrück and Deventer. Jomini, *Rév.*, vi. 211 ; *Vict. et Conq.*, iv. 62 ; François, *Journal*, 78–9.
[3] Wouters, 95–6. [4] François, *Journal*, 83.

manded the provinces of Overijssel and Gelderland, and then in succession Utrecht and Holland.[1]

Pichegru naturally was now high in favour, and on the 2nd March 1795 the Convention had decreed that he was to have the command of a new body, the ' Rhin-et-Moselle ', to be formed of the two armies, the ' Moselle ' and the ' Rhin ', both working on the Rhine. If the three armies, ' Rhin-et-Moselle ', ' Sambre-et-Meuse ', and ' Nord ', acted together, then Pichegru was to be Generalissimo.[2] The modest Jourdan, commanding the ' Sambre-et-Meuse ', was not likely to object, and Pichegru's former successful rival, Hoche, was now in La Vendée, commanding the two armies ' Côtes de Cherbourg ' and ' Côtes de Brest '. This change, however, was not carried out for some time and it was only on the 29th March 1795 that Pichegru left the ' Nord ' and, on his way to his new command, went to Paris. There on the 1st April 1795 he was put in command of the National Guard and the garrison of the Capital to suppress the Jacobin insurrection of 12e Germinal An III. Successful and acclaimed in the Convention as the Saviour of his country, he arrived at Mainz on the 16th April 1795 to take up his new command,[3] in which he was to display his incapacity, and in which he began the treachery that was to ruin him.

[1] Macdonald, *Souvenirs*, 42–3.
[2] Jomini, *Rév.*, vii. 178 ; *Vict. et Conq.*, iv. 121–2.
[3] Pajol, i. 180.

XVII

L'ARMÉE DU NORD (continued), 1795-7

Moreau succeeds Pichegru in command of the 'Nord'. Souham in retirement. Murat's quarrel with his Colonel, Landrieux. He alters his name to Marat. His regiment sent back to Brabant. Kindness of Murat to his family. He is a man of means. He is in Paris in May 1795. Movements of General Brune. Positions of future Marshals that had belonged to the 'Nord'. Strength and action of the 'Nord'. Interposition of the Prussians. Macdonald's fever forces him to go to France. Laurent's division sent up the Rhine. Correspondence of Moreau and Pichegru. Moreau goes to succeed Pichegru with the 'Rhin-et-Moselle', and Beurnonville takes his place. General Grouchy comes as Chief of the Staff. His regrets at not having gone to Italy under a young man who had done so little as Bonaparte. Wants to be sent to Hamburg to make a forced loan. The chances of Grouchy for a command. Macdonald returns from France. Good opinion of him by Beurnonville and Grouchy. Inaction of Grouchy and Macdonald whilst others are fighting in Italy and Germany. Grouchy goes to the west. The 'Nord' has to support the 'Sambre-et-Meuse', and Macdonald is sent up the Rhine. Macdonald commands the left of the 'Sambre-et-Meuse'. He goes to Belgium and Paris. His account to Vandamme of the intrigues there. Souham, who has rejoined, is placed in retirement. Macdonald commands in Holland; the 'Nord' suppressed. Unsatisfactory nature of the history of the 'Nord'. Faults of the Allies favour it. Taint of the commanders of the 'Nord'. Bad school for the future Marshals with it.

ON the departure of Pichegru on the 29th March 1795 [1] the command of the 'Nord' was given, on his recommendation, to Moreau. The two were friends, and we have seen Moreau taking Pichegru's place temporarily in October 1794 and remaining alongside of Pichegru for some time when that General resumed his post. Souham, promoted General of Division on the 13th September 1793, whilst Moreau had only obtained that rank on the 14th April 1794, would have been the natural successor of Pichegru, as his service had been of a far superior nature to that of Moreau, but, as I have said, from

[1] *Rév. franç. en Hollande*, 87.

some unexplained disgrace he seems not to have been employed with this army after the siege of Nijmegen, rejoining only on the 26th August 1796 to take command of a territorial division, the 24th, in Belgium [1] under his former junior, Moreau.

All this time, wherever Murat's Chasseur regiment, the 21st, had been, a long contest had been going on in it. The Colonel, Landrieux, had been much away whilst his Lt.-Colonels, Taillefer and Murat, had organized the squadrons and had taken them to the field. Naturally this had caused dissatisfaction. Taillefer had been got rid of by being promoted Adjutant-General on the 1st September 1793. On the 1st October 1793 Landrieux rejoined, getting wounded on the 31st. A long struggle now began between him and Murat, who was supported by a part of the officers. Finding out the former connexion of Landrieux with the Bourbons, Murat, who aimed at becoming Colonel of the regiment, denounced his chief to the Minister. Other enemies of Landrieux joined in and he was suspended on the 13th November 1793, and arrested and imprisoned on the 16th. His post, however, did not fall to Murat, as an officer from another regiment, Duprès, was appointed Colonel instead.[2] Landrieux, eventually released, attempted to regain his command, but the regiment resisted, and on the 25th October 1795 he was made Colonel of the Hussards des Alpes, and with them, as the 13th Hussars,[3] he went in 1796 to the Armée d'Italie, where in 1797 he was Chief of the Staff to Kilmaine.

Murat had had many difficulties in this warfare. In the first place, to his disgust the Minister had suspected him of being an aristocrat and belonging to the Murats d'Auvergne, whilst he, to make himself safe, represented his birth as lower than it really was. For the same reason he took the name of the then popular demagogue, Marat, to prove his patriotism. When quieter times came, the Minister objected to this, and matters looked serious for Murat, who now professed that he had only used Marat's name for a fortnight, while at Hesdin, before joining the army in the field. This was not true, for

---

[1] Fage, *Souham*, 56-7.   [2] Landrieux, i (91-115).
[3] Susane, *Cav. franç.*, i. 187, does not give this regiment, which was formed from the *Légion des Américains et du Midi*. Desbrière, *La Cav. pendant la Rév.: La crise*, 123-4, 130, 133, 140-1.

we find him described as 'Marat' in the *procès-verbal* of a curious meeting of the officers of the regiment stationed at Pont-à-Marcq, Pont-à-Breck, and Flers on the 26th November 1793.[1] Foolish as this change of name was, it must be remembered that the demagogue was not, at least originally, the vile creature he is made by historians and notably by Carlyle. Really he was a skilled physician, who had won a good position at one time in England and afterwards in Paris, and in 1777 had been appointed Médecin to the Gardes du Corps of the Comte d'Artois, the brother of the King, a fact showing his reputation at the time. I have no wish to palliate his conduct during the Revolution, but Murat, away from Paris, might at least believe he was assuming the name of a man of some position.[2]

Attempts seem to have been made to get rid of Murat by appointing him Adjutant-General, as had been done to Taillefer but, no doubt believing that this might shelve him, he steadily refused. When Murat complained of his supersession by Duprès, the Cavalry Bureau replied with the adroitness of an office that it was useless for him to produce evidence from the regiment of his fitness for command, as this evidence came after the appointment of Duprès and only showed that he had since acquired the necessary knowledge; his failure to do so before was shown by the fact that it was necessary to bring in an officer from another regiment.[3] An excellent example of official logic, 'We did a thing, which therefore was necessary'. Landrieux also struck back, and on the 17th May 1794 at 4 a.m., when about to start for Paris, Murat was arrested at Amiens on a denunciation by Landrieux for being absent from his post for doubtful reasons. Fortunately that afternoon it was known that the Representative Dumont, the supporter of Landrieux, was recalled, and by 4 p.m. Murat was released, Landrieux even apologizing from his prison, and alleging that he now believed Murat to bear different feelings towards him.[4] As at this time the 'Nord' was in full campaign, the fact that

[1] Landrieux, i (94–106).
[2] For Marat see Michaud, *Biog. univ.*, xxvi. 556–65, and an article by H. Morse Stephens in *Pall Mall Gazette* of September and October 1896, and the work, *Jean-Paul Marat*, by E. B. Bax (London, Grant Richards, 1900, 8vo).
[3] Landrieux, i (115). [4] Ibid., i (119).

Murat was going to Paris from Amiens looks as if his regiment, probably worn out, was kept in rear.[1]

The regiment seems not to have rejoined its own division, that of Michaud, which rather followed the fighting line, but it remained with Moreau for part of the campaign at least, being attached to the brigade of Vandamme,[2] with which Murat, if present, must have seen some hard fighting and have heard much strong language. In December 1794, whilst the army was resting, forage was so scarce that part of the cavalry had to be sent to the rear, Murat's regiment going to Brabant.[3]

By this time Murat had probably realized that he would have been wiser to have remained with his General as A.D.C., instead of joining such a 'wild cat' regiment. However bad his conduct as an officer had been, he seems to have been an exemplary son: his letters are full of affection for his family and he undertook to send them one hundred livres per month, the first instalment to go when he got his pay, an event probably long deferred.[4] He brought up the children of his brother Pierre, who died on the 9th October 1792, like his own.[5] On the 22nd December 1794 we find him at Cahors, selling to his brother André certain lands which he had bought from his brother-in-law Bonnafous on the 13th December that year, André paying him 5,200 livres, of which Murat got 3,000 livres and Bonnafous 2,200 livres, no doubt part of the original purchase money unpaid.[6] Murat, therefore, was a man with some means. On the 14th May 1795 he was at Paris, making a passionate defence of himself and an attack on Landrieux.[7] His regiment was quartered at or near Paris when the Jacobin insurrection of 1st Prairial, 20th May 1795, gave him an opportunity of pushing himself forward by acting against that party.

As for Brune, now General of Brigade, it is difficult to place

---

[1] For all this part of Murat's life see Landrieux, i (53–156); Murat, *Lettres*, i. 7–15, correcting date of letter of 25th Feb. to 25th April 1793; and Lumbroso, *Corr. Murat*, 10–12 and 448–51. For Dumont see also Hamel, *Robespierre*, iii. 210–14.
[2] Du Casse, *Vandamme*, I. 194.
[3] Ibid., 214; Desbrière, *La Fin de la Convention*, 137–8.
[4] Murat, *Lettres*, i. 12; Lumbroso, *Corr. Murat*, 10.
[5] Murat, *Lettres*, i, note 1, pp. 7 and 8.   [6] Ibid., 14–15.
[7] Landrieux, i (137–40); Lumbroso, *Corr. Murat*, 449–51.

him, but I think he had no direct connexion with the ' Nord ' in 1794–5. The fall of his friend Danton, and then of Robespierre in 1794 must have kept him in anxiety. He was in Paris during the 12th Germinal and probably was employed under Pichegru in suppressing the Jacobins. Then Barras took him on a mission to obtain supplies for Paris from the Channel ports, the northern Departments, Belgium, and Holland. Barras seems not to have gone farther north than Ghent,[1] and I presume Brune returned with him to Paris after 1st Prairial An III, 20th May 1795. Brune and Lt.-Colonel Murat were part of the garrison used by General Bonaparte in October 1795 at the ' Jour des Sections '.

Thus, when the fighting days of the ' Nord ' were over, the future Marshals who had belonged to it were placed as follows. Jourdan was commanding the ' Sambre-et-Meuse ', having under him Generals of Division Lefebvre and Bernadotte, and Colonels Mortier and Ney.[2] General of Brigade Brune, who had had a fitful connexion with this army, was in Paris with Lt.-Colonel Murat. General of Brigade Davout was now with the ' Rhin-et-Moselle '. Only General of Division Macdonald remained with the ' Nord ', to be joined in 1796 for a time by General of Division Grouchy. As for others, Pichegru was commanding the ' Rhin-et-Moselle ', Moreau was commanding the ' Nord ', and Hoche, in La Vendée, had the Armée des Côtes de Brest. Generals of Division Marceau and Kléber were with the ' Sambre-et-Meuse '.

Nominally the ' Nord ' remained one of the great armies of the Republic, having a strength of 136,250 against that of 170,300 for the ' Sambre-et-Meuse ', and 193,670 for the ' Rhin-et-Moselle ', but what with garrisons, sick, &c., its active force was only 67,910.[3] Henceforth it was but so many territorial divisions. A so-called peace had been made with Holland, by which that country, besides supplying a fleet, placed half its troops at the disposal of France, but in reality some 40,000 French troops had for long to be kept in Holland, as Capitaine François put it, ' pour soutenir le pays ',[4] that is,

---

[1] Barras, i. 228–33.
[2] Ney's date of promotion to Colonel was 10th Dec. 1794.
[3] Jomini, *Rév.*, vii, table, p. 56.
[4] Ibid., 8–10 ; Thiers, *Rév.* iii. 206–9 ; François, *Journal*, 79.

to keep the Dutch open to the blessings of Republican freedom. The ' Nord ' frequently lent help to the armies farther up the Rhine. In May 1795 it sent a division to Paris, 8,000 strong, which was used under Menou on the 20th May 1795 to suppress the Jacobin insurrection of 1st Prairial.[1] In September 1795 its three divisions (Souham, d'Harville, and Macdonald), with a division of Tournai and Hainault, under Dubois, had 25,198 men only [2] and the number of sick was large.

Of course the ' Nord ' could have been used with effect to turn the right of the Austrians on the right bank of the Rhine and so to support the campaign of the next army, the ' Sambre-et-Meuse ', one of whose difficulties was to cross the river, but the interposition of Prussian territory, now neutral, prevented this, whilst not only anxiety about the attitude of the Dutch, but fears of an English invasion caused a fair number of troops to be wasted in the north. As the English threatened Zeeland, Macdonald was sent to that home of fever, the island of Walcheren, with his choice of quarters between the fire of Middelburg and the frying pan of Flushing. Here he had the same experience as the English were to have in 1809 ; five-sixths of his troops went down with fever and he himself was so ill that, to save his life, he was sent to France towards the end of 1795 ; his fever recurred at the end of six weeks as such fevers do again and again, and he remained in France, no doubt nursed by his wife (he tells us nothing of such details), until the summer of 1796.[3]

In November 1795 the ' Nord ' sent the division of General Laurent, nine battalions and seven squadrons, to hold Düsseldorf and the left bank of the Rhine up to Andernach for the ' Sambre-et-Meuse '[4] whilst that force marched up the left bank of the Rhine to support the ' Rhin-et-Moselle '. Moreau seems to have supplied this body cheerfully enough : he had already been thanked by Kléber of the ' Sambre-et-Meuse ' for allowing him to procure his charger from the cavalry depot

---

[1] Jomini, *Rév.*, vii. 44-7.   [2] Saint-Cyr, *Rhin*, ii, table 99.
[3] Macdonald, *Souvenirs*, 43-4. He says that he returned in the summer of 1795 ; this must be a slip, as Beurnonville, whom he met, only took command in March 1796.
[4] Andernach, below Neuwied and Koblenz. Vogel, Atlas, xii, xvii ; Pajol, i. 260-1 ; Jomini, *Rév.*, vii. 271-2.

of the 'Nord'.[1] This division came back from Düsseldorf on the 20th January 1796, going to Belgium, where it was employed in keeping down that country.[2] Moreau kept up a correspondence with Pichegru while the latter remained at the head of the 'Rhin-et-Moselle'; some of the letters are given by M. Ernest Daudet.[3] The correspondence is in the *Dépôt de la Guerre* at Paris: it would be interesting to have it published, with that of Jourdan, the commander of the 'Sambre-et-Meuse', who also wrote to Moreau.[4]

When Pichegru left the 'Rhin-et-Moselle', he advised that Moreau should follow him in that command.[5] On the 14th March 1796 Moreau was nominated for the post [6] and went to Paris, where he met his friend. To succeed him with the 'Nord', the Directory, the new governing body of France, chose the magnificent Beurnonville, the patron and friend of Macdonald, whom we have last seen being handed over to the Austrians by Dumouriez in April 1793. After a long and irksome imprisonment, which, however, as Dumouriez had hinted, had saved his head from the guillotine, Beurnonville had been released in November 1795 in exchange, with others, for the daughter of Louis XVI.[7] Vainglorious as he was, Beurnonville besieged the Directors for a command and, according to the ill-natured account of Barras, Carnot said, ' I see one army only which can be given to this important Beurnonville; it is that which will have nothing to do'. Obviously this was the 'Nord', and accordingly Beurnonville was given that command. There is probably some exaggeration in this, but Barras most likely is nearer the truth in relating how, when the General continued his demands for the replacement of his belongings, the Director, intending a piece of irony, offered him three horses from his own stable. Beurnonville, who had much common sense under all his brag, accepted the offer and, what was more, to the disgust of Barras, he got them. Then he started for his command, having assured the Directory that he had twenty campaigns in his belly at their service.[8]

[1] Pajol, 152, 153. [2] Ibid., i. 274; Jomini, *Rév.*, vii. 277-8.
[3] Daudet, *La Conjuration de Pichegru*, 28, 58-9, 113-14, 163, 164, 179-80.
[4] Ibid., 162-3. [5] Saint-Cyr, *Rhin*, iii. 2. [6] *Fastes*, iii. 426.
[7] Thiers, *Rév.*, iii. 532; Ernest Daudet, *Hist. de l'Émigration*, ii. 128-40.
[8] Barras, ii. 83-4.

With Beurnonville, as his Chief of the Staff, came Grouchy, who almost all this time had been in La Vendée, where on the 13th June 1795 he had been promoted General of Division, and where he had served under Hoche. The west was supposed to be pacified and Grouchy, going to Paris in December 1795, had wished for this appointment to the 'Nord'. His friend, Aubert du Bayet, then War Minister, in January 1796 had first appointed him to serve in the Armée des Alpes, and then had made him Inspector-General of cavalry for the two armies, 'Alpes' under Kellermann, and 'Italie' under Bonaparte. This Grouchy looked on as a sinecure: he would have preferred a division in the Armée des Côtes de l'Océan in the north-west under Hoche, but, as that General did not answer his letter on the subject, he got the Minister to send him to the 'Nord' as Chief of the Staff to his friend, Beurnonville. Then came regrets. He had missed the first great chance of his life at the beginning of 1796, as he was to miss the second, in Bantry Bay, at the end of the year.[1]

When, as he said, he had seen Schérer replaced in command of the army of Italy by a young man who had done as little as Bonaparte, he had preferred to go to Beurnonville, and the more so as he considered his post as Inspector would be useless. But now came the news of Bonaparte's first victories, and he thought how fine it would be to pass the Alps to join the young General. He seems to have believed that he might have had the post of Chief of the Staff to 'Italie', although he allowed it might be better in the hands of Berthier, but when Stengel, the cavalry leader of the army, died on the 28th April, he thought he would have succeeded him. Not realizing how far the army of Italy would go, he wrote that, if he thought he would arrive in time, he would go to Paris and try to be appointed to it. The loss of the post of Chief of the Staff to Bonaparte he attributed to Hoche, because, if that General had told him he did not want him in the west, he would have asked for the place when he first arrived from Paris. One assumes that Bonaparte would in any case have insisted on getting Berthier, who was so well known as a good staff officer, but, as at first he had intended to take with him Duverger, his Chief of the

---

[1] Grouchy, *Méms.*, i. 199, 219-20.

Staff at Paris, it is quite possible that he might have been ready to accept a man who had held the post under Hoche. Failing Italy, Grouchy wished to command one of the divisions sent up the Rhine from time to time to support the 'Sambre-et-Meuse', but Beurnonville, often going to Holland to treat with the government there, preferred to keep Grouchy to take his place when he was absent. All this is simple enough, but it is not quite pleasant to find Grouchy suggesting to the Minister, as one way of reaping laurels, that he should be sent to Hamburg to make a forced loan there.[1]

It is interesting to get from Lacuée, one of the future Ministers of Napoleon,[2] then in the *Conseil des Anciens* and having much to do with the administration of the army, a view of what he considered to be the chances of a command for Grouchy. Writing on the 10th May 1796, he assumed that, as Berthier was in Italy, Grouchy could only serve there in charge of a division, and he preferred to see him in the north. Then, as for the Armée des Alpes, the sister force to that of Italy, it was passing under the orders of Bonaparte, and if Kellermann were to leave its direct command he probably would have no successor. In the north-west, the Armée des Côtes de l'Océan was for Hoche alone and, as he was making great steps to the perfect pacification of the district, Lacuée hoped he also would have no successor. If the Generals of the Rhine (Moreau and Jourdan) were fortunate, everything would remain as it was. Were one of them to die, or be very unsuccessful through his own fault, he might be replaced by one of his subordinates. (Here Lacuée probably was thinking of Desaix to replace Moreau, and Kléber to take the place of Jourdan.) In that case no one else would move. If Hoche were sent to succeed either of the Rhine commanders, then Hédouville (who was in the west), or Moncey (who was commanding the 11th military division at Bayonne), or Grouchy himself would succeed him. If Beurnonville went to the Rhine, then Lacuée believed Grouchy would become 'il signor generale', that is, would succeed him.[3] All this was true enough. The Armée des Alpes

---

[1] Grouchy, *Méms.*, i. 219, 224, 236–7, 239.
[2] Jean-Gérard Lacuée, Comte de Cessac (1752–1841).
[3] Grouchy, *Méms.*, i. 227–30.

was abolished, Beurnonville replaced Jourdan in September 1796, and Hoche succeeded him on the Rhine in February 1797, leaving no successor in the west. As Grouchy quitted the ' Nord ' in August 1796 for the expedition to Bantry Bay and was unfortunate there, he got no command.

In the summer of 1796 Macdonald rejoined from France, where we have seen him go to recover from fever. Beurnonville he knew before as his patron and friend. He says that the General offered to change his destination, but he refused, fearing that this preference might injure Beurnonville himself.[1] This is not quite clear, unless it means that he might have become Chief of the Staff instead of Grouchy, for Beurnonville hardly could have got him transferred to another army, and, if he had that power, Macdonald, ill with fever, should have been glad to get away. He can hardly have known Grouchy before, but that General soon professed admiration for him. Writing to Beurnonville on the 10th June 1796 a letter which shows that Macdonald's recovery did not last long, Grouchy said, ' Macdonald still has fever, my dear General; I am wretched to see him in this miserable state, and I share your opinion of his morality and powers. It is by using men that one knows them : this one gains a hundred per cent. by being known, and the frigid manner in which he receives one assuredly is worth more than those commonplace demonstrations which prove nothing, or at most some little knowledge of the customs of society,'[2] of which the *ci-devant* Noble no doubt thought he knew more than Macdonald. Beurnonville himself wrote to Grouchy of Macdonald in the same strain, ' Love this brave and loyal General ; he talks little, but he has a pure and good heart, he is an excellent comrade whom I love ; see him often ; his illness saddens him, he needs society.'[3]

Whilst Saint-Cyr, Davout, and Oudinot, with Desaix, under Moreau in the ' Rhin-et-Moselle ', and Lefebvre, Soult, Ney, and Mortier, with Kléber and Marceau, under Jourdan in the ' Sambre-et-Meuse ', were making their great advance into Germany, and Berthier, Masséna, Augereau, Victor, Lannes, Murat, Marmont, and Bessières were winning glory in Italy

[1] Grouchy, *Méms.*, i. 248 ; Macdonald, *Souvenirs*, 44.
[2] Grouchy, *Méms.*, i. 236.
[3] Ibid., 247–8.

under Bonaparte, the little group, Macdonald and Grouchy, both quaking with fever, remained inactive with the 'Nord' under Beurnonville. All three seem to have been on the most friendly terms. Beurnonville certainly treated Grouchy as an intimate friend, as his 'charmante ménagère', styling himself his husband: 'Adieu, petite coquine, soyez sage et fidèle.' When returning after an absence, he told Grouchy he was only happy in the bosom of his (military) family.[1] Beurnonville indeed was in fine form, assuring the Dutch Government, alarmed at the entry of the French troops into Amsterdam, that no blood had been shed, but much beer! Grouchy about this period was rather in the habit of finding a second father in his commander for the time and then grumbling at his father's ideas. Here he complained, perhaps with reason, at some of Beurnonville's actions. Poor as the army was, things were worse in France, so that he sent blank sheets of paper for his father to write to him on.[2] Perhaps poverty explains his coming down on General Gouvion and on his A.D.C. for their share of the expense of a ball that happened to take place when they passed through and that they attended; this seems rather hard on Gouvion and the A.D.C.[3]

Then his thoughts once more turned to Hoche, who was about to undertake an expedition to Ireland and who applied for him. On the 13th June 1796 the *Comité* nominated him for the Armée des Côtes de l'Océan, but it was only on the 19th August that he was ordered to command the troops in the island of Rhé.[4]

Leaving the 'Nord' towards the end of August 1796, Grouchy went to his own family, where fever detained him till September. For some unexplained reason we find him writing to Hoche as an injured innocent, suffering from odious calumnies, 'I will place under your eyes all the details of an event which has been so falsely misrepresented; they will convince you, as well as the heads of the Government, that my conduct has been dictated by honour and commanded by my position', which looks as if he had left Hoche in 1795 under some cloud. It was only in September that he rejoined Hoche,

---

[1] Grouchy, *Méms.*, i, note 1, pp. 222, 238.
[2] Ibid., 240.   [3] Ibid., 242.   [4] Ibid., 252-4.

whose forces were now styled the 'Quatre Divisions réunies', one of which, the 12th, fell to him.[1]

Grouchy, while with the 'Nord', had tried to get Beurnonville to support the left of the 'Sambre-et-Meuse', a thing that commander was loath to do, partly from the dislike to partake in any active operations that seems to have influenced him both now with this army and a little later with the 'Sambre-et-Meuse', and also perhaps from a suspicion not only of the Dutch, but also of the Prussians, who, Grouchy at least thought, might cease their neutrality if the French met with any great reverse on the Rhine.[2] Now, just when Grouchy had left the 'Nord', Beurnonville was forced into co-operation with Jourdan and the 'Sambre-et-Meuse'. By September 1796 the two armies, 'Rhin-et-Moselle' under Moreau, and 'Sambre-et-Meuse' under Jourdan, after advancing far, had been driven back to the Rhine by the Archduke Charles, the Government at last remembered the existence of the 'Nord', and Macdonald was sent up the river.

Struck once more by fever in the island of Walcheren, Macdonald had been very ill, and Beurnonville brought him to head-quarters at Utrecht to give him the opportunity of recovering, but a fresh attack made him worse than ever, so that Beurnonville, absent for the moment, was alarmed and hurried back to him. Getting better at last, Macdonald was sent to Deventer, where troops were assembling for the exercise camp at Gorsel:[3] these were placed under his command, his health improving as he drilled and instructed his men. By this time the 'Sambre-et-Meuse' was back on the Lahn, and Macdonald, with his own division from Gorsel and that of Castelverd[4] from Belgium, was sent up the Rhine to reinforce it.

The operations of these divisions do not come under the history of the 'Nord'. It is sufficient to say that on the 9th September 1796 Beurnonville succeeded Jourdan in the command of the 'Sambre-et-Meuse' and gave Macdonald the command of the left wing of that army. Here Macdonald may have met Ney and Mortier.

[1] Grouchy, *Méms.*, i. 253–6.   [2] Ibid., 223, 225–6, 237, 239, 245–6.
[3] Between Deventer and Zutphen. Vogel, Atlas, xii.
[4] General Jean Castelbert de Castelverd (1743–1820); see Pajol, i, note 1, p. 365.

We find him at Paris in 1797, whence in March he was writing to Vandamme and, when the latter also came to the Capital, apparently it was Macdonald who gave him such an account of the intrigues there as to shock that virtuous man.[1] Indeed, all parties in Paris were preparing for Fructidor, but Macdonald gives us no hint as to the side with which his sympathies lay. His reticence on this and on many other points is extraordinary. His silence may imply that he was in favour of the constitutional party; his former friendship with Pichegru and the disgust with Augereau that we shall find him expressing, might help that belief, but then his friendship with Vandamme would have suffered. Affection for his wife may have kept him in the Capital, but his silence is curious and very provoking; he does not even mention his being in Paris.

The *coup d'état* of Fructidor, which in a military sense was carried out by the armies of the 'Sambre-et-Meuse' and 'Italie', had one effect at the 'Nord'. Souham, who since the 26th August 1796 had been at Brussels, commanding the 24th military division, was now on the 9th September 1797 placed in retirement. No doubt this was on account of his connexion with Pichegru, the leader of the beaten party, but one can hardly imagine that he had gone beyond expressing his sympathy with his former commander. He was not employed again until the 16th August 1798.[2]

While the two divisions were absent from it with the 'Sambre-et-Meuse', the Armée du Nord was probably very weak. Beurnonville, after being appointed temporarily to command the 'Sambre-et-Meuse', had retained the command of this army as well.[3] Either under him, or else succeeding him when he went to Paris from his other command, General Dejean, junior to Macdonald, had commanded the troops left in Holland until the 24th September 1797, when he was placed in retirement, because, it is said, he would not publish the addresses the regiments of the Armée d'Italie were issuing

---

[1] 'Ô temps ! ô mœurs ! et plus haut encore, ô infernale intrigue ! ô passions, ô injustice, ô ignorance', wrote the horrified Vandamme. Du Casse, *Vandamme*, i. 353.
[2] *Fastes*, iii. 561 ; Fage, *Souham*, 57-62.
[3] Pajol, ii. 249.

against the opposition in Paris.¹ In time he became one of the Ministers of Napoleon. Macdonald, returning to Holland, he says in November 1797 (but perhaps it was earlier), took the command from Dejean.² General Moulin, from the 5th military division, was to have had the command, but he never joined,³ and on the 26th October 1797 the Armée du Nord was suppressed, its three divisions remaining in Holland in the pay of the Dutch Republic, which was bound to pay for 25,000 French troops.

In January 1798 we find Macdonald figuring in a great ceremonial at Paris.⁴ The Directory had furnished each army with a flag on which were embroidered its victories. Now peace was declared, these standards were called in. That of ' Italie ' had already been presented by Joubert and Andréossi.⁵ Now, on the 28th February 1798, the Minister for War, General Schérer, presented to the Directory Macdonald bearing the standard of the ' Nord ', and Duhesme that of the ' Rhin-et-Moselle '. Macdonald's address was remarkable for his declamation against England, whose cohorts the army, he said, had exterminated in Holland. Now it longed to form part of the expedition against England, and he offered its subscription, 31,000 odd livres, a creditable sum from a very poor force. No doubt his Scotch and Jacobite traditions explain part of his bitterness against a nation that in later years was to send a frigate to enable him to visit the early home of his family. It is to be remarked that he said that the ' Nord ' had ' partaken the opinion of the entire nation on the memorable day of Fructidor ', a point on which one would like to know what were his real sentiments. As usual, he himself says not a word of this ceremonial.

The reader probably will close this history of the Armée du Nord with a certain amount of dissatisfaction, if not of bewilderment : he will have found it difficult to form any clear picture of the events of the first campaigns, to understand why some

¹ General Comte Jean-François-Aimé Dejean (1749–1824), Pair de France. Michaud, *Biog. univ.*, lxii. 229–32 ; *Biog. des Cont.*, ii. 1262–3
² Macdonald, *Souvenirs*, 49.
³ General Jean-François-Auguste Moulin (1752–1810). One of the Directory at Brumaire. Michaud, *Biog. univ.*, lxxiv. 476–9.
⁴ *Rév. franç. en Hollande*, 169 ; Macdonald, *Souvenirs*, 49.
⁵ *Vict. et Conq.*, viii. 229–35.

of the defeats of the French did not lead to their utter ruin, and to comprehend why the final advance met with so little resistance. This is inevitable if a true description of the history of the war is here given, for neither side dreamt of following up a victory in the style of the vigorous Bonaparte. Fancy how Castiglione or Rivoli or, for the matter of that, Jena and Auerstädt would have ended, had the victor paused for days to consider his future course ! Then the commanders of the ' Nord ' seldom seemed to consider their army as one force. The wings and detachments constantly were left unsupported and exposed to danger, and the movements of the enemy were followed irrespective of the real objects of the army. If the enemy concentrated on a flank, off went the ' Nord ' to meet them on the new ground, instead of striking at their weakened centre.

General Duhesme, as I have said, apologized for many defects by representing the rawness of the French leaders, but the Allies were led by experienced men. Mack's plans were considered, with much justice, as excellent, and he and others saw the day's work clearly enough. One can only wonder that their range of view did not extend farther and show them the importance of following up the demoralized French troops when they were driven from any position, as from the Camp de César. Had blow after blow fallen on the army, destitute of cohesion as it then was, it would have broken up. The higher policy and the strategy of the Allies were deplorable. The short-sighted covetousness of Austria, which made her treat the capture of a French fortress as a conquest for herself and so brought every Frenchman against the Allies ; the equally short-sighted policy of England in insisting on the foolish raid on Dunkirk, scattering the combined army just when its victory seemed assured ; these were so many gifts of Fortune to France, the last of which, although accepted half-heartedly, still presented her with the opportunity of winning the victory at Hondschoote that animated her troops. The final triumphant sweep through Holland, which shed so much glory on Pichegru and his troops, really was due partly to the hard fighting of Jourdan and the ' Sambre-et-Meuse ', but still more to the discordant interests of the Austrians, Dutch, and English. The 'Nord' consequently was not a good school for commanders, and all the more so as it had been victorious and had met no hostile commander to 'teach' it. The connexion of Berthier, Grouchy, Kléber, and Marceau with it was but slight and, though Bernadotte, Davout, Mortier, Murat, Ney, and Hoche saw much fighting with it, they were too junior to have learnt generalship. Jourdan and Macdonald, with Moreau, were the commanders trained in the 'Nord', and their faults may be attributed to that. Jourdan never quite realized what an active, rapid antagonist could do; in his campaigns there is a certain misplaced overdaring, mixed with unnecessary caution and depression, not uncommon in commanders of an inferior class, but which I think in his case to be due to the circumstances of his first campaigns. Something also in Macdonald's style, his bull-headed rush at Souvaroff in 1799 at the Trebbia, for example, without being assured of the co-operation of Moreau and without any attempt to take advantage of the ground, recalls the 'Nord', where each part of the army fought its own battle. No doubt it was unfortunate for Macdonald that after 1795 he was kept in an eddy with the 'Nord', while the current of war was flowing fast in Germany and Italy, giving his rivals many lessons.

Moreau, the General of the plain, considered even by his admirers to be unfit to meet Bonaparte on broken ground, with his curious pauses and hesitations, his star-fish-like droppings of his divisions, was a true son of the 'Nord'. When in his campaigns in Germany he left his detached divisions exposed to the enemy, when he tamely followed the Archduke to the right bank of the Danube in 1796, careless of what happened to his comrade Jourdan, when, in the last stages of his retreat, he exposed his flank, one is at once reminded of this army. To all these men I believe the results of 1794-5 had been injurious, for a General who has seen bad tactics and worse strategy win the day is less likely to find the way to success. An army, like a bear's cub, can be licked into shape and victory, as the Allies, much to their surprise, found in 1813: a proper lesson in 1793-5 might have saved Jourdan defeats in 1796 and 1799 and have made Moreau a less dangerous commander than he was. Here, however, I am trespassing on the domain of the critics.

The history of the ' Nord ' is unpleasant, if it be only from the taint of treason which clings to so many of its commanders. First we have the weak attempt of Lafayette to resist the Convention, and his subsequent flight. Next the actual, deliberate treason of Dumouriez, failing from want of boldness and rapidity. Pichegru, under whom the ' Nord ' had its happiest times, was to fall into treachery in his next command, the ' Rhin-et-Moselle ', under very sordid circumstances. His friend and successor, Moreau, following him in his new command, was to be found screening his crime ; and then he himself, too republican, too much a lover of freedom to acquiesce in the supremacy of Bonaparte, was to be mixed up with the last conspiracy of Pichegru and was to justify the suspicions of Royalism that hung round him in his early days by joining the ranks of the Allied Monarchs when they were clustering round the maimed eagle, and by dying the adviser of the bitter enemies of France. As for truer-hearted men, besides the once ardent Dampierre, longing to be maimed, to escape honourably from his post, the fiery Custine, the brave old Houchard, who with many a gallant subordinate went to the scaffold, how melancholy is their tale ! So much of the history of the ' Nord ' is written in the blood of its officers, slaughtered by their countrymen. To be fair to the ' Nord ', however, we must remember the conduct of Macdonald. When the Empire was tottering, Moreau, spurred by his personal injuries, sprang to the attack of his country. When it fell, the sneering, jeering Macdonald, with so much to resent, was as true to the chief whom all others abandoned, as he was to the King in the ludicrous crash of the First Restoration. Be it counted unto him for righteousness, and not the less because, according to his nature, he still had a sneer ready for Emperor and for King.

INDEX

Abercromby, Lieut.-General, with British force, 183; success at Lannoy, 265; at battle of Tourcoing, 298, 302-4; in retreat from Holland, 327.

Alpes, Armée des, strength in 1794, 3; sister army to 'Italie', 4; future Marshals with, 58; Grouchy with, 63; future of, 344-5; Kellermann in command, 146.

Alvinzi, General, 61, 286.

Ardennes, Armée des, strength, 2; absorbed in 'Sambre-et-Meuse', 3; formation, 63, 65, 110-11, 114, 115; use of title, 123; Valmy campaign, 118-32; marches east, 135, 136-8; invades Belgium, 140-1, 145; takes Namur, 146; siege of Maestricht, 152; Neerwinden campaign, 154-6; at Maulde, 157; Lamarche in command, 171-2; operations in May 1793, 179; Kilmaine in command, 180; reorganized, 186; weakness of, 191-3; reinforces 'Nord', 223; absorbed in 'Sambre-et-Meuse', 314-16.

Argonne, Armée de l', 65.

Augereau, future Marshal, rise due to Napoleon, 3; classified, 42, 43; birthplace, 44; social position, 47, 48; branch of service, 37, 49, 50; political opinions, 52; 'grouped', 58; rank in April 1792, 60, 61; age in 1791, 61.

Balland, General Antoine, commands a division, 249; at Wattignies, 250-4, 262; at Le Cateau, 285-6; replaced, 290-1.

Barthel, General, 208, 209, 213, 216, 220, 223.

Beauharnais, General Alexandre, on Biron's staff, 76, 78; on Luckner's staff, 85, 102; in command of 'Rhin', 186; guillotined, 201.

Beaulieu, General, 87, 214, 240-2.

Beauregard, General, 250, 254, 256, 262, 263.

Belgique, Armée de la, designation, 63, 114, 136; moves north, 140; wins battle of Jemappes, 141-2; occupies Liége, 145; siege of Maestricht, 152; battles of Neerwinden and Louvain, 155-6; situation, 157; becomes part of 'Nord', 171-2.

Belliard, future General, 143.

Bernadotte, future Marshal, classified, 42, 43; birthplace, 45; social position, 47, 48; branch of service, 49, 50; political opinions, 52; religion, 54; 'grouped', 58; rank in April 1792, 59, 60-1; age in 1791, 61; period with 'Nord', 64; his regiment joins 'Nord', 202, 224; early career, 202-3; his regiment late, 225; battle of Hondschoote, 228-31; at Wattignies, 250, 263; Lieut.-Colonel, 276; Colonel, 277, 285; protects his General, 286; action near Landrecies, 287; joins 'Sambre-et-Meuse', 315, 319; General of Division, 340.

Berneron, General, 140, 144-5.

Berthelmy, General, on Houchard's staff, 201-2; history of, 212-13; his opinion of Hoche, 227; at Hondschoote, 229.

Berthier, future Marshal, influence of Napoleon on rise, 3; classified, 42, 43; birthplace, 44; social position, 46, 48; branch of service, 49, 50; political opinions, 53, 54; 'grouped', 58; rank in April 1792, 59, 60; age in 1791, 61; period in 'Nord', 63; on staff of 'Nord', 78; early career, 78-80; mission to Paris, 81-2; rejoins army, 85, 86; relations with Dumouriez, 88-9; moves to Metz, 94; letter to Dumouriez, 99; position after *Chassé-croisé*, 102; influence on Luckner, 115.

Berthier, César, 143.

Béru, General, in command of a force, 193; operations in August 1793, 213-16, 220-1; takes Menin, 240-1; promoted and denounced, 241-2; suspended, 265.

Bessières, future Marshal, influence of Napoleon on his rise, 1, 3; classified, 43, 44; birthplace, 45; social position, 47, 48; branch of service, 38, 50; political opinions, 53, 54; 'grouped', 58; rank in April 1792, 60, 61; age in 1791, 61.

INDEX

Beurnonville, General, takes Macdonald as A.D.C., 87, 89, 90; marches to Argonne, 123, 125, 129; his command after Valmy, 136; at Jemappes, 143; succeeds Kellermann, 146; War Minister, 151; schemes for expeditions, 153; promotes Macdonald, 157; sent with Commissioners to Dumouriez, 160; handed over to Austrians, 161; relations with Macdonald, 165; character as War Minister, 169; in command of 'Nord', 342; takes Grouchy as Chief of Staff, 343; approves of Macdonald, 345; a happy family, 346; commands 'Sambre-et-Meuse', 347.

Billaud-Varennes, Representative, 26, 211, 273.

Biron, General Duc de, plots for command of 'Nord', 76–7; advances on Mons, 78, 81; refuses command of 'Nord', 82; commands 'Rhin', 92, 102; Luckner's plan, 116; deceived by Brunswick's move, 117; guillotined, 198, 201.

Blücher, Colonel, 128, 179, 183, 214.

Bonnaud, General, 290, 294, 297–303, 305, 309, 324, 330.

Bouchotte, War Minister, spies on Dampierre, 174–5; attacks Lamarche, 185; disputes with Custine, 186–9; suspends Lamarche, 194; the 'patriots', 197; relations with Brune, 201–2; forcible promotion of Berthelmy, 212; complaint against, 217; refuses Jarry's appointment, 219; disorganizes the army, 224–5; removal of Jourdan, 273.

Bouillé, Marquis de, 13, 14, 20.

Brune, future Marshal, classified, 43, 44; birthplace, 45; social position, 47, 48; branch of service, 50; political opinions, 52; 'grouped', 58; rank in April 1792, 60, 61; age in 1791, 61; period in 'Nord', 64; in attack on Tuileries, 105; possibly at Jemappes, 143; in invasion of Holland, 153; position in April 1793, 157, 164, 174; views on War Office, 197; sketch of early career, 198–9; problem of his character, 199; General of Brigade, 199, 200; hunting down Generals, 200, 201; extraordinary influence, 201, 202; various employments, 339–40.

Brunswick, Duke of, age, 61; first meeting with Dumouriez, 72; invades France, 111–12; advance of, 117–18; pierces the Argonne, 120; Valmy, 128; recrosses frontier, 133–4; in Holland, 153.

Carle, General, 96, 98.

Carnot, Representative and Member of *Comité*, responsibility for orders, 27; as an organizer, 39; at Lille, 160; O'Moran's complaint, 211; plan for advance, 213; recommends Jourdan, 247; visit to 'Nord', 249–50; influence in battle of Wattignies, 251–4; the 'Carnot legend', 258–62; his opinion of the Generals, 262–3; urges advance, 269–71; dismissal of Jourdan, 272–3; his opinion of Beurnonville, 342.

Castelverd, General, 5, 347.

Centre, Armée du, formation, 2, 58, 62–4; commander, 66, 67; plan for movements, 76, 84–5; the *Chassé-croisé*, 90–2; in Luckner's command, 115; marches under Kellermann to Valmy, 126–8, 130; follows Allies to frontier, 134–7; becomes 'Moselle', 136.

César, Camp de, battle of, August 1793, 203–7.

Chapuis, General, 287–8, 290, 293.

Charles, Archduke, 61, 154, 155, 285, 297–302.

Chartres, Duc de, 78, 128, 142–3, 155, 161.

Chazot, General, 92, 111, 121, 129.

Choudieu, Representative, 283.

Clairfayt, General, commands an Austrian force, 117; in Valmy campaign, 118–19; attack on Camp de César, 204–6; commands a corps at Wattignies, 251–2; wounded at Menin, 292–4; at battle of Tourcoing, 296–306; battle of Tournai, 309–11; siege of Ypres, 312–13; battle of Fleurus, 317.

Coburg, Prince of, commands Allies at Neerwinden, 154–5; negotiates with Dumouriez, 159, 161–2; takes Famars, 179, 181; attack on Camp de César, 204–6; besieges Le Quesnoy, 214; siege of Maubeuge, 242–3; Wattignies campaign, 250–64; siege of Landrecies, 285; does justice to British, 305; in command of Allied army, 312; battle of Fleurus, 317–18; bad strategy of, 319–20.

Coland, General, 211–12, 228–9, 233, 234, 236, 239, 274, 276, 283–4.

Cordellier, General, 250, 255, 262.

Côtes de Brest, Armée des, 3, 335.

INDEX 355

Côtes de Cherbourg, Armée des, 3, 335.
Côtes de l'Océan, Armée des, 343, 344.
Côtes de la Rochelle, Armée des, 192, 198, 201.
Custine, General, on Rhine, 116, 117, 135, 146; in command of 'Nord', 185; career and character, 185–6; establishes order in 'Nord', 186; suspected by Jacobins, 186–8; popularity with army, 188; guillotined, 189; feeling in army, 190.

d'Abancourt, War Minister, 96, 99, 100, 101.
Daendels, General, 242, 293, 294, 301–5, 309, 310, 321.
Dampierre, General, in Valmy campaign, 123; at Jemappes, 142; relations with Dumouriez, 144–5; appointed to command 'Belgique', 171; early career and characteristics, 173; on friendly terms with Davout, 174; Murat sups with him, 175; difficulties, 178; advances and is repulsed, surrounded by spies, 179; mortally wounded, 180.
Danton, Minister, 12, 52, 111, 130, 154, 174, 199, 200, 201, 202.
Davaine, General, 264–5, 266.
Davout, future Marshal, name, 7; influence of Revolution on, 9, 10; classified, 42, 43; birthplace, 44; social position, 46, 48; branch of service, 49, 50; political opinions, 51, 52; 'grouped', 58; rank in April 1792, 59, 61; age in 1791, 61; period in 'Nord', 63, 64; position in June 1792, 87; joins 'Nord', 102; at Maulde, 106; at Condé, 130, 139; distinguishes himself at Péruwelz, 144; at siege of Antwerp, 145; in Belgium, 152; at Neerwinden, 155, 157; fires on Dumouriez, 161; characteristics and politics, 164–5, 170; Colonel, 168; relations with Dampierre, 174–5; at loss of Famars, 179, 182; commands a brigade, 183; his opinion of Custine, 188; 'suspect', 197–8; General of Brigade, imprisoned, 198; with 'Rhin-et-Moselle', 340.
de Flers, General, 143, 154.
de Grave, General, War Minister, 75.
d'Hangest, General, 111.
d'Harville, General, commanding a corps, 134, 140; at Jemappes, 141, 143; in 'Ardennes', 145, 146; strength of corps, 152; concentration after Neerwinden, 155–6; joins 'Nord', 172; in Holland, 341.

de Hesse, Charles, 70, 71, 75, 117.
Delacroix, Representative, 154.
Delbrel, Representative, 204, 206, 230, 235, 238, 239.
Dellard, General, 215, 238.
Demars, General, 241–2.
Desenfans, General, 292, 300–1, 307, 309, 312.
Devaux, Colonel, 167.
Dillon, Lieut.-General Comte Arthur, in *Chassé-croisé*, 92; at Valenciennes, 97–8; supports Dumouriez, 99–100; 'suspect', 108–9; refused Sedan command, 110–11; at council of war, 113; in Valmy campaign, 119–20, 130, 135; guillotined, 137.
Dillon, Comte Théobald, 78, 81, 125.
Drouet, Representative, 22, 23.
Dubois-Crancé, Member of *Comité*, 30–1, 39.
Dubois-Dubais, Representative, 192.
Dumas, General Alexandre, 160, 166, 214, 221, 222.
Dumas, General Mathieu, 95, 98, 101, 105.
Dumesny (or Dumesnil), General, in Hondschoote campaign, 228, 232, 233; feeble action of, 237–8; at capture of Menin, 240; defeated, 241; tried and acquitted, 242.
Dumonceau, General, 183, 265, 266.
Dumouriez, General, period in 'Nord', 63, 64; career and character, 72–5; plans for operations, 76–7; nominates Luckner for command of 'Nord', 82; resigns from Ministry, 87; posted to 'Nord', 88; reproaches Luckner, 89; takes Macdonald as A.D.C., 90; quarrel with Lafayette, 93–4; disobeys orders for *Chassé-croisé*, 96–100; action on Lafayette's emigration, 108–10; in command of 'Nord', 110; divides army, 110–11; moves to Sedan, 111; council of war, 112–13; nature of his command, 114–15; marches to Grand Pré, 118–19; clings to Argonne, his confidence, 120–3; calls Kellermann to join him, 126; at Valmy, 128–9; his audacity, opinion of Napoleon, 130–1; operations after Valmy, 133–6; at Paris, 139; invasion of Belgium, 139–40; wins battle of Jemappes, 141; relations with Dampierre, 144–5; his valet, 145; occupies Belgium, 145–6; success against War Department, 150–1; invades Holland, 152–3; brought back to Belgium, 153–4; relations with

356 INDEX

Assembly, 154-5 ; battles of Neerwinden and Louvain, 155-6 ; meeting with Macdonald, 157-8 ; negotiates with Allies and arrests Commissioners, 158-61 ; emigrates, 162 ; subsequent life, 162-3 ; Wellington's opinion of him, 163-4 ; his influence on Republic and army, 164, 168-70.
Dundas, General, 183, 295, 327.
Dunkirk, siege of, 213-35.
Dupont, General Pierre, 216-17, 221, 240-1.
Duquesnoy, General, 244, 250, 252-9, 262, 270, 271.
Duquesnoy, Representative, 211, 219-20, 221, 258-9, 270-1, 272, 273.
d'Urre de Molans, General, 148, 175, 176-7.

Élie, General, 252-3, 256-7.
Ernouf, General, 217, 229-30, 270, 272-3.

Famars, Camp de, battles in April and May 1793, 178-82.
Ferrand, General, 227, 275, 287.
Fleurus, battle of, 316-17.
Florent Guiot, Representative, 283.
Fox, General, 303-4, 310-11.
Fréron, Representative, 23.
Freytag, Hanoverian Marshal, 225, 228, 230, 231.
Fromentin, General, 253, 262, 285.

Gay de Vernon, 187-8, 205, 221, 231, 236, 237.
Gillet, Representative, 32.
Goguet, General, 285-6, 290-1.
Grouchy, future Marshal, classified, 42, 43 ; birthplace, 44 ; social position, 46, 48 ; branch of service, 37, 49, 50 ; political opinions, 52 ; ' grouped ', 58 ; rank in April 1792, 59, 60 ; age in 1791, 61 ; period in ' Nord ', 63, 64 ; joins ' Nord ', 102 ; incident near Maubeuge, 102 ; early career, 102-3 ; with Dillon's force, 119 ; in Valmy campaign, leaves ' Nord ', 130 ; a *ci-devant* Noble, 170 ; Chief of Staff to ' Nord ', 343-4 ; chances for command, 344-5 ; admires Macdonald, 345 ; leaves ' Nord ', 346-7.

Hébert, journalist, 190, 270, 271.
Hédouville, Vicomte de, General, commanding a brigade, 228 ; at Hondschoote, 229-36 ; at capture of Menin, 240-2, 344.
Hentz, Representative, 229-30, 232-3.

Hoche, age in 1791, 61 ; period in ' Nord ', 64 ; with ' Ardennes ', 137, 144, 152 ; position in Neerwinden campaign, 157 ; mission to Paris, 174 ; an incident of 1794, 188 ; in Dunkirk, 193 ; Chief of Staff at Dunkirk, 227 ; his letters to the *Comité*, 228 ; promoted Colonel Adjutant-General and then General of Brigade, 239-40 ; asked for by Souham, 265 ; attacks Nieuport, 266 ; in command of ' Moselle ', ibid. ; commands two armies in La Vendée, 335.
Hohenlohe, Prince of, 117, 206.
Hollande, Armée de la, designation, 64, 65 ; strength, 152 ; invasion of Holland, 153-4 ; recalled to Lille, 157 ; broken up, 172.
Hondschoote, campaign and battle of, 218-39.
Hope, Colonel, 326-7.
Houchard, General, in command of ' Moselle ', 186 ; given command of ' Nord ', 209 ; description of, 210 ; his cruel position, 210-12 ; takes Berthelmy as A.D.C., 212 ; movement on Ostend, 213 ; his opinion of his troops, 218-19 ; plans to relieve Dunkirk, 220-4 ; treatment by Representatives, 224-5 ; battle of Hondschoote, 226-38 ; refuses to pursue, 239 ; success at Menin, 240 ; moves to relieve Le Quesnoy, 241-3 ; arrested and tried, 244 ; guillotined, widow pensioned by Napoleon, 245.

Italie, Armée d', 3, 4, 5, 6, 58, 138, 343, 345.

Jarry, Adjutant-General, 85, 86, 219.
Jemappes, campaign and battle of, 139-45.
Jourdan, future Marshal, rise to high command, 1, 3 ; classified, 42, 43 ; birthplace, 45 ; social position, 47, 48 ; branch of service, 49, 50 ; political opinions, 52 ; grouped, 58 ; rank in April 1792, 60 ; age in 1791, 61 ; period in ' Nord ', 63-4 ; in *Chassé-croisé*, 102 ; at Sedan, 106 ; in Argonne, 121 ; panic of troops, 122 ; at Valmy, 130 ; after Valmy, 138 ; at Jemappes, 143 ; in Belgium, 152 ; in Neerwinden campaign, 156-7 ; in April 1793, 164, 174 ; at loss of Famars, 179, 182 ; General of Brigade, 183 ; General of Division, 193 ; Houchard's opinion of him, 213 ; engagement at Linselles, 215 ; transferred, 216 ; meets

INDEX 357

Ernouf, 217; action at Esquelbecq, 219; at Dunkirk, 220; at battle of Hondschoote, 223, 228-35; in command of 'Nord', 246; early career of, 247-8; battle of Wattignies, 251-8; the 'Carnot' legend, 258-9; criticisms on Wattignies, 259-62; personal vigour, 263; advance in Flanders, 264; resists order to advance, 269-71; removed from command, 272-3; commands 'Moselle', 315; wins battle of Fleurus, 317, 318; advance to Liége, 320; helps 'Nord', 329; influence of 'Nord' on his generalship, 351.

Kellermann, future Marshal, rose to high command before Bonaparte, 1; classified, 42, 43; birthplace, 45; social position, 46, 48; branch of service, 49, 50; political opinions, 52; 'grouped', 58; rank in April 1792, 59, 60; age in 1791, 61; on Rhine, 117; marches with 'Centre' to Argonne, 125; early career, 125-6; nature of his army, 127; at Valmy, 128, 130; wishes to retire on Châlons, 133; follows Allies to frontier, 134, 137; in command of Alpes, 146.

Kilmaine, General, in command of 'Ardennes', 172, 180; nominated for command of 'Nord', 185; reorganizes 'Ardennes', 186; in temporary command of 'Nord', 191; previous career, 191-2; skilful withdrawal from Camp de César, 203-7; praised by Napoleon and Marmont, 208; suspended and arrested, 209; restored to the army in 1795, 210.

Kléber, General, age in 1791, 61; joins 'Nord' from La Vendée, 291; goes to 'Sambre-et-Meuse', 315; General of Division, 340-1.

Labourdonnaye, General, in command at Lille, 96; in *Chassé-croisé*, 101; at Valenciennes, 111-12, commands 'Nord', 114-15, 122; sends reinforcements to Argonne, 123; succeeds Luckner at Châlons, 124, 139; commands 'Nord' in invasion of Belgium, 135, 140, 144; removed, 145.

Lafayette, Marquis of, commands 'Centre', 67; early career, 67-8; conference of commanders, 71; relations with Dumouriez, 75; a patron of Berthier, 79, 80; conference, 85; the *Chassé-croisé*, 90;

political objects, 91-2; hostility of Dumouriez, 93, 94; Dumouriez's disobedience, 98-100; action against Assembly, 103-7; emigrates, 107.

Lahure, Lieut.-Colonel, 179, 325, 329-31.

Lajard, War Minister, 92, 96, 97, 98.

Lake, Colonel, 183, 215.

Lamarche, General, takes Ney as A.D.C., 137; in 'Ardennes', 144, 146; in Belgium, 152; in Neerwinden campaign, 155; failure at Louvain, 156; in command of 'Ardennes', 171, 178; in command of 'Nord', 180; early services of, 180-1; resigns command, 184, 185; dismissed, 194; reports well on Ney, 197.

La Marlière, General, at la Madeleine, 174; success near Condé, 179; defends Macdonald, 182-3; at Lille, 186-7; guillotined, 193, 200-1.

Lameth, Lieut.-General Alexandre, 105, 107.

Lameth, Charles, 89.

Landrieux, Adjutant-General, 176-8, 328, 337-9.

Landrin, General, 221, 228-35.

Langeron, General, 205.

Lannes, future Marshal, influence of Napoleon on, 1, 3; effects of *amalgame*, 33; classified, 43, 44; birthplace, 45; social position, 47, 48; branch of service, 50; political opinions, 53; 'grouped', 58; rank in April 1792, 60, 61; age in 1791, 61.

La Tour-Maubourg, Marquis de (Victor), 107.

Lavalette, General, 167, 268.

Le Bas, Representative, 268, 283, 315.

Leclaire, General, 216, 219-20, 228-9, 231-6.

Lecourbe, General, 60, 255, 315.

Lefebvre, future Marshal, classified, 42, 43, 44; birthplace, 45; social position, 47, 48; branch of service, 49, 50; political opinions, 53; religion, 54-5; 'grouped', 58; rank in April 1792, 59; 61; age in 1791, 61; in Paris, 105; joins 'Centre', 137-8; in 'Moselle' and 'Sambre-et-Meuse', 315, 319; General of Division, 340.

Lemaire, General, 262, 324.

Levasseur, Representative, 224, 238, 241.

Le Veneur, General, 157, 171, 174, 227.

Louvain, battle of, 156.

Luckner, a Marshal of the Monarchy, period with 'Nord', 63; commands 'Rhin', character, 68–70; created Marshal, 71; plan of operations, 74; commands 'Nord', 82–3; conference with Rochambeau, 84–5; asks for Berthier, 85; takes Menin, 86–7; relations with Dumouriez, 89; the *Chassé-croisé*, 90–1; mediates between Lafayette and Dumouriez, 93-4; appears before *Comité*, 94–5; at Metz, 95; anger with Dumouriez, 98–101; Generalissimo, 115; distrusted by *Conseil*, 116; march of Kellermann, 116, 127; retired, 116–17; saves officers from massacre, 124; refuses to see Dumouriez, 139; guillotined, 117.

Macdonald, future Marshal, classified, 42, 43; birthplace, 44; social position, 46, 48; branch of service, 49, 50; political opinions, 53; grouped, 58; rank in April 1792, 59, 61; age in 1791, 61; period in 'Nord', 63, 64; position in June 1792, 87; A.D.C. to Beurnonville, 89; early career, 89, 90; A.D.C. to Dumouriez, 90; at Maulde, 93; position after *Chassé-croisé*, 102; at Sedan, 111; at Grand Pré, 119; in panic of troops, 122; meets Beurnonville with directions, 123; at Valmy, 129; at Paris, 139; the Jemappes campaign, 139–43; left in Paris, 150–3; his strange absence, 156–8; Colonel, 156; meets Dumouriez, 157–8; takes side of Convention, 165–7; position in April 1793, 174; made Adjutant-General, 182; success at Tourcoing, 182–3; operations near Lille, 186; General of Brigade, 193; success at Blaton, 215; praised by Representatives, 216; attack on Lannoy, 220–1; in Hondschoote campaign, 223; at capture of Menin, 240–2; operations under Souham, 264–6; denounced, 267–9; noted by Pichegru, 276; in danger as a Noble, 283, 291; new command, 292; at battle of Tourcoing, 299–307; at battle of Tournai, 309–11; siege of Ypres, 312–13; remains with 'Nord', 315, 319; attack on Boxtel, 324–5; capture of Hertogenbosch, 325; General of Division, 327; crosses Waal, 328; Lahure and Dutch fleet, 329–30; clears northern provinces, 331; his command, 334–5; fever, 341, 345, 347; reinforces 'Sambre-et-Meuse', 347; at Paris, 348; the standard of the 'Nord', 349; influence of 'Nord' on his generalship, 351; his honourable character, 352.

Mack, General, on staff of Coburg, 154; at Neerwinden, 156; in charge of negotiations with Dumouriez, 159–60; wounded at Famars, 181; Chief of Staff to Allies, 183; effect of his absence, 264; skill, 285, 290; attack on Menin, 292; battle of Tourcoing, 296–306; resigns, 312.

Malbrancq, General, 294, 301–8, 309, 312.

Mansell, Colonel, 287–8.

Marat, 80, 139, 174–5, 211, 337–8.

Marceau, General, age in 1791, 61; period in 'Nord', 64; at surrender of Verdun, 118; his opinion on *fédérés*, 124; in Valmy campaign, 130; on staff of Dillon, 137; in La Vendée, 138, 254, 315, 319; with 'Sambre-et-Meuse', 340.

Maret, future Minister, 77, 151, 337.

Marmont, future Marshal, influence of Napoleon on, 1, 3; name, 7; classified, 42, 43; birthplace, 44; social position, 46, 48; branch of service, 49, 50; political opinions, 53; musical talent, 55; 'grouped', 58; rank in April 1792, 59, 61; age in 1791, 61; opinion on Kilmaine, 208.

Masséna, future Marshal, influence of Napoleon on, 1, 3; classified, 42, 43, 44; birthplace, 45; social position, 47, 48; branch of service, 49, 50; political opinions, 53; 'grouped', 58; rank in April 1792, 60; age in 1791, 61.

Miaczinski, General, 165, 166–7.

Michaud, General, 276, 291–2, 300, 312.

Michel, General, 265.

Midi, Armée du, 2, 65, 75.

Miranda, General, 144, 145, 152, 153, 154–5, 160, 170.

Moira, Lord, 317–18.

Moncey, future Marshal, rose to high command before Bonaparte, 1; name, 7; classified, 42, 43; birthplace, 45; social position, 46, 48; branch of service, 49–50; political opinions, 53; 'grouped', 58; rank in April 1792, 59, 61; age in 1791, 61.

Moreau, General, age in 1791, 61; period in 'Nord', 63, 64; position

INDEX

in June 1792, 87; after *Chassé-croisé*, 102; not at Valmy, 137; in Belgium, 144; in invasion of Holland, 152-3; gallant conduct at Neerwinden, 155; after Neerwinden, 157, 174; his battalion and Custine, 190; at Camp de César, 193; at Hondschoote, 228; prophecy about Lecourbe, 255; commands a column, 265; General of Brigade, 267; early career, 277-80; friendship with Pichegru, 280-1; operations near Menin, 291-4; battle of Tourcoing, 296-305; battle of Tournai, 309; siege of Ypres, 312-13; conducts sieges, 321-2; the captured *émigrés*, 322-4; his division, 324; passes Meuse, 326; in temporary command of 'Nord', 327; with Pichegru, 328, 331; occupies Bentheim, 334; in command of 'Nord', 336; thanked by Kléber, 341; in command of 'Rhin-et-Moselle', 342; influence of 'Nord' on his generalship, 351; character, 352.

Mortier, future Marshal, classified, 43, 44; birthplace, 44; social position, 47, 48; branch of service, 50; political opinions, 53; 'grouped', 58; rank in April 1792, 60, 61; age in 1791, 61; period in 'Nord', 63, 64; first action, 78; early career, 80-1; position in June 1792, 87; with 'Nord', 93; after *Chassé-croisé*, 102; not at Valmy, 130; at Jemappes, 143; with 'Ardennes', 145; in Belgium, 152; in Neerwinden campaign, 156-7; in April 1793, 174, 179, 180; distinguishes himself at Famars, 182; Lieut.-Col. Adjutant-General, 193, 217; in Hondschoote campaign, 223-8; Chief of Staff to Balland, 249, 251; wounded at Wattignies, 254; attack on Le Cateau, 285; action near Landrecies, 287; his General replaced, 291; joins 'Sambre-et-Meuse', 315, 319; Colonel, 340.

Moselle, Armée de la, origin and strength, 2, 3, 62, 66, 136; relations with 'Nord', 186; Houchard in command, 210; commanded later by Jourdan, 217; reinforces 'Nord', 223; Hoche in command, 275; wins battle of Fleurus, 316-17; absorbed in 'Sambre-et-Meuse' and 'Rhin-et-Moselle', 314-15.

Murat, influence of Napoleon on, 1, 3; classified, 42, 43; birthplace, 45; social position, 47-9; branch of service, 37, 49, 50; political opinions, 52; 'grouped', 58; rank in April 1792, 59, 61; age in 1791, 61; period in 'Nord', 63, 64; joins 'Nord', 102; at Sedan, 106; with Dillon's force, 119; at Montcheutin, 121-2; probably at Valmy, 129; after Valmy, 138; early career, 146-8; letters to his family, 148-9; in Belgium, 152; at Neerwinden, 156-7; in April 1793, 164, 174; Captain and A.D.C., 175; letter from Paris, 176; 2nd Lieut.-Colonel, 177, 179; at Hesdin, 182; at Pont-à-Marcq, 194; in August 1793, 222; at capture of Menin, 241; position in October 1793, 265; his prospects, 276-7; his regiment, 291-2; battle of Tourcoing, 307; battle of Tournai, 309; siege of Ypres, 312; remains with 'Nord', 315, 319; contest with Landrieux, 337-9; family affection, 339, 340.

Napoleon, influence on career of future Marshals, 1; effect of Revolution on army, 9-10, 12; cure for difficulties of supply, 24; regiment of La Fère, 34; *pièces de régiment*, 35; his Guides, 37; music, 55-6; rank in April 1792, 61; age in 1791, 61; Rochambeau and Marshals, 81; his opinion of Lafayette, 107; of Dumouriez, 131-2; concealment of disasters, 160; knowledge of early campaigns, 188; his opinion of Kilmaine, 208; of Ernouf, 217; Houchard's widow, 245; opinion on Wattignies, 260; on Vandamme, 282.

Narbonne-Lara, General Comte de, War Minister, 68, 69, 71, 75.

Neerwinden, campaign and battle of, 153-7.

Ney, classified, 42, 43; birthplace, 45; social position, 47-9; branch of service 49, 50; political opinions, 53; musical talent, 55; 'grouped', 58; rank in April 1792, 59, 61; age in 1791, 61; period in 'Nord', 63, 64; probably at Valmy, 129; with 'Ardennes', 137; A.D.C. to Lamarche, 137, 144, 146, 152; at Neerwinden, 155-6; with Lamarche, 156, position in April 1793, 164, 174; his regiment in advanced guard, 193; tribulations of, 194; sketch of early career, 194-7; well reported on, 197; in Jourdan's

Column at Lille, 214; position in Hondschoote campaign, 223-8; at battle of Wattignies, 250, 253, 263; A.D.C. to Colaud, effect on his character, 274; Captain, 277; rejoins regiment, 283-4; regiment behaves well, 285; action near Landrecies, 287; joins 'Sambre-et-Meuse', 315, 319; Colonel, 340.

Nord, Armée du, formation, 2; strength, 3; helps to form 'Sambre-et-Meuse', 3; future Marshals with, 58, 63-8; formation, 62; attached armies, 65; Rochambeau in command, 66-7; panics among troops, 77-8, 81; Luckner in command, 82-6; the *Chassé-croisé*, 90-3; Lafayette in command, 104; Dumouriez in command, 107; Valmy campaign, 111, 112; Labourdonnaye in command, 114-15; invasion of Belgium, 139-46; strength, 152; Neerwinden campaign, 154-6; at Bruille, 157; composition, 172; Lamarche in command, 180; battles of Famars, 178-82; success at Tourcoing, 182-3; siege of Valenciennes, 183-5; Custine in command, 185; fall of Condé and Valenciennes, 189, 209; strength, 193; withdrawal from Camp de César, 203-7; battle of Hondschoote, 220-6; strength, 223; Wattignies campaign, 250-8; operations in Flanders, 264-6; state of the troops, 269-71; size of army, 284; right wing formed, 287; takes Menin, 291-5; battle of Tourcoing, 296-308; battle of Tournai, 309-11; takes Ypres, 312-13; formation of 'Sambre-et-Meuse', 314-16; future Marshals left with 'Nord', 315, 319; advance to Brussels, 318; Antwerp, 320-1; occupies Belgium and Holland, 321-34; sufferings of army, 332; future Marshals with, 340; strength, 340-1; helps 'Sambre-et-Meuse', 341-2, 347; suppressed, 349; its influence on commanders, 349-52.

O'Moran, General, 140, 143-5, 174, 201, 211, 227, 228.
Orange, Prince of, 214, 215, 241, 251, 258.
Oudinot, future Marshal, affected by *amalgame*, 33; classified, 42, 43; birthplace, 45; social position, 47, 48; branch of service, 49, 50; political opinions, 53; 'grouped', 58; rank in April 1792, 60, 61; age in 1791, 61; period with 'Nord', 63; remains with 'Centre', 93, 137, 138.
Ouest, Armée d', 3.

Pache, War Minister, 143, 148, 151, 169.
Pérignon, future Marshal, classified, 42, 43; birthplace, 45; social position, 46, 48; branch of service, 49, 50; political opinions, 53; 'grouped', 58; rank in April 1792, 59, 60; age in 1791, 61.
Pichegru, General, not a great commander, 9; commands a volunteer battalion, 60; age in 1791, 61; period in 'Nord', 64; appointed to command 'Nord', 275-6; friendship with Moreau and Souham, 280-1; generally absent from battles, 284; unsuccessful attack on Le Cateau, 285; forms a right wing, 287; operations near Menin, 291-5; absent from battle of Tourcoing, 299; attacks Allies at Tournai, 309-11; takes Ypres, 312-13; plans for advance, 316-17; enters Bruges and Brussels, 318; captured *émigrés*, 323; a slack pursuit, 324; honourable conduct towards *émigrés*, 325; crosses Meuse, 326; ill at Brussels, 327; enters Amsterdam, 328; in command of 'Rhin-et-Moselle', 335.
Pyrénées-Occidentales, Armée des, 3, 4, 58, 222.
Pyrénées-Orientales, Armée des, 3, 4, 58, 143.

Representatives of the People with the armies, 21-9, 31-2, 168, 169, 225-6. See also Billaud-Varennes, Carnot, Choudieu, Delacroix, Delbrel, Drouet, Dubois-Dubais, Duquesnoy, Florent Guiot, Fréron, Gillet, Hentz, Le Bas, Levasseur, Saint-Just.
Rhin, Armée du, formation and strength, 2, 3; errors about, 6; future Marshals with, 58; commanded by Luckner, 62-3, 66, 68-70; the 'Marseillaise', 69, 117; commanded by Biron under Luckner, 76, 91, 92, 102; plans for co-operation with 'Nord', 186; Pichegru in command, 275; reinforces 'Nord', 223.
Rhin-et-Moselle, Armée de, formation and strength, 3, 4, 66; commanded by Pichegru, 335; strength, 340; campaign of 1795, 341; Moreau in

INDEX   361

command, 342 ; campaign of 1796, 347.

Rochambeau, a Marshal of the Monarchy, commander of 'Nord', career and character, 66-7 ; plan of operations, 71 ; plots against, 76-7 ; resigns command, 81-4 ; meets Marshals of Empire in 1805, 81.

Robespierre, Member of *Comité*, 23, 27, 52, 169, 174-5, 199, 200, 209, 228, 244, 247, 251, 266, 271-3, 321, 322-4.

Saint-Cyr, future Marshal, name, 7 ; classified, 43, 44 ; birthplace, 45 ; social position, 47, 48 ; branch of service, 50 ; political opinions, 53 ; musical talent, 55 ; 'grouped', 58 ; rank in April 1792, 60, 61 ; age in 1791, 61 ; his criticism of Dumouriez, 122, note 1 ; on size of armies, 284-5.

Saint-Germain, Comte de, War Minister, 13.

Saint-Just, Representative, 21, 26, 164, 210, 268, 269, 283, 315.

Sambre-et-Meuse, Armée de, formation, 3 ; group of future Marshals with, 4, 5, 58-9, 64, 315, 319, 340 ; absorbs 'Ardennes', 65 ; Ernouf, Chief of the Staff, 217 ; effect of its formation, 277, 284 ; details of formation, 314-16 ; wins battle of Fleurus, 317 ; movements, 318-19 ; advance to Liége, 320 ; drives Austrians over Rhine, 324 ; reinforces 'Nord', 334 ; command, 335 ; reinforced from 'Nord', 341, 347 ; future Marshals with, in 1796, 345 ; Beurnonville in command, 348.

Schérer, General, 280, 315, 349.

Schwartzenberg, Prince, 61.

Sérurier, future Marshal, influence of Napoleon on career of, 1 ; classified, 42, 43 ; birthplace, 44 ; social position, 46-8 ; branch of service, 49, 50 ; political opinions, 53 ; 'grouped', 58 ; rank in April 1792, 59 ; age in 1791, 61.

Servan, War Minister, posts Berthier to 'Nord', 82, 85-6 ; withdraws muskets from Dragoons, 112 ; begs Dumouriez to march south, 114 ; appointment of Luckner as Generalissimo, 115 ; correspondence with Dumouriez, 118-19 ; opposes proposal to abandon Paris, 130 ; recommends separation of 'Nord' from 'Ardennes', 135.

Souham, General, position after *Chassé-croisé*, 102 ; at Jemappes, 143 ; in Neerwinden campaign, 157 ; commanding at Dunkirk, 226-7 ; in command near Menin, 265-7 ; supports Macdonald, 268-9 ; relations with Pichegru, 280-1 ; advice to Macdonald, 291-2 ; success at Menin, 291-4 ; in command at battle of Tourcoing, 296-308 ; his career, 308-9 ; battle of Tournai, 309-11 ; siege of Ypres, 312-13 ; his command, 320, 324 ; honourable conduct, 326 ; success at Nijmegen, 326 ; ceases to be employed, 327 ; passed over for command of 'Nord', 336-7 ; placed in retirement, 348.

Soult, future Marshal, classified, 42, 43 ; birthplace, 45 ; social position, 47, 48 ; branch of service, 49, 50 ; political opinions, 53 ; religion, 54 ; 'grouped', 58 ; rank in April 1792, 59, 61 ; age in 1791, 61 ; criticism of battle of Wattignies, 259-60 ; in 'Moselle' and 'Sambre-et-Meuse', 315, 319.

Suchet, future Marshal, influence of Napoleon on, 1 ; classified, 43, 44 ; birthplace, 45 ; social position, 47, 48 ; branch of service, 50 ; political opinions, 52 ; 'grouped', 58 ; rank in April 1792, 60, 61 ; age in 1791, 61.

Tourcoing, battle of, 296-308.
Tournai, battle of, 309-11.

Valence, General, tries to keep Berthier with 'Nord', 85-6 ; commands 'Ardennes', 137-8 ; in Jemappes campaign, 140, 145, 146 ; in Belgium, 152-3 ; Neerwinden campaign, 155-6 ; emigrates with Dumouriez, 161, 171.

Valenciennes, siege of, in 1793, 183-4, 189.

Valmy, campaign and battle of, 111-35.

Vandamme, General, at battle of Hondschoote, 228, 232-4 ; pursues York, 236-7 ; success on left, 265-6 ; in arrest, 266 ; friendship with Moreau, 279 ; career and character, 281-3 ; commands a brigade, 291, 293-4 ; at battle of Tourcoing, 300-5 ; wins a watch, 318 ; in Moreau's brigade, 321, 324 ; commands Moreau's division, 327, 331 ; care of English wounded, 331 ; Paris politics, 348.

Victor, future Marshal, influence of Napoleon on, 1 ; name, 7 ; classified, 42, 43; birthplace, 45; social position, 47–9; branch of service, 50; political opinions, 53; musical talent, 55; 'grouped', 58; rank in April 1792, 60, 61; age in 1791, 61.

Walmoden, General, 231–6, 327.
Wattignies, campaign and battle of, 250–64.
Wellington, Duke of, age in 1791, 61; his opinion of Dumouriez, 73, 163–4; of Archduke Charles, 299, note 1; at Boxtel, 325; under Dundas, 327–8; opinion on the campaign, 333.
White, General, 294.
Wurmser, General, 61, 214.

York, Duke of, action at Quiévrain, 178–9; attack on Famars, 178–82; siege of Valenciennes, 183–4, 209; attack on Camp de César, 203–7; march to Dunkirk, 213–14; the Guards at Linselles, 215; siege of Dunkirk, 218, 222, 223, 227, 234–5; marches to help Dutch, 241; marches on Maubeuge, 250, 258; action near Menin, 265; action at Troisvilles, 287–8; success at Marquain, 294–5; battle of Tourcoing, 296–306; battle of Tournai, 310–12; covers Antwerp, 320; withdraws across Meuse, 325; retires to Nijmegen, 326; leaves for England, 327 end of expedition, 333.

Milton Keynes UK
Ingram Content Group UK Ltd.
UKHW020625100524
442500UK00010B/93